M161c

The Vintage Book of

CONTEMPORARY
WORLD POETRY

The Vintage Book of

CONTEMPORARY WORLD POETRY

Edited and with an Introduction by

J. D. McCLATCHY

Vintage Books

A Division of Random House, Inc.

New York

A VINTAGE ORIGINAL, JULY 1996
FIRST EDITION

Copyright © 1996 by J. D. McClatchy

All rights reserved under International and Pan-American Copyright
Conventions. Published in the United States by Vintage Books, a division
of Random House, Inc., New York, and simultaneously in Canada by
Random House of Canada Limited, Toronto.

Library of Congress Cataloging-in-Publication Data
The Vintage book of contemporary world poetry / edited and with an
    introduction by J.D. McClatchy.—1st ed.
        p.   cm.
    "A Vintage original."
    Includes bibliographical references.
    ISBN 0-679-74115-1
    1. Poetry, Modern—20th century—Translations into English.
I. McClatchy, J. D., 1945–   .
PN6101.V56   1996
808.81'04—dc20   95-50628
                        CIP

Book design by Rebecca Aidlin

Pages 639-654 constitute an extension of this copyright page.

Random House Web address: http://www.randomhouse.com

Printed in the United States of America
10 9 8 7 6 5 4

CONTENTS

AFRICA *337*

INTRODUCTION

In Emerson's eerie definition, *the world* is everything that is not myself, including my own body. For most of us nowadays, the world is altogether less foreign, less alienated, less extremely *other*. And less dizzyingly enormous. Technology, once having created the global village, has since domesticated it, nearly internalized it. From wherever Elsewhere is, first came the explorer's account, then a map, next a postcard, now a documentary: everything seems closer. The most distant locale, the most exotic customs are now the size of a screen, and the term "remote control" is less a device than a metaphor. Over the past half-century, the ease of travel and communication, the loosening of restrictions, the availability of information and images—even that photograph of earthrise over the moon's horizon—so much has gradually changed our sense of what the world is and means. But in a way, our shifting perspectives on the world—its immensity, its immediacy—are contained within the word itself. After all, our word "world" comes from the Middle English *weorld,* in turn derived from the Germanic root *wir-,* meaning "man" (as in "werewolf"). The first use of the term in the *Oxford English Dictionary* refers to "the earthly state of human existence." For our purposes, the irony is that the abstract magnitude of "world" comes back finally to a single person, a body, the experience of an individual.

And what of the term "world poetry"? Like "world music," it is probably modeled on *Weltliteratur,* a word coined by the Romantic German philosophers to designate the extent and variety of the world's literary cultures and the fact that the spirit behind them all is one. The concept is still an appealing and useful one. The Russian poet Andrei Voznesensky recently gave the idea a late-twentieth-century spin when he referred to a poem as "a crystal, a model of the world, a structure of harmony, a method of thought penetrating to the essence of what is happening, a way of revealing the truth. Poetry knows no borders; it has no capitals and no provinces. Languages are many but poetry is one." And never before have readers had so much of the world's literature available to them. Armies of translators are continually at work. English speakers would seem to have the added advantage that theirs is now the "world language," which everyone learns and into which everything is translated. Not since Latin has there been such a common tongue. As pervasive as English is around the globe, though, for foreigners it is primarily a language for business, science, and technology. Poetry in English remains as difficult for others as their poetries are for us, and the poetry in any language must be nearly the last thing to be translated into English. Perhaps because it is intent on telling the truth in as complicated a way as possible, poetry stays quietly, defiantly, in its place. It does not travel well. In the end, every culture's poetry is a local wine, and tends to lose its unique savor—the aroma of vineyard and weather, harvest and history—when sipped abroad.

The world includes all of us, but this book does not. Some of the greatest living American, English, and Irish poets are here, to be sure—but only as translators. I have deliberately omitted from the anthology, because they are more readily available, poets from Britain and Ireland, the United States and Canada, Australia and New Zealand. That is not to say there are no poems here written directly in English. There are a few, by poets in Africa, India, and the Caribbean, where English remains for some a colonial bequest. But in much the same way that the photographer is the one missing from the picture he takes of others, the extraordinary body of contemporary poetry in English has been put to one side, under a black cloth, its eye to the lens. The test now is to see how the capaciousness of English and the ingenuity of its poets can bring so much else into brilliant focus.

Of course, poetry can be made into a commodity like anything else. This goes to the heart of a nagging question: why are some poems translated and not others? The Russians took to John Steinbeck's novels at once. How long did it take them to discover, say, Wallace Stevens, or any number of other writers whom we would consider much greater artists than Steinbeck? Excellence is often elbowed aside by ideology. Evidence rather than art can be the criterion. What gets translated is often something being used to advance a political agenda, or illustrate a point of view, or bear witness to a cause or crime. The angry energies of the exiled or the disaffected spur certain texts into print. On the other side of that coin is a publisher's commercial instinct to capitalize on some writer's passing celebrity. (And that is another reason books suddenly appear in translation—their authors may just have been given a Nobel, or issued a *fatwa*.) But poetry—good poetry—resists any sort of easy packaging. That is because it bears an oblique relationship to "events." In *The Iliad,* Homer portrayed a war, but we read his poem as an account of one man's anguished obsession. Poetry, like the "world," always returns to the private life, the hidden motive, the buried feeling. *The Odyssey* is our quintessential heroic adventure, yet it tells us more about the ordinary day-to-day life of ancient man—weaving, working, navigating—than any history does. Poetry, like the world, is always a matter of details that capture emotions: the streaked windowpane through which a longing gazes.

What can we understand of a poem originally written in French or Urdu? Emily Dickinson's poems remain—or should remain— enigmatic to Americans, yet at the same time speak powerfully to readers around the world, and have influenced poets in many other languages. What is it that *comes through*? For any good poem there are two levels of inspiration. Let's call them the "invented" and the "received." And by "invented" I mean what others would call the received—that is to say, the technical apparatus and rhythmical instincts of a native strain, the weight of historical and literary allusions, wordplay and idiom, the whole echo chamber of a tradition in whatever original combinations the new poet may devise. These, curiously, are hardest for a translation to catch, much less duplicate. The first thing to go is the music. English is a vast and subtle language, but it lacks, say, the melodic plangencies of Spanish, or the bright constellations of the Chinese ideogram. The translations gathered in this anthology are outstanding because each has set about to create an English equivalent to the music of the original.

The second inspiration is what I call the "received." Hegel thought any poem could be translated without loss because the true medium of poetry is not words but "poetic ideas." Something like this may be behind the Swedish poet Tomas Tranströmer's distinction between a poem as an expression of the life of its author's language (in his case a poem written by the Swedish language through him) and a poem as a manifestation of an invisible poem, written in a language beyond languages—a poem that has been "received," so that the version in the original language is itself already a translation. Whether in Portuguese or Arabic or English, the same

invisible poem is attempting to come into being. In this case, the po-
etry is, or can be, *found* in translation. These invisible poems finally
reveal themselves less in the actual lines of a poem than in the fig-
ures those lines create.

This, in turn, comes back to poetry's principles. The basis of all
poetry, said Aristotle, is metaphor. Nothing can be freshly or truly
seen in itself until it is seen first as something else. It is this image-
making impulse that unifies world poetry, and gives it its spiritual
force. This anthology is a book of startling images. They are not nec-
essarily drawn from the paint pots of local color. They come from
the experience of individuals—experience so private that it tran-
scends the personal. It is not the similarity, the urge toward identity,
that most intrigues us about these poems. It is the *familiar* sensation
of strangeness. We're reminded, over and over again, of the isola-
tion of each individual, the aloneness of a life. Into that isolation a
world is drawn and re-created. That isolation may be fraught with
political tensions—as it is, say, in the poems of the Palestinian Mah-
moud Darwish or the Bangladeshi Taslima Nasrin. English or Amer-
ican readers have always been insulated from the kinds of political
pressure that writers in other societies have had—sometimes subtly,
sometimes brutally—to endure. The best of those writers make an
art of evading, defying, or playfully accommodating that pressure.
But, without condescending to anyone's suffering, we shouldn't
overbid this hand. Art responds to, indeed thrives on, any sort of
pressure. Warring, deceitful politics, the upheavals of history, ideo-
logical tyrannies . . . these can also be felt or read as metaphors of
the interior life. They correspond to, and can stand for, the more pri-
vate pressures of mortality, adultery, failure, or betrayal—the whole
tangle of thwarted desires and misplaced hopes that haunts all of us.

Most of the poets in this book are what we would call cos-
mopolitan. They have traveled, explored, read. Their poetry is a
product of both necessity and choice. That is to say, their necessary
affinities are with the pleasures and rigors of their native language's
poetic tradition, but most have also chosen to learn and apply lessons
learned in other cultures. And if they resemble one another in any-
thing, it is their common experience of modernism. In the second half
of the twentieth century, is there a poet anywhere who has not ab-
sorbed Whitman, Baudelaire and Mallarmé, Yeats and Eliot and
Pound? The example of these poets has had a decisive effect world-
wide, and helped establish a modern sensibility that our contempo-

raries have inherited. The hard-bitten ironies and picked-over shards of the past, the visionary gleams, the religion of language, the splayed lyric, the astute psychologizing—in whatever dialect they may be cast, these are the qualities that have come to characterize contemporary world poetry.

When I use the word "contemporary," it may seem a sliding term. Some poets included here, after all, seem to belong to an earlier time. Some of those poets, like Pakistan's Faiz Ahmed Faiz or Turkey's Nazim Hikmet, stand like colossi astride the modern poetry of their countries; to have excluded them would have left only shadows. Others, like Paul Celan or Pablo Neruda, whose accomplishment was so influential and far-reaching, remain vital figures; to have excluded them would have diminished the account. For the rest, there are old masters and young virtuosi (some of whom died young). The selection of individual poems was not so difficult. Though all of the poets in this book have written well about their travels, I have tended to choose poems that were written, so to speak, closer to home, closer to the bone.

Most readers already have an anthology of favorite poets in their hearts, and none of those will match this one. I hope that discoveries newly made will count for far more than anyone's missing preference. Some readers will be troubled by apparent omissions of another sort. The relative scarcity of poems by women is not an omission but a sad fact. Of course, I am restricted to what has been translated into English—and that in turn depends upon the convictions and whims of publishers. On the other hand—and this is a social rather than a literary dilemma—it is also true that in large parts of the world women are discouraged from writing or publishing: a problem for enlightened politicians, not anthologists, to solve. And why not oral or "tribal" poems? There exist fascinating collections (Jerome Rothenberg has edited several of them) that have gathered from many cultures their work songs, incantations, ritual verses, chants, and lullabies. No matter how remote or primitive these cultures may seem, each has a poetry as complex as its social customs or religious ceremonies. But though poetry is a part of every culture, not every culture's poetry is retrievable by means of English translation. The aims and energies of "folk" or "shamanistic" poetry are like the stone or shell carried home from the beach: out of context, they lose their color overnight. Such collections seem finally more the stuff of anthropology than of art, and so—mindful that such material can be found elsewhere—I have kept to a "literary" tradition, to writing rather than ritual.

The omission I am most mindful of is poets, poets, and more poets. Of the tens of thousands of professional poets around the world, and the thousands of excellent ones, how many could I include? It would be easier to copy the Bible—it's frequently done—onto the head of a pin. One book per country would still be overcrowded. I have tried, instead, to taste the world's riches, to offer as broad a selection as the practicalities of space and budget would permit. I have not sought any simple geographical parity. (If the scales tip in favor of Europe, eastern Europe especially, that is because of a genuine concentration of poetic genius and the fact that more of those poets have been translated into English.) And for any one poet I have chosen work that is representative of the writer's strengths, not merely of his or her career.

The result, I think, is a book with the scope to include both the famous and the unexpected; its guiding spirit was animated by both awe and curiosity. In 1977, when the Voyager spacecraft was launched toward the outer reaches of the solar system and beyond, NASA put aboard a recording, a twelve-inch copper disc with all sorts of electronic information that an advanced extraterrestrial civilization could convert into diagrams and pictures and words that would explain our world to theirs. In addition to the photographs and schematics on the disc there were spoken greetings in sixty human languages; a compilation of earthly sounds that included rain, whales, volcanoes, heartbeats, train whistles, fire, birdsong, and laughter; and a selection of musical compositions—ranging from Bach and Stravinsky to Javanese gamelan, Indian raga, and Japanese skakuhachi—meant to represent this planet's cultural diversity. The idea was to offer not just a token of our science and culture but a portrait of our thoughts and our feelings. This book is offered to you in that same spirit. Here are the guardians of memory. Here are dozens of whispered, perplexing, gorgeous, keening, bemused, thoughtful, angry, soaring voices. Here are the songs of the earth.

The Vintage Book of

CONTEMPORARY
WORLD POETRY

EUROPE

SOPHIA DE MELLO BREYNER

Portugal (b. 1919)

In a poem called "Biography," Sophia de Mello Breyner looks back over her career and concludes: "I hated what was easy / I sought myself in the sea the wind the light." The elements, the essentials, the difficult abstractions in which we lead our particular lives—her poems are rooted in these. This same sensibility has inevitably drawn her to the luxuries of the Mediterranean landscape and the austerities of the classical world. Her poems resonate with echoes of the Greek myths, evoked both for their own life and as a judgment on hers. In her private mythology, she says, poetry "requires unflagging intransigence. It demands that I extract a seamless texture from my life, apart from what shatters, exhausts, pollutes and adulterates. It requires that I live as alert as an antenna, that I be always alive, that I never sleep or forget. It demands unflagging, concentrated, intransigent obstinacy. Because poetry is my understanding with the world, my intimacy with things, my participation in what is real, my engagement with voices and images. This is why a poem speaks not of ideal life but of actual life: the angle of a window; the reverberation of streets, cities, rooms; shadows along a wall." De Mello began publishing in 1944 and has received the Grand Prize in Poetry of the Portuguese Society of Writers. In addition to having served as a deputy in the National Assembly, she was appointed Chancellor of the National Orders by the president of Portugal.

Day of Sea

Day of sea in the sky, made
From shadows and horses and plumes.

Day of sea in my room—cube
Where my sleepwalker's movements slide
Between animal and flower, like medusas.

Day of sea in the sea, high day
Where my gestures are seagulls who lose themselves
Spiralling over the clouds, over the spume.

Translated from the Portuguese by Ruth Fainlight

Beach

The pines moan when the wind passes
The sun beats on the earth and the stones burn.

Fantastic sea gods stroll at the edge of the world
Crusted with salt and brilliant as fishes.

Sudden wild birds hurled
Against the light into the sky like stones
Mount and die vertically
Their bodies taken by space.

The waves butt as if to smash the light
Their brows ornate with columns.

And an ancient nostalgia of being a mast
Sways in the pines.

Translated from the Portuguese by Ruth Fainlight

Muse

Muse teach me the song
Revered and primordial
The song for everyone
Believed by all

Muse teach me the song
The true brother of each thing

Incendiary of the night
And evening's secret

Muse teach me the song
That takes me home
Without delay or haste
Changed to plant or stone

Or changed into the wall
Of the first house
Or become the murmur
Of sea all around

(I remember the floor
Of well-scrubbed planks
Its soapy smell
Keeps coming back)

Muse teach me the song
Of the sea's breath
Heaving with brilliants
Muse teach me the song
Of the white room
And the square window

So I can say
How evening there
Touched door and table
Cup and mirror
How it embraced

Because time pierces
Time divides
And time thwarts
Tears me alive
From the walls and floor
Of the first house

Muse teach me the song
Revered and primordial

To fix the brilliance
Of the polished morning

That rested its fingers
Gently on the dunes
And whitewashed the walls
Of those simple rooms

Muse teach me the song
That chokes my throat

Translated from the Portuguese by Ruth Fainlight

The Small Square

My life had taken the form of a small square
That autumn when your death was being meticulously organized
I clung to the square because you loved
The humble and nostalgic humanity of small shops
Where shopkeepers fold and unfold ribbons and cloth
I tried to become you because you were going to die
And all my life there would cease to be mine
I tried to smile as you smiled
At the newspaper seller at the tobacco seller
At the woman without legs who sold violets
I asked the woman without legs to pray for you
I lit candles at all the altars
Of the churches standing in the corner of that square
Hardly had I opened my eyes when I saw and read
The vocation for eternity written on your face
I summoned up the streets places people
Who were the witnesses of your face
So they would call you so they would unweave
The tissue that death was binding around you

Translated from the Portuguese by Ruth Fainlight

I Feel the Dead

I feel the dead in the cold of violets
And that great vagueness in the moon.

The earth is doomed to be a ghost,
She who rocks all death in herself.

I know I sing at the edge of silence,
I know I dance around suspension,
Possess around dispossession.

I know I pass around the mute dead
And hold within myself my own death.

But I have lost my being in so many beings,
Died my life so many times,
Kissed my ghosts so many times,
Known nothing of my acts so many times,
That death will be simply like going
From inside the house into the street.

Translated from the Portuguese by Ruth Fainlight

The Flute

In the room's corner the shadow played its little flute
It was then I remembered the cisterns and sea-nettles
And the mortal glitter of the naked beach

Night's ring was solemnly placed on my finger
And the silent fleet continued its immemorial journey

Translated from the Portuguese by Ruth Fainlight

EUGENIO DE ANDRADE

Portugal (b. 1923)

Eugénio de Andrade is the pen name of José Fontinhas, who was born in Póvoa de Atalaia, a village near the Spanish border. Since 1950 he has lived alone in Porto, and until his retirement in 1983 he worked in the Department of Public Health and Social Welfare. Although he began publishing in his teens, his mature career was launched in 1948; since then he has published prodigiously, been awarded Portugal's most prestigious literary prizes, and come to be his country's most widely known and translated poet after Fernando Pessoa. Marguerite Yourcenar once called his poetry a "well-tempered clavier," but its elegant finish works to disguise his sometimes achingly anguished feelings. Like Constantine Cavafy, de Andrade is the lyricist as abandoned romantic. The sensual surface of experience—what he calls "the rough or sweet skin of things"—and a pulsing nostalgia are his focus, and the natural world is his model: "earth and water, light and wind, unite to give a body to all the love of which my poetry is capable."

Penniless Lovers

They had faces open to whoever passed.
They had legends and myths
and a chill in the heart.
They had gardens where the moon strolled
hand in hand with the water.
They had an angel of stone for a brother.

They had like everyone
the miracle of every day
dripping from the roofs;
and golden eyes
glowing with
a wilderness of dreams.

They were hungry and thirsty like animals,
and there was silence
around their steps.
But at every gesture they made,
a bird was born from their fingers
and, dazzled, vanished into space.

Translated from the Portuguese by Alexis Levitin

Music

Poplars.

This music
of morning's white-washed walls.

Sweet vowels
of shadow and water
in a summer of tawny
lazing animals.

Morning lark
in the white
sand of June.

Acidic music
of thistles
and knives.

Music of fire
around the lips.

Unbuttoned
round the waist.

Between the legs
just there.

Music
of the first rains
upon the hay.

Fragrance only,
bee of water.

Rest and retreat
where the brief flame
of a pomegranate shines.

Music, take me:

Where are the boats?
Where are the islands?

Translated from the Portuguese by Alexis Levitin

Silence

When tenderness
seems tired at last of its offices

and sleep, that most uncertain vessel,
still delays,

when blue bursts from
your eyes

and searches
mine for steady seamanship,

then it is I speak to you of words
desolate, derelict,
transfixed by silence.

Translated from the Portuguese by Alexis Levitin

Fable

There they were, right before my eyes: it was terrible and at the same time fascinating.

At first I thought he was trying to kill her, but quickly I realized it wasn't so, maybe they both were dying, only later was some distant call made flesh in me. Then I became totally riveted to their movements, that labored, exhausted breathing, that thin gurgle rattling from their mouths.

Maria's breasts fell naked from her blouse. One of the carpenter's hands was lost in her tangled hair, the other seemed to have buried itself in the sand. The rest was that man's body, all of it: rigid and quivering at the same time, from the strain of focusing all that drive in its buttocks, the bow from which the arrow sped, to impale itself, exasperated, in the young girl's bowels. He looked like a winded horse—eyes closed, sweat dripping from the roots of his hair, spreading over his back, his loins, and his legs, almost totally exposed. A blind horse biting the white sky of August. But the earth called him, and a prolonged whinny filled the riverbed, then died high amongst the alders. At last peace descended upon the earth.

Maria looked at the carpenter through eyes brimming with astonishment, like someone who had lost everything in that one moment. Slowly, she passed her hand through his hair, in a timid caress, and began to cry. The carpenter also looked at her, but his eyes were different, they were the eyes of solitude itself.

Without a word, the man got up and began to piss. The girl also stood up and, her back turned, seemed to be cleaning her legs. I hid myself better behind the alders and saw nothing more. I heard the footsteps of both moving off, each in a separate direction, my heart tight as a knot. With a leap, I threw myself into the bed their bodies had made in the sand, breathing in eagerly, as if the air could bring me more than the warm, acrid smell of urine, and I ceased to notice the footsteps, already far off, and the snapping of dry branches here and there, and heard nothing but silence. Painful, unbearable silence.

Translated from the Portuguese by Alexis Levitin

from White on White

V

A friend is sometimes desert,
sometimes water.
Let go of August's lowest
murmur; a body

isn't always the abode of a furtive
naked light, of bird-
laden lemon trees
and summer in one's hair;

it is in the dark foliage of sleep
that wet skin
glistens,
the troubled flowering of the tongue.

What is real is the word.

XII

It's coming, it's coming to an end,
the light of March.
That's where it wandered, an intimate of every stone
and of the cats, along the grass

it tumbled with the children,
their fresh little bottoms.
No one is lord of light arrested
in a glance, no one

hesitates to sing before the silence
of a closed rose.
If you go to the window, perhaps you'll still catch
the dying of the last light.

Madness. The madness of March.

XVIII

The reasons of the world
are not exactly your reasons.
To live with burning hands isn't easy,
to live is to illuminate

with a skimming light the thickness of the body,
the blindness of the wall.
That taste of blood
which brought the spring, if spring there was,

does not lead to a crown of flame.
Black sheets of water
and the excrement of cormorants
compose your suffering.

It is a smell of semen
that the tidal breezes always bring.

XXX

It burns you, the memory of the night before
we spoke, burns you, the salt
of the mouth which bit
before it kissed.

You don't have room to die
with the morning, you only have a hole
in which to hide your tears,
a dry branch for chasing off the flies.

The soul's task is to unlearn.
Animals are the great marvel,
no memory of having been brother
to the morning star.

Perhaps already quenched or crumbling to dark.

XXXV

Sometimes one enters the house with autumn
hanging by a thread,
one sleeps better then,
even silence stills itself at last.

Perhaps out in the night I hear a rooster crow,
and a little boy climbs the stairs
with a carnation
and news of my mother.

I've never been so bitter, I tell him,
never in my shadow did the light
die so young
and so obscured.

It feels like snow.

Translated from the Portuguese by Alexis Levitin

ANGEL GONZALEZ

Spain (b. 1925)

"My poems are as much the result of my personal experience," writes Ángel González, "as they are the product of the historic time in which it has been my lot to live—or rather, to be a witness." Born in Oviedo, González's young life was stricken by the Spanish Civil War: one of his brothers was exiled, another was assassinated. He eventually became a lawyer and worked for the Civil Administration in Madrid. His first book of poems appeared in 1956 and was immediately successful. Many awards followed over the years, from the Premio Antonio Machado in 1956 to the Premio Principe de Asturias de las Letras in 1985. Growing up in a time of violence and oppression, González was determined, he says, to bear witness to the tumult "not in what the words say but in what they imply, in the spaces of shadow, of silence, of anger, or of helplessness that they discover or cover. The existence of a censorship that was ruthless, and also frequently and fortunately inept, forced me at times to have recourse to an ironical and ambiguous language, and even to transfer to a distant objective correlative many of my more immediate and urgent concerns." His civil poetry is balanced by a more lyrical side, and his poems of love are tempered by poems about mortality.

Before I Could Call Myself Ángel González

Before I could call myself Ángel González,
before the earth could support the weight of my body,
a long time
and a great space were necessary:
men from all the seas and all the lands,
fertile wombs of women, and bodies
and more bodies, incessantly fusing
into another new body.
Solstices and equinoxes illuminated
with their changing lights, and variegated skies,
the millenary trip of my flesh
as it climbed over centuries and bones.

Of its slow and painful journey,
of its escape to the end, surviving
shipwrecks, anchoring itself
to the last sigh of the dead,
I am only the result, the fruit,
what's left, rotting, among the remains;
what you see here,
is just that:
tenacious trash resisting
its ruin, fighting against wind,
walking streets that go
nowhere. The success
of all failures. The insane
force of dismay . . .

Translated from the Spanish by Steven Ford Brown and Gutierrez Revuelta

City

Things glisten. Roof tiles rise
over the tree tops.
Almost to the breaking point, tense,
the resilient streets.
There you are: beneath the intersection
of metallic cables,
where the sun fits like a halo
complimenting your image.
Rapid swallows threaten
impassive facades. Glass
transmits luminous and secretive
messages.
Everything consists of brief, invisible
gestures for habitual eyes.
And suddenly you're not there. Good-bye, love, good-bye.
You're already gone.
Nothing remains of you. The city rotates:
grinder in which everything is undone.

Translated from the Spanish by Steven Ford Brown and Gutierrez Revuelta

Yesterday

Yesterday was Wednesday all morning.
By afternoon it changed:
it became almost Monday,
sadness invaded hearts
and there was a distinct
panic of movement toward
the trolleys
that take the swimmers down to the river.

At about seven a small plane slowly
crossed the sky, but not even the children
watched it.
          The cold
was unleashed,
someone went outdoors wearing a hat,
yesterday, and the whole day
was like that,
already you see,
how amusing,
yesterday and always yesterday and even now,
strangers
are constantly walking through the streets
or happily indoors snacking on
bread and coffee with cream: what
joy!

Night fell suddenly,
the warm yellow street lamps were lit,
and no one could
impede the final dawn
of today's day,
so similar
and yet
so different in lights and aroma!

For that very same reason,
because everything is just as I told you,

let me tell you
about yesterday, once more
about yesterday: the incomparable
day that no one will ever
see again upon the earth.

Translated from the Spanish by Steven Ford Brown and Gutierrez Revuelta

The Future

But the future is different
from that destiny seen from afar,
magical world, vast sphere
brushed by the long arm of desire,
brilliant ball the eyes dream,
shared dwelling
of hope and deception, dark
land
of illusion and tears
the stars predicted
and the heart awaits
and that is always, always, always distant.

But, I think, the future is also another thing:
a verb tense in motion, in action, in combat,
a searching movement toward life,
keel of the ship that strikes the water
and struggles to open between the waves
the exact breach the rudder commands.

I'm on this line, in this deep
trajectory of agony and battle,
trapped in a tunnel or trench
that with my hands I open, close, or leave,
obeying the heart that orders,
pushes, determines, demands, and searches.

Future of mine . . . ! Distant heart
that dictated it yesterday:
don't be ashamed.
Today is the result of your blood,
pain that I recognize, light that I admit,
suffering that I assume,
love that I intend.

But still, nothing is definitive.
Tomorrow I have decided to go ahead
and advance,
tomorrow I am prepared to be content,
tomorrow I will love you, morning
and night,
tomorrow will not be exactly as God wishes.

Tomorrow, gray or luminous, or cold,
that hands shape in the wind,
that fists draw in the air.

Translated from the Spanish by Steven Ford Brown and Gutierrez Revuelta

Inventory of Places Propitious for Love

There aren't many.
Spring is highly esteemed, but
summer is better.
And also those crevices that autumn makes
when it intercedes with Sundays
in some cities
that are already as yellow as bananas.
Winter eliminates many places:
doorways facing north,
riverbanks,
public benches.
Buttresses outside
old churches

sometimes leave usable
hollows even if snow is falling.
But let's not fool ourselves: cold
temperatures and damp winds
make everything difficult.
Besides, regulations forbid
fondling (except for
predetermined areas of the skin
—of no interest at all—
of children, dogs, and other animals)
and *do not touch under peril of disgrace*
can be read in thousands of glances.
To where does one escape, then?
Everywhere squinting eyes,
tortured corneas,
implacable pupils,
reticent retinas,
are vigilant, suspicious, threatening.
Perhaps one has the option of going it alone,
of emptying the soul of tenderness
and filling it with boredom and indifference,
in this hostile time, propitious for hatred.

Translated from the Spanish by Steven Ford Brown and Gutierrez Revuelta

Whatever You Want

When you have money, buy me a ring,
when you have nothing, give me a corner of your mouth,
when you don't know what to do, come with me
—but later don't say you didn't know what you were doing.

In the morning you gather bundles of firewood
and they turn into flowers in your arms.
I hold you up grasping the petals,
if you leave I'll take away your perfume.

But I've already told you:
if you decide to leave, here's the door:
its name is Ángel and it leads to tears.

Translated from the Spanish by Steven Ford Brown and Gutierrez Revuelta

Diatribe Against the Dead

The dead are selfish:
they make us cry and don't care,
they stay quiet in the most inconvenient places,
they refuse to walk, we have to carry them
on our backs to the tomb
as if they were children. What a burden!
Unusually rigid, their faces
accuse us of something, or warn us;
they are the bad conscience, the bad example,
they are the worst things in our lives always, always.
The bad thing about the dead
is that there is no way you can kill them.
Their constant destructive labor
is for that reason incalculable.
Insensitive, distant, obstinate, cold,
with their insolence and their silence
they don't realize what they undo.

Translated from the Spanish by Steven Ford Brown and Gutierrez Revuelta

YVES BONNEFOY

France (b. 1923)

"To write poetry means thinking, but through form, through music—
music which helps, if we know how to listen. Poetry is what tries to make
music of what occurs in life," writes Yves Bonnefoy, who sometimes sees
poetry as the repudiation of *poems*. Although his treatment of them is
often elliptical and abstract, his themes are those of high romanticism:
death and longing, the natural world and the spiritual dimension. The ef-
fort of his supple, elegant style all along has been to unite these contradic-
tions. "I don't agree," he says, "with a number of contemporary critics
who see poems merely as verbal constructions, as what simply activates
and multiplies the relations that exist between words. I think, and in fact I
have always thought, that poetry is an experience of what goes beyond
words: call it the fleeting perception, then the more active remembrance,
of a state of indifferentiation, of unity—that state that characterizes real-
ity at the level that our language cannot reach, despite its definitions, its
designations, and its descriptions. This unity deserves to be perceived by
us, to be kept in mind, because in it the part becomes the whole, con-
sciousness is no longer kept separate from it, and as a consequence, death
ceases to be; it becomes simple metamorphosis, and so our anguish is qui-
eted, and the soul and body are at peace with one another." Bonnefoy
was born in Tours and studied philosophy at the University of Paris. He
has been active as an essayist, critic, translator, and editor, and since
1981 he has taught comparative poetics at the Collège de France. He is
usually regarded as the most important poet to have emerged in France
after World War II.

The Tree, the Lamp

The tree grows old in the tree, it is summer.
The bird leaps beyond birdsong and is gone.
The red of the dress illuminates and scatters
Away, in the sky, the lading of old sorrow.

O fragile country,
Like the flame of a lamp carried out-of-doors,
Sleep being close in the world's sap,
Simple the beating of the shared soul.

You too love the moment when the light of lamps
Fades and dreams into daylight.
You know it's the darkness of your own heart healing,
The boat that reaches shore and falls.

Translated from the French by Richard Pevear

The Words of Evening

The country of early October had no fruit
Not burst open in the grass, and the birds then
Came with cries of absence and of rubble
On a high, curved hull moving quickly towards us.

My words of evening,
You have the chill of late autumn grapes,
But even now the wine burns in your soul, and I find
My one true warmth in what you have begun.

The ship of a clear October's end
May come. Then we shall mingle these two lights,
O my bright ship wandering at sea,

Clarity of coming night and clarity of speech
—The mist that rises from all living things
And you, the glowing of my lamp in death.

Translated from the French by Richard Pevear

Summer Again

I step out into the snow, my eyes shut,
But the light knows how to pass
My porous lids and I can tell
That in my words it's again the snow
That swirls and clumps and shreds.

Snow:
A letter found and unfolded,
Its ink has blanched and in the signs
Is visible the clumsiness of the mind
That only manages to tangle the bright shadows.

We try to read it, we wonder
Who in our memory is thinking of us,
Except that it's summer again; and we can see
The leaves beneath the flakes, and the heat
Rising like mist from the absent soil.

Translated from the French by Lisa Sapinkopf

De Natura Rerum

Lucretius knew:
Open the casket
And you'll find it full
Of swirling snow.

Now and then two flakes
Will meet and merge,
Or else one will turn gracefully away
In its bit of death.

From where comes this brightening
In a few words

When one is merely night,
The other, dream?

From where comes this pair
Of walking, laughing shadows,
One of them all muffled
In red wool?

Translated from the French by Lisa Sapinkopf

The All, the Nothing

I

It's the last snow of the season,
The spring snow—the most skilled
At mending the rips in the dead wood
Before it's brought inside and burnt.

It's the first snow of your life,
Since yesterday there were only dots
Of color, brief pleasures, fears, chagrins—
Without substance, for lack of words.

And I can see joy overtaking the fear
In your eyes which amazement opened
In one great, bright leap: this cry, this laughter
That I love, and that I ponder.

For we're very near each other, and the child
Is the progenitor of the man who one morning
Held him, in adult hands, and lifted him up
Into the light's consenting.

II

Yes, it should be heard, and yes, made my own:
This bubbling spring, this cry of joy, which
Surges early and strong from among life's
Stones, then weakens and goes blind.

But writing is not having, nor is it being,
For within it the tremblings of joy
Are mere shadows, although the brightest ones,
In words still remembered

From the multitude of things that time
Raked long and hard with its talons,
—Thus I can only tell you
What I am not, except in my desire.

A way of taking: that of ceasing
To be oneself in the act of taking,
A way of telling: that of making it
Impossible to be alone in language.

III

May the big snow be for you the all, the nothing,
Child trying out your first uncertain steps in the grass,
Your eyes still full of the origin,
Hands grabbing at nothing but the light.

May the gleaming branches be the words
You'll have to listen to, not understanding
The meaning of their silhouette against the sky—
Otherwise you'd only name them at the price of losing.

May these two values, one sparkling, be enough for you,
Of the hill glimpsed through the opening between the trees,
Bee of life, when in your dream of the world
The world itself grows quiet.

And may the water that wells up in the meadow
Show you that joy can survive in dream,
Even when a breeze from who knows where
Is already scattering almond blossoms—and yet the other snow.

Translated from the French by Lisa Sapinkopf

A Stone

Summer passed through the cool rooms, violent,
Its eyes blind, its flanks bare;
It cried out, and its call troubled the dreams
Of those sleeping there in the simplicity of their light.

They shuddered and the rhythm of their breathing changed.
Their hands put down the heavy cup of sleep.
And already the sky was again on the earth,
Bringing the afternoon storms of summer, in the eternal.

Translated from the French by John Naughton

The Well

You hear the chain striking the wall
When the bucket goes down into the well, that other star,
Sometimes the evening star, the one that comes alone,
Sometimes the fire without rays that waits at dawn
For the shepherd and his flock to go out.

But the water at the bottom of the well is always closed,
And the star there remains forever sealed.
You can see shadows there, beneath branches,
That are travelers passing by night

Bowed down beneath a load of blackness they go
As if hesitating at a crossroads.
Some seem to wait, others withdraw
Into the glittering that flows without light.

Man's voyage, and woman's, is long, longer than life,
It is a star at the end of the road, a sky
That was shining, we thought, between two trees.
When the bucket touches the water that lifts it up,
There is joy, then the chain overwhelms it.

Translated from the French by John Naughton

The Top of the World

I

I go out,
There are thousands of stones in the sky,
I can hear
All around me the surging sounds of night.
Is it true, my friends,
That not a single star is stirring?

Is it true
That not one of these barks loaded
You would think with more than simple matter
And that seem turned toward the same pole,
Shudders suddenly and breaks free
From the mass of the others, left behind, dark?

Is it true
That not one of these figures, with eyes closed,
That smile at the prow of the world in the joy
Of the body that attends to nothing but its light,
Awakens and listens, hearing in the distance
A cry filled with love, not with desire?

II

This one would rise up, soundlessly,
And venture forth in the sea wind,
Like a young girl who goes out at night
Holding high a lamp that pours out
Its light, which frightens her, upon her shoulders,
And who looks about her, though the world is silent;
The footsteps of those who should open
Their doors beneath the trees and join her
Cannot yet be heard in the valley.

And yet, things seem so trusting,
The lamb gives itself so willingly
To the hand that kills.

And the looks one exchanges are sometimes so intense,
The voices grow so mysteriously troubled when certain
Words are spoken for tomorrow, or in the secret depths
Of the feverish invitations of night.
Is it true that words carry no promise,
A vast and senseless flash of lightning,

A glittering chest, but full of ashes?

III

There were times, my friends,
When, falling silent
All at once,
We would have listened to the sounds
Of the night rain on the dry tiles.

We would have seen the shepherd,
Bowed beneath the sudden downpour,
His head covered with a canvas sack,
Running to bring together his sheep.
We would have hoped that the knife
Of the lightning might sometimes,

In compassion,
Slip away from earth's fleecy back.

We would have caught a glimpse
Of the dreams that vanish with every dawn,
The gold-crowned dreams that set
Their glittering gifts beside the newborn child.

IV

And had she come
To sit beside us, the old woman
Who makes no sense, who has only her memories,
One of us would have said, stay,
Relax those hands blackened by the smoke,
Talk to us, teach us things, O vagabond.

The heavens were sealed, however,
As they are today,
The boat of each thing that had come in
Loaded with a wheat from the heights of the world
Remained moored at our nocturnal pier,
Shimmering faintly from just the rain
Falling in the winds of the sea.

And at evening the same weary herds were brought in,
Death served among us,
Taking in the milk that has the taste of ashes.

V

I go out.
I dream that I am going out into the snowy night.
I dream that I am carrying
With me, far, outside, there is no turning back,
The mirror from the upstairs bedroom, the mirror from
Summers past, the boat at whose prow

We, simple, pushed forward, questioning,
Deep in the sleep of summers that were brief, as life is.

In those days
It was through the sky gleaming in the mirror's waters
That the magi of our sleep, as they withdrew,
Would spread out their treasures in the darkened room.

VI

And in the rustling of the night sky
The beauty of the world bent down
To see her body reflected in the closed water
Of the sleepers, which branches out among the stones.
She brought trusting mouth and breath
Close to their lightless eyes. She would have wanted
Her brighter breast to appear beneath the shoulder
In the folds of her still closed robes,
Then day was rising around you,
Our earth in the mirror, and the sunlight
Hemmed your bare neck with a red band of mist.

But here I am now
Standing outside the house; everything is motionless
Since it is only a dream. And so I go on, leaving,
It hardly matters where, against a wall, beneath the stars,
This mirror, our life. And may night's dew
Condense and flow, over the images.

VII

O galaxies
Of the red dress
Glittering like the sands of a distant shore.

Dreams,
A flock, darker,
More tightly pressed together than stones.

I go on,
I pass by the almond trees on the terrace.
The fruit is ripe.
I open the almond and its heart sparkles.

I go on.
There is that immense flash of lightning
In front of me,
The sky,
The lamb bleeding in the straw.

Translated from the French by John Naughton

PHILIPPE JACCOTTET

France (b. 1925)

Born and educated in Switzerland, Philippe Jaccottet is a prominent critic, essayist, editor, and translator, in addition to being a poet of austere and haunting power. His first collections appeared in 1947 and 1953, and spoke to the existentialist sensibility of postwar Paris. "A stranger in this life" is how the poet first identified himself—a feeling that grows as well from his lingering fascination with surrealism, an awareness of "the other world present perhaps in this one." Although he remains a minimalist poet, his later work is warmer, reflecting both his marriage and his move to the provinces; the natural life of the senses and of the earth breathes through these poems. With an abstract lyricism, he writes about the mystery inherent in simple objects. He has wanted each poem to be "the pure water-drop." The critic Jean Starobinski has written of Jaccottet: "To be an ignorant man, to possess nothing but a fragile word, to find oneself as if relying upon darkness and nothingness: that is the position from which one must be constantly setting out. Setting out, starting again: Jaccottet doesn't resign himself to immobility, he doesn't submit to failure. When he writes, 'to start from nothing, that's my rule,' we recognize a necessary premise—nothingness—but also an indication of departure. Departure on the roads of earth, without hope of conquest, with no certain goal. But the word to which this gives rise, born of darkness and nothingness, carries within it the possibility of a journey into light. Jaccottet is one of the great poets of daybreak."

Distances

Swifts turn in the heights of the air;
higher still turn the invisible stars.
When day withdraws to the ends of the earth
their fires shine on a dark expanse of sand.

We live in a world of motion and distance.
The heart flies from tree to bird,
from bird to distant star,

from star to love; and love grows
in the quiet house, turning and working,
servant of thought, a lamp held in one hand.

Translated from the French by Derek Mahon

These wood-shadows

These wood-shadows, timid, patient,
lighter even than the grass
that survived the winter,
are the discreet, faithful,

barely perceptible shadows of death

Always in the daytime
circling our bodies
Always in the open field
these tombstones of blue slate

Translated from the French by Derek Mahon

Right at the end of night

Right at the end of night
the wind rises
and the candle goes out

Who is there to keep watch
before the first birds?
The river-cold wind knows

A flame, an inverted tear:
a coin for the ferryman

Translated from the French by Derek Mahon

Dawn

Hour when the moon mists over
at the approach of a mouth
murmuring a hidden name

so that one can scarcely make out
the comb and the hair

Translated from the French by W. S. Merwin

Swifts

At the stormy moment of dawn
at the apprehensive time
these sickles in the corn

Everything suddenly cries higher
than any ear can climb

Translated from the French by Derek Mahon

Weight of Stones

Weight of stones, of thoughts

Uneven balance
of mountain and dream

We still live in another world
perhaps the interval

Translated from the French by Derek Mahon

I Rise with an Effort

I rise with an effort and look out
at three different kinds of light—
that of the sky, that which from up there
pours into me and vanishes,
and that whose shadow my hand draws on the page.

The ink might be mistaken for shadow.

The sky descending takes me by surprise.

One would like to believe we suffer
to describe the light from above;
but pain is stronger than flight
and pity drowns everything, shining
with as many tears as the night.

Translated from the French by Derek Mahon

Glimpses

The children run shouting
in the thick grass of the playground.

The tall tranquil trees
and the torrential light
of a September morning
protect them still from the anvil
sparkling with stars up there.

♦

The soul, so chilly, so fierce, must it really
trudge up this glacier for ever,
solitary, in bare feet, no longer

remembering even its childhood prayer,
its coldness for ever punished by this cold?

◆

Wrapped in a blue bathrobe
which is wearing out too,
she goes to a mirror round
like the mouth of a child
who doesn't know how to lie.

Hair the color of ash now
in the slow burn of time;

and yet the morning sun
quickens her shadow still.

◆

At the window with its freshly whitewashed frame
(to keep out flies, to keep out ghosts)
the white head of an old man leans
over a letter or the local news.
Against the wall dark ivy grows.

Save him, ivy and lime, from the dawn wind,
from long nights and the other, eternal night.

Translated from the French by Derek Mahon

JACQUES DUPIN

France (b. 1927)

Jacques Dupin was born in Privas. With Yves Bonnefoy and André de Bouchet, he founded and has edited the prestigious literary journal *L'Éphémère*. He was also the publications editor at the Galerie Maeght and has written books about Miró and Giacometti. In the tradition of René Char and Francis Ponge, Dupin writes with an austere amplitude concentrated on the image and on ideas that images can release. It is a shadowy, minimalist search for origins. He writes, as he says in one prose poem, "as if I had never been born. Every word until this moment: pulverized, laid bare, breathed back into nothingness. To write *without any words,* as if I were being born."

Mineral Kingdom

In this country lightning quickens stone.

On the peaks that dominate the gorges
Ruined towers rise up
Like nimble torches of the mind
That revive the nights of high wind
The instinct of death in the quarryman's blood.

Every granite vein
Will unravel in his eyes.

The fire that will never be cured of us.
The fire that speaks our language.

Translated from the French by Paul Auster

My Body

My body, you will not fill the ditch
That I am digging, that I deepen each night.

Like a wild boar caught in the underbrush
You leap, you struggle.

Does the vine on the rampart remember another body
Prostrate on the keyboard of the void?

Throw off your clothes, throw away your food,
Diviner of water, hunter of lowly light.

The sliding of the hill
Will overflow the false depth,
The secret excavation underfoot.

Calm wriggles into the night air
Through disjointed stones and the riddled heart

At the instant you disappear,
Like a splinter in the sea.

Translated from the French by Paul Auster

Waiting with lowered voice

Waiting with lowered voice
For something terrible and simple
—Like the harvest of the lightning
Or the crumbling of the plaster . . .

It is the nearness of the intact sky
That emaciates the flocks,

This jut of burning rock,
And the revival of smells from the flowerless mountain . . .

Summits of wind and famine,
Insipid motet, fury of returns,
I dread the ruin which is due to me
Less than this immunity
That fetters me in its rays.

Promised land, land that crumbles,
Despite the columns, despite the drum.

Translated from the French by Paul Auster

from Songs of Rescue

1

From a thread in space, endless and unbroken. Without unravelling the fabric of the open night. Without interrupting the concert of *their* cries.

2

Dream of an afternoon: a slow exodus of clouds in the eaves. And the instinct for hanging on, my fingers clenched around a rope.

3

Staggering, out in the open . . . As if he no longer needed a name to be lost. He listens to the light patiently go into him again. Patiently, the light absolves him.

17

Two vultures, motionless in the middle of the sky. I am asleep. I am alive. Ready to pounce. From the middle of the sky, or from the edge. Cloudless, no churning in the gut.

19

Busy with your sewing: a needle pointing north, a needle pointing south, a needle pointing to the heart . . . A sharper needle penetrating the needle: pain shot through, naked light.

20

At my feet, the dried-up bed of a river. In the wrinkles of my face, a harmonica. I sleep, hiccuping like a drunkard, an infinity of windows around me.

43

The air is not religious, but in the twisted lung the air's fever is like a wick, dripping with darkness. The air is holy like a foot, like laughter . . . Like the cloven foot of the blind wanderer, like the laughter of the drug addict. Finding a way . . .

44

What could no longer *be dug*. Under a night like this one. Held captive by the white ground. By the influx of dew. What already could be written no more . . . The wet color on the edge.

45

In this forgetfulness,—hatching death like a stone, heedful of this shuddering in the grass—like a stone,—in range of the water's smell,—of signs glistening in the abundant ashes . . .

51

Scars from the plow and the stern, wheelmarks in the flesh . . . I have
no idea what comes before and after this dancing ascent of mud . . .
My dark eyes stare into the brightness of yours.

54

A profile, and the absence of a story. I am not on the point of death.
I have stopped drawing. I break down the line while listening for a
face. The sharpening of the moon in its first quarter.

56

Of you, of anyone, I know nothing about the edge and the heart.
Like a man dying on his feet . . .

Translated from the French by Paul Auster

CLAIRE MALROUX

France (b. 1935)

A respected translator of English-language poetry and fiction, known particularly for her work on Emily Dickinson, Claire Malroux has preferred, until recently, to separate her two principal activities and have her poems appear, in journals and in five published books, under the pseudonym Claire Sara Roux. Born in Albi, in southwestern France, she has from the start conducted in her work a quest for the light and clarity of her meridional childhood. The deliberately ambiguous title of her most recent book, *Entre nous et la lumière*, captures this sense of both barrier and complicity. Her poems bear the marks of an often difficult evolution, underscored by a will to "dissolve" the shadows cast by anguish, to gather the scattered, revealing fragments of life, in order to affirm the integrity of the individual faced by a blinding but always concealed mystery. Recently, she has made use of more ample, sustained forms in her poems, in which a reconstituted spoken diction opens out to its limits and recognizable cityscapes and urban interiors offset her interior geographies.

Fingers probe

Fingers probe
The desert of a face
Diviners
Tear detectors

Below the surface
They plow their furrows
Their hives
Their palaces

Passions dissolve there
Rages also

Nothing glistens
Under the arcades
No trade
On the docks

Without a harbor
A single
Boat
Heads out to sea

Translated from the French by Marilyn Hacker

In October

October its brilliance
In its arms
        the condemned leaves
        the obsession
with dying beautifully

Whorls of more carnal
        flowers
and regal silhouettes which purify themselves
        at the borders
        in the reachieved rigor of gardens

Birds shriek across
transparencies

Engraved in the actual
in the insubstantial
        grooves
the mechanism cannot fail
even if human gestures
come undone

The obstinate
light
imposes loving hands
upon the cold

Translated from the French by Marilyn Hacker

Every morning

Every morning the curtain rises
Alone, you listen to the dark dissolving
The stars slowly clicking themselves apart
The sky turns back into this breezy scarf
Shaken out by the awakened birds
You don't touch each other but you walk together
Leaning against and within each other until evening
When, alone, you chase the wild night at your gate
Sweet to weep for, like a wet stray dog
You don't want to hear the crows cry
The diminishing number of lines
To be spoken on this stage, set for how long
The shadow grows, flesh hollows itself out, another
Takes your place. Step by step you leave yourself

Translated from the French by Marilyn Hacker

Octet Before Winter

The body is immobile, left behind
On the coral leatherette train-seat.
Thoughts revolve with the wheels but
Don't advance, stopped against the present,
The future which the engines bear away.
I want to wrench myself out of time's ballast,
Switch rails. The buildings raise a hideous

Hedge. Then rocks efface themselves
Before amorous, ravaged gardens.
I relinquish the acacias, lilacs, vulnerable
Foliage. Irises on the embankments, vague fairy-tale
Grass. A pact still links me
To the tree trunks, their branches' unpolished
Diamond on grey sky. I want their lines
To keep my cindered skeleton erect.

Often, like anyone, I ask myself
What ties me to life, especially in winter
When the dying year strikes out on its graph
Three hundred and sixty-five specific days circling the sun
Revolving back, as fatally, to night:
Sometimes they are huge bodies, illuminated
Igloos, their heads shrouded in fog
Gestures slow down then, voluptuously,
Like those of someone who knows he's going to faint,
But knows a wall of glass will break his fall
Or there's the tranquil pulse of flames between
What's wished for, what's forbidden, forbidden and wished
Showing a flux, a rhythm, an outpouring
Towards a heart which only believes in mechanical laws
The great watchmaker's clock, which we take apart
Patiently, piece by piece, to convince ourselves
That the poet who holds it poised above the void
Is an unprogrammed computer, an automaton

Wisteria on a wrought-iron door, mid-boulevard,
Is not moved by the ambulance alarm
Nor are the boule-players under the fine grey hairs
Of the elms, exiled Russian princesses.
Traffic flows, on a sad and windy
Saturday before Christmas. Pedestrians
In pairs, their heads bowed, bear home fir trees
Like stags speared in some barbaric hunt.
Rue Maison Dieu: palatial cafés.
The Gare Montparnasse spreads out its entrails
Crossed by an iron bridge in its green cage,
Unlikely ramp toward an Eiffel Tower sky.

We wait for something which is not the rain,
The caress of its mourning-dove feathers,
And that rumbling which at last breaks through our apathy
Announces neither storm nor oracle
But more likely precedes some demolition:
It's the soul that's marked this time: all its flame
Sheltered in a hothouse of budding lamps.

Like noble ladies, pregnant and slightly weary,
Ascending and descending, two by two
(discussing labor laws and salaries),
A marble staircase, the sole noteworthy feature
Of a château, relic of a mythic Loire,
He hears notes pacing up and down the keyboard
Downstairs, without sorrow, or joy
Either, but with a traveler's detachment
Who sees his orbit of journeys closed on a wall.
A map of memory. His feet have kept
The imprint of rocks, of moss, of sand,
Of valley grasses, more agile than he;
His hands, calloused from tree trunks, from iron ore,
From his horses' reins as they reared up at the sea.
Still, this place remains more shadowed than a moon.
Pinned to the filmy breasts of womanly clouds,
He has passed through his legends, his fantasies.
These days, he keeps to the stubborn repetition
Of a few scales: the shuffle around a prison yard
Or the infinite spiral of a cloister.

Long luminous afternoon
Poised on the grass like a bubble
Blown by the wind
Will a breath roll it towards the estuary
Where the river, dilated but docile,
Comes to spill itself out every day
And meeting the cold spray, the sepulchral
Tongue of the sea
Will it burst with its milky flocks
Its trees budding with wings, the mirage
Of hills which will not be hills of sand?

Or, thrusting itself forward
On the powdery trail of shells,
Will it get lost in the labyrinth of marshes
Slowly rejoin the canals' long sleep
Denied by their myriad blooming eyelids,
Galaxies floating on the life-bearing liquid?
The calf who sees the pool of twilight growing
Glues itself to its mother's shadow.
Immobile group. This sculpture is
The only certainty. Today
Once again, nothing will be decided.

A storm of trucks, of tractors
Periodically breaches the valley
Blue with olive trees near an Iberian pueblo
Sometimes the town crier's trumpet, illusory
Emblem (it's recorded),
Dark rings under the eyes of the village turned
Inward toward the dethroned queen, her
Robe of state constellated with nails
The better to hide the gashes,
Thorns, blood of the desiccated wood.

Fable of the vanished one—every sentence
Unwinds the shroud, exposes
A lunar landscape of wounds
This day tasting of permanent summer
Which quenches no thirst, a sleep beneath the lashes
Of atoms shrilling through its serenity
Is death already and yourself that fly
Bumbling at its periphery to drink
A drop from the beautiful shoulder
Of the indifferent evening, never over

These lime-green chestnuts in the menacing
fire of summer set my teeth on edge
The season comes to term, completes itself
without raising the specter of any death,
not perpetuity but continuity
in after-imaginings of (bio)logical

sequences positing a mythic timelessness
Each chestnut tree will extinguish itself
candelabra after candelabra
carrying its cross in silence
on our too-human avenues
Nonetheless we must live through the winter
before exile, feel our way
among these lunar embers in the fog
toward those unrubied crowns

The lipstick poised in the air and the feeling of having
made up life as much if not more than yourself
brushed its sharp teeth then soaped rubbed
its arms its neck more rarely its private
parts without touching them. Here everything is snow
to soak up blood hairs pus shed scraps
of skin the corpse's fresh decay. A heron
at the moment it straddles the muddy pond,
a swan on narrow waters, an ugly duckling
beating its forehead against porcelain flanks.
All this transparency to push time back
into the corners or behind the swivel mirror.
The gaze is everything in this blind room,
death to those who let themselves drown in it.

Translated from the French by Marilyn Hacker

PIER PAOLO PASOLINI

Italy (1922–1975)

Poet, novelist, playwright, translator, screenwriter, actor, polemicist, film
director, and celebrity, Pier Paolo Pasolini was a gargantuan and trouble-
some figure in modern Italian culture. He was born in Bologna and stud-
ied at the university there. As a young poet after the war, he began by
writing in the Friulian dialect of the north. From the beginning, too, his
sympathies were with the poor, the excluded, the victims. His first novel,
The Ragazzi, about the hard life of street urchins in Rome, caused an up-
roar. In novels and films, his objective look at the often sordid underside
of contemporary life was always deliberately political and controversial.
This stark realism—"I don't believe in pity," he said—gave way in his
verse to a more lyrical, even vulnerable side of his imagination. His first
collection, *The Ashes of Gramsci,* which appeared in 1957, was boldly
political in inspiration; later books explore, in an intensely personal man-
ner, the social and sexual contradictions of his time. In a final, terrible
irony, Pasolini was murdered by a teenage hustler he had picked up in
Ostia. In 1970, in an introduction to a selection of his poems, he wrote
that what struck him about them was "a widespread sense of discoura-
ging unhappiness: an unhappiness that's part of the language itself, like a
datum of its own, reducible in quantity and almost in physicality. This
sense (almost a right) of being unhappy is so predominant that the sensual
joy is obscured by it; and so is its civil idealism. What strikes me further,
on reading these poems, is the realization of how ingenuous was the ex-
pansiveness with which I wrote them: it was as if I were writing for some-
one who could only love me a great deal. I understand now why I have
been the object of so much suspicion and hatred."

Prayer to My Mother

It's so hard to say in a son's words
what I'm so little like in my heart.

Only you in all the world know what my
heart always held, before any other love.

So, I must tell you something terrible to know:
From within your kindness my anguish grew.

You're irreplaceable. And because you are,
the life you gave me is condemned to loneliness.

And I don't want to be alone. I have an infinite
hunger for love, love of bodies without souls.

For the soul is inside you, it is you, but
you're my mother and your love's my slavery:

My childhood I lived a slave to this lofty
incurable sense of an immense obligation.

It was the only way to feel life,
the unique form, sole color; now, it's over.

We survive, in the confusion
of a life reborn outside reason.

I pray you, oh, I pray: Do not hope to die.
I'm here, alone, with you, in a future April . . .

Translated from the Italian by Norman MacAfee and Luciano Martinengo

Southern Dawn

I was walking near the hotel in the evening
when four or five boys appeared
on the field's tiger fur,
with no cliff, ditch, vegetation
to take cover from possible bullets—for
Israel was there, on the same tiger fur
specked with cement-block houses, useless
walls, like all slums.
I happened on them at that absurd point

far from street, hotel,
border. It was one of countless such
friendships, which last an evening
then torture the rest of your life. They,
the disinherited and, what's more, sons
(possessing the knowledge the disinherited
have of evil—burglary, robbery, lying—
and the naïve ideal sons have
of feeling consecrated to the world),
deep in their eyes, right off, was the old
light of love, almost gratitude.
And talking, talking till
night came (already one was embracing me,
saying now he hated me, now, no, he loved me,
loved me) they told me everything about themselves,
every simple thing. These were gods
or sons of gods, mysteriously shooting because
of a hate that would push them down from
the clay hills like bloodthirsty bridegrooms upon
the invading kibbutzim on the other side of Jerusalem . . .
These ragged urchins, who sleep in open air now
at the edge of a slum field—
with elder brothers, soldiers armed with
old rifles, mustached like those
destined to die the ancient deaths of mercenaries—
These are the Jordanians, terror of Israel,
weeping before my eyes
the ancient grief of refugees. One of them,
sworn to a hate that's already almost bourgeois (to blackmailing
moralism, to nationalism that has paled with neurotic
fury), sings to me the old refrain
learned from his radio, from his kings—
another, in his rags, listens, agreeing,
while puppylike he presses close to me,
not showing, in a slum field
of the Jordan's desert, in the world,
anything but love's poor simple feeling.

Translated from the Italian by Norman MacAfee and Luciano Martineng

Civil Song

Their cheeks were fresh and tender,
perhaps kissed for the first time.
Seen from behind, as they turned
to rejoin their tender group, they looked older,
coats over light trousers. Their poverty
ignores the winter's cold. Slightly bowlegged . . .
collars ragged . . . like their older brothers,
already discredited citizens. For a few more years
they won't have a price, and nothing can humiliate
those unable to judge themselves. Though they do it
with so much incredible spontaneity, they're offering themselves
    to life,
and life in turn needs them. They're so ready for it!
They return the kisses, savoring the novelty.
Then they go, as imperturbably as when they came.
But since they're still confident of that life that
cherishes them, they make sincere promises, plan a promising
    future
of embraces, even kisses. Who would make the revolution—
if it ever took place—but they? Tell them; they're ready,
as one man, as they embrace and kiss,
with the same aroma in their cheeks.
But it won't be their trust in the world that triumphs.
That the world will have to overlook.

Translated from the Italian by Norman MacAfee and Luciano Martinengo

Lines from the Testament

Solitude: you must be very strong
to love solitude; you have to have good legs
and uncommon resistance; you must avoid catching
colds, flu, sore throat; and you must not fear
thieves and murderers; if you have to walk

all afternoon or even all evening
you must do it with ease; there's no sitting down,
especially in winter, with wind striking the wet grass,
and damp mud-caked stone slabs among garbage;
there's no real consolation, none at all,
beyond having a whole day and night ahead of you
with absolutely no duties or limits.
Sex is a pretext. For however many the encounters
—and even in winter, through streets abandoned to the wind,
amid expanses of garbage against distant buildings,
there are many—they're only moments in the solitude;
the livelier and warmer the sweet body
that anoints with seed and then departs,
the colder and deathlier the beloved desert around you;
like a miraculous wind, it fills you with joy,
it, not the innocent smile or troubled arrogance
of the one who then goes away; he carries with him a
        youthfulness
awesomely young; and in this he's inhuman
because he leaves no traces, or, better, only one trace
that's always the same in all seasons.
A boy in his first loves
is nothing less than the world's fecundity.
It is the world that thus arrives with him, appearing, disappearing,
like a changing form. All things remain the same—
and you'll search half the city without finding him again;
the deed is done; its repetition is ritual. And
the solitude's still greater if a whole crowd
waits its turn: in fact the number of disappearances grows—
leaving is fleeing—and what follows weighs upon the present
like a duty, a sacrifice performed to the death wish.
Growing old, however, one begins to feel weary
especially at the moment when dinnertime is over
and for you nothing is changed; then you're near to screaming or
        weeping;
and that would be awesome if it wasn't precisely merely weariness
and perhaps a little hunger. Awesome, because that would mean
your desire for solitude could no longer be satisfied,
and if what isn't considered solitude is the true solitude,
the one you can't accept, what can you expect?

There's no lunch or dinner or satisfaction in the world
equal to an endless walk through the streets of the poor,
where you must be wretched and strong, brothers to the dogs.

Translated from the Italian by Norman MacAfee and Luciano Martinengo

Part of a Letter to the Codignola Boy

Caro ragazzo, yes, sure, let's meet,
but don't expect much from this meeting.
At the least, a new disappointment, a new
emptiness: one of those meetings good
for narcissistic dignity, like a sorrow.
At forty, I'm just as I was at seventeen.
However frustrated, the middle-aged man and the kid
are able, certainly, to *meet,* hemming and hawing
over ideas held in common, over problems
that can make two decades loom, a whole lifetime,
even though they are apparently the same.
Until one word, finding its way out of uncertain throats,
worn out from weeping and the wish to be alone—
reveals the incurable disparity of it all.
And, with you, I will have to play the poet-
father, and then fall back on irony—
which will embarrass you: the forty-year-old
by now the master of his own life,
livelier, younger than the seventeen-year-old.
Other than this likelihood, this pretense,
I have nothing else to tell you.
I'm stingy, the little I possess
I hold tight to my diabolical heart.
And the two lengths of skin between cheekbone and chin,
under the mouth disfigured by forced, timid
smiles, and the eye which has lost
its sweetness, like a fig gone sour—
there might appear before you the exact
portrait of that maturity you're pained by,

a maturity not at all brotherly. Of what use to you
is a contemporary—merely withering away
in the very leanness that devours his flesh?
What he has given he's given, the rest
is exhausted compassion.

Translated from the Italian by David Stivender and J. D. McClatchy

The Day of My Death

In a city, Trieste or Udine,
    along the linden boulevard,
when in spring
    the leaves change color,
I'll drop dead
    under the ardent sun,
        blond and tall,
and I'll close my eyes,
leaving the sky to its splendor.

Under a warm green linden
    I'll fall into my death's darkness,
    scattering linden and sun.
The beautiful boys
    will run in that light
    which I've just lost,
flying from school
with curls on their brows.

Translated from the Italian by Lawrence Ferlinghetti and Francesca Valente

ANDREA ZANZOTTO

Italy (b. 1921)

Born in Piave di Soligo, Andrea Zanzotto writes poetry rooted in the landscape and culture of his native region, the Veneto. He grew up under Fascism and, after studying at the University of Padua, joined the Resistance. After the war, he traveled in France and Switzerland, but eventually he returned to his birthplace, where he taught for forty years in a public school. His early poetry was encouraged by Giuseppe Ungaretti, Eugenio Montale, and others, and from the start he wanted both to draw on the Italian poetic tradition and to freshen it. The natural world and the round of seasons have provided the main framework of his poems. Within those boundaries he has obliquely explored the impact of history and more directly meditated on the philosophical exchanges between the self and other states of being. He has written poems in dialect and been continually fascinated by the relationship between language and identity. His voice, when not raised to an experimental pitch, maintains a quiet, almost pastoral tone, yet what Montale admired in Zanzotto's work is the heart of it: "the intensity of his lived experience."

How Long

How long between the grain and the wind
of those garrets
higher, more spun out than the sky,
how long I have left you
my writings, my withered risks.
With angel and chimera
with ancient instrument,
with the diary and the drama
the nights play by turns with the sun.
I left you up there to save
from the cauterizing light
my uncertain roof
the disoriented gables,
terraces where the crazed hail walks:

you, only shadow in winter,
shadow among the ice-demons.
Moths and noxious butterflies
rats and moles descending to hibernate
taught and refined you,
Sagittarius and Capricorn
slanted cold lances at you
and Aquarius tempered in its silences
in its transparencies
a year dripping with blood, an inexplicable
loss of mine.

Already for you with sublime tints
of fresh antennas and roofs
the new days ascend all around,
already someone rises and shakes
the mould and snow from the seas;
and if I climb to you by ledges and ropes
toward the prism that outlines you
toward dawn that shelters you,
my heart pierced by the future
ignores lightning-flashes and the chains
that still weigh down the borders.

Translated from the Italian by Ruth Feldman and Brian Swann

Distance

Now that all your distance surrounds me
I stand unarmed inside a lone evening

The honey is fragrant on the table
and there is thunder in the valley,
much anxiety between the one and the other

I am frequented space
deserted by your sun.

Come. Ask me where
shout solitude at me

And this sky tainted with dismay
with mountain lights
has learned me by heart forever.

Translated from the Italian by Ruth Feldman and Brian Swann

Epiphany

The pine pierces the hills' whiteness
and the Piave icy muscle
stirs in its snares, in the woods.
See the marvelous design
the bright steady providence
the fluency that expresses
and re-knots and unravels
echoes gems currents.
Between you changing forms and valleys scarcely
solicited by the klaxon's breath,
murmured by the dawn,
my worth the leaf that rests
with the live thistle the cocoon the gold,
my worth the tiny wave
that was your thirst one day, squirrel,
my worth beyond doubt beyond winter
that lingers blue on your balconies
my worth more than your own self
fainting with snow
which the motor, fleeing
behind the sun, abandons forever.

Translated from the Italian by Ruth Feldman and Brian Swann

If It Were Not

If it were not your face that melts
and fructifies water and mountains
and dissolves in sighs . . .

Fruit-trees overflowing in a silk dusk,
meadows that a blue sorrow roughly
untangles from the sky
and geraniums high
among birds roof-tiles and peaks

Like incense the room,
the moon
just gone by the window's hoop and all
shown through tears through flutterings
an unlucky boyhood

It is the village in a shell,
it is the village in the glass where
birds roof-tiles flags crowd
where the river freezing and fabled
slaps your cheek
and the soft apple-tree already veiled
by rain converses
rightly reclining on your heart.

Again a touch to shouting of garlands
again to dissonant winds
iron sheets
to glaciers shoulder to shoulder
limitless here.
Again a glance at the garden
at the brazier of landslides and peaks.

Translated from the Italian by Ruth Feldman and Brian Swann

Behold the Thin Green

Behold the thin green
of ribbons and geraniums
declining at the thunder and tears
tears at the dimmed panes;

Behold the scant downpour
behold the lost hour
behold the lilywhite flash
that has revealed you.

Ribbons torn from the void,
icy bare sheets,
steep piazza that at the sign
of your love opens,

ribbons and quick flashes
and you, lily-like life,
you, face, where
a mild evening prevails,

you, face, in which the rain
dies down uncertain,
bends to oblivion the exhausted
earth offered to the whirlwind,

you—bend me to trusting
darkness, to your silence.

Translated from the Italian by Ruth Feldman and Brian Swann

Campèa

I

In the cold Campèa, where ridges
quiver in clouds
vertical above sloughings
above the shadows of declining August,
the bat spreads its wings
and swoops, curled light
no longer announces anything, dark whispers
browse grass
in buried lanes.
I was here perhaps, resting
my forehead on my hand, I sighed
at the birds' refuge
bright with honey and mistletoe
at the woods proud with spindle moons.
Perhaps here I supported
your brow of blood and stone
perhaps here you knew,
I knew, what is waning
with us beyond every death.
Near Dolle all green with apple-trees
newly emerged from long ablutions,
near the woods proud with spindle moons,
when mushrooms sprout from lairs
and rays thistles spiders interweave.
When the paralyzed hand
supports the forehead and the tawny
vertical curse
burns skies of pearled atolls to ash.

II

The soul evolves in faith,
gathers and removes everything.
The embroidery that crushes and cards

the sleep of my dissatisfied temples
is ancient and alive:
tangled proud forests and waters
apple-trees with tart red berries
and the Soligo that binds the barriers
of hill and hedge with meek foam.
Slight stubborn architectures
architectures of ants,
disharmonies of hives
where honey tightens
in a coherence of rays,
you appear, laughable structures
but graceless strength without a name,
you appear, supreme
burns, unraveled backwards,
the light yesterday inextricable
the equivocal clots of bodies,
dared against the heart
that beats here
passionately, against the
immeasurable sun,
against the mind's gray asylum.

Translated from the Italian by Ruth Feldman and Brian Swann

PATRIZIA CAVALLI

Italy (b. 1947)

Born in Todi, Patrizia Cavalli went to study philosophy at the University of Rome and has lived in that city ever since. She has written radio plays and translated works by Molière and Shakespeare. Since she was young, her poems have appeared in periodicals, and they have now been collected several times. She writes as if from inside a spell—of passion and betrayal, obsession and denial, threat and defiance: the narcosis of love. Her style is hard-bitten, on the edge. The circumstances of a Cavalli poem, although private, are never merely personal; they reach out to larger, more abiding and vulnerable realities. In that way, when she writes of loss, she is writing about mortality; when she writes of love, she is writing about life.

But first one must free oneself

But first one must free oneself
of the precise greed that produces us,
that produces me sitting
in the corner of a bar
waiting with clerical passion
for the exact moment when
the little azure fires of the eyes
opposite, of the eyes acclimatized
to risk, the trajectory precalculated,
will demand a blush
from my face. And will obtain a blush.

Translated from the Italian by the author and Robert McCracken

The Moroccans with the carpets

The Moroccans with the carpets
seem like saints
but they're salesmen.

Translated from the Italian by Kenneth Koch

Now that the time seems all mine

Now that time seems all mine
and no one calls me for lunch or dinner,
now that I can stay to watch
how a cloud loosens and loses its color,
how a cat walks on the roof
in the immense luxury of a prowl, now
that what waits for me every day
is the unlimited length of a night
where there is no call and no longer a reason
to undress in a hurry to rest inside
the blinding sweetness of a body that waits for me,
now that the morning no longer has a beginning
and silently leaves me to my plans,
to all the cadences of my voice, now
suddenly I would like prison.

Translated from the Italian by Judith Baumel

To simulate the burning of the heart

To simulate the burning of the heart, the humiliation
of the viscera, to flee cursed
and cursing, to horde chastity
and to cry for it, to keep my mouth
from the dangerous taste of other mouths
and push it unfulfilled to fulfill itself with the poisons of food,

in the apotheosis of dinners when the already
swollen belly continues to swell;
to touch unreachable solitude and there
at the foot of a bed, a chair
or the stairs to recite a goodbye,
so that I can expel you from my fantasy
and cover you with ordinary clouds
so that your light will not fade my path,
will not muddle my circle from which
I send you, you unintentional star,
unexpected passage who reminds me of death.

For all this I asked you for a kiss
and you, kind and innocent accomplice, didn't give it to me.

Translated from the Italian by Judith Baumel

This time I won't permit the blue

This time I won't permit the blue, glimpsed
and seen from behind the window, from the edge of one roof
to another, in the sole grand explanation
of repetition, carrying the glance beyond
every limit, beyond the vision of the distances,
temptation and blackmail of lightness and movement, this time
I won't permit it to bribe me in the promise of light.

I won't permit the flight of odors, the air
beaten by sounds and by wings, the fast flashes
of a pigeon mirrored in the shadow
of the eaves, that, walking, embroiders the edge,
that throws itself in the vacuum only to later
rise up, I won't permit them to drag me through the streets
to beat my body, defaced of all geography,
oblivious to all tendency, in order to beat
in me the sleeping wound of stupor.

Translated from the Italian by Judith Baumel

Far from kingdoms

Far from kingdoms
how steady is the room!
Come, breathe close with me
so I may discover the sweetness
of many imperfections, some missing
tooth, some extra wrinkle, and your body
worn out slightly by carelessness.

Translated from the Italian by Judith Baumel

Ah, yes, to your misfortune

Ah, yes, to your misfortune
instead of leaving
I stayed in bed.

I, sole mistress of the house,
closed the door,
drew the blinds.
And outside, the four caged
canaries sounded like four forests
and four thousand voices of reawakening
confused by the return of light.
But beyond the door
in the dark halls, in the nearly
empty rooms that capture
the furthest sounds,
the pitiful steps of languid homecomings,
births and hazards were kindled,
indifferent and furtive deaths
were consumed.

And what do you think, that I couldn't see you
die around a corner

with the glass falling from your hands
your neck red and swollen
a little ashamed
to have been surprised
yet another time
after so much time
in the same position, the same condition,
pale, trembling, filled with excuses?

But then if I really think about your death
in whatever house, hotel or hospital bed,
in whatever street, perhaps in air
or in a tunnel; about your eyes that surrender
to the invasion; about the ultimate terrible lie
with which you will want to repulse the attack
or the infiltration; about your blood pulsing hesitant
and frantic in the final immense vision
of a passing insect, of a fold in the sheet,
of a stone or a wheel
that will survive you
well then, how can I let you go away?

Translated from the Italian by Judith Baumel

RUTGER KOPLAND

The Netherlands (b. 1934)

Rutger Kopland is the pen name of Rutger Hendrik van den Hoofdakker, a distinguished neurologist and, since 1983, professor of biological psychiatry at the University of Groningen, where he specializes in the effects of depression. He has written two controversial collections of essays on ethics in medicine and, since he started publishing poems in 1966, has become one of the Netherlands' most widely read poets. In 1989 he was given the P. C. Hooft Prize, his country's highest award for literary achievement. His free-verse style is quiet, modest, often anecdotal. He wants to explore the spaces between things: isolated figures in a landscape, the loneliness of places and of relationships, the ghosts of the past that lurk in the present.

Johnson Brothers Ltd.

In those days when my father was still big,
dangerous tools in the bulging pockets
of his jacket, in his suits the odors
of teased out twine and lead,
behind his eyes the incomprehensible world
of a man, gas-fitter, first-class,
said mother, in those days how different
my feelings were, when he would shut the doors
on her and me.

Now he is dead and I am suddenly as old as he,
it turns out to my surprise that he too had
decay built into him. In his diary I see
appointments with persons unknown, on his wall
calendars with gas-pipe labyrinths,
on the mantelpiece the portrait of a woman
in Paris, his woman, the incomprehensible
world of a man.

Looking into the little hand-basin of porcelain
dating from the 'thirties, with its silly pair of lions,
Johnson Brothers Ltd., high up in the dead-still
house the sad shuffle of mother's slippers,
Jesus Christ, father, here come the tears
for now and for then—they flow together
into the lead of the swan-neck pipe,
no longer separable from the drops that come
from the little copper tap marked "cold."

Translated from the Dutch by James Brockway

Ulumbo, a Cat

Like us he had his
quirks, but more
indifference.

In the winter he loved
stoves, in summer
little birds.

Sick and as indifferent
to death as to us.
Dying he did himself.

Translated from the Dutch by James Brockway

Breughel's Winter

Winter by Breughel, the hill with hunters
and dogs, at their feet the valley with the village.
Almost home, but their dead-tired attitudes, their steps
in the snow—a return, but almost as

slow as arrest. At their feet the depths
grow and grow, become wider and further,
until the landscape vanishes into a landscape
that must be there, is there, but only

as a longing is there.

Ahead of them a jet-black bird dives down. Is it mockery
of this labored attempt to return to the life
down there: the children skating on the pond,
the farms with women waiting and cattle?

An arrow underway, and it laughs at its target.

Translated from the Dutch by James Brockway

Natzweiler

1

And there, beyond the barbed wire, the view—
very charming landscape, as peaceful
as then.

They would need for nothing, they would
be laid down in those green pastures,
be led to those peaceful waters,

there in the distance. They would.

2

I trace the windows of the barrack huts,
watch-towers, gas-chamber.

Only the black reflection of distance
in the panes, of a peaceful landscape,

and beyond it, no one.

3

The dead are so violently absent, as though
not only I, but they too
were standing here,

and the landscape were folding their invisible
arms around my shoulders.

We need for nothing, they are saying,
we have forgotten this world,

But these are no arms,
it is landscape.

4

The yellowed photos in the display cases,
their faces ravaged by their skulls,
their black eyes,

what do they see, what do they see?
I look at them, but for what?

Their faces have come to belong
to the world, to the world
which remains silent.

5

So this is it, desertion, here is
the place where they took their leave,
far away in the mountains.

The camp has just been re-painted, in that gentle
grey-green, that gentle color
of war,

it is as new, as though nothing
has happened, as though
it has yet to be.

Translated from the Dutch by James Brockway

Thanks to the Things

1

The morning when the things again come back
to life, when low light shines out of
the mahogany, table silver, porcelain,

the bread again begins to smell of bread,
the flowered teapot of tea,
the air of old people,

when, in the dead-still room, there comes
a muttering, Lord, bless this day too,
to all eternity, amen.

2

The afternoon when things again become
the afternoon, light flecks like butterflies
begin to dance in white and waving curtains,

the fruit bowl again begins to smell of fruit,
the chairs of cane, the bouquet in the vase
of lilacs, the flower-pot of earth,

when, in the dead-still verandah, knitting needles
begin to click, the newspaper to rustle again,
the gate squeaks, the gravel softly crunches.

3

The evening when the things again begin to long
to disappear, the red carpet, the brown
velvet curtains yearn for the darkness,

the pipe in the ash-tray smells again of smoke,
the banana of its fruity flesh, the milk
of the steaming milk of bedtime,

when, in the dead-still room, the Word
is heard again, the Book claps to,
silence falls again, the pendulum clock ticks.

4

The night when the things again begin to be
but shadows of themselves,

the room again begins to smell of laundered sheets,
old woodwork, lavender,

when the dead-still window breathes again
with sleeping treetops in the wind.

5

The moment when, call it
a morning, an afternoon,
an evening, a night,

when the things begin again,
call it a house where light,
scents and sounds come
and go,

but it is death that is searching
for words for the moment when
I, and whatever he may say,
I am that.

Translated from the Dutch by James Brockway

EDDY VAN VLIET

Belgium (b. 1942)

Eddy van Vliet was born in Antwerp and now practices law. In 1989 he was awarded the Belgian State Prize for Flemish Poetry. His poems tend to be brief lyrics, and his style is straightforward. Yet each poem's suppressed narrative and emotional overtones edge toward his concern with human vulnerability. He is continually looking out from the center of an old civilization onto the prospects of contemporary life. The tensions between the two are his theme.

The Coastline

The coastline never alters for the fisherman
who day after day throws out his nets
never suspecting earthenware under the silt

The land was still just land for the farmer
who comes stepping from his field
over the graveyards of sharks

Granite is hard and eternal just like the marble
for the child who is bouncing
giant rocks that have been worn down
to pebbles above the waterline

Infallibly accurate was the time
for the Mayan priests who, after 260 days,
began a new year

And yet at times I ask you
"when are you coming back?"
while tears along your cheeks dissolve into the air
and mingle with the dust of a later century.

Translated from the Flemish by Matthew Blake

Old Champagne Glass

A cloud no bigger than a button
passes over your face

There you lie, slightly matt
and undone by the freezing air
in the Sunday market among silver spoons
and a chess board without knights

The lip rouge on your forehead is gone
the dreams were settled

Without date or emblem, neither appealing
nor worn, just old
you are waiting for a purchaser, but even more
for the fall of a bicycle bell right above your open mouth.

Translated from the Flemish by John van Tiel

Valediction—To My Father

All I want to say is that I do not know.
That it wasn't all that clear to me then
as it turned out later.

The garden fence needed greasing there and then.
The gaps in the wall needed covering and quick
quick get rid of that smell of shaving-soap.

The bald one reciting Homer. Glutton for corn.
The charmer who brought us perfume from France. And what
about
the friends on your day off? had they too packed their bags?

he walked out of the kitchen to the front door,
never to return.

Translated from the Flemish by John van Tiel

The Courtyard

In the courtyard where the cooing of pigeons
was all too easily predictable,
I heard a singing, which, freeing itself
from the whining sleet around us,
gave the impression of spring.

We looked up. The bird held its beak.

Like us he, caged and lonely having mixed up
the seasons, did not believe in
the irreversibility of time, though
his singing had delayed our parting for a while.

Translated from the Flemish by John van Tiel

The City

The city is covered with places you
took from me. Full of joint
footsteps, full of joint laughs.
They were sheltered by dreams and if need be
love grabbed the gun to protect them.

Tell my legs how to evade
what belonged to them.

Tell them. They refuse to believe
that the theaters have burnt, restaurants
were hit by plagues, terraces vanished
into thin air, hotels closed,
the courtyard was demolished.

I bow my head and think
the rain will not hit me. Thus
I shall forget what was taken from me.

Translated from the Flemish by John van Tiel

Party

After years the reunion. Brushed the dogs,
the feuds forgotten, the sons the image
of the father. Comparing weight:
belly, money, and ethics.

The late-comers are not expected earlier.
She who once was the queen, casts around
pictures of her daughters, and nobody
is surprised when the poet asks for the name
of the lady who was his big childhood love.

The laughers are talking condoms again, smoking almost
completely forbidden and anyone who does not embrace
United Europe now is lost. The cinders in the barbecue
are glowing red. No lack of cancer causes here.

The munchies are going round, the whisky works its miracles
and from the wounds of the bacon the fat is dripping.
The names of the dead are exchanged like addresses
on the last holiday. Apparently the one someone
wanted to ask something, was already buried.

Translated from the Flemish by John van Tiel

HENRIK NORDBRANDT

Denmark (b. 1945)

The northern imagination is often drawn to the south—drawn to it as an image of release and indulgence. Certainly Henrik Nordbrandt's imagination is just as much at home in the exotic cultures of the Mediterranean as in the frozen Scandinavian landscapes. As a student at the University of Copenhagen, he immersed himself in Oriental languages, and he has since spent a good deal of his time in Turkey, Greece, and Italy. He has cultivated a spiritual affinity with the great Greek poet Constantine Cavafy and is drawn to the backstreets of history and the heart. Nordbrandt's delicate love poems are especially lyrical and surprising; love is often a part of his loneliness. A prolific writer, he is widely considered the leading poet of his generation in Denmark. His work has won many awards, including the 1980 Grand Prize of the Danish Academy.

China Observed Through Greek Rain in Turkish Coffee

The drizzle
falls into my coffee
until it gets cold
and runs over
until it runs over
and clears
so the picture at the bottom
comes into sight.

The picture of a man
with a long beard
in China
in front of a Chinese pavilion
in rain, heavy rain
that has congealed
in stripes

over the windblown facade
and over the face of the man.

Under the coffee, the sugar and the milk
which is curdling
under the worn glaze
the eyes seem burnt out
or turned inward
toward China, in the porcelain of the cup
slowly emptying of coffee
and running full of rain
clear rain. The spring rain
atomizes against the eaves of the tavern
the facades on the other side of the street
resemble a huge
worn wall of porcelain
whose glow penetrates the wine leaves
the wine leaves which are also worn
as if inside a cup. The Chinaman
sees the sun appear through a green leaf
which has fallen into the cup

the cup whose contents
are now completely clear.

Translated from the Danish by the author and Alexander Taylor

No Matter Where We Go

No matter where we go, we always arrive too late
to experience what we left to find.
And in whatever cities we stay
it is the houses where it is too late to return
the gardens where it's too late to spend a moonlit night
and the women whom it's too late to love
that disturb us with their intangible presence.

And whatever streets we think we know
take us past the gardens we are searching for
whose heavy fragrance spreads throughout the neighborhood.
And whatever houses we return to
we arrive too late at night to be recognized.
And in whatever rivers we look for our reflections
we see ourselves only when we have turned our backs.

Translated from the Danish by the author and Alexander Taylor

Our Love Is Like Byzantium

Our love is like Byzantium
must have been
on the last evening. There must have been
I imagine
a glow on the faces
of those who crowded the streets
or stood in small groups
on streetcorners and public squares
speaking together in low voices
that must have resembled
the glow your face has
when you brush your hair back
and look at me.

I imagine they haven't spoken
much, and about rather
ordinary things
that they have been trying to say
and have stopped
without having managed to express
what they wanted
and have been trying again
and given up again
and have been looking at each other
and lowered their eyes.

Very old icons, for instance
have that kind of glow
the blaze of a burning city
or the glow which approaching death
leaves on photographs of people who died young
in the memory of those left behind.

When I turn towards you
in bed, I have a feeling
of stepping into a church
that was burned down long ago
and where only the darkness in the eyes of the icons
has remained
filled with the flames
which annihilated them.

Translated from the Danish by the author and Alexander Taylor

Streets

Loves that ended long ago:

Sometimes you meet them in the street
sometimes you meet them in dreams.

When you meet them in the street, they resemble dreams
when you meet them in dreams, they resemble streets

streets where half the houses are empty
because you don't remember whose faces

appear in the darkness behind the windows.

Translated from the Danish by the author and Alexander Taylor

Sailing

After having loved we lie close together
and at the same time with distance between us
like two sailing ships that enjoy so intensely
their own lines in the dark water they divide
that their hulls
are almost splitting from sheer delight
while racing, out in the blue
under sails which the night wind fills
with flowerscented air and moonlight
—without one of them ever trying
to outsail the other
and without the distance between them
lessening or growing at all.

But there are other nights, where we drift
like two brightly illuminated luxury liners
lying side by side
with the engines shut off, under a strange constellation
and without a single passenger on board:
On each deck a violin orchestra is playing
in honor of the luminous waves.
And the sea is full of old tired ships
which we have sunk in our attempt to reach each other.

Translated from the Danish by the author and Alexander Taylor

TOMAS TRANSTROMER

Sweden (b. 1931)

Tomas Tranströmer was born and educated in Stockholm and published his first collection of poems there in 1954, at once establishing himself as a major figure in Swedish literary life. His early lyrics, written in classical verse forms, have yielded over the years to weightier and more ambitious poems in free verse and prose, but his tone has remained lapidary and laconic. His world travels and his interest in music and art have broadened the range of his encounters, but he returns consistently to the northern landscape: "Out of the winter gloom / a tremolo rises / from hidden instruments." The eerily calm surfaces of his poems, disrupted by sudden metaphors that can leap across associations and moods, reflect his fascination with the dark forces that shift beneath our daily lives. "My poems," he says, "are meeting places. Their intent is to make a sudden connection between aspects of reality that conventional languages and outlooks ordinarily keep apart. What looks at first like a confrontation turns out to be a connection." All his professional life, Tranströmer has been a psychologist; in the 1960s he worked at a prison for juvenile delinquents and since then, with the handicapped. The recipient of many honors in Scandinavia and abroad, he was awarded the 1990 Neustadt Prize for Literature.

After a Death

Once there was a shock
that left behind a long, shimmering comet tail.
It keeps us inside. It makes the TV pictures snowy.
It settles in cold drops on the telephone wires.

One can still go slowly on skis in the winter sun
through brush where a few leaves hang on.
They resemble pages torn from old telephone directories.
Names swallowed by the cold.

It is still beautiful to feel the heart beat
but often the shadow seems more real than the body.

The samurai looks insignificant
beside his armor of black dragon scales.

Translated from the Swedish by Robert Bly

Sketch in October

The towboat is freckled with rust. What's it doing here so far
    inland?
It is a heavy extinguished lamp in the cold.
But the trees have wild colors: signals to the other shore.
As if people wanted to be fetched.

On my way home I see mushrooms sprouting
                        up through the lawn.
They are the fingers, stretching for help, of someone
who has long sobbed to himself in the darkness down there.
We are the earth's.

Translated from the Swedish by Robin Fulton

The Scattered Congregation

I

We got ready and showed our home.
The visitor thought: you live well.
The slum must be inside you.

II

Inside the church, pillars and vaulting
white as plaster, like the cast
around the broken arm of faith.

III

Inside the church there's a begging bowl
that slowly lifts from the floor
and floats along the pews.

IV

But the church bells have gone underground.
They're hanging in the sewage pipes.
Whenever we take a step, they ring.

V

Nicodemus the sleepwalker is on his way
to the Address. Who's got the Address?
Don't know. But that's where we're going.

Translated from the Swedish by Robert Bly

Below Freezing

We are at a party that doesn't love us. Finally the party lets the mask
fall and shows what it is: a shunting station for freight cars. In the
fog cold giants stand on their tracks. A scribble of chalk on the car
doors.

One can't say it aloud, but there is a lot of repressed violence
here. That is why the furnishings seem so heavy. And why it is so
difficult to see the other thing present: a spot of sun that moves over
the house walls and slips over the unaware forest of flickering faces,
a biblical saying never set down: "Come unto me, for I am as full of
contradictions as you."

I work the next morning in a different town. I drive there in a hum through the dawning hour which resembles a dark blue cylinder. Orion hangs over the frost. Children stand in a silent clump, waiting for the school bus, the children no one prays for. The light grows as gradually as our hair.

Translated from the Swedish by Robert Bly

PAAVO HAAVIKKO

Finland (b. 1931)

Paavo Haavikko is usually considered Finland's greatest living poet. In
1984 he was awarded the Neustadt Prize for Literature and a decade later
the prestigious Nordic Prize, given by the Swedish Academy. His output
has been enormous. His publications include novels, stories, libretti,
plays, historical studies, collections of aphorisms, and more than two
dozen books of poems. He has all along been active as a businessman and
literary editor. From the appearance of his first poems in the 1950s, he
was hailed as a leader in modern Finnish poetry as much for the vivid
rhythms and imagery of his verse as for the thematic force of his medita-
tions on love and death, history and power. Haavikko's anatomies of the
world can often seem apocalyptic in their pessimism. But, as Herbert
Lomas notes, "He is perhaps a kind of cosmic conservative, believing that
man is inhabiting a history that does not, in essence, change, his cruelty
endemic, let loose by attempts at reform, as by any shake-ups."

from The Short Year

The one who writes us is now doing four plays a year.
But the flowers fall in the summer more, and autumn's
a rich old man who can't see the limit of his resources:
                              empty rooms, unheated.
Spring's a flutter of shrieking birds,
 and even shuttered windows don't stop them piercing the psyche.
Shrieking birds, the black-throated grebe.
And a love that goes smoothly is a dream.
Winter: this play's to be played out in the dark,
                              which alters the voices;
its light in the candles enclosing the chrysanthemums
is for you. We go with open eyes, seeing nothing,
        groping with our fingers.

I light the candles each side of the winter chrysanthemums.
    I see you, your fingers splayed, counting on your fingers.
I know what you're counting: the months.
    Soon you'll talk about it.
The fingers that make you a door are now
    occupied so abstractly.
A short year, so short that at the year's end
    you'll be hugging a three-month baby;
or like a man's life, a year, and the second snow
    has already fallen without his making a single print.
Death comes abruptly to a man. A woman makes her death
    little by little, makes children,
and her happiness is to die before they do.
    When she weeps for a child, her voice and her flesh are one.

My grandfather, the Emperor, was, as you know, mad,
    wrote poems in the presence of others.
You want war,
    it's available.
        You walk stiff-legged,
like soldiers do, hysterics before an attack.
Hysteria is an illness that never gets better.
The hysteric is a winner, he never gives in.
    No use my talking. I'll read his poem:

The mist is so dense, the water's hidden from the bridge.
    The flowers are having fits,
        as they have
    to die so nonsensically.

Trees, nights are little by little a little longer,
    a little, not enough to notice.
And the dark doesn't diminish the swishing in the trees.

Still, it's sad as a child
        you speak to calmly, concealing something,
though he knows already.

In this cruel world it's useless even to beg
        not to be born again.

When women have become pictures on the walls,
                men shadows
        walking beneath trees,
conferring on perversities—
        being reborn, not dying, resurrecting—
the tree-shadows on the ground, on the snow, are brushwood.
One of them would like to saw it up.
Impossible, say the others.
                He's not convinced.
Every time they walk beneath the black
they dread a snap. It doesn't happen.
As when snowfall again reminds you of something
    .   you can't quite recall, don't like to ask about,
if I told you it straight out
        you wouldn't understand
that I love you.

And she moves in a room of nothing but waiting water,
        moves as if the room were full of mirrors,
making it meaningless to try anything
        because of existing in every direction.
She grows quite calm, as if there were no mirrors,
        or they were blind, like a masseur.
She wanted to see herself without looking—she could try
        if there were only one mirror.
And the air has breathed all her skin's perfume
        without realising, as if it were asleep.

She keeps the light on unnecessarily long in the morning—
      she's alone in the room—to stop the dark
abruptly going out, but does it intensify the pale morning moon
      when a child's paper dart sticks in the grass?

You're a long clause.
No one could claim you've not got shapely knees.
Have I ever said it's important to me?
No one could claim it's like sitting in bed,
      grabbing a grasshopper
     and not knowing where to let it go.

There are people whose feet, one could claim,
     don't quite fill up their socks.
You get uneasy, and go quite stationary.
You don't primp the lie of your hair,
     though your hand would like to.
You hear things. I see them.
I prefer a slowness in things like the dark coming in November,
     how things recur—
             those don't, do they?—
and what we're doing here, something formal.
     The candles go out when the dark does.
You start dressing by undressing.
     The water wakes.
You finally throw out two corselettes.
     Time of the waning moon.

Nights are long just now,
   short though
     when twilight is on the skin
and someone's breath is mingling with someone's hair.

Leaves want to dance, and they get wind and storm,
     and autumn days, suddenly calm, and open;

and if the pines started to shed needles
        you'd not dare query was it always so every autumn.
Nights. As only softness can be cruel,
        her soft childlike features are showing
a furious face. Her names are Nightbeauty,
        Softness, Always, Two-Shallow-Hollows,
Dimple-In-The-Pelvis-Just-Above-The-Thighs, and
        Two-Just-Near-The-Spine, as if someone had
just pressed them there with his hands,
        That-Smiling-Absentminded-Look,
The-Look-That-Comes-When-A-Hand-Is-Drawn-From-A-Glove.

You can be certain that it itself,
        not another,
no one else,
        has been introduced to you,
the world itself:
           it's not some allegorical creature
        celebrating ancient rites,
and that's why you couldn't quite catch its name,
        for it talks confusingly fast
and about everything at once.

It's a risk, using this handwriting
        that might not be readable in the morning.
When even the snowfall reminds me without avail
        of something I can't remember.

Warmer than the air around her,
           cooler than the waiting water,
        she dawdles long, alone in the room,
                without dressing,
as she's nothing to take off.
Awful to see such great despair, so few gestures.

There are many sages, but on the other hand not one
                          stupid tree.
       After writing the most difficult thing
is reading.

Translated from the Finnish by Herbert Lomas

from Darkness

Days become years. Years
       become places. Then you must go.
Thirty-three years. Said three times,
       it makes a hundred. I can count.
But I don't know if the door out
       opens out or in.

When ass's milk has turned to cowclap
       a miracle has occurred.
You can tease a tree or a person,
       not kill a frog.
You can cut an image in a birch, oozing sweetness,
       undisguised, unconcealed.
You can lash a fir, lacerate its back.
       It doesn't moan. Doesn't dare.

Windy drought. A southern damp contrives
       a blue. Many a blue backs the columns of the economy.
A dead fieldfare sprawls, wings spread,
     three bees feeding at its torn throat.
I bury it, with blessings: So long . . .
Who knows where animal souls go,
       deep down below
          or up high.

Translated from the Finnish by Herbert Lomas

PENTTI SAARIKOSKI

Finland (1937–1983)

Celebrated in his lifetime as a bohemian and political rebel, Pentti
Saarikoski was steeped in the classics from his schooldays and later trans-
lated classics ranging from Homer's *Odyssey* to Joyce's *Ulysses*. He burst
onto the scene in the 1960s, though, as a poet with an ironic edge, a reck-
less spirit who spoke with a contemporary voice. His popularity and in-
fluence were a measure of his ability to articulate the disillusionment of a
whole postwar generation. He became a Communist but quickly tired of
the party line: "Socialism's dream is different from my dream," he said.
He was a satirist but was continually drawn to mythic themes and a
dreamy, meditative manner. His work bears eloquent witness to the social
paradoxes and shifting desires of modern Finnish life. Saarikoski was
born in Karelia and after its annexation by Russia was exiled with his
family to Helsinki. In 1975 he settled in Sweden, although he continued
to write in Finnish until his early death. His last work was a trilogy of
joyous celebration.

Potato Thief

The year was as long and dark as a bed,
I slept between two winds;
the bush was filling with black berries.

I went round two museums,
the first for turn-of-the-century middle-class interiors,
the second for state-purchased paintings
suitable for turn-of-the-century middle-class interiors.
The year was long and dark
the forest was pushing through the museums.

In summer the bush bloomed,
I very nearly bought a car
but then I stole a middle-class person's potatoes

and taught them how to behave themselves. Horrible summer!
Autumn gave us the moist glad eye from afar
and I was excluded from all restaurants.

I read some cardboard cut-out poets
with speech coming out of their mouths like writing;
the poets were sitting on wooden stools
in two forests and listening to the moon.

I slept without a pillow in a long and dark bed,
the police set off after me
and the potatoes thumbed their noses at the police.
The suns were small as black berries.
I hopped on a bike and fled from the world.
I pedaled up a hill and a girl was holding a basket,
a girl in a blue skirt, she sat on the bicycle rack.
At the top of the hill I took the girl's skirt off,
the girl opened her basket and tiny lions leapt straight out
and scrambled under the snow to hibernate.

The police were after me.
I leaped off the bicycle saddle through the moon into the sky.
I yelled "Last one through's a rotten egg."

Translated from the Finnish by Herbert Lomas

from The Dance Floor on the Mountain

XXIV

Winter solstice
and the bees cling to each other
in the hive center
where Jesus is born a honey-scented child

The sun is setting
a scarlet winterball like a fatbellied man

our neighbor, the carpenter
will be rolling into bed

On the first day of the year
I place two white porcelain jugs spout to spout
after thinking all night long
about Marx's mistake

on the tablecloth there are Berghaus projections
the color
I personally call green

Marx's mistake is Lenin
as Stalin is Lenin's mistake
but Stalin didn't make mistakes

I construct a snowman
a sad fascist in the yard
so some image of this winter will remain
our neighbor the carpenter
bends his knee and takes a snap

A heavy snowfall
should mean a rich harvest

I'll build
a cold church for the fascist
a warm one for Jesus

When with summer's first ill-natured wind
and the guests gone
we come down the mountain
with no protection but each other's limbs
where shall we put our hope?

XXVI

On St. Stephen's Day
I sit in their kitchen

drink some beer and listen to language
that's their affair, their memories
and I scare: I say something
but it clatters
from mouth to floor like a horseshoe

Translated from the Finnish by Herbert Lomas

from Invitation to the Dance

V

No, Quetzalcoatl, don't come back
we adore other gods here now
your feathers are on special offer
in the supermarkets
your lakes are ice
the island-to-island bridges
are exhaust pipes of human distress
from the apartment windows
dud eyes look out
on People's Square
gone red with innocent blood
no don't come back, Quetzalcoatl
stay with the faith of your ancestors

VIII

All ye that travail and are heavy laden
you've been swindled
with every recurrent promise of a less laden life
that always piles another bale of straw on your backs
get rich to get the rich off your backs
jabber jabber

I was taxiing home
the kind of day that recalls Heraclitus
sun-blaze on the snow-studded mountain
the world close
as an arm you've leant on before

XXV

I peer from the near to the far
to Europe's edge and the world's end
The coin I've got is good
but I can't see a corpse whose tongue I could put it under

XXX

Tyrants were
people
who undressed
and got dressed
worked into the small dark hours
shuffled papers
and fellow citizens
out of the in-tray
and into the out-tray
now the heart's gone out
of government
the tyrants have been rationalized away
machines that don't tire
don't drink themselves silly
and never shimmy or rumba
are doing the work
they speak like barbed wire
and you can hear what you are
you're one-two-three or four-five-six-seven or zero
these machines would be impossible
if they hadn't been invented

L

No postman knocks at the houses of the dead
I sink a hole deep in the soil
put my invitation at the bottom
and top it with juniper twigs
I soak them with aqua vitae
and when the whole thing's flaming
there's such a smoke and stink
the dead rise they have to

they rise behind me on the mountainside
they see my shadow
and they ask me what it is

the world and the world's phenomena
are soon forgotten

Translated from the Finnish by Herbert Lomas

NIJOLE MILIAUSKAITE

Lithuania (b. 1950)

Born in Keturvalakiai in southwestern Lithuania, Nijolė Miliauskaitė
studied literature at the University of Vilnius and went on to work as an
editor. Her first poems appeared at a moment of international upheaval:
1968. Since then she has published two collections, *Ursules S. portretas*
(*Portrait of Ursula S.*, 1985) and *Namai, kuriuose negyvensim* (*A House
in Which We Will Never Live,* 1988), and is generally regarded as one of
the finest poets of the younger generation in Lithuania. She is married to
another prominent poet, Vyautas Blože. From the start she set out on
what she has called "the search for a suitable biography" of both herself
and her nation. A history of occupation haunts her work, but she reaches
beyond it to an older, almost primitive sense of the land and its people.
She writes about them in translucent textures and startling images.

on winter nights

on winter nights, when my grandmother
went to work
I carried a lantern
to light her way

large snow drifts on either side of the path
the Big Dipper, the north star, the moon
and the man who lives there
walking with a lantern, because he's cold and sad

he looks
at our lighted windows
at the burning candles, at the Christmas tree
at my eyes, filled with sleep

Translated from the Lithuanian by Jonas Zdanys

in the damp places

in the damp places
near the well
I search for horsetail—so my hair
would be light and shiny
as silk

I crumble oak bark
cut up the roots of sweet-flag
and burdock
gather cones of hops
birch leaves

spread out and dry chamomile
in the dark
rinse with stinging nettles

so my hair
would be long and soft
when you see me sitting by the window
combing it with a comb of bone

so my braids
would bind your feet

at night
I bathe in the quiet
forest lake
in moonlight

spread my linens on the grass

secretly
brew you something to drink

from grasses gathered on St. John's night
from roots

from the waters of the well of life
from magic

o grasses of sleep, bitterly sweet
grasses
of oblivion

Translated from the Lithuanian by Jonas Zdanys

these are lilacs

these are lilacs
from Jaskonis's mill, which is near crumbling
each year
I pick a huge bouquet

empty neglected ordnance yards
each year
grass overgrows
the trenches, the bunkers, and the bones
in the common grave

these are lilacs
from Jaskonis's mill, the saddest
flowers, for you, Jadvyga (the overcoat
hacked by moths rots in the attic)

and for you, Karolina, you are old already, and for you,
Barbora, the miner's
mother

and for me

Translated from the Lithuanian by Jonas Zdanys

Temporary City

walking
in the evening
along the banks
of the creek, as the sky is lighted by the glow
from the hothouses, farther on the dump, the street,
the pond, the hospital, farther still garages
and the dried tops of pine trees

here in the spring
a nurse was raped as she walked
to work one morning
and here, on this bridge,
you were beaten, kicked
by three men, healthy, uncomplicated, laughing
(it was on some holiday)

then we looked in all
the ditches for your glasses, shining our lights
into the shallow water, but could find
nothing: no frames, no lenses, not a single
face or significant mark

only muck, only pieces of things, discarded toys
a glove
and your large black beret
which we pulled from the water

◆

in the dream
some woman
young, very pale (in one ear
dangled a silver earring, the other
was torn out by the branch
of an appletree gone wild, there were once orchards here
now tall buildings line the way, through their windows
you see

only other windows, as if some other world), that woman
ran down the street screaming, and all
I could understand was: will I never
be able to see Paris!

◆

the dump, beyond the hothouses, where the spring sun
warms us so pleasantly
a brook burbles

there
from under a pile
of broken bricks, rags, newspapers, ashes
stuck
a hand

dry stalks of grass rustle in the wind

◆

old woman winter, like some beggar
stopped on the main street, is taken away
outside of town, in shock and half dead,
to die in the fields

the half-frozen
boy (with no scarf or gloves) was stopped
by two tall men near the school

(the hired
killer's knife pierces
the back)

go in (it belongs to no one)
into the empty unhappy heart
of this spring

into the blind alleys
of this city

◆

try
to give a title
to this poem

to their life
which is
and nothing more

◆

the night is ever darker
beware, those are not real stars
watch out, don't walk on the streets after dark
don't talk to strangers
fear telegrams, take no joy
in this day or in tomorrow, accept
no gifts, throw out medicine bottles, scissors, needles
hairpins, burn
letters and never
keep a diary

they don't give you an inch

eyes in every mirror, in every
face, in every brick of the walk

the walls have ears!

◆

I would not want to tie my name to it
nor my date of birth nor the place of my death

◆

Franz K., my friend
in the darkest time, when trees,

having lost their leaves, tremble through their trunks
in the wind on the dismal plain

and there is still no snow

where our corpses will be dropped
with hands and feet bound
mouths stuffed
still warm

what a comfort
it will be to believe
that we will meet

the same blood flows in our veins
and seeps
into the saturated ground

you'll croak like a bitch—someone said
and spat

and there is still no snow, Franz K.

◆

the blackened ancient coin
lands on tails
saying
yes

Translated from the Lithuanian by Jonas Zdanys

HANS MAGNUS ENZENSBERGER

Germany (b. 1929)

Born in the Bavarian town of Kaufbeuren, Hans Magnus Enzensberger studied at Hamburg and the Sorbonne, and in 1955 received his doctorate from the University of Freiburg. He has worked since as an editor, teacher, and critic. He sprang to fame, though, as an angry young man, a member of the influential Gruppe 47, a radical opponent of both romantic socialism and blind industrialism. From the start, he has wanted to be the conscience and literary catalyst of his generation. As Peter Demetz has said, Enzensberger is "more learned, cosmopolitan, and restless than any of his contemporaries," and his early work was fiercely polemical, attacking technology's insidious power. German guilt and postwar German complacence were equal targets of his embittered scorn. In 1968, drawn to revolutionary ideals, he moved to Cuba and seemed to abandon literature. But he eventually made his disillusionment with social change in Cuba and his more general despair into new and even more powerful poems, so that he seemed the true heir of Bertolt Brecht. Enzensberger's later work has returned to its more lyrical beginnings, to a concern for the individual rather than the system.

For the Grave of a Peace-Loving Man

This one was no philanthropist,
avoided meetings, stadiums, the large stores.
Did not eat the flesh of his own kind.

Violence walked the streets,
smiling, not naked.
But there were screams in the sky.

People's faces were not very clear.
They seemed to be battered
even before the blow had struck home.

One thing for which he fought all his life,
with words, tooth and claw, grimly,
cunningly, off his own bat:

the thing which he called his peace,
now that he's got it, there is no longer a mouth
over his bones, to taste it with.

Translated from the German by the author and Michael Hamburger

Middle-Class Blues

We can't complain.
We're not out of work.
We don't go hungry.
We eat.

The grass grows,
the social product,
the fingernail,
the past.

The streets are empty.
The deals are closed.
The sirens are silent.
All that will pass.

The dead have made their wills.
The rain's become a drizzle.
The war's not yet been declared.
There's no hurry for that.

We eat the grass.
We eat the social product.
We eat the fingernails.
We eat the past.

We have nothing to conceal.
We have nothing to miss.
We have nothing to say.
We have.

The watch has been wound up.
The bills have been paid.
The washing-up has been done.
The last bus is passing by.

It is empty.

We can't complain.

What are we waiting for?

Translated from the German by the author and Michael Hamburger

Song for Those Who Know

Something must be done right away
that much we know
but of course it's too soon to act
but of course it's too late in the day
oh we know

we know that we're really rather well off
and that we'll go on like this
and that it's not much use anyway
oh we know

we know that we are to blame
and that it's not our fault if we are to blame
and that we're to blame for the fact that it's not our fault

and that we're fed up with it
oh we know

and that maybe it would be a good idea to keep our mouths shut
and that we won't keep our mouths shut all the same
oh we know
oh we know

and we also know that we can't help anybody really
and that nobody really can help us
oh we know

and that we're extremely gifted and brilliant
and free to choose between nothing and naught
and that we must analyze this problem very carefully
and that we take two lumps of sugar in our tea
oh we know

we know all about oppression
and that we are very much against it
and that cigarettes have gone up again
oh we know

we know very well that the nation is heading for real trouble
and that our forecasts have usually been dead right
and that they are not of any use
and that all this is just talk
oh we know

that it's just not good enough to live things down
and that we are going to live them down all the same
oh we know oh we know

that there is nothing new in all this
and that life is wonderful
and that's all there is to it
oh we know all this perfectly well

and that we know all this perfectly well
oh we know that too

oh we know it
oh we know

Translated from the German by the author and Michael Hamburger

At Thirty-three

It was all so different from what she'd expected.
Always those rusting Volkswagens.
At one time she'd almost married a baker.
First she read Hesse, then Handke.
Now often she does crosswords in bed.
With her, men take no liberties.
For years she was a Trotskyist, but in her own way.
She's never handled a ration card.
When she thinks of Kampuchea she feels quite sick.
Her last lover, the professor, always wanted her to beat him.
Greenish batik dresses, always too wide for her.
Greenflies on her *Sparmannia*.
Really she wanted to paint, or emigrate.
Her thesis, *Class Struggles in Ulm 1500*
to 1512 and References to Them in Folksong:
Grants, beginnings and a suitcase full of notes.
Sometimes her grandmother sends her money.
Tentative dances in her bathroom, little grimaces,
cucumber juice for hours in front of the mirror.
She says, whatever happens I shan't starve.
When she weeps she looks like nineteen.

Translated from the German by the author and Michael Hamburger

The Holiday

Now that he's free, relatively, often he shuffles
round the tennis courts, pays for a shave, reads.

Black marketeers whisper, plimsolls pant past him.
Stiff with palm trees, the world expands
on Sundays. Here, in the Palace, the first whores
brood over their breakfast. All is clear, all fuzzes.
Well, if it isn't Nick! comes from the next table.
On the beach, howling misery. Complications
melt away pesetas. Chance acquaintances,
longingly primed with lotion. "What do you say, José,
if tonight we go and play? Olé, olé, olé."
Disgusting, this octopus on the plate.
The yawning bedroom. Sand in the towels.
A brilliant insect that collides with the lightbulb.
At seventeen degrees: Greek fertility goddess.
The shower smells musty. In the street someone titters.
Motorbikes rev. Then there's only the sea
that sighs away into the distance. No, it's the next room,
in the next room a woman is dying or loving herself.
Olé, olé what do you say, José? He listens.
White in his tooth-glass the sleeping tablets teem.

Translated from the German by the author and Michael Hamburger

Short History of the Bourgeoisie

That was the moment when, without
noticing it, for five minutes
we were vastly rich, magnificent
and electric, air-conditioned in July,
or, in case it was November,
the flown-in Finnish wood blazed
in Tudor fireplaces. Funny,
it was all there, just flew in
by itself, as it were. Elegant
we were, no one could bear us.
We threw solo concerts around,
chips, orchids in cellophane. Clouds
that said, I. Unique!

Flights everywhere. Even our sighs
went on credit cards. Like sailors
we bandied curses. Each one
had his own misfortune under the seat,
ready to grab at it. A waste, really.
It was so practical. Water
flowed out of taps just like that.
Remember? Simply stunned
by our tiny emotions,
we ate little. If only we'd guessed
that all this would pass
in five minutes, the roast beef Wellington
would have tasted different, quite different.

Translated from the German by the author and Michael Hamburger

Vanished Work

Rather remote, all of it.
As in a saga, darkly,
the rag-and-bone-man
with his battered top hat,
the blue hand of the woad-miller,
the corn-chandler in his cool cellar.

The rush-man has deserted his reed,
the beekeeper his hive,
the charcoal burner his flue.
The woolcarder threw her teasel away,
the trough-maker his chisel.
Trades moldered away,
extinct skills.

What has happened to the bridoons,
the hames and the terrets?

The cartwright has passed away.
Only his name survives,
like an insect congealed in amber,
in the telephone book.

But the shimmering block of light
I have lived to see
with my own eyes, heaved
easily, as if by magic
with an iron hook
onto the leathery shoulder-strap

of the iceman, on Wednesdays
at noon, punctually, and the chips
melted like fire
in my chill mouth.

Translated from the German by the author and Michael Hamburger

The Poison

Not, as it used to be, round,
little, a grain, sealed
like a berry, a pea,
tiny, concealed in a ring,
a capsule, private, minimal,
secret like an *idée fixe,*

but manifest like the sea,
ponderous and normal,
widely distributed, like the wind
unleashed, cloudy, odorless
and as impalpable, omni-
present as God was once

who, a private grain,
little, weighs less and less,

like a pea, secret,
like a deadly nightshade seed
in one's breast, sealed
like an *idée fixe*.

Translated from the German by the author and Michael Hamburger

INGEBORG BACHMANN

Austria (1926–1973)

Born in Klagenfurt, Ingeborg Bachmann spent her adolescence under Nazi
rule. Later she remembered Hitler's troops arriving in her hometown: "It
was so horrifying that my memory begins with this day . . . the terrible
brutality that one could feel, the shouting, singing, and marching—the
origin of my first death fear." She eventually went on to study law and
philosophy at universities in Innsbruck and Graz, and in 1950 at the Uni-
versity of Vienna she wrote a dissertation on Heidegger's existential phi-
losophy. Her first book of poems appeared in 1953 and won her wide
acclaim. The next year she moved to Italy, whose classical Mediterranean
landscapes enthralled her. For ten more years she wrote poems, until in
1964—the year she was given Germany's highest award for literature, the
Büchner Prize—she turned her attention exclusively to fiction. In 1973, in
her Roman apartment, she fell asleep with a lighted cigarette; three weeks
later she died of burns suffered in the resulting fire. At the heart of her
work is a sense of a lost paradise. Haunted by both the beauty of nature
and the terrors of history, her tone is that of a soul suspended between
nostalgia and despair. This may have to do with what she spoke of as
Austria's literary particularity: "Poets like Grillparzer, Hofmannsthal,
Rilke, and Robert Musil could never have been German. The Austrians
have participated in so many cultures and thus developed a sense of the
world which is different from that of the Germans. This explains their
sublime serenity, but also their sadness and many uncanny characteris-
tics." Her early work is formal; her later poems are more loosely com-
posed. Throughout her career, moral realities and mythic possibilities are
at war with each other, and the result is poems of great tension and
beauty.

Paris

> Lashed to the wheel of night,
> the lost ones sleep
> down below, in the thundering tunnels—
> but where we are, there is light.

Our arms are laden with flowers,
mimosa from many years.
Gold falls from bridge to bridge,
breathless in the river.

Cold is the light,
colder still the stone before the gate;
and all the fountain basins
are half drained.

What will happen if we stay here,
homesick to the root of our flowing hair,
and ask: what will happen
if we survive beauty's trial?

Lifted high on the wagon of light,
though waking, we are lost
in the streets of genius, above—
but where we are not, there is night.

Translated from the German by Mark Anderson

Psalm

I

Be still with me, as all bells are still!

In the afterbirth of terror
the rabble hunts for new nourishment.
On Good Friday a hand hangs in the sky
on display; it's missing two fingers
and can't swear that everything,
everything didn't happen and nothing
ever will. It dives into red dusk,
carries off the new murderers
and goes free.

At night on this earth
open the windows, fold back the sheets,
lay bare the secrets of the sick,
an ulcer full of nourishment, infinite pain
for every taste.

Butchers put on gloves
and hold the breath of the naked.
The moon in the door falls to the ground,
let the pieces lie, the handle . . .

Everything was prepared for the last anointment.
(The sacrament cannot take place.)

2

How vain everything is.
Roll a city toward you,
rise up from the city's dust,
take office
and mask yourself
to escape exposure.

Honor your promises
before a dull mirror in the air,
before a closed door in the wind.

Untraveled are the paths along the face of the sky.

3

O eyes, burned on the sun silo earth,
heavy with the rain of all eyes,
and now spun, woven
by the tragic spiders
of the present . . .

4

In the hollow of my mute being
place a word—
grow forests thick on either side
so that my mouth
lies all in shade.

Translated from the German by Mark Anderson

Invocation of the Great Bear

Great Bear, come down, shaggy night,
cloud-coated beast with the old eyes,
star eyes.
Through the thickets your paws break
shimmering with their claws,
star claws.
We guard our herds with a watchful eye,
though caught in your spell, and mistrust
your tired flanks and sharp,
half-bared fangs,
old bear.

A pine cone: your world.
You: its scales.
I hunt them, roll them
from the pines in the beginning
to the pines at the end.
Snort on them, test them with my muzzle
and set to work with my paws.

Be afraid or don't be afraid!
Just drop your coins in the collection basket and give
the blind man a good word,
let him hold the bear on its leash.
And spice the lambs well.

Perhaps this bear
will break loose, stop threatening
and chase all the cones that have fallen
from the pines, from the great, winged ones
hurled down from Paradise.

Translated from the German by Mark Anderson

Songs from an Island

Shadow fruit is falling from the walls,
moonlight bathes the house in white, and the ash
of extinct craters is borne in by the sea wind.

In the embrace of handsome youths
the coasts are sleeping.
Your flesh remembers mine,
it was already inclined to me,
when the ships
loosened themselves from shore and the cross
of our mortal burden
kept watch in the rigging.

Now the execution sites are empty,
they search but cannot find us.

◆

When you rise from the dead,
when I rise from the dead,
no stone will lie before the gate,
no boat will rest on the sea.

Tomorrow the casks will roll
toward Sunday waves,
we come on anointed

soles to the shore, wash
the grapes and stamp
the harvest into wine,
tomorrow, on the shore.

When you rise from the dead,
when I rise from the dead,
the hangman will hang at the gate,
the hammer will sink into the sea.

◆

One day the feast must come!
Saint Anthony, you who have suffered,
Saint Leonard, you who have suffered,
Saint Vitus, you who have suffered.

Make way for our prayers, way for the worshippers,
room for music and joy!
We have learned simplicity,
we sing in the choir of cicadas,
we eat and drink,
the lean cats
rub against our table,
until evening mass begins
I hold your hand
with my eyes,
and a quiet, brave heart
sacrifices its wishes to you.

Honey and nuts for the children,
teeming nets for the fishermen,
fertility for the gardens,
moon for the volcano, moon for the volcano!

Our sparks leapt over the borders,
above the night fireworks fanned their
tails, the procession
floats away on dark rafts and gives
time to the primeval world,

to the plodding lizards,
to the carnivorous plant,
to the feverish fish,
to the orgies of wind and the lust
of mountains where a pious
star loses its way, collides with their face
and dissolves into dust.

Stand firm, you foolish saints.
Tell the mainland the craters aren't resting!
Saint Roch, you who have suffered,
oh you who have suffered, Saint Francis.

◆

When someone departs he must throw his hat,
filled with the mussels he spent the summer
gathering, in the sea
and sail off with his hair in the wind,
he must hurl the table,
set for his love, in the sea,
he must pour the wine,
left in his glass, into the sea,
he must give his bread to the fish
and mix a drop of his blood with the sea,
he must drive his knife deep into the waves
and sink his shoes,
heart, anchor and cross,
and sail off with his hair in the wind.
Then he will return.
When?
        Do not ask.

◆

There is fire under the earth,
and the fire is pure.

There is fire under the earth
and molten rock.

There is a torrent under the earth,
it will stream into us.

There is a torrent under the earth,
it will scorch our bones.

A great fire is coming,
a torrent is coming over the earth.

We shall be witnesses.

Translated from the German by Mark Anderson

Aria I

Wherever we turn in the storm of roses,
thorns illuminate the night. And the thunder
of a thousand leaves, once so quiet on the bushes,
is right at our heels.

Wherever the roses' fire is put out,
rain washes us into the river. Oh distant night!
Yet a leaf that touched us now floats on the waves,
following us to the sea.

Translated from the German by Mark Anderson

A Kind of Loss

Used together: seasons, books, a piece of music.
The keys, teacups, bread basket, sheets and a bed.
A hope chest of words, of gestures, brought back, used, used up.
A household order maintained. Said. Done. And always a hand
    was there.

I've fallen in love with winter, with a Viennese septet, with
    summer.
With village maps, a mountain nest, a beach and a bed.
Kept a calender cult, declared promises irrevocable,
bowed before something, was pious to a nothing

(—to a folded newspaper, cold ashes, the scribbled piece of
    paper),
fearless in religion, for our bed was the church.

From my lake view arose my inexhaustible painting.
From my balcony I greeted entire peoples, my neighbors.
By the chimney fire, in safety, my hair took on its deepest hue.
The ringing at the door was the alarm for my joy.

It's not you I've lost,
but the world.

Translated from the German by Mark Anderson

CZESŁAW MIŁOSZ

Poland (b. 1911)

Czesław Miłosz was born into a Polish-speaking family in Lithuania and spent his childhood in czarist Russia, where his father was employed as a civil engineer. When the family returned home after World War I, their town had been made a part of the new Polish state. By the age of twenty-one, Miłosz had already published his first collection of poems and was a member of the Polish avant-garde literary movement of the 1930s. When the Nazis invaded Poland in 1939, Miłosz went underground and worked with the Resistance in Warsaw. After the war he was posted by the new Communist government to diplomatic service in Paris, but in 1951 he defected to the West, living until 1960 in Paris and since then in America, where he taught Slavic literature at the University of California at Berkeley until his retirement in 1978. In 1980 he was awarded the Nobel Prize for Literature. In his acceptance speech, he referred to his poems as bearing witness both to the natural wonders of the earth and to the demoniac doings of history in the twentieth century. Though sometimes relieved by the pleasure of the senses and always braced by a fierce intellectual prowess, memory for Miłosz is a wound, and the work of memory has been done in exile. He has written novels and essays, and worked as a translator, but his poems remain his preeminent achievement. Their authority derives from their restlessness: a shifting, ironic, heartfelt quest for spiritual balance. He freights the lyric with history and makes the historical meditation intensely personal. Over the years his vision has broadened to metaphysical matters, and he has continued to charge language— poetry and prose, high style and low—to "search for the Real."

A Poor Christian Looks at the Ghetto

Bees build around red liver,
Ants build around black bone.
It has begun: the tearing, the trampling on silks,
It has begun: the breaking of glass, wood, copper, nickel, silver,
    foam
Of gypsum, iron sheets, violin strings, trumpets, leaves, balls,
    crystals.

Poof! Phosphorescent fire from yellow walls
Engulfs animal and human hair.

Bees build around the honeycomb of lungs,
Ants build around white bone.
Torn is paper, rubber, linen, leather, flax,
Fiber, fabrics, cellulose, snakeskin, wire.
The roof and the wall collapse in flame and heat seizes the
 foundations.
Now there is only the earth, sandy, trodden down,
With one leafless tree.

Slowly, boring a tunnel, a guardian mole makes his way,
With a small red lamp fastened to his forehead.
He touches buried bodies, counts them, pushes on,
He distinguishes human ashes by their luminous vapor,
The ashes of each man by a different part of the spectrum.
Bees build around a red trace.
Ants build around the place left by my body.

I am afraid, so afraid of the guardian mole.
He has swollen eyelids, like a Patriarch
Who has sat much in the light of candles
Reading the great book of the species.

What will I tell him, I, a Jew of the New Testament,
Waiting two thousand years for the second coming of Jesus?
My broken body will deliver me to his sight
And he will count me among the helpers of death:
The uncircumcised.

Translated from the Polish by the author

Incantation

Human reason is beautiful and invincible.
No bars, no barbed wire, no pulping of books,

No sentence of banishment can prevail against it.
It establishes the universal ideas in language,
And guides our hand so we write Truth and Justice
With capital letters, lie and oppression with small.
It puts what should be above things as they are,
Is an enemy of despair and a friend of hope.
It does not know Jew from Greek or slave from master,
Giving us the estate of the world to manage.
It saves austere and transparent phrases
From the filthy discord of tortured words.
It says that everything is new under the sun,
Opens the congealed fist of the past.
Beautiful and very young are Philo-Sophia
And poetry, her ally in the service of the good.
As late as yesterday Nature celebrated their birth,
The news was brought to the mountains by a unicorn and an
        echo.
Their friendship will be glorious, their time has no limit.
Their enemies have delivered themselves to destruction.

Translated from the Polish by the author and Robert Pinsky

My Faithful Mother Tongue

Faithful mother tongue,
I have been serving you.
Every night, I used to set before you little bowls of colors
so you could have your birch, your cricket, your finch
as preserved in my memory.

This lasted many years.
You were my native land; I lacked any other.
I believed that you would also be a messenger
between me and some good people
even if they were few, twenty, ten
or not born, as yet.

Now, I confess my doubt.
There are moments when it seems to me I have squandered my
    life.
For you are a tongue of the debased,
of the unreasonable, hating themselves
even more than they hate other nations,
a tongue of informers,
a tongue of the confused,
ill with their own innocence.

But without you, who am I?
Only a scholar in a distant country,
a success, without fears and humiliations.
Yes, who am I without you?
Just a philosopher, like everyone else.

I understand, this is meant as my education:
the glory of individuality is taken away,
Fortune spreads a red carpet
before the sinner in a morality play
while on the linen backdrop a magic lantern throws
images of human and divine torture.

Faithful mother tongue,
perhaps after all it's I who must try to save you.
So I will continue to set before you little bowls of colors
bright and pure if possible,
for what is needed in misfortune is a little order and beauty.

Translated from the Polish by the author and Robert Hass

Bypassing Rue Descartes

Bypassing rue Descartes
I descended toward the Seine, shy, a traveler,
A young barbarian just come to the capital of the world.

We were many, from Jassy and Koloshvar, Wilno and Bucharest,
    Saigon and Marrakesh,
Ashamed to remember the customs of our homes,
About which nobody here should ever be told:
The clapping for servants, barefooted girls hurry in,
Dividing food with incantations,
Choral prayers recited by master and household together.

I had left the cloudy provinces behind,
I entered the universal, dazzled and desiring.

Soon enough, many from Jassy and Koloshvar, or Saigon or
    Marrakesh
Would be killed because they wanted to abolish the customs of
    their homes.

Soon enough, their peers were seizing power
In order to kill in the name of the universal, beautiful ideas.

Meanwhile the city behaved in accordance with its nature,
Rustling with throaty laughter in the dark,
Baking long breads and pouring wine into clay pitchers,
Buying fish, lemons, and garlic at street markets,
Indifferent as it was to honor and shame and greatness and glory,
Because that had been done already and had transformed itself
Into monuments representing nobody knows whom,
Into arias hardly audible and into turns of speech.

Again I lean on the rough granite of the embankment,
As if I had returned from travels through the underworlds
And suddenly saw in the light the reeling wheel of the seasons
Where empires have fallen and those once living are now dead.

There is no capital of the world, neither here nor anywhere else,
And the abolished customs are restored to their small fame
And now I know that the time of human generations is not like
    the time of the earth.

As to my heavy sins, I remember one most vividly:
How, one day, walking on a forest path along a stream,
I pushed a rock down onto a water snake coiled in the grass.

And what I have met with in life was the just punishment
Which reaches, sooner or later, the breaker of a taboo.

Translated from the Polish by Renata Gorczynski and Robert Hass

TADEUSZ ROZEWICZ

Poland (b. 1921)

Considered by many the most influential poet of postwar Poland, Tadeusz Różewicz changed the whole sensibility of Polish poetry by stripping it of its rhetorical excesses and writing in a "prosaicized" voice of somber and powerful witness. "The dance of poetry," he has said, "came to an end during the Second World War in concentration camps created by totalitarian systems." He began by chronicling the atrocities of the war and the deprivations of its aftermath: "I seek a teacher and master / let him restore to me sight hearing and speech / let him once again name things and concepts / let him separate light from dark / I am twenty-four / led to slaughter / I survived." His tone and diction were flat but nervy, aware of the violence underneath and the emptiness above. His purpose was to create "not verses but facts"—and those facts became a new kind of charged metaphor. His later work moves on the contradictions of human life, its despair and quiet pleasures; his collages of contemporary phrases and names paint a scathing portrait of modern culture's vulgar chaos. As Czesław Miłosz once said of him, "Różewicz is a poet of chaos with a nostalgia for order." He is also an important playwright, essayist, and short-story writer. After 1970 Różewicz withdrew from the literary scene; he lives now in Wrocław.

Who Is a Poet

a poet is one who writes verses
and one who does not write verses

a poet is one who throws off fetters
and one who puts fetters on himself

a poet is one who believes
and one who cannot bring himself to believe

a poet is one who has told lies
and one who has been told lies

one who has been inclined to fall
and one who raises himself

a poet is one who tries to leave
and one who cannot leave

Translated from the Polish by Magnus J. Krynski and Robert A. Maguire

Draft of a Modern Love Poem

And yet white
is best described by gray
bird by stone
sunflowers
in December

love poems of old
were descriptions of the flesh
described this and that
for instance eyelashes

and yet red
should be described
by gray the sun by rain
poppies in November
lips by night

the most tangible
description of bread
is a description of hunger
in it is
the damp porous core
the warm interior
sunflowers at night
the breasts belly thighs of Cybele

a spring-clear
transparent description
of water
is a description of thirst
ashes
desert
it produces a mirage
clouds and trees move into
the mirror

Lack hunger
absence
of flesh
is a description of love
is a modern love poem

Translated from the Polish by Magnus J. Krynski and Robert A. Maguire

Among Many Tasks

Among many tasks
very urgent
I've forgotten that
it's also necessary
to be dying

frivolous
I have neglected this obligation
or have been fulfilling it
superficially

beginning tomorrow
everything will change

I will start dying assiduously
wisely optimistically
without wasting time

Translated from the Polish by Magnus J. Krynski and Robert A. Maguire

Homework Assignment
on the Subject of Angels

Fallen
angels

resemble
flakes of soot
abacuses
cabbage leaves stuffed
with black rice
they also resemble hail
painted red
blue fire
with a tongue of gold

fallen angels
resemble
ants
moons that press
beneath the green nails of the dead

angels in paradise
resemble the inside of the thigh
of an adolescent girl

they are like stars
they shine in shameful places
they are pure like triangles and circles
they have in the middle
stillness

fallen angels
are like the open windows of a mortuary
like the eyes of cows
like the skeletons of birds
like falling airplanes
like flies on the lungs of fallen soldiers
like strings of autumn rain
that tie lips with a flight of birds

a million angels
wander
over a woman's palms

they lack a navel
on sewing machines they type
long poems in the shape
of a white sail

their bodies can be grafted
on the stump of an olive tree

they sleep on ceilings
they fall drop by drop

Translated from the Polish by Magnus J. Krynski and Robert A. Maguire

WISŁAWA SZYMBORSKA

Poland (b. 1923)

In a poem titled "Big Numbers," Wisława Szymborska writes that her imagination "doesn't cope well with big numbers. / It's still moved by singularity." Indeed, throughout her career, she has kept her eye on particulars: small creatures, overlooked objects, marginal characters, everyday habits, neglected feelings. To each as well she brings an angled perspective. It is the point of view of both a lonely skeptic and a canny ironist; as it keeps a cloying sentimentality at bay, it encourages an extraordinary detached sympathy with her subjects. "Take it not amiss, O speech," she writes, "that I borrow weighty words, / and later try hard to make them seem light." The light she makes is a sort of moral illumination, shining back from details onto the inner lives of her readers. She has published sparingly and writes with a careful precision. Her conceits are elaborated with a witty originality and spontaneity, and her work has been immensely popular in Poland. Since the age of eight, Szymborska has lived in Kraków. She graduated from the Jagellonian University, and she began publishing in 1945. Although she has tried out political themes in her poems, sometimes with a biting satirical force, her defense of the individual—of "singularity"—draws on her unique powers of observation rather than on any ideology. As an "unsurpassable model of the writer's craft and a constant encouragement to transcend the obvious with thought," she has cited Montaigne's adage "See how many ends this stick has!"

Unexpected Meeting

We are very polite to each other,
insist it's nice meeting after all these years.

Our tigers drink milk.
Our hawks walk on the ground.
Our sharks drown in water.
Our wolves yawn in front of the open cage.

Our serpents have shaken off lightning,
monkeys—inspiration, peacocks—feathers.
The bats—long ago now—have flown out of our hair.

We fall silent in mid-phrase,
smiling beyond salvation.
Our people
have nothing to say.

Translated from the Polish by Magnus J. Krynski and Robert A. Maguire

The Women of Rubens

Giantesses, female fauna,
naked as the rumbling of barrels.
They sprawl in trampled beds,
sleep with mouths agape for crowing.
Their eyes have fled into the depths
and penetrate to the very core of glands
from which yeast seeps into the blood.

Daughters of the Baroque. Dough rises in kneading-troughs,
baths are asteam, wines glow ruby,
piglets of cloud gallop across the sky,
trumpets neigh an alert of the flesh.

O meloned, O excessive ones,
doubled by the flinging off of shifts,
trebled by the violence of posture,
you lavish dishes of love!

Their slender sisters had risen earlier,
before dawn broke in the picture.
No one noticed how, single file, they
had moved to the canvas's unpainted side.

Exiles of style. Their ribs all showing,
their feet and hands of birdlike nature.
Trying to take wing on bony shoulder blades.

The thirteenth century would have given them a golden
    background,
the twentieth—a silver screen.
The seventeenth had nothing for the flat of chest.

For even the sky is convex,
convex the angels and convex the god—
mustachioed Phoebus who on a sweaty
mount rides into the seething alcove.

Translated from the Polish by Magnus J. Krynski and Robert A. Maguire

Pietà

In the small town where the hero was born:
seeing the monument, praising it for its size,
shooing two hens off the steps of the abandoned museum,
finding out where the mother lives,
knocking and pushing the creaking door open.
She holds herself erect, hair combed straight, eyes clear.
Saying I've come from Poland.
Exchanging pleasantries. Asking questions loud and clear.
Yes, she loved him very much. Yes, he was always like that.
Yes, she was standing by the prison wall then.
Yes, she heard the salvo.
Regretting not bringing a tape recorder
and movie camera. Yes, she knows what those things are.
On the radio she had read his last letter.
On the television she had sung old lullabies.
Once she had even acted in a film, staring into
the klieg lights till the tears came. Yes, she is moved by the
    memory.
Yes, she's a little tired. Yes, it will pass.

Getting up. Expressing thanks. Saying goodbye. Going out,
walking past the next batch of tourists.

Translated from the Polish by Magnus J. Krynski and Robert A. Maguire

Theater Impressions

For me a tragedy's most important act is the sixth:
the resurrecting from the stage's battlegrounds,
the adjusting of wigs, of robes,
the wrenching of knife from breast,
the removing of noose from neck,
the lining up among the living
to face the audience.

Bows solo and ensemble:
the white hand on the heart's wound,
the curtsey of the lady suicide,
the nodding of the lopped-off head.

Bows in pairs:
fury extends an arm to meekness,
the victim looks blissfully into the hangman's eyes,
the rebel bears no grudge as he walks beside the tyrant.

The trampling of eternity with the tip of a golden slipper.
The sweeping of morals away with the brim of a hat.
The incorrigible readiness to start afresh tomorrow.

The entry in single file of those who died much earlier,
in the third, the fourth, or between the acts.
The miraculous return of those lost without trace.
The thought that they've been waiting patiently backstage,
not taking off costumes,
not washing off makeup,
moves me more than the tragedy's tirades.

But truly elevating is the lowering of the curtain,
and that which can still be glimpsed beneath it:
here one hand hastily reaches for a flower,
there a second snatches up a dropped sword.
Only then does a third, invisible,
perform its duty:
it clutches at my throat.

Translated from the Polish by Magnus J. Krynski and Robert A. Maguire

Under a Certain Little Star

I apologize to coincidence for calling it necessity.
I apologize to necessity just in case I'm mistaken.
Let happiness be not angry that I take it as my own.
Let the dead not remember they scarcely smolder in my memory.
I apologize to time for the muchness of the world overlooked per
    second.
I apologize to old love for regarding the new as the first.
Forgive me, far-off wars, for bringing flowers home.
Forgive me, open wounds, for pricking my finger.
I apologize to those who cry out of the depths for the minuet-
    record.
I apologize to people at railway stations for sleeping at five in the
    morning.
Pardon me, hounded hope, for laughing now and again.
Pardon me, deserts, for not rushing up with a spoonful of water.
And you, O falcon, the same these many years, in that same cage,
forever staring motionless at that self-same spot,
absolve me, even though you are but a stuffed bird.
I apologize to the cut-down tree for the table's four legs.
I apologize to big questions for small answers.
O Truth, do not pay me too much heed.
O Solemnity, be magnanimous unto me.
Endure, mystery of existence, that I pluck out the threads of your
    train.
Accuse me not, O soul, of possessing you but seldom.

I apologize to everything that I cannot be everywhere.
I apologize to everyone that I cannot be every man and woman.
I know that as long as I live nothing can justify me,
because I myself am an obstacle to myself.
Take it not amiss, O speech, that I borrow weighty words,
and later try hard to make them seem light.

Translated from the Polish by Magnus J. Krynski and Robert A. Maguire

Reality Demands

Reality demands
that we also mention this:
Life goes on.
It continues at Cannae and Borodino,
at Kosovo Polje and Guernica.

There's a gas station
on a little square in Jericho,
and wet paint
on park benches in Bilá Hora.
Letters fly back and forth
between Pearl Harbor and Hastings,
a moving van passes
beneath the eye of the lion at Chaeronea,
and the blooming orchards near Verdun
cannot escape
the approaching atmospheric front.

There is so much Everything
that Nothing is hidden quite nicely.
Music pours
from the yachts moored at Actium,
and couples dance on their sunlit decks.

So much is always going on
that it must be going on all over.

Where not a stone still stands,
you see the Good Humor man
besieged by kids.
Where Hiroshima was,
Hiroshima is again,
producing many products
for everyday use.

This terrifying world is not devoid of charms,
of the mornings
that make waking up worthwhile.
The grass is green
on Maciejowice's fields,
and studded with dew,
as is usually the case with grass.

Perhaps all fields are battlefields,
all grounds are battlegrounds,
those we remember
and those that are forgotten:
the birch, cedar, and fir forests, the white snows,
the yellow sands, gray gravel, the iridescent swamps,
the canyons of black defeat,
where, in times of crisis,
you can cower under a bush.

What moral flows from this? Probably none.
Only the blood flows, drying quickly,
and, as always, a few rivers, a few clouds.

On tragic mountain passes
the wind rips hats from unwitting heads,
and we can't help
laughing at that.

Translated from the Polish by Stanislaw Baranczak and Clare Cavanagh

The End and the Beginning

After every war
someone's got to tidy up.
Things won't pick
themselves up, after all.

Someone's got to shove
the rubble to the roadsides
so the carts loaded with corpses
can get by.

Someone's got to trudge
through sludge and ashes,
through the sofa springs,
the shards of glass,
the bloody rags.

Someone's got to lug the post
to prop the wall,
someone's got to glaze the window,
set the door in its frame.

No sound bites, no photo opportunities
and it takes years.
All the cameras have gone
to other wars.

The bridges need to be rebuilt,
the railroad stations, too.
Shirt sleeves will be rolled
to shreds.

Someone, broom in hand,
still remembers how it was.
Someone else listens, nodding
his unshattered head.
But others are bound to be bustling nearby

who'll find all that
a little boring.

From time to time someone still must
dig up a rusted argument
from underneath a bush
and haul it off to the dump.

Those who knew
what this was all about
must make way for those
who know little.
And less than that.
And at last nothing less
than nothing.

Someone's got to lie there
in the grass that covers up
the causes and effects
with a cornstalk in his teeth,
gawking at clouds.

Translated from the Polish by Stanislaw Baranczak and Clare Cavanagh

ZBIGNIEW HERBERT

Poland (b. 1924)

Zbigniew Herbert was born in Lvov, in a part of eastern Poland that was invaded by both the Soviet Union and Germany during World War II and was annexed by the Soviets after the war. Herbert himself fought in the Resistance against the Nazis and began writing poetry during these tumultuous years. After the war he studied economics, law, and philology, and eventually worked in clerical jobs in Warsaw. Because of Communist censorship, he could only "write for the drawer," but meanwhile he perfected a style that has since come to be recognized as the most powerful and influential of all contemporary Polish poets. Czesław Miłosz has described Herbert's voice as "casual and whispering." Like many poets of his generation, he thought the war had rendered the old literary styles useless. "You understand," he once wrote, "I had words in abundance to express my rebellion and protest. I might have written something of this sort: 'O you cursed, damned people, so-and-sos, you kill innocent people, wait and a just punishment will fall on you.' I didn't say this because I wanted to bestow a broader dimension on the specific, individual, experienced situation, or rather, to show its deeper, general human perspectives." Like Samuel Beckett's, his diction is both antirhetorical and rich, the movement of his lines abrupt and riddling. His real virtuosity lies in his sensibility: alert to history, skeptical of its fictions, ducking behind metaphor the better to tell a bitter truth. With his impulse toward the parable, he often uses a pseudopersona, Mr. Cogito, both to express and to satirize his longings. The ironic, even "playful" side of his imagination has been a way to counter the modern tyrannies, whether Communist or capitalist. "We are despite everything / guardians of our brothers," says one poem. Herbert's canny, clear-eyed moral sensibility and guarded but pulsing compassion guide his poems toward their true ambition. "Beyond the poet's ego," he says, "there extends a different, obscure but real world. One should not cease to believe that we can grasp this world in language and do justice to it." With his increasing fame, Herbert was allowed to travel to the West, and he has taught in Berlin and Los Angeles. Prizes have been heaped on him, although he remains unaffected. In recent years he has lived in Paris—he's perhaps the most famous European poet alive.

To Marcus Aurelius

for Professor Henryk Elzenberg

Good night Marcus put out the light
and shut the book For overhead
is raised a gold alarm of stars
heaven is talking some foreign tongue
this the barbarian cry of fear
your Latin cannot understand
Terror continuous dark terror
against the fragile human land

begins to beat It's winning Hear
its roar The unrelenting stream
of elements will drown your prose
until the world's four walls go down
As for us?—to tremble in the air
blow in the ashes stir the ether
gnaw our fingers seek vain words
drag off the fallen shades behind us

Well Marcus better hang up your peace
give me your hand across the dark
Let it tremble when the blind world beats
on senses five like a failing lyre
Traitors—universe and astronomy
reckoning of stars wisdom of grass
and your greatness too immense
and Marcus my defenseless tears

Translated from the Polish by Czesław Miłosz and Peter Dale Scott

Hen

The hen is the best example of what living constantly with humans leads to. She has completely lost the lightness and grace of a bird.

Her tail sticks up over her protruding rump like a too large hat in bad taste. Her rare moments of ecstasy, when she stands on one leg and glues up her round eyes with filmy eyelids, are stunningly disgusting. And in addition, that parody of song, throat-slashed supplications over a thing unutterably comic: a round, white, maculated egg.

The hen brings to mind certain poets.

Translated from the Polish by Czesław Miłosz and Peter Dale Scott

Drawer

O my seven-stringed board
in you I dried and pressed my tears
my rebel's frozen fist and paper
on which one cold night I wrote down
my youthful comic testament

and now it's empty and cleaned out
I've sold the tears and the bunch of fists
in the market place they fetched a price
a little fame a penny or two
and now nothing scares off sleep
now not for me the lice and concrete

o drawer o lyre I have lost
and still so much that I could play
with fingers drumming your empty floor
and how good was a desperate heart
and how difficult to part
from nourishing pain which had no hope

I knock on you open forgive me
I could be silent no more I had
to sell the mark of my discontent
such is freedom one has afresh

to invent and to abolish gods
when Caesar wrestles with song at last

and now an empty seashell hums
about the seas which lapsed into sand
the storm congealed to a crystal of salt
before the drawer receives the body
such is my unwieldy prayer
to four boards of consciousness

Translated from the Polish by Czesław Miłosz and Peter Dale Scott

Our Fear

Our fear
does not wear a night shirt
does not have owl's eyes
does not lift a casket lid
does not extinguish a candle

does not have a dead man's face either

our fear
is a scrap of paper
found in a pocket
"warn Wójcik
the place on Długa Street is hot"

our fear
does not rise on the wings of the tempest
does not sit on a church tower
it is down-to-earth

it has the shape
of a bundle made in haste
with warm clothing

provisions
and arms

our fear
does not have the face of a dead man
the dead are gentle to us
we carry them on our shoulders
sleep under the same blanket

close their eyes
adjust their lips
pick a dry spot
and bury them

not too deep
not too shallow

Translated from the Polish by Czeslaw Milosz and Peter Dale Scott

Elegy of Fortinbras

for C.M.

Now that we're alone we can talk prince man to man
though you lie on the stairs and see no more than a dead ant
nothing but black sun with broken rays
I could never think of your hands without smiling
and now that they lie on the stone like fallen nests
they are as defenseless as before The end is exactly this
The hands lie apart The sword lies apart The head apart
and the knight's feet in soft slippers

You will have a soldier's funeral without having been a soldier
the only ritual I am acquainted with a little
There will be no candles no singing only cannon-fuses and bursts
crepe dragged on the pavement helmets boots artillery horses
    drums drums I know nothing exquisite

those will be my maneuvres before I start to rule
one has to take the city by the neck and shake it a bit

Anyhow you had to perish Hamlet you were not for life
you believed in crystal notions not in human clay
always twitching as if asleep you hunted chimeras
wolfishly you crunched the air only to vomit
you knew no human thing you did not know even how to breathe

Now you have peace Hamlet you accomplished what you had to
and you have peace The rest is not silence but belongs to me
you chose the easier part an elegant thrust
but what is heroic death compared with eternal watching
with a cold apple in one's hand on a narrow chair
with a view of the ant-hill and the clock's dial

Adieu prince I have tasks a sewer project
and a decree on prostitutes and beggars
I must also elaborate a better system of prisons
since as you justly said Denmark is a prison
I go to my affairs This night is born
a star named Hamlet We shall never meet
what I shall leave will not be worth a tragedy

It is not for us to greet each other or bid farewell we live on
    archipelagos
and that water these words what can they do what can they do
    prince

Translated from the Polish by Czesław Miłosz and Peter Dale Scott

Remembering My Father

His face severe in clouds above the waters of childhood
so rarely did he hold my warm head in his hands
given to belief not forgiving faults

because he cleared out woods and straightened paths
he carried the lantern high when we entered the night

I thought I would sit at his right hand
and we would separate light from darkness
and judge those of us who live
—it happened otherwise

a junk-dealer carried his throne on a hand-cart
and the deed of ownership the map of our kingdom

he was born for a second time slight very fragile
with transparent skin hardly perceptible cartilage
he diminished his body so I might receive it

in an unimportant place there is shadow under a stone

he himself grows in me we eat our defeats
we burst out laughing
when they say how little is needed
to be reconciled

Translated from the Polish by John Carpenter and Bogdana Carpenter

Mr. Cogito Meditates on Suffering

All attempts to remove
the so-called cup of bitterness—
by reflection
frenzied actions on behalf of homeless cats
deep breathing
religion—
failed

one must consent
gently bend the head

not wring the hands
make use of the suffering gently moderately
like an artificial limb
without false shame
but also without unnecessary pride

do not brandish the stump
over the heads of others
don't knock with the white cane
against the windows of the well-fed

drink the essence of bitter herbs
but not to the dregs
leave carefully
a few sips for the future

accept
but simultaneously
isolate within yourself
and if it is possible
create from the matter of suffering
a thing or a person

play
with it
of course
play
entertain it
very cautiously
like a sick child
forcing at last
with silly tricks
a faint
smile

*Translated from the Polish by John Carpenter
and Bogdana Carpenter*

What Mr. Cogito Thinks About Hell

The lowest circle of hell. Contrary to prevailing opinion it is inhabited neither by despots nor matricides, nor even by those who go after the bodies of others. It is the refuge of artists, full of mirrors, musical instruments, and pictures. At first glance this is the most luxurious infernal department, without tar, fire, or physical tortures.

Throughout the year competitions, festivals, and concerts are held here. There is no climax in the season. The climax is permanent and almost absolute. Every few months new trends come into being and nothing, it appears, is capable of stopping the triumphant march of the avant-garde.

Beelzebub loves art. He boasts that already his choruses, his poets, and his painters are nearly superior to those of heaven. He who has better art has better government—that's clear. Soon they will be able to measure their strength against one another at the Festival of the Two Worlds. And then we will see what remains of Dante, Fra Angelico, and Bach.

Beelzebub supports the arts. He provides his artists with calm, good board, and absolute isolation from hellish life.

Translated from the Polish by John Carpenter and Bogdana Carpenter

ADAM ZAGAJEWSKI

Poland (b. 1945)

Adam Zagajewski was born in Lvov in the Polish Ukraine and moved to Kraków in 1963. He read philosophy and psychology at the Jagellonian University, and during the 1970s he was a part of the opposition democratic movement in Poland. His first volume of poems was published in 1972, and in the years following he has written three novels, four more collections of poems, and four volumes of essays. In 1982 he moved to France, and he now divides his time between Paris, where he edits the literary quarterly *Cahiers littéraires,* and Texas, where he teaches at the University of Houston. Zagajewski's poems can strike an astute political note, but they are finally concerned more with states of soul than with states of society. The tangled branches of a cherry tree are as likely to engage him as any socialist argument. The primary task of his poetry—its tone so melancholy, at once romantic and ironic—is to locate the self in the backwash of history and culture. Displacement rather than engagement preoccupies him, almost a posthistorical world. The silence of a landscape, the solitude of the observer: these are what his poems maneuver around or through, and they do so with uncanny overtones.

Betrayal

The greatest delight, I sense,
is hidden sublimely in the act of betrayal
which can be equal only to fidelity.
To betray a woman, friends, an idea,
to see new light in the eyes
of distant shadows. But choices are
limited: other women, other
ideas, the enemies of our
long-standing friends. If only
we could encounter some quite different
otherness, settle in a country which has
no name, touch a woman before

she is born, lose our memories, meet
a God other than our own.

Translated from the Polish by Renata Gorczynski

At Daybreak

From the train window at daybreak,
I saw empty cities sleeping,
sprawled defenselessly on their backs
like great beasts.
Through the vast squares, only my thoughts
and a biting wind wandered;
linen flags fainted on towers,
birds started to wake in the trees,
and in the thick pelts of the parks
stray cats' eyes gleamed.
The shy light of morning, eternal
debutante, was reflected in shop windows.
Carousels, finally possessing themselves, spun
like prayer wheels on their invisible fulcrums;
gardens fumed like Warsaw's smoldering ruins.
The first van hadn't arrived yet
at the brown slaughterhouse wall.
Cities at daybreak are no one's,
and have no names.
And I, too, have no name,
dawn, the stars growing pale,
the train picking up speed.

Translated from the Polish by Renata Gorczynski, Benjamin Ivry, and C. K. Williams

Electric Elegy

for Robert Hass

Farewell, German radio with your green eye
and your bulky box,
together almost composing
a body and soul. (Your lamps glowed
with a pink, salmony light, like Bergson's
deep self.)
              Through the thick fabric
of the speaker (my ear glued to you as
to the lattice of a confessional), Mussolini once whispered,
Hitler shouted, Stalin calmly explained,
Bierut hissed, Gomulka held endlessly forth.
But no one, radio, will accuse you of treason;
no, your only sin was obedience: absolute,
tender faithfulness to the megahertz;
whoever came was welcomed, whoever was sent
was received.
              Of course I know only
the songs of Schubert brought you the jade
of true joy. To Chopin's waltzes
your electric heart throbbed delicately
and firmly and the cloth over the speaker
pulsated like the breasts of amorous girls
in old novels.
              Not with the news, though,
especially not Radio Free Europe or the BBC.
Then your eye would grow nervous,
the green pupil widen and shrink
as though its atropine dose had been altered.
Mad seagulls lived inside you, and Macbeth.
At night, forlorn signals found shelter
in your rooms, sailors cried out for help,
the young comet cried, losing her head.
Your old age was announced by a cracked voice,
then rattles, coughing, and finally blindness
(your eye faded), and total silence.
Sleep peacefully, German radio,

dream Schumann and don't waken
when the next dictator-rooster crows.

Translated from the Polish by Renata Gorczynski, Benjamin Ivry, and C. K. Williams

Watching *Shoah* in a Hotel Room in America

There are nights as soft as fur on a foal
but we prefer chess or card playing. Here,
some hotel guests sing "Happy Birthday"
as the one-eyed TV nonchalantly shuffles its images.
The trees of my childhood have crossed an ocean
to greet me coolly from the screen.
Polish peasants engage with a Jesuitical zest
in theological disputes: only the Jews are silent,
exhausted by their long dying.
The rivers of the voyages of my youth flow
cautiously over the distant, unfamiliar continent.
Hay wagons haul not hay, but hair,
their axles squeaking under the feathery weight.
We are innocent, the pines claim.
The SS officers are haggard and old,
doctors struggle to save them their hearts, lives, consciences.
It's late, the insinuations of drowsiness have me.
I'd sleep but my neighbors
choir "Happy Birthday" still louder:
louder than the dying Jews.
Huge trucks transport stars from the firmament,
gloomy trains go by in the rain.
I am innocent, Mozart repents;
only the aspen, as usual, trembles,
prepared to confess all its crimes.
The Czech Jews sing the national anthem: "Where is my home . . ."
There is no home, houses burn, the cold gas whistles within.
I grow more and more innocent, sleepy.
The TV reassures me: both of us

are beyond suspicion.
The birthday is noisier.
The shoes of Auschwitz, in pyramids
high as the sky, groan faintly:
Alas, we outlived mankind, now
let us sleep, sleep:
we have nowhere to go.

Translated from the Polish by Renata Gorczynski, Benjamin Ivry, and C. K. Williams

When Death Came

I wasn't with you when death came.
The municipal hospital was your last home:
white room, cobwebs, chipped
paint, a jar of cherry preserves,
an old issue of a rotogravure, a tin fork
with a tine gone, two glasses.
In the next bed, a tailor with cancer.
You were so old the doctors thought
you'd hardly weigh
in the numbers of death.
So old that the children on your street
thought you another century,
an empire slouching on the broken sidewalk.
As death came, though, youth came:
you suddenly spoke the language of childhood,
the white screen between you and the living
was the wing of a glider.
The intravenous drip muttered, a pigeon
impatiently paced on the sill.
You were taking all of yourself
from that dreary place into your death:
the dandy of eighteen, the mature thirty-year-old,
the German teacher with no truck
for indolent students, the pensioner
with his long daily walk

that may at the end have measured
the distance from earth
to heaven.
You'd regenerated yourself
for your death.
In the hall, the muffled laughter
of nurses; at the window,
sparrows fighting for crumbs.

Translated from the Polish by Renata Gorczynski, Benjamin Ivry, and C. K. Williams

AGNES NEMES NAGY

Hungary (1922–1991)

Ágnes Nemes Nagy was born in Budapest, the daughter of a lawyer whose roots were in Transylvania. With the outbreak of the war, having just graduated from the University in Budapest, she joined in civilian Resistance work. After the war she worked for the literary journal *New Moon,* which was eventually banned. For ten years she published no poetry but continued to write for children. After that period she published steadily; volumes of her essays appeared, along with a *Collected Poems* in 1981. Two years later she won the prestigious Kossuth Prize. The textures of Nemes Nagy's poems are richly worked, allusive, and formally shaped. "I am," she wrote, "what is called an objective lyric poet, in the sense that objects attract me and also in the sense that the objectivity of the lyric tone attracts me. At the same time I could also say that I am attracted by the intense tension which is generated by these objects at the moment when they rise above the general feeling of peril, as expressions or perhaps counterpoints of that endangerment. Because, when all is told, I love objects. Even the threatening ones. Objects have a comforting force-field. . . . I might say that I hold poetry to be one of the great roads to human cognition, of recognition through the emotions, that I consider our poetic campaigns into the land of the Nameless crucially important, a factor in the spiritual survival of twentieth-century man." By the time of her death, Nemes Nagy was considered the best woman poet in Hungary.

Sincerity

I wince in self-revelation.
Happy is the free spirit.
I should have been a coachman
who just washes silently
the big blonde horses, washes.

Translated from the Hungarian by Hugh Maxton

Between

The great sleeves of air,
air on which the bird
and the science of birds bear
themselves, wings on the fraying argument;
incalculable result
of a moment's leafy silhouette
bark and branch of a haze living upwards
like desire into the upper leaves
to inhale every three seconds
those big, frosty angels.

Downweight. On the plain
the mountain's motionless shocks
as they lie or kneel
peaks and escarpments,
geology's figure-sculpture,
the glen's a moment's distraction
and once more the forms and rocks,
chalky bone to outline
into identity of pleated stone.

Between the sky and the earth.

Creaking of rocks. As
the sun's clear ores
into themselves almost, stone into metal, as
a creature steps on in his claws smoke,
and up above the escarpment
ribbons of burning hoof,
then night in the desert, night as
quenching and reaching
its stony core, night below zero, and as
the tendons, joints, plaques
split and tear, as
they are strained in endless
splitting ecstasy

by routine dumb lightning
in black and white—

Between the day and the night.

Aches and stabbings,
visions, voiceless aqueducts,
inarticulate risings,
unbearable tension
of verticals between up and down.

Climates. Conditions.
Between. Stone. Tanktraces.
A strip of black reed rimming the plain
written in two lines, in the lake, the sky,
two black plaques of signsystem,
diacritic on the stars—

Between the sky and the sky.

Translated from the Hungarian by Hugh Maxton

Like One Who

Like one who brought news from far
and then forgets his message,
and of all that gritty light only
a handful stuck with him, knotted . . .

so wanders the amnesiac
in his body's crumpled coat.

Translated from the Hungarian by Hugh Maxton

A Four-Light Window

1

The first is a park.
A garden path between bare boughs
path at one side, mass of a yew tree
flecked with winter fruit
the glass beads of *art nouveau*
and more
more—to what end?

The mark of the square picture
is the garden path, bird's neck path
as it turns, impossible in words
only in the hand's gesture,
and cranes its unwritable bird's head
into the dull bushes.

2

The second is clouded.

3

The third is of concrete.
I mean a garage roof
(the window sill cuts in two, and below
the vintage-animals invisible
in bespoke tarpaulin
retracting light
from varnish & polish & chrome
and the unheard four strokes
resound emptily in their cylinders
with the viscous chill of winter garages)
while outside the burning winter sunlight
and the mix of climates

and the mix of woodpecker overalls
as it cuts over the snow field
and turns the horizon
like a steering wheel,
noon spin through bright meridian.

4

The fourth is the sky,
drum-tight, without a line.
Rare silence of earth's atmosphere
as it does not write, thick slate
its inextinguishable vaporings.
A few strokes only, broken signals,
broached interpretations,
remnant of prefix, an auspice.

Translated from the Hungarian by Hugh Maxton

SANDOR CSOORI

Hungary (b. 1930)

"From the first," Sándor Csoóri has written, "there has been present in my work, in whichever genre, a general sense of unease about how to maintain the existence of the human personality in the world amid the great campaigns of depersonalization." This unease must have been imprinted early. In 1945, after the brutalities of the war, Csoóri returned to his native Zámoly to help bury the dead after the village had "changed hands" seventeen times. Then followed the years of Communist rule, during which his career, launched with lyrical hopes, took a more skeptical turn. Still, he was determined to link his work to that of such great nationalist predecessors as Gyula Illyés and Sándor Petöfi: to take up the nation's fate as his subject, to join its rural longings to its urban voice, to combine European sophistication with the folklore of Hungary. The task for the poet is that of the individual, to survive as a paradox without illusions. "Hopelessness is self-defense," he has written, "the source of final calmness. And without that, how could anyone act? In other words, the Eastern European is not only doomed to existence, but also to existentialism, because he can preserve his sanity and honesty only through the conscious or instinctive undertaking, or perhaps the religion, of hopeless action." Csoóri's work has won many awards, including Hungary's Attila József Prize, Austria's Herder Prize, and the Grand Prize at the Cannes Film Festival for his film *Ten Thousand Days*.

My Masters

Where, where are my masters?
In the past they'd appear without even being called.
They'd come before the first peal of the bells,
across barren yards: madmen, poets,
alcoholic saints; they'd come from the night's marshes,
holding Hungary's broken peony in their hands.

One of them would come with a flood,
another from between clattering tracks,
another limping, with the white frost of Bakony on his back.

And I always read the words
from their motionless lips.
Where might they linger now? Where might they be kept waiting?
With whom do they share their deaths,
the way prisoners of war share a lone potato?
As though they are ashamed
of this fouled landscape that's sunk into itself,
and their dirtied mission.

Translated from the Hungarian by Len Roberts

A Thin, Black Band

Since I don't wake with her,
since I don't sit at the table to have dinner with her,
since death flowed into my laughing mouth
and I am caught between the rains,
as between the slats of the iron fence in my childhood days:
I can see a thin, black band wavering for a long time
before my eyes.
It comes closer, vanishes, once again rises,
as if an eye's swaying bloodshot vein hypnotized
me from morning till night.

I can see it, too, among the museum's massive columns
in the slanted, falling sunshine,
before the January statues' snow-mouths,
and near women's faces in the market, in the street,
standing on the escalator of the subway.
America fades away within me, the Great Lakes' light,
like when the lamp is turned off.
Startled, I look about, and haltingly I begin to believe
that the dead, too, are fickle,
and they won't stop their secret game
once, while living, they've started it.

The wind whirls, whirls upon the lean docks,
tips hats and roofs,
lures water from the middle of the Danube aloft,
and that black marvel dances there, there too, about
the prancing waterspout,
it draws my eyes, lures them after it,
like a strand of black hair that cannot be caught.

Translated from the Hungarian by Len Roberts and Tibor Tengerdi

Postponed Nightmare

I'm sitting in the sunshine,
    getting warm as the rocks
        after a rough, rheumatic winter.
    At my ankle a small wind stirs in the grass,
your breath from down below, perhaps.

They say I wept months for you.
    That may be; I can't recollect.
        On either side of me the nights blackened
    and horses reared with blood-frothed mouths,
as they do when a shell bursts among them.

And trains and cities and a flock
    of crows plummeting headfirst
        and the skidding, burning wrecks after
    midnight on America's roads,
where I waited, mid-dream, for a crash.

I yelled to you: come, there is a renewal
    in my madness, my pain that is
        greater than pain: the severed
    head, the arm, fly toward you
and our eyes meet again—

I'm sitting in the sunshine,
    getting warm as the rocks.

A winter's postponed nightmare cries out in my bones.
At my ankle a small wind stirs in the grass,
your breath from down below, perhaps.

Translated from the Hungarian by Len Roberts and László Vértes

We Were Good, Good and Obedient

for my generation

We were good, good and obedient,
like the little boys hung with cherries in the promenade,
we didn't trample the grass and didn't undermine
the dahlias planted in the park.
We were good, good and obedient:
we hissed out even in our sleep
for the stray dogs kicked in the back,
but we avoided the eyes of cowering men
as though they were puddles of blood at an accident.
We were good, good and obedient,
we saw Georgia's cliffs in brave sunlight,
we drank its wine,
we saw the Black Sea trudging home at night
and the ancient gods left without mouths,
and, with velvet stomachs, we ate dinner out of sheer spite.
Mozart, standing on his cold star, played music for us
to the horse-radished rump of beef.
We were good, good and obedient,
the wind blew, the years swayed to the side with us,
like an airplane circling slowly over
a lit city,
the fine, drifting ashes of the advertisements' fires
and the world's fires shot up to us,
the epaulets of generals hurrying to receptions glowed yellow,
but we watched, instead, with chattering teeth, Jancso's*
paradisiacal
women on the movie screen
and the perverse little panties they hung on the crosses

                    of graves.
          We were good, good and obedient,
misfortune stepped, in her skirt, over
               our aching nose-bones,
          through us the past was brought to pass,
but we still fondled the memory of a trumpet-resounding ball
               from the time of the war,
as though stuffed pink sacks
          had taken our places, dreaming, those nights.

*Miklós Jancso, famous Hungarian film director and producer, who presented naked
women in his films during the 1960s and 1970s, causing some public outcries.

Translated from the Hungarian by Len Roberts and László Vértes

Everyday History

To rise
and make fire in the stove,
in the brain after the reeling of the smoke,
in the ducts of the bones cold from sleeplessness,
and to seek the way to the hand,
from the hand to the drinking glass,
the remnants of yesterday's ashes in the hollows of the face,
perhaps a bird-blown windstorm will revive them yet,
and to wander
from one body to another,
and like nomadic kings: to seek the everyday motherland,
and, having found it
or not,
to spend the night in a single smile's tent,
and to walk in the Creation like a stranger,
to breathe in the dawn
poison of the trees,
the iron dust of the towns,
to go to all the wars,
to wear the lilac leaves around the neck

like a dogtag
and, understanding everything
and understanding nothing, to part with what I love
and rage for what I loved,
brazenly, like my own life's
hired man.

Translated from the Hungarian by Len Roberts

GYORGY PETRI

Hungary (b. 1943)

With the collapse of the Communist empire in 1989, the lives of millions were changed irrevocably. For György Petri it meant he was "not obliged to participate in political life anymore." Since the 1956 Uprising and the subsequent Soviet invasion, he had lived under a stultifying regime that fed the bitterness, ennui, and dissident behavior of Petri and many of his colleagues. Born in Budapest, he has lived at the center of events, political and moral, that have shaped the modern Hungarian imagination, but because he is a member of the younger generation of artists, his attitude toward those events and regimes is contemptuous or satirical. "My use of language," he says, "was partly a provocation against the unbelievable prudishness of socialist realism and state culture. There's a great silence about sexual life and bodily functions. There's also a sociological prudery, a refusal to talk about the disturbing facts of social or private life." His poem "Night Song of the Personal Shadow" is written in the voice of the man sent to spy on Petri because of his political beliefs. When Petri writes, in his dramatic monologue "Electra," about the bloated traitor Aegisthus in the Greek myth, he is portraying János Kádár, the Communist leader of Hungary for decades. Although his first two books had been issued by a state publishing house, by the early 1980s many of his poems were found "politically unacceptable." He defied official channels and—until the government fell—published his work in samizdat. All along his underlying theme has been the freedom of the individual, its possibilities and impossibilities.

By an Unknown Poet
from Eastern Europe, 1955

It's fading,
            like the two flags that, year by year,
we'd put out for public holidays
in the iron sheaths stuck over the gate—
like them the world's looking pale, it's fading now.

Where have they gone, the days of pomp and cheer?

Smothered with dust
in the warmth
of an attic room,
a world dismantled holds its peace.

The march has gone and disappeared.

It metamorphosed into a howl
the wind winnowed.
And now, instead of festive poets here,
the wind will recite into thin air,

it will utter scurrying dust and pulsating heat
above the concrete square.

That our women have been loved seems quite incredible.

Above the era
of taut ropes and white-hot foundries,
the tentative, wary
present—dust settling—hovers.

Above unfinished buildings:
imperial frauds, fantasies.

I no longer believe
what I believed once.
But the fact that I have believed—
that I compel myself
day by day to recall.

And I do not forgive anyone.

Our terrible loneliness
crackles and flakes
like the rust on iron rails in the heat of the sun.

Translated from the Hungarian by Clive Wilmer and George Gömöri

To S.V.

The bus was taking me
over the bridge and I looked
on into the tunnel. At
the far end of that pipe
padded with shadows, there were
vehicles hanging about—
quarantined
in an unreachably distant
sandy sun-strip.

A long time since
we were last watching together—
looking out for occasions
to enrich our occasional
poetry with occasions of pain.
Filing away at lyric skeleton-keys
we gauge by sight
for a small circle of friends.

I amble on alone—
the prisoner of a condition it'd be
going too far to call loneliness
and deceiving myself to call independence—on
among parched sights.
I walk down to the embankment looking for shade.
In glass-melting heat
the bus I have just got off
is crawling away somewhere.

An airless tent of chestnuts. But up there
already, the infant stars, as yet
tenderly spiked, herald the autumn.
The water's putrescent slate.
But at least it gets broken up
by a boat putting out from here.
A sight, a view: I've no one
to share it with.

Summer's fruits have ripened
in me and they taste soapy.

I could already tell we were in for a bad year
the morning after New Year's Eve.
In a city of iron shutters, all pulled down,
we slithered about on insidious snow
looking for soak-up soup or hair-of-the-dog.
We ended up drinking iodine-yellow beer
in a surgically tiled café.
And time we stepped outside,
the street was wearing eyesore white.

Our weak brains stop working.
Sailors on ships that are locked in ice,
as is well-known, will devour each other.
Just like the modern Theatre of Provocation—
it all degenerates, banter
into argument, teasing
into insult. Till finally the background
cracks the backbone of the situation.

Translated from the Hungarian by Clive Wilmer and George Gömöri

Gratitude

The idiotic silence of state holidays
is no different
from that of Catholic Sundays.
People in collective idleness
are even more repellent
than they are when purpose has harnessed them.

Today I will not
in my old ungrateful way
let gratuitous love decay in me.
In the vacuum of streets

what helps me to escape
is the memory of your face and thighs,
your warmth,
the fish-death smell of your groin.

You looked for a bathroom in vain.
The bed was uncomfortable
like a roof ridge.
The mattress smelt of insecticide,
the new scent of your body mingling with it.

I woke to a cannonade
(a round number of years ago
something happened). You were still asleep.
Your glasses, your patent leather bag
on the floor, your dress on the window-catch
hung inside out—so practical.

One strap of your black slip
had slithered off.
And a gentle light was wavering
on the downs of your neck, on your collar-bones,
as the cannon went on booming

and on a spring poking through
the armchair's cover
fine dust was trembling.

Translated from the Hungarian by Clive Wilmer and George Gömöri

To Be Said Over and Over Again

I glance down at my shoe and—there's the lace!
This can't be gaol then, can it, in that case.

Translated from the Hungarian by Clive Wilmer and George Gömöri

Night Song of the Personal Shadow

The rain is pissing down,
you scum.
And you, you are asleep
in your nice warm room—
that or stuffing the bird.
Me? Till six in the morning
I rot in the slackening rain.
I must wait for my relief, I've got to wait
till you crawl out of your hole,
get up from beside your old woman.
So the dope can be passed on
as to where you've flown.
You are flying, spreading your wings.
Don't you get into my hands—
I'll pluck you while you're in flight.
This sodding rain
is something I won't forget,
my raincoat swelling
double its normal weight
and the soles of my shoes.
While you
were arsing around
in the warm room.

The time will come
when I feed you to fish in the Danube.

Translated from the Hungarian by Clive Wilmer and George Gömöri

Christmas 1956

On the twentieth, at a certain moment
(6:45 A.M.), I, a child of ill omen,
born between Joe S. and Jesus,

become thirteen. It's my last year
of Christmas being a holiday. There's
plenty to eat: the economy of scarcity
was to my Gran as the Red Sea: she crossed over
with dry feet and a turkey. There's a present too—
for me: I control the market still—my one
cousin a mere girl, only four, and I
the last male of the line
(for the time being). Wine-soup, fish, there's everything,
considering we've just come up from the shelter—
where G.F. kept flashing a tommy-gun
with no magazine in it ("Get away, Gabe," he was told,
"d'you want the Russkies after us?").
Gabe (he won't be hanged till it's lilac-time)
comes in wishing us merry Christmas, there's no
midnight mass because of the curfew;
I concentrate on *Monopoly,* my present—
my aunt got it privately, the toyshops
not having much worth buying. My aunt has come,
in a way, to say goodbye: she's getting
out via Yugoslavia, but at the border (alas)
she'll be left behind, and so (in a dozen years
about) she will have to die of cancer of the spine.
Nobody knows how to play *Monopoly,* so
I start twiddling the knob on our Orion,
our wireless set, and gradually tune in
to London and America, like Mum in '44,
only louder: it's no longer forbidden—yet.
The Christmas-tree decorations, known by heart,
affect me now rather as many years on
a woman will, one loved for many years.
In the morning, barefoot, I'm still to be found
rummaging through the *Monopoly* cards, inhaling
the smell of fir-tree and candles. I bring in
a plateful of brawn from outside, Gran
is already cooking, she squeezes a lemon,
slices bread to my brawn. I crouch on a stool
in pyjamas. There's a smell of sleep and holiday.
Grandad's coughing in what was the servant's room,
his accountant's body, toothpick-thin,

thrown by a fit of it from under the quilt,
Mother's about too, the kitchen is filling up
with family, and it's just as an observer
dropped in the wrong place that I am here:
small, alien and gone cold.

Translated from the Hungarian by Clive Wilmer and George Gömöri

Electra

What *they* think is it's the twists and turns of politics
that keep me ticking; they think it's Mycenae's fate.
Take my little sister, cute sensitive Chrysosthemis—
to me the poor thing attributes a surfeit of moral passion,
believing I'm unable to get over
the issue of our father's twisted death.
What do I care for that gross geyser of spunk
who murdered his own daughter! The steps into the bath
were slippery with soap—and the axe's edge too sharp.
But that this Aegisthus, with his trainee-barber's face,
should swagger about and hold sway in this wretched town,
and that our mother, like a venerably double-chinned old whore,
should dally with him simpering—everybody pretending
not to see, not to know anything. Even the Sun
glitters above, like a lie forged of pure gold,
the false coin of the gods!
Well, that's why! That's why! Because of disgust, because it all
      sticks in my craw,
revenge has become my dream and my daily bread.
And this revulsion is stronger than the gods.
I already see how mold is creeping across Mycenae,
which is the mold of madness and destruction.

Translated from the Hungarian by Clive Wilmer and George Gömöri

Morning Coffee

I like the cold rooms of autumn, sitting
early in the morning at an open window,
or on the roof, dressing-gown drawn close,
the valley and the morning coffee glowing—
this cooling, that warming.

Red and yellow multiply, but the green
wanes, and into the mud the leaves
fall—fall in heaps,
the devalued currency of summer:
so much of it! so worthless!

Gradually the sky's
downy grey turns blue, the slight
chill dies down. The tide
of day comes rolling in—
in waves, gigantic, patient, barreling.

I can start to carry on. I give myself up
to an impersonal imperative.

Translated from the Hungarian by Clive Wilmer and George Gömöri

MIROSLAV HOLUB

Czech Republic (b. 1923)

Born in Plzeň, the son of a lawyer and a linguist, Miroslav Holub studied medicine at the Charles University in Prague and later took another advanced degree in immunology. He began his career as a pathologist, then worked for many years as a microbiologist at the Czechoslovak Academy of Sciences, and he is now chief research immunologist at the Institute of Clinical and Experimental Medicine in Prague. He didn't start writing poetry until he was thirty—at about the time his scientific interests shifted to immunology—but since then he has been prolific. (He is a prolific author, too, of scientific papers in cellular immunology; he also writes a popular newspaper column and edits a science magazine.) Devoted to his two professions, Holub has wanted, he says, to "find poetic equivalents for the new reality of the micro-world," so he has drawn on science for both metaphors and perspectives. "I like the play or dance of metaphors, just as I like the play of ideas in a poem. My poems, by the way, always begin with an idea, an obsessive idea of some sort." Because he had signed a street petition after the 1968 Soviet invasion of Czechoslovakia, the Communist authorities banned his poems, and—though he continued to work in the laboratory—he published nothing between 1970 and 1982. His poems remain anti-Romantic, often minimalist, sometimes surrealist. "There are lines," he explains, "which are just intended as a sort of graphic image of something, and which are not obscure by nature or because I couldn't find a better solution, but because I wanted to make them less comprehensible in order to describe a certain difficulty."

Man Cursing the Sea

Someone
just climbed to the top of the cliffs
and began to curse the sea.

Dumb water, stupid pregnant water,
slow, slimy copy of the sky,
you peddler between sun and moon,
pettifogging pawnbroker of shells,

soluble, loud-mouthed bull,
fertilizing the rocks with your blood,
suicidal sword
dashed to bits on the headland,
hydra, hydrolizing the night,
breathing salty clouds of silence,
spreading jelly wings
in vain, in vain,
gorgon, devouring its own body,

water, you absurd flat skull of water—

And so he cursed the sea for a spell,
it licked his footprints in the sand
like a wounded dog.

And then he came down
and patted
the tiny immense stormy mirror of the sea.

There you go, water, he said,
and went his way.

Translated from the Czech by Stuart Friebert and Dana Hábová

The Fly

She sat on the willow bark
watching
part of the battle of Crécy,
the shrieks,
the moans,
the wails,
the trampling and tumbling.

During the fourteenth charge
of the French cavalry

she mated
with a brown-eyed male fly
from Vadincourt.

She rubbed her legs together
sitting on a disemboweled horse
meditating
on the immortality of flies.

Relieved she alighted
on the blue tongue
of the Duke of Clervaux.

When silence settled
and the whisper of decay
softly circled the bodies

and just
a few arms and legs
twitched under the trees,

she began to lay her eggs
on the single eye
of Johann Uhr,
the Royal Armorer.

And so it came to pass—
she was eaten by a swift
fleeing
from the fires of Estrés.

Translated from the Czech by Stuart Friebert and Dana Hábová

On the Origin of the Contrary

As if the sky broke up,
only it was just two palms of a hand.

It flapped its wings for a while,
but the palms closed
a little more. The wings got stuck.
It kicked its feet, but the palms
closed, one of its feet broke off.

Each time it moved something,
the palms closed and something broke off.
So it grew torpid. It could be
catalepsy.

But it could be the creeping realization
that blue sky did not exist any more.
                    On the contrary.
That there is no meadow with a flower
here and there.
                    On the contrary.
That there is nothing irresistible any more.
                    On the contrary.
That there is no glucosis,
            no droning,
            no time,
                    On the contrary.

And thus will it be. Until
someone gets bored. By that life,
that death, or that tickling in the palm.

Translated from the Czech by Stuart Friebert and Dana Hábová

Vanishing Lung Syndrome*

Once in a while somebody fights for breath.
He stops, getting in everyone's way.

*Burke.

The crowd flows around, muttering
about the flow of crowds,
but he just fights for breath.

Inside there may be growing
a sea monster within a sea monster,
a black, talking bird,
a raven Nevermore that
can't find a bust of Athena
to perch on and so just grows
like a bullous emphysema with cyst development,
fibrous masses and lung hypertension.

Inside there may be growing
a huge muteness of fairy tales,
the wood-block baby that gobbles up everything,
father, mother, flock of sheep,
dead-end road among fields,
screeching wagon and horse,
I've eaten them all and now I'll eat you,
while scintigraphy shows
a disappearance of perfusion, and angiography
shows remnants of arterial branches
without the capillary phase.

Inside there may be growing
an abandoned room,
bare walls, pale squares where pictures hung,
a disconnected phone,
feathers settling on the floor
the encyclopaedists have moved out and
Dostoevsky never found the place,

lost in the landscape
where only surgeons
write poems.

Translated from the Czech by David Young and Dana Hábová

Immanuel Kant

The philosophy of white blood cells:
this is self,
this is non-self.
The starry sky of non-self,
perfectly mirrored
deep inside.
Immanuel Kant,
perfectly mirrored
deep inside.

And he knows nothing about it,
he is only afraid of drafts.
And he knows nothing about it,
though this is the critique
of pure reason.

Deep inside.

Translated from the Czech by Dana Hábová and David Young

Interferon

Always just one demon in the attic.
Always just one death in the village. And dogs
howl in that direction, while from the other way
the newborn child comes, just one,
to fill the empty space in the big air.

Likewise, cells infected by a virus
send signals out, defenses
are mobilized, and no other virus
gets a chance to settle down
and change the destiny. This phenomenon
is called interference.

And when a poet dies, deep in the night,
a lone black bird wakes up in the thicket
and sings for all it's worth,
while a black rain trickles down
like sperm or something,
the song is bloodstained, the suffocating bird
sings perched on an empty thorax
where the imaginary heart
wakes up to face its forever interfering
futility. And in the morning, the sky's swept clean,
the bird's sleepy, the soil's fertilized,
and the poet is gone.

In Klatovska Street, in Pilsen,
by the railway bridge, there was
a small shop that sold quilts and comforters.
In times when what is needed
is a steel cover for the whole continent,
the quilt business is slack.
The shopkeeper was in trouble.
In such times men of the world
usually turn to art.

In the big shop window
the shopkeeper built
a cottage of quilts and comforters
and staged a performance every night
about a quilted cake-house and a red-quilted
Little Red Riding Hood, while his wife,
in this stuffed masquerade,
played the wolf or the witch,
and he was the padded Hansel,
Gretel, Red Riding Hood or Granny.
To see the two old people
crawling in monstrous floods of textile
around the plump cottage
was not unambiguous.

It was something like the life
of sea cucumbers in the mud
under a cliff. Outside
the surf of war roared and they
carried on their puffy
pantomime, out of time and out of action.

Children used to watch from the street
and then go home. Nothing was sold,
but it was the only pantomime around.

The black bird sang
and the rain poured into the thorax
marked with the Star of David.

But in the actors under the quilts,
l'anima allegra must have woken up
at that moment, so that,
sweating and rapt, they played
the undersea *commedia dell'arte*
thinking there was no backstage
until a scene was over, moving jerkily
from shopwindow to cottage and back,
with the gaiety of polio-stricken Columbines,
while the sound of drums and bugles never reached them.

Or else they thought such a deep
humiliation of old age
and its traditional dignity
interfered with the steps
of men in leather coats
and departures of trains
for human slaughterhouses.
It did.

The black bird sang
and the ravaged sclerotic hearts
hopped in their chests,
and then one morning they did not play,
did not raise the shutters,

the sky was swept clean, the soil fertilized,
the comforters confiscated for the eastern front
and the actors transferred to
the backstage of the world
called Bergen-Belsen.
In place of the quilt shop now
a greengrocer peddles rubbery kohlrabies.

Always just one death in the village.
Always just one demon.
How great is the power of the theater, even if
it ends up collapsing
and vanishing backstage.
Dogs howl in that direction.
And the butterfly pursues
those who stole the flowers.

When we did autopsies
at the psychiatric ward in Bohnice,
in air thick with the urban pollution
of relative futility,
the car would pull up before the barracks
and the inmates would wave
some sort of Labor Day parade flags
from the windows
as one went, hugely alone,
to the solitary mortuary
beyond a grove of trees
where the naked bodies
of ancient schizophrenics
waited, along with two live inmates,
one pulling the corpses up from the basement
on a dumbwaiter and putting them gently
on tables, as a mother would
her unbaptized child,
the other lurking in a dark corner
with a pen dipped in ink
to write the Latin protocol,
his spelling faultless,
and nobody uttering a sound, only

the moan of the elevator shaft . . . and the knife
slicing the epidermis and dermis made
a sound like tearing silk . . . and it was always
powerful and unprecedented pneumonias
and tumors big as dragon's eggs,
the rain soaked the thorax
and in the roaring silence
one had to break the line of an angel's fall
and dictate the logical sentence
for the ghoul, doomed ages ago . . .
and the schizophrenic's pen in the corner
diligently scratched the paper
like an eager mouse.

We need no prompter,
the puppets said proudly.

The air of this anatomic theater
was filled with interferon,
it was a spectacular personal charge
against the malignant growth, it was
a general amnesty of walls, entropy
was forsworn for the moment,

because there are no bubbles at the bottom
to be cracked by the breeze.

The red balloon outside
soared to the unseen heaven, its chains
stretched by knowing
the nearer the inferno
the greater the paradise,
the nearer the prison cell
the greater the freedom.

Cantabit coram latrone omne vacuus viator.

And that is the fierce essence of the theater,
when the actor stripped of everything
rises to the top of the conflagration

and everything else is hushed
like a much-hunted animal
with muscles still trembling
but with endorphins
and an immense peace in the brain.

Yes, even a whale will sometimes leave the herd
to hurl itself into shallow water and die in the sun
like a collapsed cathedral, with a pushed-out penis,
and death is buried instantly
in a tiny grain of sand
and the sea is laughing.

Ask felled trees; in broken speech
they preach about saplings. In the galactic
jargon of white dwarves
stars of the main sequence
shine forever.

In the non-Euclidean curved space
which passes comprehension as
the interference of the theater does,
you hear forever the voices of children
from the elementary school of death,
children from kitchen puppet tragedies,
and children from military junkets
when spearing and subsequent flinging of legs
was something like curry,
the condiment of mercenary marches,
voices of children passing comprehension—

But we washed behind our ears,
we didn't pull the cat's tail,
we haven't put
our fingers into sockets—

What else is left
in the universe of hominization
slow as the decay of tritium,
except learning about the growing shame of demons—

since the time of the Aztecs, high priests
haven't presented offerings while dressed
in the skin of a freshly skinned prisoner.

We need no prompter, said—

One Christmas, a drunk
dressed up as a devil
fell down the stairs and lay there,
and a child, experiencing
that embarrassing joy just inches from fright,
ran out, upon hearing the noise, and called—

Mummy, come here, there's a dead devil—

And he was, although the actor got up
after another sip. Maybe dogs howled,
but only by a dark mistake.
The stars of the main sequence shone,
the bird was about to sing in the saplings,
the child trembled a little
from the chill of three million years,
in the big air, and was told,
poetically,

it's all just a game,
look, the butterfly's bringing
the flowers back . . . and
there's no other devil . . . and
the nearer the paradise . . .

It believed and it didn't—

Translated from the Czech by Dana Hábová and David Young

VASKO POPA

Serbia (1922–1991)

Born in Grebenac to Romanian parents, Vasko Popa studied in Vienna,
Bucharest, and Belgrade. During the war he fought with the Communist
partisans and was held in a Nazi concentration camp. For most of his life,
he worked as an editor at several publishing houses. As a poet he worked
steadily—by his death he had published forty-three collections, which had
been awarded many prizes, and was considered the leading poet of the
language. He first fell under the sway of French surrealism, then of Ser-
bian folklore. From both influences he derived a unique idiom: surfaces
that are succinct and deceptively simple, yielding to metaphysical puzzles.
Terse, aphoristic, elliptical, his poems were usually conceived as parts of
longer sequences, which is why some critics have referred to his work as
"epic" in impulse. He preferred the concrete to the abstract, the legend to
the ledger, the stark to the baroque. Love and fate were the poles of his
imagination. As Ted Hughes has written of Popa's work, "No poetry
could carry less luggage than his, or be freer of predisposition and precon-
ception. No poetry is more difficult to outflank, yet it is in no sense defen-
sive. His poems are trying to find out what does exist, and what the
conditions really are. The movement of his verse is part of his method of
investigating something fearfully apprehended, fearfully discovered."

In the Ashtray

A tiny sun
With yellow tobacco hair
Is burning out in the ashtray

The blood of cheap lipstick suckles
The dead stumps of stubs

Beheaded sticks yearn
For sulphur crowns

Blue roans of ash whinny
Arrested in their prancing

A huge hand
With a burning eye in its palm
Lurks on the horizon

Translated from the Serbian by Anne Pennington

Pig

Only when she felt
The savage knife in her throat
Did the red veil
Explain the game
And she was sorry
She had torn herself
From the mud's embrace
And had hurried so joyfully
From the field that evening
Hurried to the yellow gate

Translated from the Serbian by Anne Pennington

Heaven's Ring

Stargazer's Death

He had to die they say
Stars were closer to him
Even than people

The ants ate him they say
He fancied stars give birth to ants

And ants to stars
So he filled his house with ants

His celestial debauches
Cost him his head they say
And that silly rumor about a dagger
With human fingerprints

He found himself out of this world
They say he went to find a sunflower
In which every heart's every star's
Road comes together

He had to die they say

Heaven's Ring

Ring nobody's ring
How did you get lost
Fall out of the blue somewhere
More likely everywhere than somewhere

Why did you instantly marry
Your old your age-old shine
To your young emptiness

They neither remember you
Nor their wedding night

Your shine has taken to drink
Your emptiness has put on weight
And you're lost again

Here's my ring finger
Calm down on it

Good for Nothing

You slept good for nothing
And dreamt you were something

Something caught fire
The flames writhed
Their suffering blind

You woke up good for nothing
Warmed your back
On a dream flame

You didn't see the flame's suffering
Whole worlds of suffering
Your back's nearsighted

The flame went out
Its suffering got its eyes back
Then it too went out blissfully

Orphan Absence

You didn't have a real father
The day you first saw the world within you
Your mother was not at home
It was a mistake you were born

Built like an empty gorge
You smell of absence
Alone you gave birth to yourself

You fidget with rags on fire
Break your heads one after the other
Jump in and out of your mouths
To give youth back to your old mistake

Bend down naked if you can
Down to my last letter
And follow its track

It seems to me my little orphans
That it leads
Into some sort of presence

The Shadow Maker

You walk forever and ever
Over your own individual infinity
From head to heel and back

You're your own source of light
The zenith is in your head
In your heel its setting

Before it dies you let your shadows out
To lengthen to estrange themselves
To work miracles and shame
And bow down only to themselves

At zenith you reduce the shadows
To their proper size
You teach them to bow to you
And as they bow down to disappear

You're coming this way even today
But the shadows won't let us see you

The Starry Snail

You crawled after the rain
The starry rain

The stars made a house for you
Out of their bones
Where are you taking it now on your towel

Time limps behind you
To overtake you to run you over
Let your horns out snail

You crawl on a huge cheek
That you'll never glimpse
Straight into the plow of nothingness

Turn to the life-line
On my dream hand
Before it's too late

Make me the inheritor
Of your wonder-working silver towel

Immigrant Stars

You looked at each other stars
On the sly so the sky won't see you
You meant well

Got it all backwards

The morning found you cold
Far from the hearth
Far from the heaven's gate

Look at me stars
On the sly so the earth won't see it
Give me secret signs
I'll give you a stick of cherry wood

One of my wrinkles for a path
One of my eyelashes for a guide
To take you back home

Translated from the Serbian by Charles Simic

Burning Shewolf

1

On the bottom of the sky
The shewolf lies

Body of living sparks
Overgrown with grass
And covered with sun's dust

In her breasts
Mountains rise threatening
And forgive as they lower themselves

Through her veins rivers thunder
In her eyes lakes flash

In her boundless heart
The ores melt with love
On seven stems of their fire

Before the first and last howl
Wolves play on her back
And live in her crystal womb

2

They cage the shewolf
In the earth's fire

Force her to build
Towers of smoke
Make bread out of coals

They fatten her with embers
And have her wash it down
With hot mercury milk

They force her to mate
With red-hot pokers
And rusty old drills

With her teeth the shewolf reaches
The blonde braid of a star
And climbs back to the base of the sky

3

They catch the shewolf in steel traps
Sprung from horizon to horizon

Tear out her golden muzzle
And pluck the secret grasses
Between her thighs

They sick on her all-tied-up
Deadbeats and bloodhounds
To go ahead and rape her

Cut her up into pieces
And abandon her
To the carcass-eating tongs

With her severed tongue the shewolf
Scoops live water from the jaws of a cloud
And again becomes whole

4

The shewolf bathes herself in the blue
And washes away the ashes of dogs

On the bottom of a torrent
That runs down the stones of her motionless face
Lightnings spawn

In her wide-open jaw
The moon hides its ax during the day
The sun its knives at night

The beatings of her copper-heart
Quiet the barking distances
And lull to sleep the chirping air

In the ravines
Below her wooded eyebrows
The thunder means business

5

The shewolf stands on her back legs
At the base of the sky

She stands up together with wolves
Turned to stone in her womb

She stands up slowly
Between noon and midnight
Between two wolf lairs

Stands up with pain
Freeing from one lair her snout
And from the other her huge tail

She stands up with a salt-choked howl
From her dry throat

Stands up dying of thirst
Toward the clear point at the summit of the sky
The watering place of the long-tailed stars

Translated from the Serbian by Charles Simic

NOVICA TADIC

Yugoslavia (b. 1949)

Novica Tadić was born in a small village in Montenegro but was educated and has since lived in Belgrade. He is considered the leading poet of his generation and a disciple of Vasko Popa's riddling, innovative work. His poems are chilling, often grotesque in the manner of Bosch paintings. "For Tadić," writes Charles Simic, "reality is unstable, prone at any moment to break into separate and unfamiliar pieces, only to suddenly reassemble itself. He is the poet who questions appearances and catalogues new species. . . . It is the poetry of the new dark ages that Tadić writes. This is the natural history of a feverish brain full of dark premonitions at the end of a long and vile century."

Dogs Gambol

Here's what I see:
Old masters
      the hawk and the snake
that the rat conquered
A long ribbon of fireflies
makes a miraculous rainbow
around the earth
In love and gluttony
unknown monsters
lie in a forest clearing
Do you hear
the thunder and hiss
of magnificent crawlers
Out of her bloody valley
Mother Terror blesses
her five-legged sucklings
who eat earth and air
The severed fingers of god lead
the living hard-working army

of unconquerable worms
Under the huge trees
hungry bushes sprout
Nimble little beasts
drag their after-births in their wake
Under the black stones
the black spring thunders
From caves and pits
a wild sound is heard
Dead angels and dead lightning
hang from a cliff
Families of many evils
struggle in the warm air
The huge forest hen
decorates herself with fire-feathers
too soon much too soon
she will fly down on our heads
from such eggs
    a truly MONSTROUS WORLD
    will hatch

Translated from the Serbian by Charles Simic

Nobody

He shows me tonight
his hair of wire glass and flowers
double-edged lips
five-pointed tongue

Ah he unbuttons
his silk vest—
he has a body after all—
a gold watch

And in the meantime meantime
in the shadow of his trousers
instead of feet

he has two little wheels
devilish little wheels

Translated from the Serbian by Charles Simic

Man from the Death Institute

Here comes one more looking pale
behind his dark glasses

A haystack of rotted hair
sits on his skull

On his tightly closed lips
a firefly scurries

Out of his sleeve a moon-hand
flashes in the night

While he
with a theatrical gesture
leaves the night mail
by my pillow
and as if jesting
threatens me
with his finger

Translated from the Serbian by Charles Simic

Jesus

Jesus
Our Jesus
Our Jesus a pincushion

Translated from the Serbian by Charles Simic

Antipsalm

Disfigure me, Lord. Take pity on me.
Cover me with bumps. Reward me with boils.
In the source of tears open a spring of pus mixed with blood.
Twist my mouth upsidedown. Give me a hump. Make me
    crooked.
Let moles burrow through my flesh. Let blood
circle my body. Let it be thus.
May all that breathes steal breath from me,
all that drinks quench its thirst in my cup.
Turn all vermin upon me.
Let my enemies gather around me
and rejoice, honoring You.

Disfigure me, Lord. Take pity on me.
Tie every guilt around my ankles.
Make me deaf with noise and delirium. Uphold me
above every tragedy.
Overpower me with dread and insomnia. Tear me up.
Open the seven seals, let out the seven beasts.
Let each one graze my monstrous brain.
Set upon me every evil, every suffering,
every misery. Every time you threaten,
point your finger at me. Thus, thus, my Lord.
Let my enemies gather around me
and rejoice, honoring You.

Translated from the Serbian by Charles Simic

Little Picture Catalogue

I

In a ghost town
dogs roam
among dead dogs

2

in a blind alley
a boy wheels the halo
of the holy mother

3

in someone's backyard
a crucified
hen

4

from the pipe of a customer
in a whorehouse
a woman's black stocking
rises like smoke

5

in the anteroom
many shoes overcoats
hats gloves
but the house empty
not one human face
    to be seen

6

unknown massive gray
objects above the
waters of salvation

Translated from the Serbian by Charles Simic

Laocoon/Serpent

It's only a trickle
of dirty water
dirty water
spilled somewhere

Down the steep street
it winds narrowly
down the steep street
I'm climbing wearily

But where oh where
is the mighty serpent
and where the hell are
my sons now

Translated from the Serbian by Charles Simic

PAUL CELAN

Romania (1920–1970)

The poet known as Paul Celan was born Paul Antschel to German-speaking Jewish parents in Czernovitz, in the Romanian province of Bukovina. (His surname was later spelled Ancel, and in 1947 he adopted an anagram of it.) He started premedical studies in France in 1938, but with the outbreak of World War II, he returned to his homeland. His parents were deported to a concentration camp, where his father died of typhus and his mother was shot to death. Celan himself was sent to a labor camp from which he eventually escaped. His early "Death Fugue" remains the most powerful poem ever written about the Holocaust. After the war he lived in Bucharest and—fluent in Russian and French—worked as a translator. He soon moved to Vienna, falling in with an avant-garde circle of painters and writers, but in 1948 he settled in Paris, where he wrote short, enigmatic prose pieces and began publishing collections of poems. He continued with his translations and his studies but never abandoned his intense relationship with the German language. "Only in one's mother tongue," he wrote, "can one express one's own truth. In a foreign language, the poet lies." From 1959 until his death, he taught German literature at L'École Normale Supérieure. Subject to breakdowns, he finally committed suicide by drowning himself in the Seine. Surrealism and Jewish mysticism were influences on Celan, but strongest was his own drive to remake the language of poetry. The results were poems dense with paradox, disjunctive leaps, fractured lines, eerie compounds, and startling images. Their themes of hopelessness and distrust echo continually; the absurd was Celan's bread, and in his work God seems to be the tear in the world's eye. However oblique, these are poems of an astonishing intensity, written in a German that, as he said, "had to pass through a frightful muting, pass through the thousand darknesses of deathbringing speech." He is generally considered the finest lyric poet to have emerged in Europe after the war.

Death Fugue

Black milk of daybreak we drink it at sundown
we drink it at noon in the morning we drink it at night

we drink and we drink it
we dig a grave in the breezes there one lies unconfined
A man lives in the house he plays with the serpents he writes
he writes when dusk falls to Germany your golden hair Margarete
he writes it and steps out of doors and the stars are flashing he
    whistles his pack out
he whistles his Jews out in earth has them dig for a grave
he commands us strike up for the dance

Black milk of daybreak we drink you at night
we drink in the morning at noon we drink you at sundown
we drink and we drink you
A man lives in the house he plays with the serpents he writes
he writes when dusk falls to Germany your golden hair Margarete
your ashen hair Shulamith we dig a grave in the breezes there one
    lies unconfined

He calls out jab deeper into the earth you lot you others sing now
    and play
he grabs at the iron in his belt he waves it his eyes are blue
jab deeper you lot with your spades you others play on for the
    dance

Black milk of daybreak we drink you at night
we drink you at noon in the morning we drink you at sundown
we drink and we drink you
a man lives in the house your golden hair Margarete
your ashen hair Shulamith he plays with the serpents
He calls out more sweetly play death death is a master from Ger-
    many
he calls out more darkly now stroke your strings then as smoke
    you will rise into air
then a grave you will have in the clouds there one lies unconfined

Black milk of daybreak we drink you at night
we drink you at noon death is a master from Germany
we drink you at sundown and in the morning we drink and we
    drink you
death is a master from Germany his eyes are blue
he strikes you with leaden bullets his aim is true

a man lives in the house your golden hair Margarete
he sets his pack on to us he grants us a grave in the air
he plays with the serpents and daydreams death is a master from
    Germany

your golden hair Margarete
your ashen hair Shulamith

Translated from the German by Michael Hamburger

I am the first

I am the first to drink of the blue that still looks for its eye.
I drink from your footprint and see:
you roll through my fingers, pearl, and you grow!
You grow, as do all the forgotten.
You roll: the black hailstone of sadness
is caught by a kerchief turned white with waving goodbye.

Translated from the German by Michael Hamburger

Tenebrae

    We are near, Lord,
    near and at hand.

    Handled already, Lord,
    clawed and clawing as though
    the body of each of us were
    your body, Lord.

    Pray, Lord,
    pray to us,
    we are near.

Wind-awry we went there,
went there to bend
over hollow and ditch.

To be watered we went there, Lord.

It was blood, it was
what you shed, Lord.

It gleamed.

It cast your image into our eyes, Lord.
Our eyes and our mouths are so open and empty, Lord.
We have drunk, Lord.
The blood and the image that was in the blood, Lord.

Pray, Lord.
We are near.

Translated from the German by Michael Hamburger

Language Mesh

Eye's roundness between the bars.

Vibratile monad eyelid
propels itself upward,
releases a glance.

Iris, swimmer, dreamless and dreary:
the sky, heart-grey, must be near.

Athwart, in the iron holder,
the smoking splinter.
By its sense of light
you divine the soul.

(If I were like you. If you were like me.
Did we not stand
under *one* trade wind?
We are strangers.)

The flagstones. On them,
close to each other, the two
heart-grey puddles:
two
mouthsfull of silence.

Translated from the German by Michael Hamburger

Matière de Bretagne

Gorselight, yellow, the slopes
suppurate heavenward, the thorn
woos the wound, bells ring
within, it is evening, Nothing
rolls its seas to the service,
the blood sail makes for you.

Dry, the bed behind you
fills with silt, its hour
clogs with rushes, above,
by the star, the milky
tideways jabber through mud, date shell,
below, bunched, yawns into blueness, a shrub
of transience, beautiful,
meets your memory, greets it.

(Did you know me,
hands? I went
the forked way you showed me, my mouth
spewed out its chippings, I went, my time,
a shifting snow-wall, cast its shadow—did you know me?)

Hands, the thorn-
wooed wound, hands,
Nothing is ringing its seas.
Hands, in the gorselight, the
blood sail
makes for you.

You
you teach
you teach your hands
you teach your hands you teach
you teach your hands
                    how to sleep

Translated from the German by Michael Hamburger

Alchemical

Silence, cooked like gold, in
charred
hands.

Great, grey
sisterly shape
near like all that is lost:

All the names, all those
names
burnt with the rest. So much
ash to be blessed. So much
land won
above
the weightless, so weightless
rings
of souls.

Great, grey one. Cinder-
less.

You, then.
You with the pale
bit-open bud,
you in the wine-flood.

(Us too, don't you think,
this clock dismissed?
Good,
good, how your word died past us here.)

Silence, cooked like gold, in
charred, charred
hands.
Fingers, insubstantial as smoke. Like crests, crests of air
around——

Great, grey one. Wake-
less.
Re-
gal one.

Translated from the German by Michael Hamburger

Thread suns

Thread suns
above the grey-black wilderness.
A tree-
high thought
tunes in to light's pitch: there are
still songs to be sung on the other side
of mankind.

Translated from the German by Michael Hamburger

In Prague

That half-death,
suckled big with our life,
lay around us, true as an ashen image—

we too
still drank, soul-crossed, two daggers,
sewn on to stones of the sky, born of word blood
in the night bed,

bigger and bigger
we grew interlaced, there was
no longer a name for
that which drove us (one of the how many
and thirty
was my live shadow
that climbed the delusory steps towards you?),

a tower
the halved one built for himself into where,
a Hradshin
made of pure gold-makers' No,

bone-Hebrew
ground into sperm
ran through the hourglass
through which we swam, two dreams now, chiming
against time, in the squares.

Translated from the German by Michael Hamburge

When you lie

When you lie in
the bed of lost flag cloth,

with blue-black syllables, in snow eyelash shade,
through thought-
showers
the crane comes gliding, steely—
you open to him.

His bill ticks the hour for you
into every mouth—in each hour,
with a red-hot rope, bell-rings a
millennium of silence,
unrespite and respite
mint each other to death,
the florins, the pennies
rain hard through your pores,
in
the shape of seconds
you fly there and bar
the doors yesterday and tomorrow,—phosphorescent,
like eternity teeth,
your one breast buds, and the other
breast buds too,
towards the graspings, under
the thrusts—: so densely,
so deeply
strewn
is the starry
crane-
seed.

Translated from the German by Michael Hamburger

Little night

Little night: when you
take me inside, take me
up there,
three pain-inches above the
floor:

all those shroud coats of sand,
all those can'thelps,
all that still
laughs
with the tongue—

Translated from the German by Michael Hamburger

All those sleep shapes

All those sleep shapes, crystalline,
that you assumed
in the language shadow,

to those
I lead my blood,

those image lines, them
I'm to harbor
in the slit-arteries
of my cognition—,

my grief, I can see,
is deserting to you.

Translated from the German by Michael Hamburger

MARIN SORESCU

Romania (b. 1936)

Marin Sorescu, the son of farmworkers, was born in Oltenia and studied
philosophy at the University of Iasi. His professional life has been spent as
an editor for newspapers and magazines, interspersed with teaching stints
abroad. He has gained some fame as a playwright, although during
Ceauşescu's regime his pointed and subversive plays were rarely seen for
long. His first collection of poems appeared in 1965 and proved immedi-
ately popular. Sorescu prefers to take ordinary experiences and make
metaphysical parables out of them. Sometimes his wit is mere whimsy,
but his laconic, intelligent voice often rises to the sort of comedy that can
encompass both satire and pathos.

With a Green Scarf

With a green scarf I blindfolded
the eyes of the trees
and asked them to catch me.

At once the trees caught me,
their leaves shaking with laughter.

I blindfolded the birds
with a scarf of clouds
and asked them to catch me.

The birds caught me
with a song.

Then with a smile I blindfolded
my sorrow
and the day after it caught me
with a love.

I blindfolded the sun
with my nights
and asked the sun to catch me.

I know where you are, the sun said,
just behind that time.
Don't bother to hide any longer.

Don't bother to hide any longer,
said all of them,
as well as all the feelings
I tried to blindfold.

Translated from the Romanian by Michael Hamburger

Start

Often the start went wrong,
the bang wasn't loud enough
or it wasn't heard,
and the competitors, sent back again and again to their places,
became so nervous that they began to brawl,
covered themselves in ashes, broke
their legs and threw sand into
the spectators' eyes.

The track, the whole stadium,
was often red with blood,
the start went wrong so many times.

Once
a man with the starting-gun
out of fear of the imminent disaster
fired not into the air
but through his head.
As though by a miracle this time
all the runners won.

The death of the shot man
was hardly noticed.

Ever since, tradition demands,
whoever signals the start
puts the weapon to his forehead.

The instrument that brought in so many gold medals
has landed up with me.

Already the runners rest
their left knees on the chalk line,
their eyes have run on far ahead,
their nostrils quiver.

All they're waiting for is the bang.
It's all up to me.

Translated from the Romanian by Michael Hamburger

Precautions

I pulled on a suit of mail
made of pebbles
worn smooth by water.

I balanced a pair of glasses
on my neck
so as to keep an eye
on whatever
was coming behind me.

I gloved and greaved
my hands, my legs, my thoughts,
leaving no part of my person
exposed to touch
or other poisons.

Then I fashioned a breastplate
from the shell
of an eight-hundred-year-old
turtle.

And when everything was just so
I tenderly replied:
—I love you too.

Translated from the Romanian by Paul Muldoon and Joana Russell-Gebbett

Fresco

In hell, maximum use
Is made of the sinners.

With the help of tweezers,
Brooches and bracelets, hairpins and rings,
Linen and bedclothes
Are extracted from the heads of the women.
Who are subsequently thrown
Into boiling cauldrons
To keep an eye on the pitch,
And see that it doesn't boil over.

Then some of them
Are transformed into dinner pails
In which hot sins are carried to the domiciles
Of pensioned-off devils.

The men are employed
For the heaviest work,
Except for the hairiest of them,
Who are spun afresh
And made into mats.

Translated from the Romanian by D. J. Enright and Joana Russell-Gebbett

Perseverance

I shall look at the grass
Till I obtain the degree
Of Doctor of Grass.

I shall look at the clouds
Till I become a Master
Of Clouds.

I shall walk beside the smoke
Till out of shame
The smoke returns to the flame
Of its beginning.

I shall walk beside all things
Till all things
Come to know me.

Translated from the Romanian by D. J. Enright and Joana Russell-Gebbett

Map

First let me show you with the pointer
The three parts of water
That can be seen very clearly
In my bones and tissues:
The water is colored blue.

Then the two eyes,
My sea stars.

The driest part,
The forehead,
Goes on carbon-copying
The wrinkles
Of the earth's crust.

This island of fire is the heart—
Inhabited, I seem to recall.
If I see a road
I think that's where
My legs should be,
Otherwise the road wouldn't make sense.

If I see the sea
I think that's where my soul should be,
Otherwise its marble
Would not make waves.

There are of course
A few other bright spots
On my body,
Such as my thoughts and experiences
Of tomorrow.

With the senses,
The five continents,
I describe two circles every day:
The merry-go-round around the sun
And the roundabout
Of death . . .

That, more or less, is the map of my world
Which will stay unrolled a little longer
In front of you.

Translated from the Romanian by Michael Longley and Joana Russell-Gebbett

Fountains in the Sea

Water: no matter how much, there is still not enough.
Cunning life keeps asking for more and then a drop more.

Our ankles are weighted with lead, we delve under the wave.
We bend to our spades, we survive the force of the gusher.

Our bodies fountain with sweat in the deeps of the sea,
Our forehead aches and holds like a sunken prow.
We are out of breath, divining the heart of the geyser,
Constellations are bobbing like corks above on the swell.

Earth is a waterwheel, the buckets go up and go down,
But to keep the whole aqueous architecture standing its ground
We must make a ring with our bodies and dance out a round
On the dreamt eye of water, the dreamt eye of water, the dreamt
    eye of water.

Water: no matter how much, there is still not enough.
Come rain, come thunder, come deluged dams washed away,
Our thirst is unquenchable. A cloud in the water's a siren.
We become two shades, deliquescent, drowning in song.

My love, under the tall sky of hope
Our love and our love alone
Keeps dowsing for water.
Sinking the well of each other, digging together.
Each one the other's phantom limb in the sea.

Translated from the Romanian by Seamus Heaney and Joana Russell-Gebbett

The Tear

I weep and weep a tear
Which will not fall
No matter how much I weep.

Its pang in me
Is like the birth of an icicle.

Colder and colder, the earth
Curves on my eyelid,
The northern ice-cap keeps rising.

O, my arctic eyelid.

Translated from the Romanian by Seamus Heaney and Joana Russell-Gebbett

YANNIS RITSOS

Greece (1909–1990)

Yannis Ritsos was the most popular and prolific of modern Greek poets, having published nearly a hundred collections of poems in his lifetime. An unorthodox Communist since the late 1920s, he was imprisoned after World War II and then again during the military dictatorship that ruled Greece from 1967 to 1974. Although before and after these tumultuous periods he wrote overtly political poems, most of his work explores, more subtly, themes of exile, alienation, futility, dispossession, and terror. Beyond that, Ritsos meditated on the history, mythology, and landscape of Greece. In his work the past and present become images of each other. His revisionist ironies focus on the failures of history, the death of the gods, the absence of heroes. His tremendous vitality—which also pulses through long narrative and dramatic poems, fiction, essays, plays, and translations—finally drew its strength from the abiding features of Greece: sun, sea, rock, olive tree. In a poem called "Last Will and Testament," he wrote: "I believe in poetry, in love, in death, / which is precisely why I believe in immortality, I write a verse, / I write the world; I exist; the world exists. / A river flows from the tip of my little finger."

Miniature

The woman stood up in front of the table. Her sad hands
begin to cut thin slices of lemon for tea
like yellow wheels for a very small carriage
made for a child's fairy tale. The young officer sitting opposite
is buried in the old armchair. He doesn't look at her.
He lights up his cigarette. His hand holding the match trembles,
throwing light on his tender chin and the teacup's handle. The
    clock
holds its heartbeat for a moment. Something has been postponed.
The moment has gone. It's too late now. Let's drink our tea.
Is it possible, then, for death to come in that kind of carriage?
To pass by and go away? And only this carriage to remain,
with its little yellow wheels of lemon

parked for so many years on a side street with unlit lamps,
and then a small song, a little mist, and then nothing?

Translated from the Greek by Edmund Keeley

Penelope's Despair

It wasn't that she didn't recognize him in the light from the
    hearth: it wasn't
the beggar's rags, the disguise—no. The signs were clear:
the scar on his knee, the pluck, the cunning in his eye. Frightened,
her back against the wall, she searched for an excuse,
a little time, so she wouldn't have to answer,
give herself away. Was it for him, then, that she'd used up twenty
    years,
twenty years of waiting and dreaming, for this miserable
blood-soaked, white-bearded man? She collapsed voiceless into a
    chair,
slowly studied the slaughtered suitors on the floor as though
    seeing
her own desires dead there. And she said "Welcome,"
hearing her voice sound foreign, distant. In the corner, her loom
covered the ceiling with a trellis of shadows; and all the birds
    she'd woven
with bright red thread in green foliage, now,
on this night of the return, suddenly turned ashen and black,
flying low on the flat sky of her final enduring.

Translated from the Greek by Edmund Keeley

The End of Dodona II

With the gods overthrown like that, nobody knew which way to
    turn.

The sick stayed in bed with their eyes closed.
Their woolen socks rotted away in their shoes, along with two
     flowers in a glass.
The cunning ones adjusted quickly. They put on their best clothes
     again,
circulated in the marketplace, discussed things, did business. They
     undertook
the defense against the invader. They changed the names of streets
and temples: improvised substitutions. Zeus and Dione
gave way to Jesus and the Virgin. Theodosius
added the finishing touches—what altars and sanctuaries, and
     that huge tree
overwhelmed by votive offerings.
                         And still
a number of people (including the best) haven't yet come to their
     senses. They're waiting once again
for better gods and people. They fume, protest,
dream, hope. We, the few (who, to some degree anyway, use their
     heads),
we've given up such luxuries, given up thinking itself.
We plow our small plot of land, look at the clouds once in a
     while,
calm now, almost secure. One day we found, thrown into a ditch,
that statuette that used to strike metal tools with its wand
and give out prophetic sounds. For a moment that moved us. We
     said
we'd set it aside for safekeeping somewhere. But what's the point?
     Are we supposed to cling to relics these days?
And what if they dug it up on us? We left it there. Covered it with
     two handfuls of dirt.
The dog was in a hurry. It smelled the trees. Large raindrops were
     already falling.

Translated from the Greek by Edmund Keeley

Marpessa's Choice

It wasn't by chance that Marpessa preferred Idas over Apollo,
despite her passion for the god, despite his incomparable beauty—
the kind that made myrtle tremble into blossom as he went by.
   She
never dared raise her glance above his knees.
Between his toenails and his knees, what an inexhaustible world,
what exquisite journeys and discoveries between his toenails and
      his knees. Still,
at the ultimate moment of choice, Marpessa lost her nerve: What
      would she do
with a bequest as grand as that? A mortal, she would grow old
      one day.
She suddenly imagined her comb with a tuft of white hair in it
left on a chair beside the bed where the immortal one would rest
      shimmering;
she thought also of time's fingerprints on her thighs, her fallen
      breasts
in front of the black metal mirror. Oh no—and she leaned as
      though dead
against Idas's mortal shoulder. And he lifted her up in his arms
      like a flag
and turned his back on Apollo. But as he was leaving, almost
      arrogantly,
one could hear something like the sound of cloth ripping (a
      strange sound):
a corner of the flag was held back, trapped by the god's foot.

Translated from the Greek by Edmund Keeley

Requiem on Poros

We keep forgetting the gods. And if we happened to remember
      Poseidon tonight
as we returned to the desolate shores of Calauria,

it's because over here, in the sacred grove one July evening,
while oars gleamed in the moonlight and one could hear
the guitars of ivy-crowned young men in the rowboats,
here in the pine-covered spot, Demosthenes took poison—
he, a stammerer, who struggled until he became the best orator of
    the Greeks,
and then, condemned by the Macedonians and the Athenians,
    learned, in the course of one night,
the most difficult, the greatest art of all: to be silent.

Translated from the Greek by Edmund Keeley

The Distant

O distant, distant; deep unapproachable; receive always
the silent ones in their absence, in the absence of the others
when the danger from the near ones, from the near itself, burdens
during nights of promise with many-colored lights in the gardens,
when the half-closed eyes of lions and tigers scintillate
with flashing green omissions in their cages
and the old jester in front of the dark mirror
washes off his painted tears so that he can weep—
O quiet ungrantable, you with the long, damp hand,
quiet invisible, without borrowing and lending, without
    obligations,
nailing nails on the air, shoring up the world
in that deep inaction where music reigns.

Translated from the Greek by Edmund Keeley

ODYSSEUS ELYTIS

Greece (1911–1996)

Born Odysseus Alepoudhelis in Heraklion on the island of Crete, Elytis
was educated at the University of Athens and at the Sorbonne, served in
the army during World War II, and later worked in broadcasting and as
an art critic. His first collection of poems appeared in 1936; his early
work reflects his fascination with French surrealism. "I have always been
preoccupied," he said, "with finding the analogies between nature and
language in the realm of the imagination, a realm to which the surrealists
also gave much importance, and rightly so. Everything depends on imagi-
nation, that is, on the way a poet sees the same phenomenon as you do,
yet *differently* from you." Elytis's work focused on both the physical and
the sublime, and his tone was always lyrical and vigorous. His major
work, *The Axion Esti,* a long sequence based on the Byzantine liturgy,
was published in 1959. In 1979 he was awarded the Nobel Prize for Lit-
erature. Lawrence Durrell once wrote of Elytis: "Using the most up-to-
date methods in technique, he has, at the same time, insisted that at
bottom poetry is not simply a craft or skill but an act of divination. His
poems are spells, and they conjure up that eternal Greek world which has
haunted and continues to haunt the European consciousness with its hints
of a perfection that remains always a possibility."

Aegean Melancholy

What linking of soul to the halcyons of the afternoon!
What calm in the voices of the distant shore!
The cuckoo in the trees' mantilla,
And the mystic hour of the fishermen's supper,
And the sea playing on its concertina
The long lament of the woman,
The lovely woman who bared her breasts
When memory found the cradles
And lilac sprinkled the sunset with fire!

With caïque and the Virgin's sails
Sped by the winds they are gone,
Lovers of the lilies' exile;
But how night here attends on sleep
With murmuring hair on shining throats
Or on the great white shores;
And how with Orion's gold sword
Is scattered and spilled aloft
Dust from the dreams of girls
Scented with mint and basil!

At the crossroad where the ancient sorceress stood
Burning the winds with dry thyme, there,
Lightly, holding a pitcher full with the waters of silence,
Easily, as though they were entering Paradise,
Supple shadows stepped . . .
And from the crickets' prayer that fermented the fields
Lovely girls with the moon's skin have risen
To dance on the midnight threshing floor . . .

O signs, you who pass in the depths
Of the mirror-holding water—
Seven small lilies that sparkle—
When Orion's sword returns
It will find poor bread under the lamp
But life in the star's embers;
It will find generous hands linked in space,
Abandoned seaweed, the shore's last children,
Years, green gems . . .

O green gem—what storm-prophet saw you
Halting the light at the birth of day,
The light at the birth of the two eyes of the world!

Translated from the Greek by Edmund Keeley and Philip Sherrard

from The Axion Esti

Praised be the wooden table
the blond wine with the sun's stain
the water doodling across the ceiling
the philodendron on duty in the corner

The walls hand in hand with the waves
a foot that gathered wisdom in the sand
a cicada that convinced a thousand others
conscience radiant like a summer

Praised be the heatwave hatching
the beautiful boulders under the bridge
the shit of children with its green flies
a sea boiling and no end to it

The sixteen deckhands hauling the net
the restless seagull slowly cruising
stray voices out of the wilderness
a shadow's crossing through the wall

The islands with all their minimum and lampblack
the islands with the vertebrae of some Zeus
the islands with their boat yards so deserted
the islands with their drinkable blue volcanoes

Facing the meltemi with jib close-hauled
Riding the southwester on a reach
the full length of them covered with foam
with dark blue pebbles and heliotropes

Sifnos, Amorgos, Alonnisos
Thasos, Ithaka, Santorini
Kos, Ios, Sikinos

Praised be Myrto standing
on the stone parapet facing the sea

like a beautiful eight or a clay pitcher
holding a straw hat in her hand

The white and porous middle of day
the down of sleep lightly ascending
        the faded gold inside the arcades
and the red horse breaking free

Hera of the tree's ancient trunk
the vast laurel grove, the light-devouring
        a house like an anchor down in the depths
and Kyra-Penelope twisting her spindle

The straits for birds from the opposite shore
a citron from which the sky spilled out
        the blue hearing half under the sea
the long-shadowed whispering of nymphs and maples

Praised be, on the remembrance day
of the holy martyrs Cyricus and Julitta,
        a miracle burning threshing floors in the heavens
priests and birds chanting the *Ave:*

Hail Girl Burning and hail Girl Verdant
Hail Girl Unrepenting, with the prow's sword

Hail you who walk and the footprints vanish
Hail you who wake and the miracles are born

Hail O Wild One of the depths' paradise
Hail O Holy One of the islands' wilderness

Hail Mother of Dreams, Girl of the Open Seas
Hail O Anchor-bearer, Girl of the Five Stars

Hail you of the flowing hair, gilding the wind
Hail you of the lovely voice, tamer of demons

Hail you who ordain the Monthly Ritual of the Gardens
Hail you who fasten the Serpent's belt of stars.

Hail O Girl of the just and modest sword
Hail O Girl prophetic and daedalic

Translated from the Greek by Edmund Keeley and George Savidis

The Origin of Landscape
or the End of Mercy

Suddenly the swallow's shadow reaped the glances of its nostalgia:
Noon.

With a sharp flint, slowly, skilfully, the sun engraved the wings of
the west wind above the shoulders of the Daughter of Justice.

Light working on my flesh, the violet mark appeared for a mo-
ment on my chest just where remorse had touched me and I
ran madly. Then sleep among steep leaves desiccated me and I
was left alone. Alone.

I envied the waterdrop that, unperceived, glorified the lentisk.
Would that I could be like that in the miraculous eye privi-
leged to see the end of Mercy.

Or was I perhaps like that? In the harshness of the rock, uncleft
from peak to base, I recognized my obstinate jaw. In another
age it tore the beast to pieces.

And the sand beyond, settled by the delight the sea once gave me
when men blasphemed and I opened my arms wide in my
hurry to find solace within her. Was it this I was looking for?
Purity?

Water reversing its current, I entered the spirit of the myrtle where
lovers take refuge from persecution. Again I heard the silk

brushing the hairs of my chest as it panted. And the sound,
"my darling," at night, in the ravine where I cut the stars' last
moorings and the nightingale was trying to take shape.

Truly, what yearnings and what derision I had to pass through,
    with a fragment of an oath in my two eyes and my fingers
    free from corruption. Yes, they were like that, the years when
    I was struggling to make the endless azure sky so tender.

I spoke. And, turning my face, I again confronted it in the light as
    it gazed steadfastly at me. Merciless.

It was purity.

Beautiful, and pensive from the shadow of years, under the sun's
    semaphore the Daughter of Justice wept

As she watched me walking once more through this world, with-
    out gods, but weighed down with what I had snatched from
    death while still living.

Suddenly the swallow's shadow reaped the glances of its nostalgia:
Noon.

Translated from the Greek by Edmund Keeley and Philip Sherrard

NAZIM HIKMET

Turkey (1902–1963)

No figure towers over modern Turkish literature so commandingly as
Nâzim Hikmet—as novelist, playwright, journalist, and especially poet.
He was born in Salonika (now a part of Greece). For his early and pas-
sionate Communist sympathies, he was several times imprisoned in
Turkey; he eventually fled to the Soviet Union in 1951 and lived there for
the rest of his life. Only after his death did his fame spread abroad, but
his impact on Turkish literature was immediate. He revitalized the stulti-
fying literary conventions in his homeland, because his poems were writ-
ten in free verse. His humanistic and ideological themes are raised above
the merely political by their strongly personal concerns and lyrical details.
When not merely declamatory, Hikmet's poems at their best are what we
mean by *public* poetry: the self opened and given over. Terrence Des Pres
wrote that Hikmet is "in the best sense, a writer of primitive poetry, po-
etry which depends for its power on primary techniques—repetition, con-
trast, line-break, basic imagery of earth, man, and nature (which to the
Western ear sounds Biblical), and finally a use of metaphor mainly to en-
large rather than to refine and complicate. These, along with Hikmet's
distinctness of voice and mystical overtones, his moral energy and faithful
delight in life itself, provide the foundation of his art."

Angina Pectoris

> If half my heart is here, doctor,
>   the other half is in China
> with the army flowing
>   toward the Yellow River.
> And every morning, doctor,
> every morning at sunrise my heart
>   is shot in Greece.
> And every night, doctor,
> when the prisoners are asleep and the infirmary is deserted,
> my heart stops at a run-down old house
>   in Istanbul.

And then after ten years
all I have to offer my poor people
is this apple in my hand, doctor,
one red apple:
                    my heart.
And that, doctor, that is the reason
for this angina pectoris—
not nicotine, prison, or arteriosclerosis.
I look at the night through the bars,
and despite the weight on my chest
my heart still beats with the most distant stars.

Translated from the Turkish by Randy Blasing and Mutlu Konuk

The Cucumber

to Ekber Babayev

The snow is knee-deep in the courtyard
and still coming down hard:
it hasn't let up all morning.
We're in the kitchen.
On the table, on the oilcloth, spring—
on the table there's a very tender young cucumber,
                              pebbly and fresh as a daisy.
We're sitting around the table staring at it.
It softly lights up our faces,
and the very air smells fresh.
We're sitting around the table staring at it,
amazed
          thoughtful
                    optimistic.
We're as if in a dream.
On the table, on the oilcloth, hope—
on the table, beautiful days,
a cloud seeded with a green sun,
an emerald crowd impatient and on its way,
loves blooming openly—

on the table, there on the oilcloth, a very tender young cucumber,
pebbly and fresh as a daisy.
The snow is knee-deep in the courtyard
and coming down hard.
It hasn't let up all morning.

Translated from the Turkish by Randy Blasing and Mutlu Konuk

Things I Didn't Know I Loved

it's 1962 March 28th
I'm sitting by the window on the Prague-Berlin train
night is falling
I never knew I liked
night descending like a tired bird on a smoky wet plain
I don't like
comparing nightfall to a tired bird

I didn't know I loved the earth
can someone who hasn't worked the earth love it
I've never worked the earth
it must be my only Platonic love

and here I've loved rivers all this time
whether motionless like this they curl skirting the hills
European hills crowned with chateaus
or whether stretched out flat as far as the eye can see
I know you can't wash in the same river even once
I know the river will bring new lights you'll never see
I know we live slightly longer than a horse but not nearly as long
as a crow
I know this has troubled people before
and will trouble those after me
I know all this has been said a thousand times before
and will be said after me

I didn't know I loved the sky
cloudy or clear

the blue vault Andrei studied on his back at Borodino
in prison I translated both volumes of *War and Peace* into Turkish
I hear voices
not from the blue vault but from the yard
the guards are beating someone again

I didn't know I loved trees
bare beeches near Moscow in Peredelkino
they come upon me in winter noble and modest
beeches are Russian the way poplars are Turkish
"the poplars of Izmir
losing their leaves . . .
they call me The Knife . . .
                          lover like a young tree . . .
I blow stately mansions sky-high"
in the Ilgaz woods in 1920 I tied an embroidered linen handkerchief
                                    to a pine bough for luck

I never knew I loved roads
even the asphalt kind
Vera's behind the wheel we're driving from Moscow to the Crimea
                                    Koktebele
                          formerly "Goktepé ili" in Turkish
the two of us inside a closed box
the world flows past on both sides distant and mute
I was never so close to anyone in my life
bandits stopped me on the red road between Bolu and Geredé
                                    when I was eighteen
apart from my life I didn't have anything in the wagon they could take
and at eighteen our lives are what we value least
I've written this somewhere before
wading through a dark muddy street I'm going to the shadow play
Ramazan night
a paper lantern leading the way
maybe nothing like this ever happened
maybe I read it somewhere an eight-year-old boy
                                    going to the shadow play
Ramazan night in Istanbul holding his grandfather's hand
    his grandfather has on a fez and is wearing the fur coat
        with a sable collar over his robe

and there's a lantern in the servant's hand
and I can't contain myself for joy

flowers come to mind for some reason
poppies cactuses jonquils
in the jonquil garden in Kadikoy Istanbul I kissed Marika
fresh almonds on her breath
I was seventeen
my heart on a swing touched the sky
I didn't know I loved flowers
friends sent me three red carnations in prison

I just remembered the stars
I love them too
whether I'm floored watching them from below
or whether I'm flying at their side

I have some questions for the cosmonauts
were the stars much bigger
did they look like huge jewels on black velvet
                                   or apricots on orange
did you feel proud to get closer to the stars
I saw color photos of the cosmos in *Ogonek* magazine now don't
      be upset comrades but nonfigurative shall we say or abstract
      well some of them looked just like such paintings which is to
      say they were terribly figurative and concrete
my heart was in my mouth looking at them
they are our endless desire to grasp things
seeing them I could even think of death and not feel at all sad
I never knew I loved the cosmos

snow flashes in front of my eyes
both heavy wet steady snow and the dry whirling kind
I didn't know I liked snow

I never knew I loved the sun
even when setting cherry-red as now
in Istanbul too it sometimes sets in postcard colors
but you aren't about to paint it that way

I didn't know I loved the sea
                          except the Sea of Azov
or how much

I didn't know I loved clouds
whether I'm under or up above them
whether they look like giants or shaggy white beasts

moonlight the falsest the most languid the most petit-bourgeois
strikes me
I like it

I didn't know I liked rain
whether it falls like a fine net or splatters against the glass my
        heart leaves me tangled up in a net or trapped inside a drop
        and takes off for uncharted countries I didn't know I loved
        rain but why did I suddenly discover all these passions sitting
        by the window on the Prague-Berlin train
is it because I lit my sixth cigarette
one alone could kill me
is it because I'm half dead from thinking about someone back in
        Moscow
her hair straw-blond eyelashes blue

the train plunges on through the pitch-black night
I never knew I liked the night pitch-black
sparks fly from the engine
I didn't know I loved sparks
I didn't know I loved so many things and I had to wait until sixty
        to find it out sitting by the window on the Prague-Berlin train
        watching the world disappear as if on a journey of no return

Translated from the Turkish by Randy Blasing and Mutlu Konuk

ANDREI VOZNESENSKY

Russia (b. 1933)

Andrei Voznesensky was born in Moscow, the son of an engineer and a
teacher. As a teenager he sent some of his poems to Boris Pasternak, who
summoned the boy to visit. The older writer became, Voznesensky has
said, "my god, my father, and for a long time, my university." One thing
Pasternak taught his protégé, he remembers, was that "a book is a cubic
chunk of smoking conscience." The innovation and technical brilliance of
Voznesensky's lyrics were themselves a form of political commentary, and
his early collections led Khrushchev to denounce him as a "bourgeois for-
malist." Over the years he has been in and out of official favor. But he
has always remained immensely popular among Russian readers, for
whose anxieties and restlessness he became a powerful voice. He had once
studied to become an architect, and although he abandoned that plan, his
poetry is carefully structured, often cerebral and darkly ironic. As an
elegist, he has written of national horrors that range from the Nazi mas-
sacre of Soviet Jews to the Chernobyl disaster. "Every word he writes,"
W. H. Auden once observed about Voznesensky, "even when he is criti-
cizing, reveals a profound love for his native land and its traditions." The
poet himself, whose later work has grown more intimate and relaxed,
broods on his own language: "There is a kind of drawn-out music in
Russian speech that comes from the great distances of the Russian
steppes. This cello-like note resounds in the lengths of our names—in our
surnames and patronymics. Language is the music of thought; it is what
our ancestors called the soul. . . . Russian is especially suited to the trans-
mission of psychological states; the mood landscapes that it can evoke are
unique and untranslatable."

I Am Goya

> I am Goya
> of the bare field, by the enemy's beak gouged
> till the craters of my eyes gape
> I am grief

I am the tongue
of war, the embers of cities
on the snows of the year 1941
I am hunger

I am the gullet
of a woman hanged whose body like a bell
tolled over a blank square
I am Goya

O grapes of wrath!
I have hurled westward
                  the ashes of the uninvited guest!
and hammered stars into the unforgetting sky—like nails
I am Goya

Translated from the Russian by Stanley Kunitz

Someone Is Beating a Woman

Someone is beating a woman.
In the car that is dark and hot
Only the whites of her eyes shine.
Her legs thrash against the roof
Like berserk searchlight beams.

Someone is beating a woman.
This is the way slaves are beaten.
Frantic, she wrenches open the door
and plunges out—onto the road.

Brakes scream.
Someone runs up to her,
Strikes her and drags her, face down,
In the grass lashing with nettles.

Scum, how meticulously he beats her,
Stilyága, bastard, big hero,

His smart flatiron-pointed shoe
Stabbing into her ribs.

Such are the pleasures of enemy soldiers
And the brute refinements of peasants.
Trampling underfoot the moonlit grass,
Someone is beating a woman.

Someone is beating a woman.
Century on century, no end to this.
It's the young that are beaten. Somberly
Our wedding bells start up the alarm.
Someone is beating a woman.

What about the flaming weals
In the braziers of their cheeks?
That's life, you say. Are you telling me?
Someone is beating a woman.

But her light is unfaltering
World-without-ending.

There are no religions,
                              no revelations,
There are women.

Lying there pale as water
Her eyes tear-closed and still,
She doesn't belong to him
Any more than a meadow deep in a wood.

And the stars? Rattling in the sky
Like raindrops against black glass,
Plunging down,
                              they cool
Her grief-fevered forehead.

Translated from the Russian by Jean Garrigue

The Call of the Lake

To the Memory of the Victims of Fascism

Pevsner 1903, Lebedev 1916, Birman 1938, Birman 1941, Drobot 1907 . . .

As if our sneakers froze to the ground . . .
Stillness.
Ghetto in the lake. Ghetto in the lake.
Three bottom acres teeming with life.

A fellow in a pea-green jacket
hails us with news the fishing's good;
but look at the blood
                      on his tiny hook,
blood!

"No! No!"—says Volodka—
"I want to smack him on the jaw;
it's really more
              than I can bear.

"It would be desecrating life
to wash myself in this place,
like smearing Mary or Moishe
over my face.

"Your boat is muddying the lake.
Don't, buddy.
Just touch the water with your palm,
feel how it burns!

"Hands that liquefy below
could belong to my bride—
not some girl who lived long ago—
her breasts, her hair, her need."

No word.
The lake is close to the border.
Three pines.

The stunned reservoir
of life, of a cloud, of height.

Lebedev 1916, Birman 1941, Rumer 1902, Boiko (twice) 1933.

Translated from the Russian by Stanley Kunitz

Old Song

to G. Dzhagarov

The janissaries carry off our children from village after village.
Bulgarian folk song

The past hurts, George, but sing and be merry,
with horses' urine our icons burn.
Each stolen baby becomes a janissary
who will scourge his homeland on his return.

You and I, George, let us drink together,
in our eyes the wild fires of centuries glow.
Each sister is raped by her own brother,
and nobody knows whose brother is who.

With the mother's uterus cut out,
whose son is whose no need to ask.
Our wounded motherland cries out
beneath God knows what enemy mask.

Let us say that we are Turkish soldiers;
aren't we burning our own altars then?
We can understand who our enemies are,
but fail to recognize our own men.

Now ruining forest, field, and stream,
who cut me off, George, tell me please,

the moment I became a human being
from my oldest ancestors, the trees?

Your slashed breast dragging the earth, Mother,
transfixed with love more than surprise,
reel back now from your murderer, Mother!

Mother, look—he has your eyes!

Translated from the Russian by William Jay Smith and Vera Dunham

A Chorus of Nymphs

I'm 41st in line for Plisetskaya,
26th for plaid blankets from Czechoslovakia,
30th for a ticket to the Taganka,
35th for a place in Vagankovo Cemetery,
whoever wants to see the Madonna—sign up
at Seaport Hall—hey, you with the kid,
you weren't in line before!
Whoever was ninth goes back to tenth,
Rimskaya becomes Korsakova,
I'm 16th at the optician's,
and 75th for Glazunov,
110th for an abortion
(not pregnant now, but ready when my turn comes).
You with the kid, you weren't here before,
47th for spare car parts
(they signed me up at birth).
No. 1000 for a new car
(signed up before birth).
What are they giving out? Who should be bribed?
And you're a mother besides!
I'm 45th behind everybody with a 35,
and, you with the kid, what are you staring at?
Those who want to see the Madonna, check in at ten o'clock.
But, you with the kid, you won't make it.

Because I'm first for Wednesday,
and you're first to go to hell.

Translated from the Russian by Vera Dunham and H. W. Tjalsma

Two Poems

I

Over a dark and quiet empire
alone I fly—and envy you,
two-headed eagle who at least
have always yourself to talk to.

II

To hang bare light bulbs from a ceiling
simple cord will always serve;
it's only the poet who must hang
by his glaring white spinal nerve.

Translated from the Russian by William Jay Smith and Patricia Blake

YEVGENY YEVTUSHENKO

Russia (b. 1933)

Yevgeny Alexandrovich Yevtushenko was born in Siberia, the son of geologists. From his impetuous start in the early 1950s, he has been perhaps the most celebrated and slippery figure in contemporary Russian poetry. Because his early poetry was tolerated by the Soviet authorities and he was allowed to travel in Europe and America to give readings, his fame spread among both foreigners and the Russian young, even as his critics smelled complicity and corruption. Still, the poet sometimes went too far and was reprimanded, thereby earning back a measure of moral respect. His best-known poem, "Babii Yar," written in 1961, is an elegy for the 96,000 Jews executed during the war by Nazis in a ravine near Kiev; it is also a fierce indictment of Russian anti-Semitism. In 1968 he wrote a letter condemning the Soviet invasion of Czechoslovakia; in 1974 he criticized the arrest of Alexander Solzhenitsyn. For both these gestures, he paid in official sanctions. Yet he has never been able to shake, either in Russia or in the West, the aura of cynical hypocrisy: he complained about the totalitarian authorities but accepted their medals. He has portrayed himself as a poet of the people and has held throngs enthralled; he has been prolific as a poet and novelist, essayist and screenwriter, film director, actor, and cultural emissary. "My fate is supernatural, / my destiny astonishing," says one poem. Set against thuggish opponents, he seems brilliant. Set against the moral and poetic standard of the greatest Russian poets of this century, his achievement is quickly diminished. Still, at his best, Yevtushenko can rise to a febrile rhetorical power or capture the common rhythms of daily life.

Babii Yar

No monument stands over Babii Yar.
A drop sheer as a crude gravestone.
I am afraid.
   Today I am as old in years
as all the Jewish people.
Now I seem to be

a Jew.
Here I plod through ancient Egypt.
Here I perish crucified, on the cross,
and to this day I bear the scars of nails.
I seem to be
                    Dreyfus.
The Philistine
                    is both informer and judge.
I am behind bars.
                    Beset on every side.
Hounded,
            spat on,
                    slandered.
Squealing, dainty ladies in flounced Brussels lace
stick their parasols into my face.
I seem to be then
                    a young boy in Byelostok.
Blood runs, spilling over the floors.
The barroom rabble-rousers
give off a stench of vodka and onion.
A boot kicks me aside, helpless.
In vain I plead with these pogrom bullies.
While they jeer and shout,
                    "Beat the Yids. Save Russia!"
some grain-marketeer beats up my mother.
O my Russian people!
                    I know
                    you
are international to the core.
But those with unclean hands
have often made a jingle of your purest name.
I know the goodness of my land.
How vile these anti-Semites—
                    without a qualm
they pompously called themselves
the Union of the Russian People!
I seem to be
            Anne Frank
transparent
            as a branch in April.

YEVGENY YEVTUSHENKO • 253

And I love.
                    And have no need of phrases.
My need
            is that we gaze into each other.
How little we can see
                    or smell!
We are denied the leaves,
                        we are denied the sky.
Yet we can do so much—
                    tenderly
embrace each other in a darkened room.
They're coming here?
                        Be not afraid. Those are the booming
sounds of spring:
                    spring is coming here.
Come then to me.
                    Quick, give me your lips.
Are they smashing down the door?
                                No, it's the ice breaking . . .
The wild grasses rustle over Babii Yar.
The trees look ominous,
                        like judges.
Here all things scream silently,
                            and, baring my head,
slowly I feel myself
                    turning gray.
And I myself
            am one massive, soundless scream
above the thousand thousand buried here.
I am
        each old man
                    here shot dead.
I am
        every child
                    here shot dead.
Nothing in me
            shall ever forget!
The "Internationale," let it
                        thunder
when the last anti-Semite on earth

is buried forever.
In my blood there is no Jewish blood.
In their callous rage, all anti-Semites
must hate me now as a Jew.
For that reason
                    I am a true Russian!

Translated from the Russian by George Reavey

The Heirs of Stalin

Mute was the marble.
                         Mutely glimmered the glass.
Mute stood the sentries,
                   bronzed by the breeze.
But thin wisps of breath
                      seeped from the coffin
when they bore him
                   out of the mausoleum doors.
Slowly the coffin floated by,
                     grazing the fixed bayonets.
He was also mute—
            he also!—
                      but awesome and mute.
Grimly clenching
              his embalmed fists,
he watched through a crack inside,
                      just pretending to be dead.
He wanted to fix each pallbearer
                  in his memory:
young recruits from Ryazan and Kursk,
in order somehow later
                  to collect strength for a sortie,
and rise from the earth
            and get
                to them,

                              the unthinking.
He has worked out a scheme.
                         He's merely curled up for a nap.
And I appeal
              to our government with a plea:
to double,
           and treble, the guard at this slab,
so that Stalin will not rise again,
                              and with Stalin—the past.
We sowed crops honestly.
                    Honestly we smelted metal,
and honestly we marched,
                    in ranks as soldiers.
But he feared us.
               Believing in a great goal, he forgot
that the means must be worthy
                          of the goal's greatness.
He was farsighted.
                Wily in the ways of combat,
he left behind him
                many heirs on this globe.
It seems to me
             a telephone was installed in the coffin.
To someone once again
                    Stalin is sending his instructions.
Where does the cable yet go
                      from that coffin?
No, Stalin did not die.
                   He thinks death can be fixed.
We removed
          him
          from the mausoleum.
But how do we remove Stalin
                      from Stalin's heirs?
Some of his heirs
               tend roses in retirement,
but secretly consider
                  their retirement temporary.
Others,

from platforms rail against Stalin,
but,
    at night,
          yearn for the old days.
It is no wonder Stalin's heirs,
                with reason today
visibly suffer heart attacks.
             They, the former henchmen,
hate a time
      when prison camps are empty,
and auditoriums, where people listen to poetry,
                 are overfilled.
My motherland commands me not to be calm.
Even if they say to me: "Be assured . . ."—
                I am unable.
While the heirs of Stalin
        are still alive on this earth,
it will seem to me
      that Stalin still lives in the mausoleum.

Translated from the Russian by George Reavey

Hand-Rolled Cigarettes

If, in a fisherman's hut, you poke
behind the sagging sideboard with a stick,
you'll find his stock for making cigarettes,
a pile of newspapers, many years' thick.

There you'll meet mobs of secret agents
and doctor-poisoners of the age.
Bedbugs and roaches with mustaches
huddle, and crawl along the page.

Returning late, the tired fisherman
enjoys his ladled kvass's tang,

and sifts tobacco at his ease
onto some bureaucrat's harangue.

Cool in practice of his skill.
with fingers confident and strong,
he coils the speech in a narrow tube
and neatly wets it with his tongue.

The contents?—they're not his affair!
That glowing edge of nicotine
advancing, at the end of day,
eats up the newsprint, line by line.

He would have liked a sunny day,
wind in his sails and a lucky catch.
His yellow nail gleams salmon-bright,
flicking dead words reduced to ash.

Old eulogies and exposés
fulfill their destiny and rise,
with trashy articles and poems,
in spiral columns to the skies.

When evening falls in the north country,
cigarette-tips pinpoint the gray,
as, caught in the mood of dirty weather,
fishermen sit and puff away.

Their worn tobacco pouches rustle
till dawn sweeps inland on the tide.
Listen! They roll another cigarette:
and history is on their side.

Translated from the Russian by Stanley Kunitz

Siberian Wooing

In Siberia there once was what at first seemed a barbaric but canny custom. During wooing the bride was required to wash the feet of the groom and then drink the water. Only in this way was the bride considered worthy to be taken as a wife.

The bridegroom of forty-one,
                  who tomorrow goes off to war
                        in a heated van,
is planted by his Zima relatives
                  on a creaky stool,
and new, still pale, bootstraps
                     stick out of his smashing kid boots
where the wickedly elegant upper part
                    is turned back
and where a golden
              kerosene light plays.
The bride of forty-one
              enters with a heavy washbowl
                  painted with roses,
in which the softly steaming water
              shifts uneasily,
and pulling the groom's boots off,
                soiling both hands at once
                     with shoeblack,
she unwinds his leg wrappings,
              all without shame.
Now she immerses
             his bare feet with their little-boy red spots
so that when he winces in reflex
              water spills over the rim
                  onto the patterned floor mat,
and caresses his feet with water
              and the female tenderness
                  of shaking girlish fingers,
diamond after diamond
             dropping from her eyes into the washbowl.
She stands on her knees

before her future dead husband,
washing him in advance, so that if he is killed—

he is cleansed,
and the tips of her fingers

caress on his feet

each tiny hair,
the way a peasant woman's fingers caress

every tiny ear of corn in
the field.
And her future husband sits there—

neither alive

nor dead.
She bathes his feet,

but his cheeks and Cossack forelock are soaked.
He breaks into such a sweat

that his eyes spend tears,
relatives

and icons

break into tears.
And when the bride bends over

to drink the water of her beloved,
he jumps up,

raises her up in a single motion,

sits her down, as his wife,
falls on his own knees,

and instantly pulls from her

the garishly painted, combed felt boots,
and thrusts her feet into the washbowl,

shaking as in a chill of fever.
How he washes her feet—

each toe,

each nail!
How he kneads

her sweet-apple ankles

in his trembling palms!
How he washes her!

As though she were his yet unborn daughter,
whose father,

after his own future demise,

he will become!

And then he raises the washbowl
                and presses his teeth—biting
                        until the enamel crunches
and his adam's apple dances on his neck—
                    drinking that cup to the bottom,
and across his face,
          across his chest,
                  quivering, like a transparent flag
                      of greatest purity,
flows the water from the feet of lovers,
                water from the feet of lovers . . .

Translated from the Russian by Albert C. Todd and James Ragan

JOSEPH BRODSKY

Russia (1940–1996)

When Joseph Brodsky was awarded the Nobel Prize for Literature in 1987—the second youngest person ever given the prize—the Swedish Academy cited his "all-embracing authorship imbued with clarity of thought and poetic intensity." Born in Leningrad, he left school at fifteen and worked at menial jobs, from farmhand to machine operator and coroner's assistant. He began writing poems a few years later and at the same time taught himself English and Polish in order to read and translate the works of poets like John Donne and Czesław Miłosz, whom he admired. Because as a teenager he had joined a dissident political group, the Soviet authorities arrested him in 1964 and put him on trial for "social parasitism." The case drew wide protests, but Brodsky was sentenced to five years of hard labor in the Arctic. He was released after eighteen months and worked as a translator, but by 1972 he was forced into exile. He headed first to Austria, in order to meet W. H. Auden, one of his muses. Eventually he emigrated to the United States and in 1977 became an American citizen. Despite the tumult of his personal life, his poetry is largely uninterested in politics. "Language and, presumably, literature," he wrote, "are more ancient and inevitable, more durable than any form of social organization. The revulsion, irony, or indifference often expressed by literature toward the state is essentially the reaction of the permanent—better yet, the infinite—against the temporary, against the finite." Steeped in the traditional themes and verse technique of lyric poetry, his work took up both the abiding metaphysical perplexities and the fleeting intimate moments of the individual life. He drew his inspiration from the great modern poets of Russia—Osip Mandelstam, Marina Tsvetaeva, and Anna Akhmatova—as well as from poets of other cultures: Cavafy, Hardy, Eliot, Montale, Frost, and Auden. Though often grittily realistic, his poems manifest a deeply religious aura; they are laced as well with a rueful wit, considerable learning, and a vigorously moral point of view.

Six Years Later

So long had life together been that now
The second of January fell again
On Tuesday, making her astonished brow
Lift like a windshield-wiper in the rain,
    So that her misty sadness cleared, and showed
    A cloudless distance waiting up the road.

So long had life together been that once
The snow began to fall, it seemed unending;
That, lest the flakes should make her eyelids wince,
I'd shield them with my hand, and they, pretending
    Not to believe that cherishing of eyes,
    Would beat against my palm like butterflies.

So alien had all novelty become
That sleep's entanglements would put to shame
Whatever depths the analysts might plumb;
That when my lips blew out the candle-flame,
    Her lips, fluttering from my shoulder, sought
    To join my own, without another thought.

So long had life together been that all
That tattered brood of papered roses went,
And a whole birch-grove grew upon the wall,
And we had money, by some accident,
    And tonguelike on the sea, for thirty days,
    The sunset threatened Turkey with its blaze.

So long had life together been without
Books, chairs, utensils—only that ancient bed,
That the triangle, before it came about,
Had been a perpendicular, the head
    Of some acquaintance hovering above
    Two points which had been coalesced by love.

So long had life together been that she
And I, with our joint shadows, had composed

A double door, a door which even if we
Were lost in work or sleep, was always closed:
    Somehow, it would appear, we drifted right
    On through it into the future, into the night.

Translated from the Russian by Richard Wilbur

I Sit by the Window

I said fate plays a game without a score,
And who needs fish if you've got caviar?
The triumph of the Gothic style would come to pass
And turn you on—no need for coke, or grass.
    I sit by the window. Outside, an aspen.
    When I loved, I loved deeply. It wasn't often.

I said the forest's only part of a tree.
Who needs the whole girl if you've got her knee?
Sick of the dust raised by the modern era,
The Russian eye would rest on an Estonian spire.
    I sit by the window. The dishes are done.
    I was happy here. But I won't be again.

I wrote: The bulb looks at the floor in fear,
And love, as an act, lacks a verb; the zer-
o Euclid thought the vanishing point became
Wasn't math—it was the nothingness of Time.
    I sit by the window. And while I sit
    My youth comes back. Sometimes I'd smile. Or spit.

I said that the leaf may destroy the bud;
What's fertile falls in fallow soil—a dud;
That on the flat field, the unshadowed plain
Nature spills the seeds of trees in vain.
    I sit by the window. Hands lock my knees.
    My heavy shadow's my squat company.

My song was out of tune, my voice was cracked,
But at least no chorus can ever sing it back.
That talk like this reaps no reward bewilders
No one—no one's legs rest on my shoulders.
    I sit by the window in the dark. Like an express,
    The waves behind the wavelike curtain crash.

A loyal subject of these second-rate years,
I proudly admit that my finest ideas
Are second-rate, and may the future take them
As trophies of my struggle against suffocation.
    I sit in the dark. And it would be hard to figure out
    Which is worse: The dark inside, or the darkness out.

Translated from the Russian by Howard Moss

October Tune

A stuffed quail
on the mantelpiece minds its tail.
The regular chirr of the old clock's healing
in the twilight the rumpled helix.
Through the window, birch candles fail.

For the fourth day the sea hits the dike with its hard horizon.
Put aside the book, take your sewing kit;
patch my clothes without turning the light on:
golden hair
keeps the corner lit.

Translated from the Russian by the author

Belfast Tune

Here's a girl from a dangerous town.
She crops her dark hair short

JOSEPH BRODSKY ♦ 265

so that less of her has to frown
    when someone gets hurt.

She folds her memories like a parachute.
    Dropped, she collects the peat
and cooks her veggies at home: they shoot
    here where they eat.

Ah, there's more sky in these parts than, say,
    ground. Hence her voice's pitch,
and her stare stains your retina like a gray
    bulb when you switch

hemispheres, and her knee-length quilt
    skirt's cut to catch the squall.
I dream of her either loved or killed
    because the town's too small.

Roman Elegies

to Benedetta Craveri

I

The captive mahogany of a private Roman
flat. In the ceiling, a dust-covered crystal island.
At sunset, the windowpanes pan a common
ground for the nebulous and the ironed.
Setting a naked foot on the rosy marble,
the body steps toward its future: to its attire.
If somebody shouted "Freeze!" I'd perform that marvel
as this city happily did in its childhood hour.
The world's made of nakedness and of foldings.
Still, the latter's richer with love than a face, that's certain.
Thus an opera tenor's so sweet to follow
since he yields invariably to a curtain.
By nightfall, a blue eye employs a tear,
cleansing, to a needless shine, the iris;

and the moon overhead apes an emptied square
with no fountain in it. But of rock as porous.

II

The month of stalled pendulums. Only a fly in August
in a dry carafe's throat is droning its busy hymn.
The numerals on the clock face crisscross like earnest
anti-aircraft searchlights probing for seraphim.
The month of drawn blinds, of furniture wrapped in cotton
shrouds, of the sweating double in the mirror above the cupboard,
of bees that forget the topography of their hives and, coated
with suntan honey, keep staggering seaward.
Get busy then, faucet, over the snow-white, sagging
muscle, tousle the tufts of thin gray singes!
To a homeless torso and its idle, grabby
mitts, there's nothing as dear as the sight of ruins.
And they, in their turn, see themselves in the broken Jewish
r no less gladly: for the pieces fallen
so apart, saliva's the only solution they wish
for, as time's barbarous corneas scan the Forum.

III

The tiled, iron-hot, glowing hills: midsummer.
Clouds feel like angels, thanks to their cooling shadows.
Thus the bold cobblestone eyes, like a happy sinner,
the blue underthings of your leggy blond friend. A bard of
trash, extra thoughts, broken lines, unmanly,
I hide in the bowels of the Eternal City
from the luminary that rolled back so many
marble pupils with rays bright enough for setting
up yet another universe. A yellow square. Noontime's
stupor. A Vespa's owner tortures the screaming gears.
Clutching my chest with my hand, at a distance
I reckon the change from the well-spent years.
And, like a book at once opened to all its pages,
the laurels scratch the scorched white of a balustrade.

And the Colosseum looms, the skull of Argus,
through whose sockets clouds drift like a thought of the vanished
      herd.

IV

Two young brunettes in the library of the husband
of the more stunning one. Two youthful, tender
ovals hunch over pages: a Muse telling Fate the substance
of several things she tried to render.
The swish of old paper, of red crepe de Chine. A humming
fan mixes violets, lavender, and carnations.
Braiding of hair: an elbow thrusts up its summit
accustomed to cumulus-thick formations.
Oh, a dark eye is obviously more fluent
in brown furniture, pomegranates, oak shutters.
It's more keen, it's more cordial than a blue one;
to the blue one, though, nothing matters!
The blue one can always tell the owner
from the goods, especially before closing—
that is, time from living—and turn the latter over,
as tails strain to look at heads in tossing.

V

Jig, little candle tongue, over the empty paper,
bow to the rotten breath as though you were courted,
follow—but don't get too close!—the pauper
letters standing in line to obtain the content.
You animate the walls, wardrobe, the sill's sweetbriar:
more than handwriting is ever after;
even your soot, it appears, soars higher
than the holiest wish of these musings' author.
Still, in their midst you earn yourself a decent
name, as my fountain pen, in memory of your tender
commas, in Rome, at the millennium's end, produces
a lantern, a cresset, a torch, a taper,
never a period—and the premises look their ancient

selves, from the severed head down to a yellow toenail.
For an ink pot glows bright whenever someone mentions
light, especially in a tunnel.

VI

Clicking of a piano at the siesta hour.
Stillness of sleepy mews acquires
C-flats, as scales coat a fish which narrows
round the corner. Exhaling quarrels,
inhaling a fusty noon's air, the stucco
flaps its brown gills, and a sultry, porous
cavity of a mouth scatters
around cold pearls of Horace.
I've never built that cloud-thrusting stony
object that could explain clouds' pallor.
I've learned about my own, and any
fate, from a letter, from its black color.
Thus some fall asleep while hugging
a Leica, in order to take a picture
of the dream, to make themselves out, having
awakened in a developed future.

VII

Eggshells of cupolas, vertebrae of bell towers.
Colonnades' limbs sprawled wide in their blissful, heathen
leisure. The square root of a skylark scours
the bottomless, as though prior to prayers, heaven.
Light reaps much more than it has sown: an awkward
body hides in a crack while its shadow shutters
walls. In these parts, all windows are looking northward,
where the more one boozes the less one matters.
North! A white iceberg's frozen-in piano;
smallpoxed with quartz, vases' granite figures;
a plain unable to stop field-glass scanning;
sweet Ashkenazy's ten running fingers.
Never again are the legions to thread those contours:

to a creaking pen, even its words won't hearken.
And the golden eyebrow—as, at sunset, a cornice—
rises up, and the eyes of the darling darken.

VIII

In these squinting alleyways, where even a thought about
one's self is too cumbersome, in this furrowed clutter
of the brain which has long since refused to cloud
the universe, where now keyed up, now scattered,
you trundle your boots on the cobbled, checkered
squares, from a fountain and back to a Caesar—
thus a needle shuffles across the record
skipping its grooves—it is altogether
proper to settle now for a measly fraction
of remaining life, for the past life craving
completeness, for its attempts to fashion
an integer. The sound the heels are scraping
from the ground is the aria of their union,
a serenade that what-has-been-longer
hums to what's-to-be-shorter. This is a genuine
Caruso for a gramophone-dodging mongrel.

IX

Lesbia, Julia, Cynthia, Livia, Michelina.
Bosoms, ringlets of fleece: for effects, and for causes also.
Heaven-baked clay, fingertips' brave arena.
Flesh that renders eternity an anonymous torso.
You breed immortals: those who have seen you bare,
they too turned Catulluses, statues, heavy
Neros, et cetera. Short-term goddesses! you are
much more a joy to believe in than a permanent bevy.
Hail the smooth abdomen, thighs as their hamstrings tighten.
White upon white, as Kazimir's dream image
one summer evening, I, the most mortal item
in the midst of this wreckage resembling the whole world's rib
    cage,

sip with feverish lips wine from a tender collar-
bone; the sky is as pale as a cheek with a mole that trembles;
and the cupolas bulge like the tits of the she-wolf, fallen
asleep after having fed her Romulus and her Remus.

X

Mimicking local pines, embrace the ether!
The fingertips won't cull much more than the pane's tulle quiver.
Still, a little black bird won't return from the sky blue, either.
And we, too, aren't gods in miniature, that's clear.
That's precisely why we are happy: because we are nothings;
        speckled
pores are spurned by summits or sharp horizons;
the body is space's reversal, no matter how hard you pedal.
And when we are unhappy, it's perhaps for the same small
        reasons.
Better lean on a portico, loose the white shirt that billows,
stone cools the spinal column, gray pigeons mutter,
and watch how the sun is sinking into gardens and distant villas,
how the water—the tutor
of eloquence—pours from the rusted lips, repeating
not a thing, save a nymph with her marble truants,
save that it's cold and fresh, save that it's splitting
the face into rippling ruins.

XI

Private life. Fears, shredded thoughts, the jagged
blanket renders the contours of Europe meager.
By means of a blue shirt and a rumpled jacket
something still gets reflected in the wardrobe mirror.
Let's have some tea, face, so that the teeth may winnow
lips. Yoked by a ceiling, the air grows flatter.
Cast inadvertently through the window,
a glance makes a bunch of blue jays flutter
from their pine tops. A room in Rome, white paper,
the tail of a freshly drawn letter: a darting rodent.

Thus, thanks to the perfect perspective, some objects peter
out; thus, still others shuffle across the frozen
Tanaïs, dropping from the picture, limping,
occiputs covered with wilted laurels and blizzards' powder—
toward Time, lying beyond the limits
of every spraddling superpower.

XII

Lean over. I'll whisper something to you: I am
grateful for everything: for the chicken cartilage
and for the chirr of scissors already cutting
out the void for me—for it is your hem.
Doesn't matter if it's pitch-black, doesn't matter if
it holds nothing: no ovals, no limbs to count.
The more invisible something is,
the more certain it's been around,
and the more obviously it's everywhere. You
were the first to whom all this happened, were you?
For a nail holding something one would divide by two—
were it not for remainders—there is no gentler quarry.
I was in Rome. I was flooded by light. The way
a splinter can only dream about.
Golden coins on the retina are to stay—
enough to last one through the whole blackout.

Translated from the Russian by the author

ELENA SHVARTS

Russia (b. 1948)

When in 1703 Peter the Great founded St. Petersburg, he called the city his "Paradise." It is this czar whom a poem by Elena Shvarts describes as the man "who split Russia in two with his new-whetted knife: / and spread the dark jam of his serfs on the streets— / but their souls skipped away as he swatted, like flies." St. Petersburg, where she was born and educated, is both Shvarts's home and her obsessive subject. In its sky are crows like "scraps of burnt archives." It is a "glorious dump," a "gulf of chiming bells," or the "spawn of a country-hovel brain, / Reeking of cabbage soup." She is haunted by religious mysticism and by the neoclassicism of the city's traditions. As a result her poems are both ecstatic in their impulses and restrained by their technique. Her first book was not published until 1989; before then her work appeared only underground or abroad. Shvarts is a quintessential city poet: gulping, allusive, entangled, tense, sometimes raucous, a gatherer of lost souls.

What That Street Is Called

What that street is called—you can read it on the sign,
For me its name is paradise, my lost paradise.
What the whole town's called—you can ask a passer-by,
For me its name is paradise, my lost paradise.
Because it's lost, its parks are still in blossom,
My heart throbs, my heart thrashes, a happy captured bream.
Black rats nest over the shining river, in undergrowth,
They're permitted, welcome, nothing can ruin paradise on earth.
You were radiant even when you thoughtfully advised
That when you drink beer you should salt the rim of the glass.
What a time that was—I'll look it up in the calendar,
You're like a house-coat, you are worn, God is above you and
    inside.
You're delicate, frail, you crumble like a porcelain cup—God's
    glow

Is shining through it, probably, it's all becoming clearer now.
He's pecking through your mortal shell before our very eyes,
You're stooping—and no wonder!—look who's sitting on your
    shoulders.
Oh, I'd accept that burden, but my name's not written down,
Let's stroll along the boulevard, watch the band play in the rain,
As warm torrents pour into the thundering gullets of horns, over a
    precipice,
Playing the *Slavyanka,* down it drops,
                          my "Paradise."

Translated from the Russian by Michael Molnar

Remembrance of Strange Hospitality

Once I had a taste
Of a girlfriend's milk,
My sister's milk—
Not to quench my thirst
But satisfy my soul.
Into a cup she squeezed
Milk from her left breast
And in that simple vessel
It gently frothed, rejoiced.
There was something birdlike in its odor,
Whiffs of sheep and wolf, and something older
Than the Milky Way, it was
Somehow warm and dense.
A daughter in the wilderness,
Once let her aged father drink
From her breasts and thus became
His mother. By this act of grace
Her whiteness drove away the dark,
A cradle substituted for a tomb.
From the duct next to your heart
You offered me a drink—
I'm not a vampire, am I?—Horror.

It frothed and tinkled, warm
And sweet, soft, everlasting,
Crowding time back in a corner.

Translated from the Russian by Michael Molnar

Elegy on an X-ray Photo of My Skull

The flautist boasts but God's enraged—
He stripped the living skin from Marsyas—
Such is the destiny of earthly flautists:
Grown jealous, He will say to each in turn:—
"You've licked the honey of music but you're just muck,
You're still a lump of that same dirt
And lodged inside you is the stone of death."
Apollo was the god of light
But he grew dark
When round his hands, you Marsyas,
Twisted in pain.
And now he is a god of glimmer,
But eternal also are your groans.

And my God, growing dark,
Slipped me this photograph
In which my glowing skull,
Etched from the invisible,
Swam, blocking out the dusk
And the stripped naked park—
It was a mass of fog
Embraced in liquid dark.
In it shadow and cloud were blended
And my hand began to tremble.
This skull was my own
But it didn't know me,
Its intricate pattern
Like a damascene dagger

Is skilfully crafted,
How pure and how strong.
But the mouth is bared,
Still alive its grin.

Bone, you yellowed a long time,
Grew as heavy as sin,
Like a walnut you aged and you ripened,
A present for death.
Grown brazen inside me, this yellow bone
Has lapped itself in a sleigh-rug of skin
And taking my reins sped off headlong
But come to a halt at my brow.
In anguish here before my God I stand
Holding my skull in a trembling hand—
O Lord, what shall I do with it?
Spit in its eyesockets?
Fill it up with wine?
Or put it on my neck and wear it once again?
So I hurl it aside—this light-looking shell
And it flies off thundering among the stars like a pail.
But it returned and landing on my neck, reminded me in
      consolation:
Way back at someone's house, its fellow stood as a table
      decoration
And led the deathlife of a dehydrated plant
As if it were a temple or a chalice.
There was a lot to drink but not enough—
And someone took this skull and began to pass it round
To collect the money for a vodka bottle.
Small change was scattered clinking on the dark occiput
But straightaway I confiscated it,
Put it back where it belonged—calm down—
And like a kitten it rubbed against my palm.
For this I shall be granted as reward
That nobody will desecrate my skull—
No worm will crawl inside, no new Hamlet take it in his hands.
When my end comes—I shall walk up the aisle in flames.
But something else strikes me as weird,

That I can't sense my skeleton inside—
Neither skull nor flesh nor bones—
More like a crater after the explosion
Or a memory of missing news,
Mistiness or mist
Or a spirit drunk on its new life.

But you will be my lodgings when
They start to pipe the Resurrection.
You, my spirit's navel, fly
Sooner to the East. And I
All around you as a dusty cloud
Erupting, swirling, setting as the Word.
But what a shame you won't be filled again
With all that soft old curd.

Translated from the Russian by Michael Molnar

Elegies on the Cardinal Points

I North

for M. Sh.

Down the winding lanes of Moscow, down its hopeless
    convolutions
Someone's shadow flew past in sweet desperation.
On a pool she kissed an emerald duck,
Pressed some crusted leaves against her eyeballs,
Shrieking with laughter dodged a tramcar-bull
And warmed herself up on a tramwire spark.

At night—come to the picture show, they pleaded,
"Bergman films!" Moments from your life repeated
Hundreds of times. Who knew that nightly cinemas are hired by
    hell?

That strapped into their seats the dead sit in the hall
Gazing with tilted heads into the past?
Escorted there like soldiers to the baths?
"Waiting. Love. Your Marat."—for Charlotte, a telegram.

I've cast off seven skins, eight souls, all my clothes,
And in my breast I've tracked a ninth soul down,
A gentle mole, it trembled in my hand,
Pale-blue iceborn snow-wife with a broomstick,
I poked two little eyes in and she died.

Look—the vault of heaven's bestrewn and snowing wings and
    feathers,
No sweeping them up in a week, stay buried in them forever.
Look—under the moon fly Lion and Eagle and Bull,
And you sleep, you lie back in your body's serpentine coils.
Where's the angel?—you ask, and I will most surely respond:
Where there's gloom—there's a radiance, all the world is maimed,
The angel twined in gloom like a tenacious plant.
Steer for black point, for desolation and gloom,
Steer for darkness, for dark, for the rocks, the muddle, the pit.
The angel plays hide-and-seek?—but he's there!—in earth-
    underfoot.
He's no worm. Don't try to dig for him in a field.
See—towards winter shining birds fly to the pole?

She gave a glance, began to groan
And stumbling on crenellations flew all night,
Her bloodspots dripping on hospitals, boulevards, mills . . .
Don't worry! Your death is the birth of an angel of light.

II South
On a marble statuette

for I. Burikhin

Young lady! Did you drop something?
Too bad, that's how it is. A foot
Narrow as a glove. And the calf
Has dispersed into resonant dust.

And when I looked at you I missed myself—
Old loves do not exist, nor does this winter
Or the next—but on the topmast fire
Burns bluely and there's howling from the darkness
And flocks of hands circle above my head
Like seagulls, pecking and bearing off memory,
And darkness ossifies and boulders snore
And nearby, furiously, it seems that cloth's being torn
And life seeps out into an oily blot—
That once was a point of anguish. Flotsam drifts.
Tell me, darling—was it me who lived
On earth? And floated, gliding through the azure?
With a goose, nipping and tearing out emerald grass,
She and me whispering together tra-la-la, tra-la-la?
Eternity lay in a pool, from it I took a drink,
This pool drained like a sea with knives in waves
That hack and slash. O lengthy farewells—life!
But surely God Himself constructed us—diamonds
Set within a frame of bone.
But surely God Himself constructed us—
Like the cyclamens he sowed in snow,
And doing so He trembled all over and burnt and shivered,
And saw that everything should tremble, shiver, whistle,
Shattering like fire and blood, and into darkness hurtle—
Where straightaway they'll rip you into shreds
Sinking unsated fangs into your shoulders,
Take out the honeycombs of memory—they're no longer in your
        power.
And only love like Lot's wife glistens,
A spear suspended in this dreadful chasm.

Where is the pole of the Universe, tell me, diamond magnet!
Where is He, radiant, icy, white,
Whom Nansen, Peary, Scott now speed towards
Driving through darkness a team of hungry shades?
I'm headed that way too—where buried in ice-blocks sleeps
The lilac bear, the way shown by the diamond magnet.
In the heavens ethereal fires blaze
And a flight of eyes wings to the South.

Birds—crosses worn by God against His skin!
Many of you are torn off and once again you are many,
You come with us up to the very brink
Of inky darkness, where we'll find teams and a sleigh,
Where through the eternal tundra there's a track,
And there we'll no more wander from our way . . .

III East

for E. Feoktistov

Get up! Shame on you, sleeping in common view.
Get up! the resurrection's shortly due.
A crematorium—fine place she's picked to sleep!
Get up! I'll have a wine-flask set.
Lord! that reflection in the window—is that me?
Am I now incarnated as that poppy-seed?
So what! I'll take a look at cyclamens in crunchy snow,
Creep under their glass like a little bird and scuttle away.
And everyone's a little bird caroling on a bough,
And nobody wants to listen, but it trills out all the louder.
I'll deck myself more lavishly in golden plumes,
Read, read my fortune in the coffee grounds.
Because I'm similar to that snuffed-out cordial,
Because I feel the strength to face some future torment.
O God, I feel—I'm like such countries as Korea,
Just try to step on me, I'll scorch your heels.
O God, just peck the grains off me as fast as possible.
I'll be salt of your tears and I'll drink myself sick.

Everyone's a caroling bird—just take a look.
Drawing breath through snow a burning flower sprouts.
Ranks of backbones fly towards the East.
Wind is the angel's form, it enters unnoticed.
Death gnaws your edges, etches out your borders,
That vitriolic brew, that aquafortis.
On crowded sails fly off into the blue,
Wind is the angel's form, it blows around your brow.

IV West

for N. Guchinskaya

Westward, westward along the shadow's track,
Everything's carried off howling—into the deepest black.
Old rags and rings and faces, like a ball down a bowling alley,
Like refuse down a chute—everything melts into mist.
And what am I? Vessel of pre-eternal abysses,
As it ebbs and it flows within me the Mediterranean shimmers.
I'll block my ears and hear—the sound inside a shell,
And seas and all their hearts run dry.
On the fast-drying sands what remnants linger?
I'll list it for you woefully on my fingers:
Molluscs and verses, slugs and a curl,
But rising sands began to smack their lips.
The human voice crescendoes, climaxing in a bird's shriek, in a
          singing,
Oh, squall like a seagull and you will obtain acquiescence.
I'm so subdued as it is it's simply disgusting.
(Flowers bloomed in horror although there was frost.
Antichrist walked across the sky in clouds and stars,
Now his descent begun, he grew before one's eyes.
He walked in a slender, sky-blue ray of light,
Behind him, faithful as lapdogs, helicopters in flight.
And the people kneeled and crossed themselves in the darkness.
He approached—eternal cold streamed out of his eyes,
Wooden he seemed and painted and still unborn.
No, *you* were never crucified for us!

But with a precise and rhythmic touch he laid hands on bowed
    heads.)
Everything's carried off howling and only the saints come back.
(There's Kseniya, barefoot—see?—Guards' greatcoat down to her
    heels,
Under a blazing halo of ice, Kseniya is carrying bricks.)
Wind carries off everything westward along the shadows' track.
Space ripped the cardinal points to form a cross.
How can you stand your ground among these tremors and
    crevasses?
Best, let's just flutter off into the sky
Towards the sunset where Persephone, pale
And in despair, stares at a telephone dial.
Where howl in yearning shades and parts of shades—
You will assuage both thirst and hunger with a pomegranate seed.

Translated from the Russian by Michael Molnar

THE MIDDLE EAST

ADONIS

Lebanon (b. 1930)

Ali Ahmad Said was born and educated in Syria and as a young writer adopted the pen name Adonis. In 1956, harassed and imprisoned for his political views, he moved to Beirut; four years later he became a Lebanese citizen. In 1958 he founded the journal *Mawāqif,* which championed the renovation of Arabic literary conventions. Adonis is now usually considered the most influential poet and critic in the Arab world. In both his closely argued criticism and his often symbolist and visionary poetry, he has called for "a leap outside of established concepts, a change in the order of things and in the way we look at them." A student of classical Arab poetry, he has revived older forms and experimented with prose poems. "I come from a land," he has written, "where poetry is like a tree which watches over man and where a poet is a guard who understands the rhythm of this world. He travels with history and feels the rhythm of history. By heeding this rhythm, he realizes the gaps and distances that separate man from man. I see this separation between men as a darkness which science cannot dispel despite its transformative power. Only poetry can illuminate this darkness."

The Passage

> I sought to share
> the life of snow
> and fire.
>   But neither
> snow nor fire
> took me in.
>   So,
> I kept my peace,
> waiting like flowers,
> staying like stones.
> In love I lost
> myself.
>   I broke away

and watched until
I swayed like a wave
between the life
I dreamed and the changing
dream I lived.

Translated from the Arabic by Samuel Hazo

Tree of Fire

The tree by the river
is weeping leaves.
It strews the shore
with tear after tear.
It reads to the river
its prophecy of fire.
I am that final
leaf that no one
sees
          My people
have died as fires
die—without a trace.

Translated from the Arabic by Samuel Hazo

Song of a Man in the Dark

To ascend? How?
These mountains are not torches.
No stairs await me
in the higher snows.

Thus for you
from here—
these messages of grief . . .

Each time I rise,
the mountains in my blood
say no, and darkness
holds me in its narrow sorrows.

Translated from the Arabic by Samuel Hazo

Elegy for the Time at Hand

I

Chanting of banishment,
exhaling flame,
the carriages of exile
breach the walls.

Or are these carriages
the battering sighs of my verses?

Cyclones have crushed us.
Sprawled in the ashes of our days,
we glimpse our souls
passing
on the sword's glint
or at the peaks of helmets.

An autumn of salt spray
settles on our wounds.
No tree can bud.
No spring . . .

Now in the final act,
disaster tows our history
toward us on its face.
What is our past
but memories pierced like deserts

prickled with cactus?
What streams can wash it?
It reeks with the musk
of spinsters and widows
back from pilgrimage.
The sweat of dervishes
begrimes it as they twirl
their blurring trousers into miracles.

Now blooms the spring of the locust.
Over the dead nightingales
the night itself weighs and weighs.
The day inches to birth
while the shut and bolted door
of the sea
rejects us.

We scream.
We dream of weeping,
but tears refuse our eyes.
We twist our necks
in zero hurricanes.

O my land,
I see you as a woman in heat,
a bridge of lust.

The pharaohs take you when they choose,
and the very sand applauds them.
Through the clay of my eyeshells,
I see what any man can see:
libations at the graves of children,
incense for holy men,
tombstones of black marble,
fields scattered with skeletons,
vultures,
mushy corpses with the names of heroes.

Thus we advance,
chests to the sea,

grieving for yesterday.
Our words inherit nothing,
beget nothing.
We are islands.

From the abyss we smell ravens.
Our ships send out their pleas
to nothing but the moon's crescent
of despair that broods
a devil's spawn.
At riverfall, at the dead sea,
midnight dreams its festivals,
but sand and foam and locusts
are the only brides.

Thus we advance,
harvesting our caravans
in filth and tears,
bleeding the earth
with our own blood
until the green dam of the sea
alone
stops us.

2

What god shall resurrect us
in his flesh?
After all, the iron cage is shrinking.
The hangman will not wait
though we wail from birth
in the name of these happy ruins.

What narrow yesterdays,
what stale and shriveled years . . .
Even storms come begging
when the sky matches the gray
of the sand,
leaving us stalled between seasons,

barricaded by what we see,
marching under clouds that move
like mules and cannon.
The dust of graveyards blinds us
until our eyes rime
with ash.
No lashes fringe the sun.
No brows can shade the day,
and life comes moment by moment
as it comes to the poor only.
Shadowed by ice and sand,
we live.

And so live all men.

All men . . . mere scraps from everywhere,
fresh baits of arsenic.
Under their sky what green can sprout?

All men . . . choked by ashes,
crushed by the rocks of silence,
mounted by empire builders,
paraded in arenas for their sport,
so many footstools,
so many banners . . .
No one whispers in Barada or the Euphrates.
Nothing breeds or stirs.
O my dry and silent land,
who left you like a fossil?
On the map you're virile,
rich with wheat, oil, ports,
countercolored by migrations.
Shall a new race grow in the poppy fields?
Shall fresh winds rearrange the sand?

Let the rain come.
Let rain wash us in our ruins,
wash the corpses, wash our history.
Let the poems strangled on our lips

be swept away like rocks in the street.
Let us attend to cows, doves, flowers, gods.
Let sounds return
to this land of starving frogs.
Let bread be brought by locusts
and the banished ants . . .

My words become a spear in flight.
Unopposable as truth,
my spear returns to strike me
dead.

3

Braid your hair, my boys, with greener leaves.
We still have verse among us.
We have the sea.
We have our dreams.
"To the steppes of China
we bequeath our neighing horses,
and to Georgia, our spears.
We'll build a house of gold
from here to the Himalayas.
We'll sail our flags in Samarkand.
We'll tread the treasured mosses
of the earth.
We'll bless our blood with roses.
We'll wash the day of stains
and walk on stones as we would walk on silk.

"This is the only way.
For this we'll lie with lightning
and anoint the mildewed earth
until the cries of birth
resound, resound, resound.

"Nothing can stop us.
Remember,

we are greener than the sea,
younger than time.
The sun and the day are dice
between our fingers."

Under the exile's moon
tremble the first wings.
Boats begin to drift
on a dead sea, and siroccos
rustle the gates of the city.
Tomorrow the gates shall open.
We'll burn the locusts in the desert,
span the abyss
and stand on the porch
of a world to be.

"Darkness,
darkness of the sea,
be filled with the leopard's joy.
Help us to sacrifice,
name us anew.
The eagle of the future waits,
and there are answers in its eyes.

"Darkness,
darkness of the sea,
ignore this feast of corpses.
Bring the earth to blossom
with your winds.
Banish plague and teach the very rocks
to dance and love."

The goddess of the sand prostrates herself.
Under brichthorn
the spring rises like clocynth from the lips
or life from the sea.
We leave the captive city
where every lantern is a church
and every bee more sacred than a nun.

4

"Where is your home?
Which country?
Which camp without a name?"

"My country is abandoned.
My soul has left me.
I have no home."

When pharaohs ruled and men were cannibals,
the words of poets died.
While pharaohs rule,
I take my books and go,
living in the shade of my heart,
weaving from my verse's silk
a new heaven.

The sea cleanses our wounds
and makes of wounds the salt's kin . . .
The white sea,
the daily Euphrates,
the Orontes in its cradle,
the Barada—
I have tasted them all,
and none could slake me.
Yet I learned their love,
and my despair deserved such waters.

Though desperate, I still hate death.
Though lost, I seek my way
through all the lies and doubts
that are the crust and quicksand
of the earth.

Give me the exile's sail,
the pilgrim's face.
I turn my back on jails and holocausts.
I leave the dead to death.

And I go,
keeping my endless sorrows,
my distance from the stars,
my pilgrimage,
my girl
and my verses.
I go with the sweat
of exile on my forehead
and with a lost poem
sleeping in my eyes.
I go,
dreaming of those buried
in orchards and vineyards,
and I remember those I love,
those few.
When the sea rages my blood
and the wind kisses my love's hair,
I remember my mother,
and I weave in memory for her
a mat of straw
where she can sit and weep.

Amen to the age of flies.

Because the earth survives beneath my feet,
the pale god of my despair rejoices.
A new voice speaks my words.
My poems bloom naked as roses.

Find me some paper,
some ink.
Despair is still my star,
and evil is always being born.
Silence rises on the sand.
There are hearts to touch.
Some ink . . .
Some paper . . .

"Where is your home?
What camp without a name?"

"My country is abandoned.
My soul has left me.
I have no home."

Translated from the Arabic by Samuel Hazo

MAHMOUD DARWISH

Palestine (b. 1942)

His life and his work have one theme: exile. Mahmoud Darwish was born
in the village of Birwe, east of Acre in Galilee. During the war of 1948, he
fled with his family to Lebanon, and his village was destroyed by the Is-
raeli army. When the family returned home, they were too late to be in-
cluded in the census of Palestinian Arabs and were thereby denied identity
papers. He could not travel and was continually harassed by the authori-
ties; in the 1960s he was several times imprisoned or put under house ar-
rest. In 1971 he left Israel for Cairo, where he worked for the newspaper
Al Ahram. Two years later, in Beirut, he joined the Palestine Liberation
Organization and became editor of its scholarly journal. In 1987 he be-
came a member of the PLO Executive Committee, a position he resigned
in 1993 after the peace accord signed by the PLO and Israel. "My role on
the Executive Committee," he explained, "was that of a symbol. I was
there to provide a moderating influence on the tension and to help recon-
cile differences. I have never been a man of politics. I am a poet with a
particular perspective on reality." Darwish's perspective includes a plan-
gent nostalgia for his lost homeland and a roiling anger at the blood that
has been shed over it. The hypocrisies of politics and the sufferings of a
displaced people cast a deep shadow. Darwish uses many traditional Arab
images and seeks to invest them with an urgent new reference. In addition
to fourteen collections of poems, he has written many prose works and
has long since emerged as the leading poet not only of the Palestinian
struggle but of contemporary Arabic literature. He lives in Paris.

Identity Card

> Put it on record.
>   I am an Arab
> And the number of my card is fifty thousand
> I have eight children
> And the ninth is due after summer.
> What's there to be angry about?

Put it on record.
    I am an Arab
Working with comrades of toil in a quarry.
I have eight children
For them I wrest the loaf of bread,
The clothes and exercise books
From the rocks
And beg for no alms at your door,
    Lower not myself at your doorstep.
    What's there to be angry about?

Put it on record.
    I am an Arab.
I am a name without a title,
Patient in a country where everything
Lives in a whirlpool of anger.
    My roots
    Took hold before the birth of time
    Before the burgeoning of the ages,
    Before cypress and olive trees,
    Before the proliferation of weeds.

My father is from the family of the plough
    Not from highborn nobles.
And my grandfather was a peasant
    Without line or genealogy.
My house is a watchman's hut
    Made of sticks and reeds.
Does my status satisfy you?
    I am a name without a surname.

Put it on record.
    I am an Arab.
Color of hair: jet black.
Color of eyes: brown.
My distinguishing features:
    On my head the *'iqal* cords over a *keffiyeh*
    Scratching him who touches it.
My address:
    I'm from a village, remote, forgotten,

Its streets without name
And all its men in the fields and quarry.

What's there to be angry about?

Put it on record.
    I am an Arab.
You stole my forefathers' vineyards
    And land I used to till,
    I and all my children,
    And you left us and all my grandchildren
    Nothing but these rocks.
    Will your government be taking them too
    As is being said?

So!
    Put it on record at the top of page one:
    I don't hate people,
    I trespass on no one's property.
And yet, if I were to become hungry
    I shall eat the flesh of my usurper.
    Beware, beware of my hunger
    And of my anger!

Translated from the Arabic by Denys Johnson-Davies

On Wishes

Don't say to me:
    Would I were a seller of bread in Algiers
    That I might sing with a rebel.
Don't say to me:
    Would I were a herdsman in the Yemen
    That I might sing to the shudderings of time.
Don't say to me:
    Would I were a café waiter in Havana
    That I might sing to the victories of sorrowing women.

Don't say to me:
    Would I worked as a young laborer in Aswan
    That I might sing to the rocks.

My friend,
The Nile will not flow into the Volga,
Nor the Congo or the Jordan into the Euphrates.
Each river has its source, its course, its life.
My friend, our land is not barren.
Each land has its time for being born,
Each dawn a date with a rebel.

Translated from the Arabic by Denys Johnson-Davies

Victim Number 48

They found in his chest a lamp of roses and a moon
And he thrown dead upon the stones.
In his pocket they found a few piastres,
A box of matches, a travel pass,
And tattoo marks upon his young arm.

His mother missed him,
Mourned him year after year.
Boxthorn sprouted in his eyes
And darkness thickened.

When his brother grew up
And went looking for work in the city's markets
They put him in prison:
He carried no travel pass.
All he carried in the street was a box of garbage
And other boxes.

So, children of my country,
Thus did the moon die.

Translated from the Arabic by Denys Johnson-Davies

Steps in the Night

Always,
    We hear at night approaching steps
And the door flees from our room,
Always,
Like departing clouds.

Your blue shadow, who draws it away
Each night from my bed?
The steps come on, and your eyes are countries,
Your arms a blockade around my body.
And the steps come on,
Why does the shadow that depicts me flee,
O Shahrzad?
And the steps come on and do not enter.
Be a tree,
That I may see your shade.
Be a moon,
That I may see your shade.
Be a dagger,
That I may see your shade in mine,
A rose in ashes.
Always,
I hear at night approaching steps,
And you become my places of exile,
You become my prisons.
Try to kill me
Once and for all.
Do not kill me
With approaching steps.

Translated from the Arabic by Denys Johnson-Davies

We Walk Towards a Land

We walk towards a land not of our flesh,
Not of our bones its chestnut trees,
Its stones unlike the curly goats
Of the Song of Songs.
We walk towards a land
That does not hang a special sun for us.
Mythic women clap:
A sea around us,
A sea upon us.
If wheat and water do not reach you,
Eat our love and drink our tears.
Black veils of mourning for the poets.
You have your victories and we have ours,
We have a country where we see
Only the invisible.

Translated from the Arabic by Rana Kabbani

Sirhan Drinks His Coffee in the Cafeteria

They arrive.
Our doors are the sea.
The rain surprised us.
No God but God.
The rain surprised us, and the bullets.
The earth here is a carpet,
And they continue to arrive.

You do not know the day.
You cannot tell the color,
Nor the taste. Nor the voice.
You do not know the shape.
Sirhan is born, and Sirhan grows.
He drinks the wine and raves,

He draws his killer and he tears the picture,
He kills him when he sees his final shape.

Sirhan writes upon his jacket's sleeve
And memory takes a bird's beak
And eats the wheat of Galilee.

What was love?
Hands that were expressive,
Chains and prisons being formed,
Exiles being born.
We wrap around your name.
We were a people now we are of stone.
You were a country now you are of smoke.
Old chains are bracelets of blown roses
Old chains are maidenhead and passion
In this new exile.

Sirhan lies when he says he drank your milk.
Sirhan grew up in the kitchens of a ship
Which never touched your shores.

    What is your name?
    I've forgotten.
    What is your father's name?
    I've forgotten.
    And your mother's?
    I've forgotten.
    Did you sleep last night?
    I slept for an eternity.
    Did you dream?
    I dreamt.
He cried suddenly:
    Why did you drink the oil you smuggled
    From the wounds of Christ?

We saw his fingers begging.
We saw him measuring the sky with chains.
Lands that change their people,
Stars that spread like pebbles.

He sang:
Our generation passed and died.
The killers bred in us the victims grew in us
Blood like water.
Mothers who married enemies.
We called out, "wheat!"
The echo came back "war"
We called out, "home!"
The echo came back "war"
We called out, "Jaffa!"
The echo came back "war"
From that day on we measured skies with chains.

Sirhan laughs in the kitchens of the ship.
He holds a tourist and is lost.
All lands are far that lead to Nazareth.
All lands are far except for Nazareth.

Songs speak to him, and holidays make him lonely.
The smell of coffee is geography.
They exiled you.
They murdered you.
Your father hid behind the texts
And watched them come.
The smell of coffee is a tender hand.
The smell of coffee is a voice that takes you.
The smell of coffee is a sound that gurgles
Like the water in the alleys when it rains.

Sirhan knows more than one language
Or one woman. He has a pass to leave the ocean
He has another pass to enter it.
He is a drop of blood looking for its wound.
The smell of coffee is geography.
He drinks his coffee and he dreams.

You were born here. Yet you live there.
Your city does not sleep. It has no lasting names.
Houses change inhabitants,
Windows leave their places as they enter memory.

Sirhan draws a shape then cancels it.
He does not read the papers, so how does sorrow
Reach him?

What is Jerusalem but a stance for speeches,
But a step to hungry power?
What is Jerusalem but cigarettes and liquor?
Yet it is my country.
You would not find a difference
Between its curved fields
And my palm.
You could not find the difference
Between the night that sleeps in memory
And the night upon the Carmel.

He tears the clouds apart
And throws them at the winds.

I ate. I drank. I slept. I dreamt.
I learnt a vowel.
He writes: ص ط ض ع ظ
And they disappear before him,
The dins of oceans in them,
The din of silence in them.
Letters to distinguish us from others.
We stone them with our diphthongs.
Shall we fight?
What matter,
Since the Arab revolution
Remains preserved in anthems,
In flags and at the bank.
In your wounds' name they speak their speech.
Christ becomes a dealer
Who signs away his merchandise of cloth.
No sky for you except this tent:
It burns, you burn.

We come to you as prisoners or corpses.
Sirhan a prisoner of the peace and war.
He reads the details of his fate

On the wall behind the stripper's legs:
Your war is two wars,
Your war is two wars.

Sirhan!
Did you kill?
Sirhan is silent.
He drinks his coffee and he dreams.
He draws a map without a border in it.
He measures earth with chains.
He draws a picture of his killer,
He rips it up,
Then kills it when it takes a final shape.

Translated from the Arabic by Rana Kabbani

Words

When my words were wheat
I was earth.
When my words were anger
I was storm.
When my words were rock
I was river
When my words turned honey
Flies covered my lips.

Translated from the Arabic by Rana Kabbani

Guests on the Sea

Guests on the sea: Our visit is short
our talk is notes from the past shattered an hour ago
from what Mediterranean will the creation begin?

We set up an island
for our southern cry. Farewell, small island of ours.

We did not come to this country from a country
we came from pomegranates, from the glue of memory
from the fragments of an idea we came to this foam
Do not ask us how long we will stay among you, do not ask us
anything about our visit. Let us
empty the slow ships from the remains of our souls and our
    bodies.
Guests on the sea. Our visit is short.
And the earth is smaller than our visit. We shall send another
    apple
to the waters, circles within circles, where are we to go
when we leave? Where are we to go back to when we return? My
    God
what is left of the resistance of our souls? What directions are left
What earthen frontiers are left? Is there another rock
over which to offer a new sacrifice for your mercy?
What is left of us that we may set out once again?

Sea, do not give us the song that we do not deserve.

The sea has its ancient craft:
ebb and flow;
woman has her first task: seduction
it is for poets to fall from melancholy
it is for martyrs to explode in dream
it is for wise men to lead a people on towards happy dreams

Sea, do not give us the song that we do not deserve

We did not come to this place from the language of place
the plants of the distance have grown tall, the shadow of the sand
    has grown long within us and spread out
our short visit has grown long. How many moons have given their
    rings to one who is not of us. How many stones
has the swallow laid in the distance. How many years
shall we sleep as guests on the sea, wait for a place
and say: In a little while we shall leave here.

We have died from sleep and have broken here.
It is only the temporary that will last in us, age of the sea.

Sea, do not give us the song that we do not deserve

We want to live for a time, not for nothing
but just that we can set out again
Nothing of our ancestors remains in us, but we want
the country of our morning coffee
we want the fragrance of primitive plants
we want a special school
we want a special cemetery
we want a freedom
the size of a skull . . . and a song.

Sea, do not give us the song that we do not deserve

we did not come just for the sake of coming . . .
the sea tossed us up at Carthage as shells and a star
who can remember how the words lit up into a homeland for
    those who have no doorway?
Who remembers the ancient bedouins when they seized the world
    . . . with a word?
Who remembers the slain as they rushed to break the secrets of
    the myths?
They forget us, we forget them, life lives its own life.
Who now remembers the beginning and the end?
We wish to live for a time just to return to something
anything
anything
to a beginning, an island, a ship, an ending
a widow's prayer, a cellar, a tent.
Our short visit has grown long
and the sea died within us two years ago . . . the sea has died
    within us.

Sea, do not give us the song that we do not deserve

Translated from the Arabic by Lena Jayyusi and W. S. Merwin

YEHUDA AMICHAI

Israel (b. 1924)

Yehuda Amichai was born to a merchant family of Orthodox Jews in southern Germany—his ancestors had lived there since the Middle Ages—and grew up speaking both German and Hebrew, and steeped in the German literary tradition. At age eleven he emigrated with his parents to Palestine. He fought with the British army during World War II and as a commando with the Haganah underground during the 1948 war. His work began to appear in the 1950s, and he was among the first to compose poems in colloquial Israeli Hebrew. He is now generally considered Israel's most important and influential poet, and in addition to his many collections of poetry he has written novels, plays, and essays. History is an inevitable subject, but his poems remain resolutely autobiographical and ironic, rich with anecdote and fantasy. Amichai thinks of himself as hurling metaphors against violence. "I am politically engaged," he has said, "because everyone in Israel—on the right or left—exists under political pressures and existential tensions. . . . My personal history has coincided with a larger history. For me it's always been one and the same." He uses religion rather than believes in it and turns to love as a source of wonder and perplexity. The slyness of his voice and its straightforward tone ("saying emotional things dryly" is his aim) sometimes disguise his technical virtuosity. He has said: "A modern, or postmodern, composer might take the heart of a Bach fugue and break it open, expand it; what I do is put jazzy language and techniques within classical forms, juxtaposing different, sometimes competing, languages and forms."

Letter

> To sit on the veranda of a hotel in Jerusalem
> and to write: Sweetly pass the days
> from desert to sea. And to write: Tears, here,
> dry quickly. This little blot
> is a tear that has melted ink. That's how
> they wrote a hundred years ago. "I have
> drawn a circle round it."

Time passes—like somebody who, on a telephone,
is laughing or weeping far away from me:
whatever I'm hearing I can't see.
And whatever I see I don't hear.

We were not careful when we said "next year"
or "a month ago." These words are like
glass splinters, which you can hurt yourself with,
or cut veins. Those who do things like that.

But you were beautiful, like the interpretation
of ancient books.
Surplus of women in your far country
brought you to me, but
other statistics have taken you
away from me.

To live is to build a ship and a harbor
at the same time. And to complete the harbor
long after the ship was drowned.

And to finish: I remember only
that there was mist. And whoever
remembers only mist—
what does he remember?

Translated from the Hebrew by Ted Hughes and the author

Quick and Bitter

The end was quick and bitter.
Slow and sweet was the time between us,
slow and sweet were the nights
when my hands did not touch one another in despair
but in the love of your body
which came between them.

And when I entered into you
it seemed then that great happiness
could be measured with the precision
of sharp pain. Quick and bitter.

Slow and sweet were the nights.
Now is bitter and grinding as sand—
"Let's be sensible" and similar curses.

And as we stray further from love
we multiply the words,
words and sentences so long and orderly.
Had we remained together
we could have become a silence.

Translated from the Hebrew by Assia Gutmann

A Man in His Life

A man in his life has no time to have
Time for everything.
He has no room to have room
For every desire. Ecclesiastes was wrong to claim that.

A man has to hate and love all at once,
With the same eyes to cry and to laugh
With the same hands to throw stones
And to gather them,
Make love in war and war in love.

And hate and forgive and remember and forget
And order and confuse and eat and digest
What long history does
In so many years.

A man in his life has no time.
When he loses he seeks

When he finds he forgets
When he forgets he loves
When he loves he begins forgetting.

And his soul is knowing
And very professional,
Only his body remains an amateur
Always. It tries and fumbles.
He doesn't learn and gets confused,
Drunk and blind in his pleasures and pains.

In autumn, he will die like a fig,
Shriveled, sweet, full of himself.
The leaves dry out on the ground,
And the naked branches point
To the place where there is time for everything.

Translated from the Hebrew by Benjamin Harshav and Barbara Harshav

Anniversaries of War

Tel Gath

I brought my children to the mound
Where once I fought battles,
So they would understand the things I did do
And forgive me for the things I didn't do.

The distance between my striding legs and my head
Grows bigger and I grow smaller.
Those days grow away from me,
These times grow away from me too,
And I'm in the middle, without them, on this mound
With my children.

A light afternoon wind blows
But only a few people move in the blowing wind,
Bend down a little with the grass and the flowers.
Dandelions cover the mound.
You could say, as dandelions in multitude.

I brought my children to the mound
And we sat there, "on its back and its side"
As in the poem by Shmuel Ha-Nagid in Spain,
Like me, a man of hills and a man of wars,
Who sang a lullaby to his soldiers before the battle.

Yet I did not talk to my heart, as he did,
But to my children. To the mound, we were the resurrection,
Fleeting like this springtime, eternal like it too.

Ruhama

In this wadi, we camped in the days of the war.
Many years have passed since, many victories,
Many defeats. Many consolations I gathered in my life
And wasted, much sorrow have I collected and spilled out in vain,
Many things I said, like the waves of the sea
In Ashkelon, to the west, always saying the same things.
But as long as I live, my soul remembers
And my body ripens slowly in the flame of its own annals.

The evening sky bends down like the sound of a trumpet
Above us, and the lips move like lips in a prayer
Before there was any God in the world.

Here we lay by day, and at night we went to battle.
The smell of the sand as it was, and the smell of eucalyptus leaves
As it was, and the smell of the wind as it was.

And I do now what every memory dog does:
I howl quietly

And piss a turf of remembrance around me,
No one may enter it.

Huleikat—the Third Poem About Dicky

In these hills, even the towers of oil wells
Are a mere memory. Here Dicky fell,
Four years older than me, like a father to me
In times of trouble and distress. Now I am older than him
By forty years and I remember him
Like a young son, and I am his father, old and grieving.

And you, who remember only faces,
Do not forget the hands stretched out,
The feet running lightly,
The words.

Remember: even the departure to terrible battles
Passes by gardens and windows
And children playing, a dog barking.

Remind the fallen fruit
Of its leaves and branches,
Remind the sharp thorns
How soft and green they were in springtime,
And do not forget,
Even a fist
Was once an open palm and fingers.

The Shore of Ashkelon

Here, at the shore of Ashkelon, we reached the end of memory,
Like rivers reaching the sea.
The near past sinks into the far past,
And from the depths, the far overflows the near.
Peace to him that is far off and to him that is near.

Here, among broken statues and pillars,
I ask how did Samson bring down the temple
Standing eyeless, saying: "Let me die with the Philistines."

Did he embrace the pillars as in a last love
Or did he push them away with his arms,
To be alone in his death.

What Did I Learn in the Wars

What did I learn in the wars:
To march in time to swinging arms and legs
Like pumps pumping an empty well.

To march in a row and be alone in the middle,
To dig into pillows, featherbeds, the body of a beloved woman,
And to yell "Mama," when she cannot hear,
And to yell "God," when I don't believe in Him,
And even if I did believe in Him
I wouldn't have told Him about the war
As you don't tell a child about grown-ups' horrors.

What else did I learn. I learned to reserve a path for retreat.
In foreign lands I rent a room in a hotel
Near the airport or railroad station.
And even in wedding halls
Always to watch the little door
With the "Exit" sign in red letters.

A battle too begins
Like rhythmical drums for dancing and ends
With a "retreat at dawn." Forbidden love
And battle, the two of them sometimes end like this.

But above all I learned the wisdom of camouflage,
Not to stand out, not to be recognized,
Not to be apart from what's around me,
Even not from my beloved.

Let them think I am a bush or a lamb,
A tree, a shadow of a tree,
A doubt, a shadow of a doubt,
A living hedge, a dead stone,
A house, a corner of a house.

If I were a prophet I would have dimmed the glow of the vision
And darkened my faith with black paper
And covered the magic with nets.

And when my time comes, I shall don the camouflage garb of my
    end:
The white of clouds and a lot of sky blue
And stars that have no end.

Translated from the Hebrew by Benjamin Harshav and Barbara Harshav

Four Resurrections in the Valley of the Ghosts

First Resurrection

A woman who looks like my mother sees a man who looks like
    me,
They pass each other without turning around.

Mistakes are marvelous and simple as life and death,
As the arithmetic book of a small child.

In the shelter for wayward girls, girls singing on the balcony
Hang their clothes out to dry, banners of love.

In the fiber institute they make ropes of fiber
To bind souls in the bundle of life.

An afternoon wind blows, as if asking:
What did you do, what did you talk about.

In old stone houses young women do in the day
What the mothers of their mothers dreamed of doing at night.

The Armenian church is empty and closed
Like an abandoned wife whose husband went far off and
   disappeared.

Wayward girls sing, "God will bring the dead to life
In His great mercy" and fold their dried clothes.
"Blessed forever be His name."

Second Resurrection

In the public park, pots that once held plants—
Now empty and crumpled like discarded wombs.

Seesaws and slides, like instruments of torture,
Or like wings of a big bird or a falling angel.

And the ancient ceremony begins,
A father tells his little son:

"So I'm going,
And you stay here alone."

So are summer and winter in their due time, so are
Generations in their changes, so those who remain, those who go.

Third Resurrection

With the pleading voice of a beggar
I praise the world.

With a voice crying for help from the depths,
I laud.

A young woman curses her mother
Who left her fat thighs.

I bless her,
And her too.

The sadness of parted lovers is empty here, hollow as a drum.

People wrote on the gate of their home:
"Strangers No Entrance"
But they themselves are strangers.

At the wall of the Christian cemetery
A violated telephone booth,
The torn wires hanging, like veins
And arteries: waiting for their time.

Fourth Resurrection

I saw the seats of a torn-down movie house
Lying in an empty lot,
Taken out of their dark home
And abandoned to the cruel sun,
Broken seats with fragments of numbered rows:
24, 26, 28, 30 with 7, 9, 11, 13.

And I asked myself: Where are the feats and where are the words
That were on the screen. *Who in fire and who in water,*
And where are those who sat in these seats,
Where is their lament and where is their laughter,
Where are their roads and where are their oaths,
And what are the sights and the images they see,
And what are the words they hear now.
Are they still sitting in numbered rows
Or standing in long lines,
And how will they arise to life and where.

Translated from the Hebrew by Benjamin Harshav and Barbara Harshav

Little Ruth

Sometimes I remember you, little Ruth,
We were separated in our distant childhood and they burned you
    in the camps.
If you were alive now, you would be a woman of sixty-five,
A woman on the verge of old age. At twenty you were burned
And I don't know what happened to you in your short life
Since we separated. What did you achieve, what insignia
Did they put on your shoulders, your sleeves, your
Brave soul, what shining stars
Did they pin on you, what decorations for valor, what
Medals for love hung around your neck,
What peace upon you, *peace unto you.*
And what happened to the unused years of your life?
Are they still packed away in pretty bundles,
Were they added to my life? Did you turn me
Into your bank of love like the banks in Switzerland
Where assets are preserved even after their owners are dead?
Will I leave all this to my children
Whom you never saw?

You gave your life to me, like a wine dealer
Who remains sober himself.
You sober in death, lucid in the dark
For me, drunk on life, wallowing in my forgetfulness.
Now and then, I remember you in times
Unbelievable. And in places not made for memory
But for the transient, the passing that does not remain.
As in an airport, when the arriving travelers
Stand tired at the revolving conveyor belt
That brings their suitcases and packages,
And they identify theirs with cries of joy
As at a resurrection and go out into their lives;
And there is one suitcase that returns and disappears again
And returns again, ever so slowly, in the empty hall,
Again and again it passes.
This is how your quiet figure passes by me,

This is how I remember you until
The conveyor belt stands still. *And they stood still. Amen.*

Translated from the Hebrew by Benjamin Harshav and Barbara Harshav

We Have Done Our Duty

We did our duty.
We went out with our children
To gather mushrooms in the forest
Which we planted ourselves when we were children.

We learned the names of wildflowers
Whose aroma was
Like blood spilled in vain.
We laid a big love on small bodies,
We stood enlarged and shrunken in turn,
In the eyes of the holder of the binoculars,
Divine and mad.

And in the war of the sons of light and the sons of darkness
We loved the good and soothing darkness
And hated the painful light.
We did our duty,
We loved our children
More than our homeland,
We dug all the wells into the earth
And now we dig into the space of the skies,
Well after well, with no beginning, no end.

We did our duty,
The words *you shall remember* we changed to "we will forget"
As they change a bus schedule
When the direction of the route changes,
Or as they change the plaques
Of *Dew and Showers* and *He Who Brings Rain* in the synagogue
When the seasons change.

We did our duty,
We arranged our lives in flowerbeds and shadows
And straight paths, pleasant for walking,
Like the garden of a mental hospital.

Our despair is domesticated and gives us peace,
Only the hopes have remained,
Wild hopes, their screams
Shatter the night and rip up the day.

We did our duty.
We were like people entering a moviehouse,
Passing by those coming out, red-faced
Or pale, crying quietly or laughing aloud,
And they enter without a second glance, without
Turning back, into the light and the dark and the light.
We have done our duty.

Translated from the Hebrew by Benjamin Harshav and Barbara Harshav

DAN PAGIS

Israel (1930–1986)

Dan Pagis was born in German-speaking Bukovina, at the time a part of Austria, later of Romania, and now of Russia. During World War II he spent three years in a Nazi concentration camp. In 1946 he emigrated to Israel, learned Hebrew, and began writing poetry in that language within a few years. At first he taught in a kibbutz, but eventually he earned his doctorate from Hebrew University in Jerusalem. He became a professor there of medieval Hebrew literature, a field in which he published important books. Eight collections of his poems appeared, all marked by a subtle lyric power and haunted by the past. Wit, learning, nostalgia, irony: Pagis used the resources of poetry to confront suffering.

Autobiography

I died with the first blow and was buried
among the rocks of the field.
The raven taught my parents
what to do with me.

If my family is famous,
not a little of the credit goes to me.
My brother invented murder,
my parents invented grief,
I invented silence.

Afterward the well-known events took place.
Our inventions were perfected. One thing led to another,
orders were given. There were those who murdered in their own
    way,
grieved in their own way.

I won't mention names
out of consideration for the reader,

since at first the details horrify
though finally they're a bore:

you can die once, twice, even seven times,
but you can't die a thousand times.
I can.
My underground cells reach everywhere.

When Cain began to multiply on the face of the earth,
I began to multiply in the belly of the earth,
and my strength has long been greater than his.
His legions desert him and go over to me,
and even this is only half a revenge.

Translated from the Hebrew by Stephen Mitchell

Footprints

From heaven to the heaven of heavens to the heaven of night
                                    Yannai

Against my will
I was continued by this cloud: restless, gray,
trying to forget in the horizon, which always receded

Hail falling hard,
like the chatter of teeth:
refugee pellets pushing eagerly
into their own destruction

In another sector
clouds not yet identified.
Searchlights that set up
giant crosses of light
for the victim.
Unloading of cattle cars.

Afterward the letters fly up,
after the flying letters mud
hurries, snuffs, covers for a time

It's true, I was a mistake, I was forgotten
in the sealed car, my body tied up
in the sack of life

Here's the pocket where I found bread,
sweet crumbs, all from the same world
Maybe there's a window here—if you don't mind,
look near that body, maybe you can open up
a bit. That reminds me
(pardon me) of the joke about the two Jews
in the train, they were traveling to

Say something more; talk.
Can I pass from my body and onward—

•

From heaven to the heaven of heavens to the heaven of night
long convoys of smoke

The new seraphim who haven't yet understood,
prisoners of hope, astray in the empty freedom,
suspicious as always: how to exploit
this sudden vacuum, maybe
the double citizenship will help,
the old passport,
maybe the cloud? what's new in the cloud,
here too of course
they take bribes. And between us: the biggest bills
are still nicely hidden away, sewn
between the soles—
but the shoes have been piled up below:
a great gaping heap

Convoys of smoke. Sometimes
someone breaks away,

recognizes me for some reason, calls my name.
And I put on a pleasant face, try to remember:
who else
who

Without any right to remember, I remember
a man screaming in a corner, bayonets rising
to fulfill their role
in him

Without any right to remember. What else
was there? Already I'm not afraid
that I might say

without any connection at all:
there was a heart, blue from excessive winter,
and a lamp, round, blue, kindhearted.
But the kerosene disappears with the blood, the flame flickers—

Yes, before I forget:
the rain stole across some border, so did I,
on forbidden escape routes, with forbidden hope,
we both passed the mouth of the pits

Maybe now
I'm looking in that rain
for the scarlet thread

Where to begin?
I don't even know how to ask.
Too many tongues are mixed in my mouth. But
at the crossing of these winds,
very diligent, I immerse myself
in the laws of heavenly grammar: I am learning
the declensions and ascensions of
silence.

Who has given you the right to jest?
What is above you you already know.

You meant to ask about what is within you,
what is abysmally through you.
How is it that you did not see?

But I didn't know I was alive.
From the heaven of heavens to the heaven of night
angels rushed, sometimes one of them
would look back, see me, shrug his shoulders,
continue from my body and onward

◆

Frozen and burst, clotted,
scarred,
charred, choked.

If it has been ordained that I pull out of here,
I'll try to descend rung by rung,
I hold on to each one, carefully—
but there is no end to the ladder, and already
no time. All I can still do is fall
into the world

And on my way back
my eyes hint to me:
you have been, what more did you want to see?
Close us and see:
you are the darkness, you are the sign.

And my throat says to me:
if you are still alive, give me an opening, I
must praise.

And my upside-down head is faithful to me,
and my hands hold me tight:
I am falling   falling
from heaven to the heaven of heavens to the heaven of night

◆

Well then: a world.
The gray is reconciled by the blue.
In the gate of this cloud, already a turquoise
innocence, perhaps light green. Already sleep.
Heavens renew themselves, try out their wings, see me

and run for their lives. I no longer wonder.
The gate bursts open:
a lake
void   void   pure of reflections

Over there,
in that arched blue, on the edge of the air,
I once lived. My window was fragile.
Maybe what remained of me
were little gliders that hadn't grown up:
they still repeat themselves in still-clouds, glide,
slice the moment
        (not to remember now, not to remember)

And before I arrive
        (now to stretch out to the end, to stretch out)
already awake, spread to the tips of my wings,
against my will I feel that, very near,
inside, imprisoned by hopes, there flickers
this ball of the earth,
scarred, covered with footprints.

Translated from the Hebrew by Stephen Mitchell

Conversation

Four talked about the pine tree. One defined it by genus, species, and
variety. One assessed its disadvantages for the lumber industry. One
quoted poems about pine trees in many languages. One took root,
stretched out branches, and rustled.

Translated from the Hebrew by Stephen Mitchell

Picture Postcard from Our Youth

On your piano a plaster Beethoven stands
and thinks: Thank goodness I've gone deaf.
Even the neighborhood sparrows are singing out of tune this
    morning.

Only the Kurdish peddler is being true to himself
as he limps along the street shouting *Old clothes!*
in his bargain-basement Hebrew.

It doesn't matter. From the tangle of voices, the one voice ascends.
A blue bell of air
arches above us.

Translated from the Hebrew by Stephen Mitchell

Wall Calendar

December. An arctic wind, new
And bitter. Angels and polar bears
Sink into their winter slumber.
Just then,
Above, in the folds of soft snow,
The traps of spring get set.

June. In a military ceremony
Filled with sunshine,
The man is buried at noon.
Just then
It is midnight in the woman's belly. The fetus
Reports for duty: he recognizes the code.

December. Suddenly the boat
Turns over, I drown in a squalid
Sea, and watch, as expected,

Just then
All my stolen years drift by
Like sweet water.

Translated from the Hebrew by Tsipi Keller

DAHLIA RAVIKOVITCH

Israel (b. 1936)

Born in Ramat Gan, a suburb of Tel Aviv, Dahlia Ravikovitch studied at Hebrew University in Jerusalem and has since worked as a teacher and journalist. She has written fiction, books for children, and several collections of poems, which have been awarded many literary prizes in Israel. Her poetry is always lyrical and often visionary; she kneads her images into intense, sometimes startling epiphanies. Over the years her style has grown more colloquial, her verse more relaxed. After her country's 1982 invasion of Lebanon, she joined with many other Israeli poets in writing to protest its brutality. Antiwar poems rarely survive their occasion, but when Ravikovitch writes of the rape of a young Arab shepherdess—as she does in "Hovering at a Low Altitude"—she makes a military horror into a moral fable of violence and detachment that continues to haunt.

Trying Again

If I could only get all of you,
how could I ever get all of you—
even more than beloved icons,
more than a quarried mountainside,
more than mines
of burning coal,
say the mines of extinguished coal
and the breath of day burning like a furnace.

If I could get you for all the years,
how could I ever get you from all the years—
how to stretch out one arm
like a river branching in Africa,
like dreaming the Bay of Storms,
dreaming a ship that went down,
the way you imagine clouds as a bed,
lilies of clouds spread beneath you,

but when you need them they won't support you,
don't believe they'll support you.

If I could get hold of every particle of you,
if I could get hold of you like metal—
say pillars of copper,
a pillar of purple copper (that pillar
I remembered last summer)—
and the bottom of the ocean I've never seen,
the bottom of the ocean I see
under the weight of a thousand layers of air,
a thousand and one held breaths.

If I could only have all of you
as you are now,
how could you ever become
like a part of me.

Translated from the Hebrew by Chana Bloch and Ariel Bloch

Surely You Remember

After they all leave,
I remain alone with the poems,
some poems of mine, some of others.
I prefer poems that others have written.
I remain quiet, and slowly
the knot in my throat dissolves.
I remain.

Sometimes I wish everyone would go away.
Maybe it's nice, after all, to write poems.
You sit in your room and the walls grow taller.
Colors deepen.
A blue kerchief becomes a deep well.

You wish everyone would go away.
You don't know what's the matter with you.

Perhaps you'll think of something.
Then it all passes, and you are pure crystal.

After that, love.
Narcissus was so much in love with himself.
Only a fool doesn't understand
he loved the river, too.

You sit alone.
Your heart aches, but
it won't break.
The faded images wash away one by one.
Then the defects.
A sun sets at midnight. You remember
the dark flowers too.

You wish you were dead or alive or
somebody else.
Isn't there a country you love? A word?
Surely you remember.

Only a fool lets the sun set when it likes.
It always drifts off too early
westward to the islands.

Sun and moon, winter and summer
will come to you,
infinite treasures.

Translated from the Hebrew by Chana Bloch and Ariel Bloch

A Dress of Fire

You know, she said, they made you
a dress of fire.
Remember how Jason's wife burned in her dress?
It was Medea, she said, Medea did that to her.

You've got to be careful, she said,
they made you a dress that glows
like an ember, that burns like coals.

Are you going to wear it, she said, don't wear it.
It's not the wind whistling, it's the poison
seeping in.
You're not even a princess, what can you do to Medea?
Can't you tell one sound from another, she said,
it's not the wind whistling.

Remember, I told her, that time when I was six?
They shampooed my hair and I went out into the street.
The smell of shampoo trailed after me like a cloud.
Then I got sick from the wind and the rain.
I didn't know a thing about reading Greek tragedies,
but the smell of the perfume spread
and I was very sick.
Now I can see it's an unnatural perfume.

What will happen to you now, she said,
they made you a burning dress.
They made me a burning dress, I said. I know.
So why are you standing there, she said,
you've got to be careful.
You know what a burning dress is, don't you?

I know, I said, but I don't know
how to be careful.
The smell of that perfume confuses me.
I said to her, No one has to agree with me,
I don't believe in Greek tragedies.

But the dress, she said, the dress is on fire.
What are you saying, I shouted,
what are you saying?
I'm not wearing a dress at all,
what's burning is me.

Translated from the Hebrew by Chana Bloch and Ariel Bloch

The Sound of Birds at Noon

This chirping
is not in the least malicious.
They sing without giving us a thought
and they are as many
as the seed of Abraham.
They have a life of their own,
they fly without thinking.
Some are rare, some common,
but every wing is grace.
Their hearts aren't heavy
even when they peck at a worm.
Perhaps they're light-headed.
The heavens were given to them
to rule over day and night
and when they touch a branch,
the branch too is theirs.
This chirping is entirely free of malice.
Over the years
it even seems to have
a note of compassion.

Translated from the Hebrew by Chana Bloch and Ariel Bloch

You Can't Kill a Baby Twice

By the sewage puddles of Sabra and Shatila,
there you transported human beings
in impressive quantities
from the world of the living to the world
of eternal light.

Night after night.
First they shot,
they hanged,

then they slaughtered with their knives.
Terrified women climbed up
on a ramp of earth, frantic:
"They're slaughtering us there,
in Shatila."

A thin crust of moon
over the camps.
Our soldiers lit up the place with searchlights
till it was bright as day.
"Back to the camp,
beat it!" a soldier yelled at
the screaming women from Sabra and Shatila.
He was following orders.
And the children already lying in puddles of filth,
their mouths gaping,
at peace.
No one will harm them.
You can't kill a baby twice.

And the moon grew fuller and fuller
till it became a round loaf of gold.

Our sweet soldiers
wanted nothing for themselves.
All they ever asked
was to come home
safe.

Translated from the Hebrew by Chana Bloch and Ariel Bloch

Hovering at a Low Altitude

I am not here.
I am on those craggy eastern hills
streaked with ice,
where grass doesn't grow

and a wide shadow lies over the slope.
A shepherd girl appears
from an invisible tent,
leading a herd of black goats to pasture.
She won't live out the day,
that girl.

I am not here.
From the deep mountain gorge
a red globe floats up,
not yet a sun.
A patch of frost, reddish, inflamed,
flickers inside the gorge.

The girl gets up early to go to the pasture.
She doesn't walk with neck outstretched
and wanton glances.
She doesn't ask, Whence cometh my help.

I am not here.
I've been in the mountains many days now.
The light will not burn me, the frost
won't touch me.
Why be astonished now?
I've seen worse things in my life.

I gather my skirt and hover
very close to the ground.
What is she thinking, that girl?
Wild to look at, unwashed.
For a moment she crouches down,
her cheeks flushed,
frostbite on the back of her hands.
She seems distracted, but no,
she's alert.

She still has a few hours left.
But that's not what I'm thinking about.
My thoughts cushion me gently, comfortably.
I've found a very simple method,

not with my feet on the ground, and not flying—
hovering
at a low altitude.

Then at noon,
many hours after sunrise,
that man goes up the mountain.
He looks innocent enough.

The girl is right there,
no one else around.
And if she runs for cover, or cries out—
there's no place to hide in the mountains.

I am not here.
I'm above those jagged mountain ranges
in the farthest reaches of the east.
No need to elaborate.
With one strong push I can hover and whirl around
with the speed of the wind.
I can get away and say to myself:
I haven't seen a thing.
And the girl, her palate is dry as a potsherd,
her eyes bulge,
when that hand closes over her hair, grasping it
without a shred of pity.

Translated from the Hebrew by Chana Bloch and Ariel Bloch

AFRICA

LEOPOLD SEDAR SENGHOR

Senegal (b. 1906)

Léopold Sédar Senghor was born in the small coastal town of Joal, then a part of French West Africa. When Senegal gained its independence in 1960, Senghor became his country's first president and served in that office for two decades. In 1983 he was elected to the French Academy, the first black African ever so honored. But many awards preceded his elevation, just as he had served in many important government posts before becoming president. As a young writer in Paris, along with Aimé Césaire and Léon Gontran Damas, he helped found the *négritude* movement. After graduating from the Sorbonne, he stayed on in France, teaching classical literature and African history. His first mature poems were written in the 1930s and often dwell on the conflicts between the African sensibility and European culture. Following his service in the French Colonial Army during World War II, he lived in Paris, New York, and Dakar, and was active in promoting—by means of journals and anthologies—the establishment of an African literature with a worldwide audience. His longer poems have a rapturous amplitude and are composed as if their emotional rhetoric were meant to be heard accompanied by African musical instruments. Yet for all their grand, outsized gestures, his poems remain the expression of a very personal, sometimes even private, point of view, a perspective fraught with loneliness and longing.

Pearls

White pearls,
Slow droplets,
Droplets of fresh milk,
Lights fleeing along telegraph lines,
Along the long monotonous gray days!
Where are you going?

To which paradise? Which paradise?
The first lights of my childhood
Never found again . . .

Translated from the French by Melvin Dixon

I Am Alone

I am alone in the plains
And in the night
With trees curled up from the cold
And holding tight, elbow to body, one to the other.

I am alone in the plains
And in the night
With the hopeless pathetic movements of trees
That have lost their leaves to other islands.

I am alone in the plains
And in the night.
I am the solitude of telegraph poles
Along deserted
Roads.

Translated from the French by Melvin Dixon

Before Night Comes

Before night comes I think of you and for you before I fall
Into the white net of anguish, and before twilight I walk
Along the borders of dreams and desires, among the sand gazelles
To bring poetry back to the Childhood Kingdom.

They stare at you astonished, like the young girl from Ferlo,
You remember her Fulani breasts and thighs, hills more melodious
Than saitic bronzes and her braided hair dancing as she danced,
And her huge, vacant eyes that lit up my night.

Is the light still so weightless in your limpid country
And the women too beautiful to be real?
If I saw the young girl again, or the woman now,

She would be you in the September sun,
Golden skin, melodious bearing, and those huge eyes
Like fortresses against death.

Translated from the French by Melvin Dixon

Song of the Initiate

to Alioune Diop

Tâgu-gûtût, nydyulê mômé!
Mûsê mbûbân, ndyulê mômé!
Let the circumcised wear their bonnets!
Let the circumcised wear their robes!
                    Wolof poem

(for three flutes)

Pilgrimage along the migratory roads, a voyage to ancestral
        sources.

Ebony flute, smooth and shiny, penetrates the mists of my
        memory
O flute! The haze is a pagne over my sleep and my original face.
O sing of the elemental light and sing of the silence announcing
The ivory gong of the rising Sun, clearing my befuddled memory,
Light on her twin hills, on the melodious curve and her cheeks.
I sit under the peace of a mahogany tree in the odor of herds
And wild honey. The Sun of her smile!
And the dew shining on the indigo grass of her lips.
The hummingbirds shriek, airborne flowers, the inexpressible
        grace
Of her words, the kingfishers dive into her eyes
In a sparkling blue naïveté of joy by the streaming
Rice fields, her lashes rustle rhythmically in the clear air
And I hear the hour, O delights! rising to the white center
Of the sky draped with flags.

CONTEMPORARY WORLD POETRY

The herds and the cooing doves will soon be immobile
In the noon shade, but I must rise to pursue my pure passion.

(for two horns and one gorong)

O horn to my rescue! I was lost in the forest of her hair,
Horn beneath your black patina, ivory slowly ripened in black
  mud.
I slip on the elephants' footprints on the soapy bridge
Of her riddles. How can I unravel the ruse of vines,
Appease the hissing snakes? And once again a wounded call,
And only an evil siren responds. Once again a moaning call,
But only the cries of mute birds answer me,
Like children slaughtered at night, and the flight of red
Monkeys. The tsetses and hummingbirds aggravate my anguish,
And I sweat and tremble from the cold. But the response
Of her clear song in the clearing is the assurance that guides me
And the scents of remembered flowers in whose happy shouts I
  bathe.
The green gold of her complexion softer than copper
Was as smooth as her soul exhausted in the sun and trade wind,
Bouquets of palm fronds above primal fears,
O Ancient Forest, lost roads, hear this Pilgrim's toneless song.

(for two balaphons and one gorong)

Beyond the putrid swamp of entrails lies the freedom
Of the plains, a savanna as black as I, a fire of Death
That prepares the rebirth, a rebirth of Feeling and Spirit.
Then the white gold of sand under sunlight where my desire
Is consumed in pure vibration and fervent spaces.
But sing to my willing ears the mirage of oases,
For the temptation of dry mists assails me, trying to oppress
My faith. Ah! May the twin chimes sound lively!
Let the drum of the Initiates grumble!
As one who is circumcised, I pass the test. The flames
Of a thousand *aderas* will guide me along the straight paths,
Candles on the sanctuary road that will guide me again
With its smell, the aroma of sweet gum in the harmattan.

(for three drums: gorong, talmbatt, *and* mbalakh*)*

There emerging from the Night, the pure high altar
And its granite brow, then the line from its eyebrows
Like the fresh shadow of a *kori.*
To the Pilgrim whose eyes are washed by fasting, ashes,
And keeping watch, the red Lion's head appears in surreal
Majesty in the rising Sun, above the supreme zenith.
O Killer! O Terrifying One! I surrender and grow weak.
I have no antelope's horn, only an empty trumpet and my full
Double sack. O! may you strike me down with your twin flashes,
—The fearful sweetness of their roar! the unrelenting.
Delight of their claws! And may I die suddenly
To be reborn in the revelation of Beauty!
Silence, silence in the shade . . . muffled tom-tom . . .
Slow tom-tom . . . heavy tom-tom . . . black tom-tom . . .

(for two horns and one balaphon)

She flees, she flees through the white flat land, while I take
Careful aim, giddy with desire. Is she in the bush of games,
Passions of thorns and thickets? Then shall I force her
To the chains of time, inhaling the sweet breath of her flanks
Of speckled shadows, and at stupefying High Noon shall I
Twist her fragile arms. The antelope's rattle will intoxicate me
Like fresh palm wine and I shall drink for a long time
The wild blood that rises from her heart, the bloody milk
That flows to her mouth, the scent of the wet earth.

Am I not the son of Dyogoye, the hungry Lion?

(for two horns and a balaphon)

Listen to the barking dogs, bullets in the black stall of my belly.
Where are my yellow watchdogs with their hungry mugs?
Just my rifle girdled with sacred blood. I whistle to you
With a charming cry, dogs of my arms, dogs of my legs,
For I lost my heart in a basement cabaret in Montmartre.

Listen to the barking dogs, bullets in the black stall of my belly.
I have to hold back my blood at the end of its long cinnabar leash,
The son of Man, son of Lion, who roars in the hollow hills
Setting fire to a hundred villages with his male harmattan voice.

I will go leaping above the hills, defying the fear of wind
And steppes, defying the river-seas where virgin bodies drown
In the depth of their anguish. Then I will climb back up the sweet
    belly
Of dunes and the gleaming thighs of the day, up to the dark throat
Where a quick blow kills the striped fawn of my dream.

Translated from the French by Melvin Dixon

KOFI AWOONOR

Ghana (b. 1935)

Kofi Awoonor was born in the small farming village of Wheta, not far
from the sea, the son of a tailor and a chieftain's daughter. He was edu-
cated at the University of Ghana and studied further in London and New
York. He has served variously as the director of the film division of the
Ghana Ministry of Information, a professor at the State University of
New York at Stony Brook, and Ghana's ambassador to Brazil. In the
mid-1970s he was imprisoned for a year on charges of subversion, and he
wrote a strong series of poems about his captivity in Ussher Fort. He has
also written criticism, novels, plays, and screenplays. Awoonor's poetry
has been "very much an effort to move the oral poetry from which I
learnt so much into perhaps a higher literary plane." He has kept close to
the vernacular rhythms of African speech and poetry. "The written
word," he says, "came almost as if it had no forebears. So my poetry as-
says to restate the oral beginnings, to articulate the mysterious relation
between the *word* and the magical dimensions of our cognitive world. I
work with forces that are beyond me, ancestral and ritualized entities
who dictate and determine all my literary endeavors. Simply put, my
work takes off from the world of all our aboriginal instincts. It is for this
reason I have sat at the feet of ancient poets whose medium is the voice
and whose forum is the village square and the market place."

At the Gates

I do not know which god sent me,
to fall in the river and fall in the fire
these have failed me.
I move into the gates
demanding which war is it;
which war is it?
The dwellers in the gates
answer us; we will let that war come
they whom we followed to come

sons of our mothers and fathers
bearing upon our heads nothing
save the thunder that roars
who knows when evil matters will come.
Open the gates!
It is Akpabli Horsu* who sent me

Open the gates, my mother's children,
and let me enter.
Our thunder initiates have run amok
and we sleep in the desert land
not moving our feet.
We will sleep in the desert
guns in our hands we cannot fire
machetes in our hands we cannot throw
the death of a man is not far away.
I will drink it; it is my god who gave it to me
I will drink this calabash
for it is God's gift to me.
Bachelor, never go too far**
for the drummer boys will cook and let you eat.

Don't cry for me over
my daughter, death called her.
She is an offering of my heart.
The ram has not come to stay;
three days and it has gone.
Elders and chiefs, whom will you trust?
A snake has bitten my daughter and
whom will I trust?
Walk on gently; give me an offering
that I will give to God
and he will be happy.

---

*Akpabli Horsu: a famous Anlo warrior whose fame was widespread, and his name still is sung in songs.
**Bachelor, never go too far: The bachelor must not travel too far afield lest he suffer from hunger. There are many jokes about the bachelor. One famous one is: When you hear a bachelor scream, do not be in a hurry to go to his aid, for it is either his corn-flour bag or his beard which has caught fire.

Uproot the yams you planted
for everything comes from God
it is an evil god who sent me
that for all I have done
I bear the magic of the singer that has come
I have no paddle, my wish,
to push my boat into the river.

This Earth, My Brother

The dawn crack of sounds known
rending our air
shattering our temples toppling
raising earthwards our cathedrals of hope,
in demand of lives offered on those altars
for the cleansing that was done long ago.
Within the airwaves we carry
our hutted entrails; and we pray;
shrieks abandoned by lonely road-sides
as the gunmen's boots tramp.
I lift up the chalice of hyssop and tears
to touch the lips of the thirsty
sky-wailing in a million spires
of hate and death; we pray
bearing the single hope to shine
burnishing in the destiny of my race
that glinting sword of salvation.
In time my orchestra plays my music
from potted herbs of anemone and nim
pour upon the festering wounds of my race,
to wash forever my absorbent radiance
as we search our granary for new corn.
There was that miracle we hoped for
that salvation we longed for

for which we said many prayers
offered many offerings.

In the seasons of burning feet
of bad harvest and disastrous marriages
there burns upon the glint edge of that sword
the replica of the paschal knife.
The sounds rounded our lonely skies
among the nims the dancers gather their cloths
stretching their new-shorn hides off offered cows
to build themselves new drums.
Sky-wailing from afar the distant tramp
of those feet in rhythm
miming underneath them violence.
Along the roads lined with mimosas
the mangled and manacled are dragged
to the cheers of us all.
We strew flowers at the feet of the conquerors
beg for remission of our sins.

Lead the lame ram unto the sacrifice
and erect the final totem
to pierce the vaginal whole
await for the sacrifice coming.
Along those lonely paths lead
where we carry out gutted souls unto battle
to wage the war our fores waged
and lose those victories they lost
and rush home with songs of the harvest.
We pray.

Wayfarers attend upon the victors
cover my foot with unfurled flags.
For the moon rides its lonely horse
across my tarnished sky.
And I pray;
In the dusk I sit and count
marking off upon my heart strings
the beats registered. And I pray

to him who breathes me
washes me.

The crows fly upon the waves
glistening
rending apart the seams of our air
romping through to an eternal beginning
carrying away our entrails
on the ballast of my lonely earth.
Is this carnival of hate
my festival
and my talisman of hope?

He will come out of the grave
His clothes thrown around him;
worms shall not have done their work.
His face shall beam the radiance of many suns.
His gait the bearing of a victor,
On his forehead shall shine a thousand stars
he will kneel after the revelation
and die on this same earth.

    And I pray
That my hills shall be exalted
And he who washes me,
    breathes me
    shall die.
They led them across the vastness
As they walked they tottered
and rose again. They walked
across the grassland to the edge of the mound
and knelt down in silent prayer;
they rose again led to the mound,
they crouched
like worshippers of Muhammed.
Suddenly they rose again
stretching their hands to the crowd
in wasteful gestures of identity
Boos and shrieks greeted them

as they smiled and waved
as those on a big boat going
on a long long journey.
A sudden silence fell
as the crowd pushed and yelled
into the bright sharp morning of a shooting.

They led them unto the mound
In a game of blindman's bluff
they tottered to lean on the sandbags
Their backs to the ocean
that will bear them away.
The crackling report of brens
and the falling down;
a shout greeted them
tossing them into the darkness.

and my mountains reel and roll
to the world's end.

The First Circle

I

the flat end of sorrow here
two crows fighting over New Year's Party
leftovers. From my cell, I see a cold
hard world.

2

So this is the abscess that
hurts the nation—
jails, torture, blood
and hunger.
One day it will burst;
it must burst.

3

When I heard you were taken
we speculated, those of us at large
where you would be
in what nightmare will you star?
That night I heard the moans
wondering whose child could now
be lost in the cellars of oppression.
Then you emerged, tall, and bloody-eyed.

It was the first time
      I wept.

4

         The long nights I dread most
         the voices from behind the bars
     the early glow of dawn before
the guard's steps wake me up,
the desire to leap and stretch
and yawn in anticipation
of another dark home-coming day
only to find that
      I cannot.
   riding the car into town,
hemmed in between them
    their guns poking me in the ribs,
    I never had known that my people
    wore such sad faces, so sad
    they were, on New Year's Eve,
    so very sad.

They Shall Know

Voices, single row of nights
    where the birds long died;
    the iron clang of the door.
What dreams are possible here?
John pitted with smallpox
    sat near the wayside shop
    weary.

Outing once in three weeks
flags, buntings
    signs announce the fair.
Silence over the city
we wind our way through the sleep walkers
    My keepers chatting gaily
    of power and politics and power
    for governments, national language
    trials and reprieves.
At the end they gave me an egg
    and two pieces of white bread
    which I broke before my wife.
It is exactly one month today

So the World Changes

Where are they?
Awlesi's mother's trade collapsed
the children cried and cried
"call her for me, please call her for me"

The day the desert tree blossoms
is the feasting day for the fowls of the air
The evil fowls and the good fowls
The owner of the earth covers them in his cloth

promised them
when he holds the promise
Thirst shall not kill them
so the world changes
rain comes after the drought
the yam festival after the sewing time.
Do not lose heart,
have arms, we have shields
When the powder house falls
the mother fails to make war.
Some rivers there are you cannot swim
some strong rivers there are you cannot ford.

CHRISTOPHER OKIGBO

Nigeria (1932–1967)

Christopher Okigbo, the son of an Igbo schoolteacher, was born in Ojoto, in eastern Nigeria, and educated at the University of Ibadan, where he read classics. Although he was raised as a Catholic, his parents' home had a shrine to their ancestral gods, the male Ikenga and the female Udo. "I am believed to be a reincarnation," he said, "of my maternal grandfather, who used to be the priest of the shrine called Ajani, where Idoto, the river goddess, is worshipped. When I was born it was believed that I should carry on his duties. And although someone else had to perform his functions, this other person was only, as it were, a regent. And in 1958, when I started taking poetry very seriously, it was as though I had felt a sudden call to begin performing my full functions as the priest of Idoto." His own poems, as much a product of his reading as of his background, are hieratic, almost priestly in their devotion to a high literary vision. In part his style evolved from his conviction that the modern African writer embodies a complex of values that are part indigenous and part exotic. Tribal chants or T. S. Eliot were equally sources for Okigbo. He played jazz clarinet and worked as a librarian and editor. But in 1966, when civil war broke out in Nigeria and the new state of Biafra seceded, Okigbo joined the Biafran cause. He was already considered the country's foremost poet, but his political convictions impelled him to action. By special commission he was appointed a major in the Biafran army. In August 1967 he was killed in action, defending the university town of Nsukka.

Elegy of the Wind

White light, receive me your sojourner; O milky way,
    let me clasp you to my waist;
And may my muted tones of twilight
Break your iron gate, the burden of several centuries,
    into twin tremulous cotyledons . . .

Man of iron throat—for I will make broadcast with
    eunuch-horn of seven valves—

I will follow the wind to the clearing,
And with muffled steps seemingly out of breath break
     the silence the myth of her gate.

For I have lived the sapling sprung from the bed
     of the old vegetation;
Have shouldered my way through a mass of ancient
     nights to chlorophyll;

Or leaned upon a withered branch,
A blind beggar leaning on a porch.

I have lived the oracle dry on the cradle of a new generation . . .
The autocycle leans on a porch, the branch dissolves into embers,

The ashes resolve their moments
Of twin-drops of dew on a leaf:
And like motion into stillness is my divine rejoicing—
The man embodies the child
The child embodies the man; the man remembers
The song of the innocent,
Of the uncircumcised at the sight of the flaming razor—

The chief priest of the sanctuary has uttered
     the enchanted words;
The bleeding phallus,
Dripping fresh from the carnage cries out for
     the medicinal leaf . . .

O wind, swell my sails; and may my banner run
     the course of wider waters:

The child in me trembles before the high shelf
     on the wall,
The man in me shrinks before the narrow neck of
     a calabash;

And the chant, already all wings, follows
In its ivory circuit behind the thunder clouds.
The slick route of the feathered serpent . . .

Come Thunder

Now that the triumphant march has entered the last street
    corners,
Remember, O dancers, the thunder among the clouds . . .

Now that laughter, broken in two, hangs tremulous between the
    teeth,
Remember, O dancers, the lightning beyond the earth . . .

The smell of blood already floats in the lavender-mist of the after-
    noon.
The death sentence lies in ambush along the corridors of power;
And a great fearful thing already tugs at the cables of the open air,
A nebula immense and immeasurable, a night of deep waters—
An iron dream unnamed and unprintable, a path of stone.

The drowsy heads of the pods in barren farmlands witness it,
The homesteads abandoned in this century's brush fire witness it:
The myriad eyes of deserted corn cobs in burning barns witness it:

Magic birds with the miracle of lightning flash on their
      feathers . . .
The arrows of God tremble at the gates of light,
The drums of curfew pander to a dance of death;

And the secret thing in its heaving
Threatens with iron mask
The last lighted torch of the century . . .

Elegy for Alto

(With Drum Accompaniment)

AND THE HORN may now paw the air howling goodbye . . .

For the Eagles are now in sight:
Shadows in the horizon—

THE ROBBERS are here in black sudden steps of showers, of
    caterpillars—

THE EAGLES have come again,
The eagles rain down on us—

POLITICIANS are back in giant hidden steps of howitzers, of
    detonators—

THE EAGLES descend on us,
Bayonets and cannons—

THE ROBBERS descend on us to strip us of our laughter, of our
    thunder—

THE EAGLES have chosen their game,
Taken our concubines—

POLITICIANS are here in this iron dance of mortars, of generators—

THE EAGLES are suddenly there,
New stars of iron dawn;

So let the horn paw the air howling goodbye . . .

O mother mother Earth, unbind me; let this be my last testament;
    let this be
The ram's hidden wish to the sword the sword's secret prayer to
    the scabbard—

THE ROBBERS are back in black hidden steps of detonators—

FOR BEYOND the blare of sirened afternoons, beyond the
    motorcades;
Beyond the voices and days, the echoing highways; beyond the
    latescence
Of our dissonant airs; through our curtained eyeballs, through our
    shuttered sleep,
Onto our forgotten selves, onto our broken images; beyond the
    barricades
Commandments and edicts, beyond the iron tables, beyond the
    elephant's
Legendary patience, beyond his inviolable bronze bust; beyond
    our crumbling towers—

BEYOND the iron path careering along the same beaten track—

THE GLIMPSE of a dream lies smouldering in a cave, together with
    the mortally wounded birds.
Earth, unbind me; let me be the prodigal; let this be the ram's
    ultimate prayer to the tether . . .

AN OLD STAR departs, leaves us here on the shore
Gazing heavenward for a new star approaching;
The new star appears, foreshadows its going
Before a going and coming that goes on forever . . .

WOLE SOYINKA

Nigeria (b. 1934)

In 1986 Wole Soyinka became the first African writer to win the Nobel Prize for Literature. His work—as dramatist, novelist, memoirist, critic, and screenwriter as well as poet—is impressive both for its range and for its searching honesty. "I have," he has written, "one abiding religion—human liberty. Conditioned to the truth that life is meaningless, insulting, without this fullest liberty, and in spite of the despairing knowledge that words alone seem unable to guarantee its possession, my writing grows more and more preoccupied with this theme of the oppressive boot, the irrelevance of the color of the foot that wears it, and the struggle for individuality." Soyinka was born and educated in Nigeria. He later took a doctorate at the University of Leeds and worked at the Royal Court Theatre in London, where his first play was produced in 1955. Returning to his homeland, he continued to write plays and poems that incorporate the myths and folklore of the Yoruba tribe, to which he belongs. His parables of African life take an unsparing view of both the brutal heritage of colonialism and the corruption of contemporary African politics. In 1967 he was imprisoned by the government, charged with helping the Biafran independence movement. He spent two years in solitary confinement. Since 1975 he has taught comparative literature at the University of Ife and at colleges around the world.

The Hunchback of Dugbe

> I wondered always where
> He walked at night, or lay
> Where earth might seem
> Suddenly in labour when he sighed.
>
> By day, stooped at public drains
> Intense at bath or washing cotton holes,
> An ant's blown load upon
> A child's entangled scrawl

The calmest nudist
Of the roadside lunatics.

The devil came one sane night
On parole from hell, lace curtains
Sieved light dancing pebbles
On his vast creation egg

His cement mixer borne
On crossed cassava sticks.

Not in disdain, but in truth immune
From song or terror, taxi turns
And sale fuss of the mad, beyond
Ugliness or beauty, whom thought-sealing
Solemnly transfigures—the world
Spins on his spine, in still illusion.

But the bell-tower of his thin
Buttocks rings pure tones on Dugbe
A horse penis loin to crooked knees
Side-slapping on his thighs

At night he prowls, a cask
Of silence; on his lone matrix
Pigeon eggs of light dance in and out
Of dark, and he walks in motley.

Funeral Sermon, Soweto

We wish to bury our dead. Now, a funeral
Is a many-cultured thing. Some races would
Rope a heifer to the slaughter stone, or
Goat/ram/pig or humble cockerel,
Monochrome or striped, spotted, seamless—
The soothsayer rules the aesthetics or,

Rank and circumstance of the dear deceased.
Market rates may ruin devout intentions.
Times austere are known to sanction disrespect,
Spill thinner blood than wished. Still,
Flow it must. Rank tunnels of transition
Must be greased, the bolt of passage loosened,
Home-brewed beer or smuggler's brands, prestigious,
Froth and slosh with ostentation, belch
In discreet bubbles like embarrassed mourners
At the wake. The dead record no disavowal.

We wish to mourn our dead.
Is custom overlooked? No. Our heads
Are shaven clean. Cropped close. Neglected. Matted
Thick with ritual unguents, spiked with clay
Or fiber. Ceremonials well rehearsed,
All outward acts of group cohesion, smothering
Loss, performed. Our headgears bear clan colors.
Portraits, mementos, icons, elders' mats
Laid out in proud parade, mute debts
Of honor, surrogates to vanished breath.
Mummers, griots, play out lineage roles.
The feats, the voices, reverential anecdotes . . .
All to bind us to the "dead but not forgotten."

O dearly beloved, we wish to mourn. But first,
Shall we lance some ancient tumuli? Probe
Some birthly portents, glorified demise?
"When beggars die . . ." You know the verse . . .
But if the heavens launch comets to proclaim
The death of kings, archeological probes
Catalogue our earthly supplement—spent
Rhetoric of skills our earth hoards yield:
Vaults of coins to bribe the other world,
Inlaid bowls, golden lamps, cryptic stellae,
Astral calculus engraved on marble
Mausoleums—the astrologer's final computation?
The jewelled sword hilt, "rich beyond all dreams."
A geography of stasis and cerebral feats
Cheek by jowl across the centuries.

Heliolatrous Incas. Slave and palm oil
Aristocracy on blood-soaked Niger creeks—
Their sportive obsequies arced human skulls,
Fresh-tissued, point to point of silver lances—
Innovative variants of the polo game!
Have we treasures to inter, dear brothers
And sisters? Do we play polo in Soweto?

We wish to bury our dead. Others
Boast horsemen sentinels, ranged in Chinese
Catacombs, silent guards on vanished
Dynasties. Or their Nilotic counterparts—
Did time stand still for these? The labor hours—
Gathering, grading, grinding, mixing,
Mapping the hour of star and moon alignment
To stuff the royal orifice with spices.
Draining toes swelled tuberose with pomp
To ease the slide of rings and golden anklets.
Calf amulets of ivory. Seals on each finger
Equal a nation's ransom. Casque or death mask,
Mines to rival Nature's undiscovered hoards.
Queen, princeling, favorite cat, each
Scrolled in own sarcophagus surround the god-king.
Antechambers lined with lesser beings
Extend the ministry beyond the end
To imagined wants of their lone, lordly dead.

O dearly beloved, seeking solace ever,
Distractions of the mind to ease keen pangs
As we move to bury our dead, we pause only
To contemplate these ancient vanities—
Mongol, Pharaoh, proud Asantehene
All, too lean in frame to fill their grandiose
Subterranean schemes, a troubled sleep
Of ranked retainers swells. Nerveless arms
Redress lost battles, amplify the dream
That thrust a mildewed gauntlet at mortality.
Awesome pyramids on burning sands,
Cunning combs of mind in mountain wombs,
Absentee landlords of necropolis, peopled

By vassals, serfs you dared not leave behind—
How phrased your priests their Final Unction?
Even in death, beware insurrection of life,
And life after debt? Of blood?

We wish to bury our dead. Let all take note,
Our dead were none of these eternal hoarders—
Does the buyer of nothing seek after-sales service?
Not as prophetic intuitions, or sly
Subversive chant do we invoke these ancient
Ghosts, but as that ritual homily
Time-honored in the offices of loss.
Not seeking martyrdom, the midnight knock,
Desecration of our altar, vestments,
Not courting ninety-day detention laws,
The state seal on the voice of man—and God. . . .

We wish only to bury our dead. Shorn
Of all but name, our indelible origin,
For indeed our pride once boasted empires,
Kings and nation builders. Seers. Too soon
The brace of conquest circumscribed our being
Yet found us rooted in that unyielding
Will to life bequeathed from birth, we
Sought no transferred deed of earthly holdings.
Slaves do not possess their kind. Nor do
The truly free.

We wished to bury our dead,
We rendered unto Caesar what was Caesar's.
The right to congregate approved;
Hold procession, eulogize, lament
Procured for a standard fee. All death tariff
Settled in advance, receipted, logged.
A day to cross the barriers of our skin,
Death was accorded purchase rights, a brief license
Subject to withdrawal—we signed acceptance
On the dotted line—"orderly conduct" et cetera.
We now proceed to render earth's to earth.

We wish to mourn our dead. No oil tycoons
We, Mandela, no merchant princes, scions
Of titled lineage. No peerage aspirants
Nor tribal chieftains. Only the shirtless
Ghetto rats that briefly left
The cul-de-sac of hunger, stripes,
Contempt. The same that rose on hind legs
That brief hour in Sharpeville, reddening
The sleepy conscience of the world. We,
The sludge of gold and diamond mines,
Half-chewed morsels of canine sentinels
In nervous chain stores, snow-white parks.
Part-crushed tracks of blinded Saracens,
The butt of hippo trucks, water cannon mush.
We, the bulldozed, twisted shapes of
Shanty lots that mimic black humanity.
Our dead bore no kinship to the race
Of lordly dead, sought no companion dead
To a world they never craved.
We set out to mourn our dead, bugling
No Last Post, no boom of guns in vain salute.

But others donned a deeper indigo than the bereaved.
Unscheduled undertakers spat their lethal dirge
And fifty-eight were sudden bright-attired,
Flung to earth in fake paroxysms of grief.
And then we knew them, counted, laid them out,
Companion voyagers to the dead we mourned.

And now, we wish to bury our dead. . . .

EDOUARD MAUNICK

Mauritius (b. 1931)

Edouard Maunick was born on Mauritius, a volcanic island midway between Africa and India, and like his native land he is of mixed African, Indian, and French ancestry. By his midtwenties he had published his first collection of poems and moved to Paris, where he went to work for the French Overseas Radio Service and joined the circle of black West Indian and African intellectuals. His work is less concerned with indigenous culture than with the broader themes of modernism: identity, meaning, and mortality.

from Carousels of the Sea

6

Further off is the measured force the word of the sea
Further without leeway for the blueing shoulders of the horizon

harm is born of the light
when it capsizes under the voyages' assault
when it watches oblivion like a beast
and seeks the shipwreck of ten-year-old villages
conclusive shifts of time in exile

further off is risk without defeat
the ever renewed patience of the shadow
to find words beyond language
further the serpent in the blood
broken by all the betrayals
victories of voluntary resignation

I did not leave in order to forget
I am mulatto

the Indian ocean will never give way to the city of today
but harm compromises in me harm however come by

I repeat further off to stain the liquid mirrors
to cross a threshold where you await me since the poem

20

I love to encounter you in strange cities
where every broil every noise every clock
betrays your body beating in my pulses

I love to release you in foreign beds
when night becomes a tree by the force of its nudity

I love what separates us in our resemblance
frontiers of dawn resembling our faces
the proofs of life are only found elsewhere
never say no when I speak to you from afar . . .

Translated from the French by Gerald Moore

Seven Sides and Seven Syllables

for Aimé Césaire and Pierre Emmanuel

I

happen you come on your own
to this contradicted place
re-celebrate ebony
the original metal

happen you essay the dream
before you outlive yourself
before the blood surges back
before your father expires

this land once was a mirror
which was silvered by the sea
in the sweat of oars, islands
with keys girded up their loins

        good fortune surrounded us
        in no way surprising us
        if we wager on the sea
        for the last possible time

but what can be the last time
for the deracinated?
again, those who oppose him
share the flesh of the poet

        unaware, he keeps going
        not heeding all the mad ways
        all countries merge dizzily
        in this country of his own

II

my love is improbable
let the saliva well up
neutrality, its token
skimming the garden of birth

        here the roses are roses
        sword-lilies prohibited
        a man who speaks standing up
        has his eyes bandaged with rain

we all take powerful root
on assassination day
with the garden's iron pickets
stained bright by the equinox

here a man who speaks standing
is submerged in the symbol:
I say rose and it means hope
but who will live by this game?

who will take up sword-lilies
in their form of machetes
to knot up with blood once more
what survives as a mongrel?

the whole world I name garden
I leave no place unbaptized
who will plant garden fences
if not I, or my kinfolk?

I, the child of all races
soul of India, Europe,
my identity branded
in the cry of Mozambique

III

thus I am anonymous
while holding the heritage
of your ancestral truncheons
and your black man's evasions

I could accept your labels
and stay unidentified
be tattooed by your numbers
while remaining uncounted

command all your battlements
cloak myself in your panic
recognizing the thunder
and recognizing the wind

know the substance of exile:
on the sea, wind and thunder
recognizing all the roots
of the tree that rejects me

        recognizing all the roots
        tongue-ties me with bereavement
        on the shore of denial
        I will choose to be Negro

I've read Senghor and Césaire
and Guillén and Richard Wright
but Lorca and St.-John Perse
Dylan Thomas and Cadou

        Paul Éluard, vertical
        all reinvent memory
        you step out of the mirror
        to marry morning with night

IV

rising in me, the promise
my mouth will spit bitterness
to crack the rejecting rock
at the end of all stanzas

        utterance moves toward a place
        where snow, thunder cohabit
        of words fouled by long weeping
        of visions searing the skin

with desires pure and bitter
tumultuous silences
I here spell out my poem
releasing my love of you

withholding what must be said
dividing my blood from blood
inhabiting somewhere else
than the habitable space

exile is no easy thing
despite obscure boundaries
open doors and living hands
no, it is never easy!

to accept is to refuse
refusal reveals anger
fling open your registers!
bring your mortal crucifix!

I swear to understand flesh
transparent as lake water
I shall murder ancient seas
set fire to their slave cargoes

V

but CHRIST, this odor of chains
and this rattling of metal
against the defeated bones
these quincunxes of ropes!

I can force my eyes to see
but the sight is too tragic:
dogs trained to attack the blacks
and their spirituals stabbed

yes, to watch the capsizing
of women and child voices
whose offense is vertical
because they refuse to crawl

is this Christmas and manger?
are these our poems pure white?
are these our poems deep black?
this the summation of poems?

VI

what right have I to denounce
while shooting with your own guns?
or healing with your own hands?
I freeze and starve for us all

If I could find a kingdom
between midday and midnight
I would go forth and proclaim
my mixed blood to the core

for I choose the you-in-me
without color or passport
they say we all long for God
and we are all forgiven

VII

happen you come on your own
to this contradicted place
to embrace the bitter dream
of the solar boundaries

discover the point of light
which is the true equator
having no need of the sea
to conceal your departures

happen you come without wrath
to this place of denial

open your eyes to the rain
lave the body till it splits

at last, for a final time
adjust your steps to the steps
of the sole presence in you:
a man the size of a man

my love may only exist
when endorsed by your absence
I no longer need the past
to stand up in the present

the carousels of the sea
are not mad carousels now
I had to silence my fate
with this, my derisive voice.

Translated from the French by Carolyn Kizer

DENNIS BRUTUS

South Africa (b. 1924)

Dennis Brutus was born in Salisbury, Southern Rhodesia (now Harare,
Zimbabwe). Both his parents were teachers, and Brutus himself graduated
from Fort Hare University, later studied law at the University of the Wit-
watersrand, and went on to teach English and Afrikaans in high school
from 1948 until 1961. Because of his antiapartheid activities, he was dis-
missed from his teaching post by the South African government and for-
bidden to write. In 1963 he was arrested for his defiance, but he escaped.
He was tracked down in Mozambique, returned to the South African se-
cret police, and again tried to escape. This time he was shot, tortured, and
imprisoned for eighteen months on Robben Island, off Cape Town. After
his release, he was permitted to leave the country, and after living some
years in London, he emigrated to the United States. Imprisonment, exile,
injustice—these are his subjects. In his work the personal is subsumed by
the public struggle. Brutus is not afraid of the blunt rhetoric of liberation,
and he has always seen his poetry as a part of the struggle against his
homeland's barbarous policies.

There Was a Time When the Only Worth

There was a time when the only worth
was other men—
their saleable value;
one felt the steady venom
in the gaze of another shackled
and knew the relief of escaping,
and in another day bowed down
accepting this ignominious ultimate:

war did not make captors—
for captors one made war:
and captives were the purpose of the war:

so, for alien almost-humans
we made hunted beasts of humans.
Till time brings its reverses.

They Hanged Him, I Said Dismissively

They hanged him, I said dismissively
having no other way to say he died
or that he was a dear friend
or that work wove us most intimately
in common tasks, ambitions, desires.
Now he is dead: and I dare not think
of the anguish that drove him to where he was
or the pain at their hands he must have faced
or how much he was racked by my distress:
now, it is still easiest to say, they hanged him,
dismissively.

Robben Island Sequence

I

neonbright orange
vermilion
on the chopped broken slate
that gravelled the path and yard
bright orange was the red blood
freshly spilt where the prisoners had passed;
and bright red
pinkbright red and light
the blood on the light sand by the sea
the pale lightyellow seas and
in the light bright airy air
lightwoven, seawoven, spraywoven air
of sunlight by the beach where we worked:

where the bright blade-edges of the rocks
jutted like chisels from the squatting rocks
the keen fine edges whitening to thinness
from the lightbrown masses of the sunlit rocks,
washed around by swirls on rushing wave water,
lightgreen or colourless, transparent with a hint of light:

on the sharp pale whitening edges
our blood showed light and pink,
our gashed soles winced from the fine barely felt slashes,
that lacerated afterwards:
the bloody flow
thinned to thin pink strings dangling
as we hobbled through the wet clinging sands
or we discovered surprised
in some quiet backwater pool
the thick flow of blood uncoiling
from a skein to thick dark red strands.

The menace of that bright day was clear as the blade of a knife;
from the blade edges of the rocks,
from the piercing brilliance of the day,
the incisive thrust of the clear air into the lungs
the salt-stinging brightness of sky and light on the eyes:
from the clear image, bronze-sharp lines of Kleynhans laughing
Khaki-ed, uniformed, with his foot on the neck of the convict who
      had fallen,
holding his head under water in the pool where he had fallen
while the man thrashed helplessly
and the bubbles gurgled
and the air glinted dully on lethal gunbutts,
the day was brilliant with the threat of death.

II

sitting on the damp sand
in sand-powdered windpuff,
the treetops still grey in the early morning air

and dew still hanging tree-high,
to come to the beginning of the day
and small barely-conscious illicit greetings
to settle to a shape of mind, of thought,
and inhabit a body to its extremities:
to be a prisoner, a political victim,
to be a some-time fighter, to endure—
find reserves of good cheer, of composure
while the wind rippled the tight skin forming on the cooling
    porridge
and sandspray dropped by windgusts depressed it:
to begin, at the beginning of a day, to be a person
and take and hold a shape to last for this one day. . . . .

(afterwards the old lags came along
with their favourite warders, to select
the young prisoners who had caught their eye,
so that these could be assigned to their span)

III

some mornings we lined up for "hospital"
—it meant mostly getting castor oil—
but what a varied bunch we were!
for all had injuries—but in such variety
split heads; smashed ankles, arms;
cut feet in bandages, or torn and bloodied legs:
some, under uniform, wore their mass of bruises
but what a bruised and broken motley lot we were!

At Night

    At night
    on the smooth grey concrete of my cell
    I heard the enormous roar of the surf
    and saw in my mind's eye
    the great white wall of spray rising

like a sheet of shattering glass
where the surge broke
on the shore and rocks and barbed wire
and going to the shed
in hope of a visitor
I greeted the great cypresses
green and black
dreaming in their poised serenity
in the limpid stillness of the brilliant afternoon
gracious as an Umbrian Raphael landscape
but more brilliant and more sharp.

Endurance

. . . is the ultimate virtue—more,
the essential thread
on which existence is strung
when one is stripped to nothing else
and not to endure is to end in despair.

I

Cold floors
bleak walls
another anteroom:
another milestone behind
fresh challenges ahead:
in this hiatus
with numb resolution
I coil my energies
and wait.

II

Stripped to the waist
in ragged pantaloons

long ago I sweated over bales,
my stringy frame—strained—
grew weary but sprang back
stubbornly
from exhaustion:
the lashes now,
and the labors are different
but still demand,
wound and stretch to breaking point:
and I still snap back, stubbornly.

III

All day a stoic
at dawn I wake, eyelids wet
with tears shed in dreams.

IV

My father, that distant man,
grey hair streaked with silver,
spoke of St. Francis of Assisi
with a special timbre in his voice:
loved him not, I think, for the birds
circling his head, nor the grace
of that threadbare fusty gown
but for his stigmata: the blood
that gleamed in the fresh wounds
on his palms and insteps:
in my isolation cell in prison,
the bullet wound in my side still raw,
those images afflicted me.

V

When we shook hands in the Athenian dusk
it closed a ring that had opened twenty-four years before

when a wisp of off-key melody had snaked into my grey cell
whistled by a bored guard in the sunlit afternoon outside:
it circled the grey walls like a jeweled adder
bright and full of menace and grew
to a giant python that encircled me, filling the cell
then shrank and entered me where it lay
coiled like my gut, hissing sibilantly
of possession;
twice I breathed death's hot fetid breath
twice I leaned over the chasm, surrendering
till some tiny fibre at the base of my brain
protested in the name of sanity and dragged me
from the precipice of suicide that allured
with its own urgent logic

Our hands meeting, uncordially, your gaze
quizzical, perhaps affronted
sealed a circle in the gathering dusk,
like the ring of dark waves advancing
on the island's jagged shore
and the dark enclosure of wire
whose barbs are buried in my brain.

VI

Wormwood grey shadows take shape
as night drains from the moon:
objects assume outlines
and some backdrop is suggested
and still the noose of time's expiring closes in

shapes, like bats-upended
hover and circle
holy men chanting their mantras
as darkness dissolves
in a purgatorial stasis.

VII

In the air pungent with asepsis
the raucous guards swagger
their uniforms and holsters bulk
in a perennial twilight
the sweat of newly dead corpses
makes rigid the smoke-laden fug
the collapsed lung labors stertoriously
strained iterations of emergencies
thread the air like steel bobbins
stitching towards finality, mortality

corpselike, in the gloom
bodies clutter the floor in rows
a gloom threaded with sighs
yearnings, griefs and lusts
overhead, the silhouette of guard and gun
prowl against the discolored glass
men's hungers, tears, groans

tall expanses, concrete brick, glass
encircle the harsh cement
dull grey against fresh blood
and a circle of gaping mouths
the faces swallowed away
life bleeding away, the blood pooled

only redeeming this crepuscular acesis
one bright voice, bright eyes, welcoming flesh
one bright ribbon in the encircling gloom
long torn, long lost and tattered
but still cherished at the center of the brain

No, it redeems nothing
cannot stave off the end
nor offer any relief from this
encompassing gloom

BREYTEN BREYTENBACH

South Africa (b. 1939)

The son of an itinerant worker, Breyten Breytenbach was born in the village of Bonnievale in the Western Cape and studied at the Michaelis School of Art, a part of the University of Cape Town. (Painting has been central to his life as an artist ever since.) He dropped out of school, though, and went to Paris, where he painted and wrote. A friend took his poems back to South Africa, where they were published to immediate acclaim in 1964. He continued to publish and won major literary prizes, but when he sought to visit South Africa to accept his awards, he was denied a visa because of his interracial relationship: in Paris he had married a Vietnamese woman. His poems, fueled by an exile's love for his native land, grew bitter. "Looking into South Africa," he has written, "is like looking into the mirror at midnight when one has pulled a face and a train blew its whistle and one's image stayed there, fixed for all eternity. A horrible face, but one's own." Outraged by the insult to his wife, Breytenbach fell in with antiapartheid groups in Paris and was eventually recruited for an undercover espionage mission in South Africa. His celebrity made him conspicuous; he was arrested, tried, and sentenced to nine years in prison. Under pressure during his trial and in prison, he made compromising statements that confused his admirers, but before and after his release in 1982 he has been a passionate opponent of apartheid. His style, loose and associative, invigorated the Afrikaans language, and it has been a sharp instrument of protest and assertive individuality.

Breyten Prays for Himself

There is no need for Pain Lord
We could live well without it
A flower has no teeth

It is true we are only fulfilled in death
But let our flesh stay fresh as cabbage
Make us firm as pink fish
Let us tempt each other, our eyes deep butterflies

Have mercy on our mouths our bowels our brains
Let us always taste the sweetness of the evening sky
Swim in warm seas, sleep with the sun
Ride peacefully on bicycles through bright Sundays

And gradually we will decompose like old ships or trees
But keep Pain far from Me o Lord
That others may bear it
Be taken into custody, Shattered
              Stoned
              Suspended
              Lashed
              Used
              Tortured
              Crucified
              Cross-examined
              Placed under house arrest
              Given hard labor
Banished to obscure islands till the end of their days
Wasting in damp pits down to slimy green imploring bones
Worms in their stomachs heads full of nails
But not *Me*
But we never give Pain or complain

Translated from the Afrikaans by Denis Hirson

Asylum

por el "C"

I

at first those closest to you shot holes in you
and the sly spider of the night
he who waits in every corner of every room
swarmed right through these red doors of daybreak
and the trail of shiny thread choked your veins

the blood sinks for ever into the ground
the broken body lies, obscene
raped, in a manger, in a stable
the lips grin—did they want to say a last "goodbye"?
the teeth are a trampled gate
a broken-down wall
the eyes are open but there's nothing to see
small sentry boxes of an uninhabited realm
two bees in the honey and the light petrified
the breath trembles somewhere far off among birds in trees
and the body is already embalmed
with the erotic perfume of decay—
you become a web of dazzling bone . . .

come and slaver up the holes again
make the body airtight please
and spin a film over our eyes
so that we can never see how a hero dies
how the secrets of his carcass are looked upon by mortals

2

the journey in the land of the lonely
is a journey without hostels through a land without borders
all along a sea without shores
only with love as beacons

in the land of the blind all colors are unbelievable
every sound is the witness
of the silver language of mutes
with only love as darkness

with only love as lighthouses
a barrier against the sea
of the notes in a throat where foam
must break open
like a machine-gun's whispered message
stuttered out in code by the mute
in the ears of the deaf

who can write it down for the blind
with only love as ink

because the machine-gun gives away the secret
to reveal all secrets
because the machine-gun opens the way
and washes your feet
and places before you the bread and the wine
and so you come back home
only with love as the body for your death

Translated from the Afrikaans by Stephen Gray and A. J. Coetzee

Firewing

when you think of your country
you see
plaits and glasses; an old dog full of blood;
and a horse drowned in the river; a mountain on fire;
a space and two people without teeth in bed;
dark figs against sand; a road, poplars,
house, blue, ships of cloud;
reeds; a telephone;
you see

when you think of your country
you see
we must be strong; guts full of craters and flies;
the mountain is a butcher's shop without walls;
over the thousand hills of Natal
the fists of the warriors like standards;
prisoners lie in the mud: you see
mines bursting with slaves; the rain
spatters high like sparks against the evening;
amongst the reeds the skeleton of the dwarf rots

when you think of your country
it is the end of all thought;

if it's bright outside you throw the windows open,
you see the stars are arrows in the void;
you hear, as quiet as a rumor, don't you?
"we are the people. we are black, but we don't sleep.
we hear in the dark how the thieves guzzle in the trees.
we listen to our power they cannot know. we listen
to the heart of our breathing. we hear the sun
shaking in the reeds of the night. we wait until
the devourers rotten and glutted fall from the branches—
a glutton will be known by his fruits—
or we'll teach the pigs to climb trees."

Translated from the Afrikaans by Ernst van Heerden

Dreams Are Also Wounds

thus every dream secretly and small inscribes its letters
at dawn we search for scabs of ink in the glass
to store them away in safe archives

but the wounds never heal

the darkest blood continues to bloom
orchards of revolutions on the sheets
or the bubbling of love in gardens

of wounds that never heal

even the deaf are allowed to dream
as the mad are free to whisper their letters
and the blind to look at the wind

pain bruises us all to a more intimate shade—
how green were the birds in the gardens
of my youth, how ripe and painted the sun

and the snow never heals

the earth is a ruler rich in people
people are kings rich in trees
of fear or of hate, or trees of yearning

which can never heal the dreams

for this is our only unending paradise—
we are rich like a fisherman
sorting and counting his ultimate eggs

returning the fish to the sea
in order to speak like eggs talk
to sing like waves bleeding for years

with blood that never heals

the soldiers have eyes like peas
the peasants have hands of earth
and they all dream messages and worlds

filled with flowers that can never heal

now even a parrot enters the poem, a yellow parrot
airing its complaints from verse
to line with a wail in the black sails of its tongue

so that its songs can never heal

so my nights will never learn to heal or read
for *you* have come to let the last drops of my blood
would you too be no more than a scar in my flesh?

without blood we cannot possibly bleed
and our dreams are the blood of the night
just as we are blood and dreamt in blood

and so I remain a bed-marshal
emptying my armies night after night
pressing the inkdrops from my heart

for you, dreamt up, who can never heal

our bodies are mere husks of flesh
destined to wither into walking sticks
when, finally, undreaming, we go to sleep

and only then will water turn to vinegar
and silence stretch its rainbows in the sky
and then our dreams will meet

and may these letters never heal
assuredly, these wounds will never heal

Translated from the Afrikaans by André Brink

Out There

"if words could speak words should have told . . ."
                    not so, Federico?
did you see it looming?
sparkspanking black horses in the night
with a jingling of stirrups
the way stars chink when you tread on them
to release a bruised odor,
was that the secret sign of fate
through the dark-hearted joy of the villages—
                how did it go again?
                —open wide the shutters
                and put flowers
                on balcony and windowsill
                and sing for me
                ah, the day smells of oranges—
divine this liberty and sweet is the sound!

or just beyond the orchard down by the river
where a rider might slice the moon
with his knife from its water

(and she no virgin),
did you know it then?
in Cordoba, no, Granada?
where gardens grow an Arabian calm
and each palmtree deep like deepsong
rising in the coiled night of the blood—
               did you know
               as you were taken to dig the grave
               grey and grave the faint break of day
               where you and your carcass would lie
               with a bullet-hole between the
                     buttocks—
               why?

and you, Osip?
               faulty like the very future,
you with the words a glass-clear bell in the nocturnal
bungle and botch of being human
               making your lips to tremble
               all down the thingamabody
               to the fingers on the pad
               where phalanxes are lips
               beseeching a tongue
               when paper is pale wasteland—
you who identified the predator lurking
behind the withered hand and the paranoid whiskers,
you who saw man indignifying man—
surely you must have recognized your destiny
snuffling for you,
the fool, the amnesiac
caricature with the shivers in a greatcoat,
wedged, lice-infested, in a cattle-truck
among the errant dead—
crazed one in the irrevocable extremes of some Siberia,
holy clown in a slave-camp—
               till you were no more Osip, poet-person
               but just a pile of rotted-bare
               decay
               spoor in the snow
               twist in time

muttered muttering become wind in the wind—
why?

is yours the only course then, Hanshan?
shrieking monk on Cold Mountain
with your verses penned in brush and cloud
pearls of tears and frosted footfalls
going past Fate and Why
the way everything that lives must die
                    and live, and die,
and emerge from illusion's total truth,
and you never to have existed anyway?
that *so?*

is it thus,
                    you shadows of conceit and phantoms of
                        the well-versed heart?
unbolt those doors with their spider's work of locks
and push aside the bars of light—
behold, the night out there smells of oranges,
listen, there's windrhyme there are dreams there
                    the voices of survivors

                    I must go up to the ridges
                    where aloes smolder red bait for planets
                    where ants build fortresses around a
                        bride
                    and a finger carelessly predicts the
                        seasons in dust,
                    I want to stroke the celestial dome
                    must lie on earth
                    to see mountains gambol,
                    I wish to be a life
                    as only death can still be pulsation . . .

                    Translated from the Afrikaans by the author

There Is Life

there are christs spiked against trees
prophets in the wilderness seized with fits
worshipers whose eyes bud under the sun
buddhas on one side conversing with figs

there is life greening in the clouds
while dolphins shred through loops of waves
the seagull's swerving gutlean shriek
and barefooted scragginess against mountainflanks

behind magnifying sky the crater's firespeech
inclines of snow like silences shifted
when heaven cracks open hairline wide
and out spill black legends the swallow the dove

there are bones that bind the earth
delight that breaks through what's time-bound
and blunderer droll notion though I may be
I'll still grow rich on daylight's beam

the scales flamed the whole night through
I might once have been a prisoner too
but here the heart's pulsing contract is spelled out:
we will all be naked a hundred years from now

Translated from the Afrikaans by the author

Lullaby

Schluf mine faygele
Mach tzu dine aygele
Eye lu lu lu

Close tight your eyes my love
Hush now my little dove

For the mouse in the kiss
For the blood in the shoe

Guernica Madrid Babi-Yar
Cyprus Belfast Suez
Athens Luanda Santiago
Santiago Hanoi My Lai Pnom-Penh
Hué Praha Budapest
Sabra Chatilla

Schluf geshmak mine kind
Schluf un zai-gezund
Eye lu lu lu

Ai
Sleep deep my wondrous child
Sleep stiff and still and blind

Ravensbrücken Belzec
Sobibor Bergen-Belsen
Majdanek Chelmno Treblinka
Auschwitz

The people are in the kraal
And with first light of morrow
Here's two socks bone-white as sorrow

And sleep pickaninny
And all the night-hooded names
I'm not yet allowed to say

What blackens the tongue
With the stone of its closeness
The tongue makes black

Aia lu du-du

Translated from the Afrikaans by the author

ASIA

FAIZ AHMED FAIZ

Pakistan (1911–1984)

The son of a lawyer and wealthy landowner, Faiz Ahmed Faiz was born in Sialkot in the Punjab, then a part of India under British rule. He studied both English and Arabic literature at the university and in the 1930s became involved with the leftist Progressive Movement. During World War II he served in the Indian army, but with the 1947 division of the subcontinent, he moved to Pakistan, where he served as editor of *The Pakistan Times*. He was also closely involved with the founding of labor unions in the country and in 1962 was awarded the Lenin Peace Prize by the Soviet Union. But before that he spent some years in solitary confinement, under a sentence of death, accused of helping to overthrow the government. The very government that had imprisoned him came, after his release, to praise him, and he was eventually put in charge of the National Council of the Arts. By the time of his death in Lahore—after another period of exile in Lebanon—his popularity with both the literary elite and the masses was enormous. He charged the traditional romantic imagery of Urdu poetry with a new political tension, so that when his poems speak of the "beloved," they may be referring both to a woman or muse and to the idea of revolution.

Don't Ask Me for That Love Again

That which then was ours, my love,
don't ask me for that love again.
The world then was gold, burnished with light—
and only because of you. That's what I had believed.
How could one weep for sorrows other than yours?
How could one have any sorrow but the one you gave?
So what were these protests, these rumors of injustice?
A glimpse of your face was evidence of springtime.
The sky, wherever I looked, was nothing but your eyes.
If you'd fall into my arms, Fate would be helpless.

All this I'd thought, all this I'd believed.
But there were other sorrows, comforts other than love.
The rich had cast their spell on history:
dark centuries had been embroidered on brocades and silks.
Bitter threads began to unravel before me
as I went into alleys and in open markets
saw bodies plastered with ash, bathed in blood.
I saw them sold and bought, again and again.
This too deserves attention. I can't help but look back
when I return from those alleys—what should one do?
And you still are so ravishing—what should I do?
There are other sorrows in this world,
comforts other than love.
Don't ask me, my love, for that love again.

Translated from the Urdu by Agha Shahid Ali

A Prison Evening

Each star a rung,
night comes down the spiral
staircase of the evening.
The breeze passes by so very close
as if someone just happened to speak of love.
In the courtyard,
the trees are absorbed refugees
embroidering maps of return on the sky.
On the roof,
the moon—lovingly, generously—
is turning the stars
into a dust of sheen.
From every corner, dark-green shadows,
in ripples, come towards me.
At any moment they may break over me,
like the waves of pain each time I remember
this separation from my lover.

This thought keeps consoling me:
though tyrants may command that lamps be smashed
in rooms where lovers are destined to meet,
they cannot snuff out the moon, so today,
nor tomorrow, no tyranny will succeed,
no poison of torture make me bitter,
if just one evening in prison
can be so strangely sweet,
if just one moment anywhere on this earth.

Translated from the Urdu by Agha Shahid Ali

Fragrant Hands

For the Anonymous Woman Who Sent Me a Bouquet of Flowers in Prison

A strange arrangement to comfort the heart—
someone has made that possible
in a corner of the cell
with giving, generous hands,

and the air is now so softened,
I compare it with the Beloved's hair,
the air is so drowned,
I think a body, wearing a jewelry of blossoms,
has just passed this way.

And as the air holds itself together,
a bouquet of compassion,
I can say:

Let thousands of watches be set on cages
by those who worship cruelty,
fidelity will always be in bloom—
this fidelity on which are grafted
the defeats and triumphs of the heart.

Should you, Oh air, ever come across her,
   my friend of fragrant hands,
recite this from Hafiz of Shiraz to her:
   "Nothing in this world is without terrible barriers—
   Except love, but only when it begins."

Translated from the Urdu by Agha Shahid Ali

Vista

Deserted street, shadows of trees and houses, locked doors—
We watched the moon become a woman,
baring her breast, softly, on the edge of a rooftop.
Below the earth was blue, a lake of stilled shadows,
on which a leaf, the bubble of a second, floated
and then burst, softly.
Pale, very pale, gently, very slowly,
wine that is cold color
was poured into my glass,
and the roses of your hands, the decanter and the glass,
were, like the outline
of a dream, in focus, for a moment.
Then they melted, softly.
My heart once again promised love, softly.
You said, "But softly."
The moon, breathing as it went down, said,
"More, yet more softly."

Translated from the Urdu by Agha Shahid Ali

So Bring the Order for My Execution

The Day of Judgment is here.
A restless crowd has gathered all around the field.
This is the accusation: that I have loved you.

No wine is left in the taverns of this earth.
But those who swear by rapture,
this is their vigil:

they've made sure,
simply with a witnessing thirst,
that intoxication is not put out today.

In whose search is the swordsman now?
His blade red, he's just come from the City of Silence,
its people exiled or finished to the last.

The suspense that lasts between killers and weapons
as they gamble: who will die and whose turn is next?
That bet has now been placed on me.

So bring the order for my execution.
I must see with whose seals the margins are stamped,
recognize the signatures on the scroll.

Translated from the Urdu by Agha Shahid Ali

You Tell Us What to Do

When we launched life
on the river of grief,
how vital were our arms, how ruby our blood.
With a few strokes, it seemed,
we would cross all pain,
we would soon disembark.
That didn't happen.
In the stillness of each wave we found invisible currents.
The boatmen, too, were unskilled,
their oars untested.
Investigate the matter as you will,
blame whomever, as much as you want,

but the river hasn't changed,
the raft is still the same.
Now *you* suggest what's to be done,
you tell us how to come ashore.

When we saw the wounds of our country
appear on our skins,
we believed each word of the healers.
Besides, we remembered so many cures,
it seemed at any moment
all troubles would end, each wound heal completely.
That didn't happen: our ailments
were so many, so deep within us
that all diagnoses proved false, each remedy useless.
Now do whatever, follow each clue,
accuse whomever, as much as you will,
our bodies are still the same,
our wounds still open.
Now tell us what we should do,
you tell us how to heal these wounds.

Translated from the Urdu by Agha Shahid Ali

TASLIMA NASRIN

Bangladesh (b. 1962)

Taslima Nasrin was born in Mymensingh, Bangladesh, the daughter of a doctor. Like her father, she studied medicine and, after graduating in 1984, worked as a gynecologist and anesthesiologist in hospitals in Dacca, the capital. During her medical studies, she gained prominence as a strongly feminist newspaper columnist; she also began to publish poetry and fiction. In 1993 her novel *Shame* was banned by the Bangladeshi government on the ground that its "inflammatory" tone excited tensions between Muslims and Hindus. Her work continues to call for secular, liberal solutions to deeply ingrained injustices. As she has written in one poem, "From now on let religion's other name be humanity." Conservative mullahs began to offer rewards to anyone who would murder her. In 1994, during an interview with a Calcutta newspaper, she asserted—and later claimed she has been misquoted—that the Koran should be revised. Fundamentalists demanded her execution for blasphemy. Nasrin went into hiding and eventually sought asylum in Sweden, where she continues to live. In 1994 the European Parliament awarded her the Sakharov Prize for Freedom of Thought. She has published eight collections of poems; most of them are rallying cries against the oppression of Bangladeshi women.

Character

You're a girl
and you'd better not forget
that when you step over the threshold of your house
men will look askance at you.
When you keep on walking down the lane
men will follow you and whistle.
When you cross the lane and step onto the main road
men will revile you and call you a loose woman.

If you've got no character
you'll turn back,
and if not
you'll keep on going,
          as you're going now.

Translated from the Bengali by Carolyne Wright and Farida Sarkar

Border

I'm going to move ahead.
Behind me my whole family is calling,
my child is pulling at my *sari*-end,
my husband stands blocking the door,
but I will go.
There's nothing ahead but a river
I will cross.
I know how to swim but they
won't let me swim, won't let me cross.

There's nothing on the other side of the river
          but a vast expanse of fields
but I'll touch this emptiness once
and run against the wind, whose whooshing sound
makes me want to dance. I'll dance someday
and then return.

I've not played keep-away for years
          as I did in childhood.
I'll raise a great commotion playing keep-away someday
and then return.

For years I haven't cried with my head
          in the lap of solitude.
I'll cry to my heart's content someday
and then return.

There's nothing ahead but a river
and I know how to swim.
Why shouldn't I go? I'll go.

Translated from the Bengali by Carolyne Wright and Farida Sarkar

At the Back of Progress . . .

The fellow who sits in the air-conditioned office
is the one who in his youth raped
                    a dozen or so young girls
and at the cocktail party, he's secretly stricken with lust
fastening his eyes on the belly button of some lovely.
In the five-star hotels, this fellow frequently
          tries out his different tastes
          in sex acts with a variety of women.
This fellow goes home and beats his wife
                    over a handkerchief
                    or a shirt collar.
This fellow sits in his office and talks with people
                    puffing on a cigarette
                    and shuffling through his files.

          Ringing the bell he calls his employee
                              shouts at him
                    orders the bearer to bring tea
                              and drinks.
          This fellow gives out character references for people.

The employee who's speaking in such a low voice
that no one knows or would ever suspect
how much he could raise his voice at home,
               how foul his language could be
               how vile his behavior.
Gathering with his buddies, he buys some movie tickets
and kicking back on the porch outside, indulges
          in loud harangues on politics, art and literature.

Someone is committing suicide   his mother
                         or his grandmother
                  or his great-grandmother.

Returning home he beats his wife
                 over a bar of soap or
                 the baby's pneumonia.

The bearer who brings the tea
who keeps the lighter in his pocket
and who gets a couple of *takā* as a tip:
he's divorced his first wife for her sterility,
his second wife for giving birth to a daughter,
he's divorced his third wife for not bringing dowry.
Returning home, this fellow beats his fourth wife
over a couple of green chilis or a handful of cooked rice.

Translated from the Bengali by Carolyne Wright and Mohammad Nurul Huda

Eve Oh Eve

Why won't Eve eat of the fruit?
Didn't Eve have a hand to reach out with,
fingers with which to make a fist;
didn't Eve have a stomach to feel hunger with,
a tongue to feel thirst,
a heart with which to love?

But then why won't Eve eat of the fruit?

Why would Eve merely suppress her wishes,
regulate her steps?
Subdue her thirst?
Why would Eve be so compelled
to keep Adam moving around in the Garden of Eden
                 all their lives?

Because Eve has eaten of the fruit
                    there are sky and earth,
because she has eaten
                    there are moon, sun, rivers and seas.
Because she has eaten, trees, plants and vines,
because Eve has eaten of the fruit
                    there is joy, because she has eaten there is joy,
joy, joy—
Eating of the fruit, Eve made a heaven of the earth.

Eve, if you get hold of the fruit
                    don't ever refrain from eating.

Translated from the Bengali by Carolyne Wright and Mohammad Nurul Huda

Another Life

Women spend the afternoon squatting on the porch
                    picking lice from each other's hair,
they spend the evening feeding the little ones
                    and lulling them to sleep in the glow of the bottle
                      lamp.
The rest of the night they offer their backs
                    to be slapped and kicked by the men of the house
or sprawl half-naked on the hard wooden cot—

Crows and women greet the dawn together.
Women blow into the oven to start the fire,
tap on the back of the winnowing tray with five fingers
                    and with two fingers pick out stones.

Women spend half their lives picking stones from the rice.

Stones pile up in their hearts,
there's no one to touch them with two fingers . . .

Translated from the Bengali by Carolyne Wright

A. K. RAMANUJAN

India (1929–1993)

Attipat Krishnaswami Ramanujan was born in Mysore, the son of a mathematician and astronomer, and was raised with a strange family custom. On the first floor of the house, Tamil was spoken; upstairs English and Sanskrit were spoken; from the roof terrace, the local Kannada language could be heard. The boy grew up fluent in all these languages. After graduating from Maharaja's College in Mysore, he began writing poems in several languages. He taught for some years and developed a fascination with Indian folklore. He came to the United States and earned a doctorate in linguistics at Indiana University in 1963 but afterwards moved to Sri Lanka, planning to become a Buddhist. In the end he accepted a job teaching South Asian languages and literature at the University of Chicago, a post he held until his death; he edited and translated many volumes of verse, including the acclaimed *Speaking of Siva*. In 1976 he was awarded the honorary title of Padma Sri by the Indian government, and his many prizes included a MacArthur Fellowship in 1983. The flux of life was his principal theme. "To see such flowing continuity," he once wrote, "is truly to be an alvar, truly to be the 'immersed one.' " The swirl of images and repetitive changes within poetic forms embodied his concerns. Throughout his career he tried to express the richness of Tamil and Kannada culture and literary traditions in English verse, to combine several imaginations within a single sensibility.

Elements of Composition

Composed as I am, like others,
of elements on certain well-known lists,
father's seed and mother's egg

gathering earth, air, fire, mostly
water, into a mulberry mass,
moulding calcium,

carbon, even gold, magnesium and such,
    into a chattering self tangled
in love and work,

scary dreams, capable of eyes that can see,
    only by moving constantly,
the constancy of things

like Stonehenge or cherry trees;

add uncle's eleven fingers
    making shadow-plays of rajas
and cats, hissing,

becoming fingers again, the look
    of panic on sister's face
an hour before

her wedding, a dated newspaper map
    of a place one has never seen, maybe
no longer there

after the riots, downtown Nairobi,
    that a friend carried in his passport
as others would

a woman's picture in their wallets;

add the lepers of Madurai,
    male, female, married,
with children,

lion faces, crabs for claws,
    clotted on their shadows
under the stone-eyed

goddesses of dance, mere pillars,
    moving as nothing on earth
can move—

I pass through them
    as they pass through me
taking and leaving

affections, seeds, skeletons,

millennia of fossil records
    of insects that do not last
a day,

body-prints of mayflies,
    a legend half-heard
in a train

of the half-man searching
    for an ever-fleeing
other half

through Muharram tigers,
    hyacinths in crocodile waters,
and the sweet

twisted lives of epileptic saints,

and even as I add,
    I lose, decompose
into my elements,

into other names and forms,
    past, and passing, tenses
without time,

caterpillar on a leaf, eating,
   being eaten.

In the Zoo

A Tour with Comments

And these
these are scavenger birds
          fit emblems
for a city like Calcutta
or Madurai
crammed to the top of its gates

They are known generally
as adjutant storks
        yes they have a long-legged dignity
that's slightly vulgar

Adjutant storks come in three shades
a faded black
      like Madras lawyers *a grey*
a dirty white
     like grandmother's maggoty curds

They are rather noisy and heavy
in their take-off
and flap themselves into air
        like father
into the rain, his baggy umbrellas with three ribs
broken by his sons in a fencing match and three
by last year's winds

But once air-borne
      this furry spider-legged auntie
of a bird
    it circles
on motionless wings
      filling the sky's transparency

with slow sleepy perfect circles
like father's Magic Carpet story
that rowdy day when the rainstorm leaked
through the roof
and mother was ill
and he had to mop
the kitchen of our pattering feet

Pleasure

A naked Jaina monk
ravaged by spring
fever, the vigour

of long celibacy
lusting now as never before
for the reek and sight

of mango bud, now tight, now

loosening into petal,
stamen, and butterfly,
his several mouths

thirsting for breast,
buttock, smells of finger,
long hair, short hair,

the wet of places never dry,

skin roused even by
whips, self touching self,
all philosophy slimed

by its own saliva,
cool Ganges turning
sensual on him,

smeared his own private

untouchable Jaina
body with honey
thick and slow as pitch,

and stood continent
at last on an anthill
of red fire ants, crying

his old formulaic cry

at every twinge,
"Pleasure, Pleasure,
Great Pleasure!"—

no longer a formula
in the million mouths
of pleasure-in-pain

as the ants climb, tattooing

him, limb by limb,
and covet his body,
once naked, once even intangible.

At Forty,

our Jatti, palace wrestler of Mysore,

teacher at the gym, has the grey
eyes of a cat, a yellow moustache,
and a whorl of tabby hair
on his chest.

No shirts under his military pea-coat
except on special days, when he wears

ribbons, medals and stripes—his father's
from World War One.

Someone in the palace is said to have said
one day, "Jatti, the Wrestler, our teacher at the gym,
is now in top form, our state's very best,"
and so they trim

his hair, give him all-body shaves to bring out
the fury of his yellow moustache.
Eggs and meat for breakfast, massages
of iguana fat,

till he glows in the dark, a lit medallion
figure. No sex, they whisper, for even
a look at your wife or that rumoured Muslim mistress
will drain

your power, loosen your grip. They weigh him,
measure his chest, his belly, his thigh,
and they pat his treasure. One April day,
they take him out

in a procession of purple turbans,
urchins, and burnished brass, the raucous
palace band on hire, from clocktower
to market square

to the white ropes of the red arena
in the Town Hall, where he is thrown
round after round, rolled over, jeered at
by rowdies

and sat upon by a nobody from nowhere,
a black hulk with a vulgar tiger's name
strutting in pink satin shorts. Jatti,
the Wrestler,

our teacher at the gym, walks away,
shaking off a swarm of eyes and hands, walks fast

and slow, in white trunks and bare feet,
through backstreet mats

of drying grain, straight to the gym,
to the red earth pit where he'd sparred
all year. Neck-deep he buries his body
in familiar ground,

only his bloodshot eyes moving in his head
and sometimes his short-haired scalp,
tabby-grey; his moustache unwaxed, turned down,
caked with mud.

Five disciples, we fumble and exercise
under a dusty bulb with dumb-bells
and parallel bars, over and over,
all eyes,

not knowing where to look
or when to leave, till he suddenly
shakes his body free, showers at full blast
under the corner tap,

and gently booms, "I've to go home, boys,"
like every day, and leaves, never
to come back, but to become
a sulphurous foreman

in a matchstick factory, well-known
for the fury of his yellow moustache,
once Jatti, wrestler, our teacher
at the gym.

Some People

Others see a rush, a carnival, a million,
why does he see nothing, or worse, just one:

a singular body, a familiar head?
You'd worry too, wouldn't you, if,

in a whole milling conference
on Delhi milk and China soybean, in all

that human hair, national
smells and international fragrance,

you saw your wife from another life,
wed and left behind in childhood,

now six weeks dead, yet standing there
in raw-silk sari, in sandalwood footwear?

JAYANTA MAHAPATRA

India (b. 1928)

Jayanta Mahapatra was born in Cuttack, in Orissa, and has lived there most of his life. He went away to school, studied science, and for some years was a lecturer in physics at Ravenshaw College. His meditative poems survey the tumult and tedium of Indian life with a lonely calm. "Mystery has always fascinated me," he has said, "a sense of the unknown, of things unexplainable, and this has found its way into my poetry. And it is this quality of the ununderstandable which somehow goes to make the beauty of a poem. And this is how I feel: that one must try somehow to reach the border between things understandable and ununderstandable in a poem, between life and death, between a straight line and a circle. . . . Recurrent themes of women appear in my poetry, particularly the Indian woman, who seems to have suffered so much, and who still fascinates me by her seeming contentment."

A Summer Poem

Over the soughing of the sombre wind
priests chant louder than ever:
the mouth of India opens.

Crocodiles move into deeper waters.

Mornings of heated middens
smoke under the sun.

The good wife
lies in my bed
through the long afternoon;
dreaming still, unexhausted
by the deep roar of funeral pyres.

Main Temple Street, Puri

Children, brown as earth, continue to laugh away
at cripples and mating mongrels.
Nobody ever bothers about them.

The temple points to unending rhythm.

On the dusty street the colour of shorn scalp
there are things moving all the time
and yet nothing seems to go away from sight.

Injuries drowsy with the heat.

And that sky there,
claimed by inviolable authority,
hanging on to its crutches of silence.

Taste for Tomorrow

At Puri, the crows.

The one wide street
lolls out like a giant tongue.

Five faceless lepers
move aside
as a priest passes by.

And at the street's end
the crowds thronging the temple door:

a huge holy flower
swaying in the wind of greater reasons.

Sanskrit

Awaken them; they are knobs of sound
that seem to melt and crumple up
like some jellyfish of tropical seas,
torn from sleep with a hand lined by prophecies.
Listen hard; their male, gaunt world sprawls the page
like rows of tree trunks reeking in the smoke
of ages, the branches glazed and dead;
as though longing to make up with the sky,
but having lost touch with themselves
were unable to find themselves, hold meaning.

And yet, down the steps into the water at Varanasi,
where the lifeless bodies seem to grow human,
the shaggy heads of word-buds move back and forth
between the harsh castanets of the rain
and the noiseless feathers of summer—
aware that their syllables' overwhelming silence
would not escape the hearers now, and which
must remain that mysterious divine path
guarded by drifts of queer, quivering banyans:
a language of clogs over cobbles, casting
its uncertain spell, trembling sadly into mist.

Ash

The substance that stirs in my palm
could well be a dead man; no need
to show surprise at the dizzy acts of wind.
My old father sitting uncertainly three feet away

is the slow cloud against the sky:
so my heart's beating makes of me a survivor
over here where the sun slowly sets.
The ways of freeing myself:

the glittering flowers, the immensity of rain
which were limited to promises once
have had the lie to themselves. And the wind,
that had made simple revelation in the leaves,

plays upon the ascetic-faced vision of waters;
and without thinking
something makes me keep close to the walls
as though I were afraid of that justice in the shadows.

Now the world passes into my eye:
the birds flutter towards rest around the tree,
the clock jerks each memory towards the present,
to become a past, floating away like ash, over the bank.

My own stirrings like the wind's
keep hoping for the solace that would be me
in my father's eyes
to pour the good years back on me;

the dead man who licks my palms
is more likely to encourage my dark intolerance
rather than turn me
towards some strangely solemn charade:

the dumb order of the myth
lined up in the life-field,
the unconcerned wind perhaps truer than the rest
rustling the empty, bodiless grains.

A Monsoon Day Fable

The fable at the beginning of the monsoon
echoes alone, like a bell ringing in a temple
far from home. The furrows of earth that turned
year after year do not change shape or colour:

is it music, this immortality? Crouching silence
that takes cover inside a lump of shadow,
simply mocking man? Suddenly the face of the girl
I cannot have appears before me.
And the tune of the latest hit song interrupts itself,
then resumes in my head. I think
of visiting the afternoon movie hoping to see
the ageing dancer who lives by herself across the street.
I feel the silence of a woman's secret whiteness
where her petticoat, loose and undone, lies open
sorrowfully, as though after an act of love.
I feel the silence of the ugly, squint-eyed girl
as she paces the street, between the taunting buildings.
All this adds up to a silence the meaning of which
I cannot reach; or was it a destiny, a fable,
a scent of the same rain on the earth?
Or the pull of a loose muscle in the dancer's startled leg?
The Cuttack dawn herds the emaciated cows
toward the municipal slaughter-house, their feet
slipping, their eyes following the vague light
into silence. Wet, as though with glue, they haunt
me through the nights, perhaps equipped with designs
to show man his true nature, perhaps
like the eyes of Einstein. For me to deny
the thought that I am in a sort of exile.
My observation is limited to the process of my falling,
and neither the law of falling bodies
nor the general theory of relativity stills the wing.
The day stands like a mature prime minister
but a thousand thoughts away, a thousand voices above
the level of mournful lowing in my room.
I pick up the morning newspaper and see
how a nation goes on insulting itself
with its own web of rhetoric. And remember how
some of us poets had participated at the Silver Jubilee
Celebrations of the *Sahitya Akademi* in New Delhi,
and with plagiarized smiles and abstract talk
convinced ourselves that in harmony there was
no deception. It seems so strange looking at one another
and finding ourselves go into the distances of our eyes;

even my wife does not look as if she belonged to me,
and even the spittle I swallow every hour
has nothing perhaps to do with me, like
that unreachable Girl who leads me to a dim corner
of my conscience, alone. Alone, I look at her
as though I do not understand, the heart dry
in the midst of all this wetness.
At dawn when rain scratches against my skin
I hear again that familiar beat which did nothing
but merely quicken for someone's presence,
and I hear the silence of today
in its song of dead refrains:
a lonely halo of earth
that gazes aimlessly about the footprints
of someone going home.

NGUYEN CHI THIEN

Vietnam (b. 1933)

Nguyên Chí Thiên was born in Hanoi and grew up in Haiphong. In 1958, swayed by the Let-a-Hundred-Flowers-Bloom movement in North Vietnam, he tried to publish a journal independent of government control; for doing so he was sentenced to two years in a "reeducation" camp. Still defiant after his release, he was arrested again and condemned to one camp after another until 1978. He returned to Haiphong but was denied employment by the Communist authorities. To survive he rented out his room to prostitutes, and with the money he made he bought pen and paper to write down the poems he had composed and memorized during his long years in prison camps. On April 2, 1979, he ran into the British Embassy in Hanoi and left his collection of poems with a clerk. He was soon arrested again. But his poems made it to London and were published. Once his work and fate were known, international pressure was brought to bear on Hanoi, and Thiên was released from prison in 1991. One quality prized by Vietnamese poets, in addition to clever wordplay, is that a poem be *hung,* forthright from the heart. Thiên's poems, recounting his days and nights in prison, are just that.

A Jungle Night

A jungle night—it rains and rains, roofs leak.
Shivering with cold, we hug our knees, trade stares.
The pale blue dot of fire on an oil lamp.
The can for piss, the can for shit.
The bed with stinging bugs.
A prisoner's New Year's Eve, in Sixty-one.

Translated from the Vietnamese by Huynh Sanh Thông

This Land's No Joy

This land's no joy.
By day they wipe off sweat, and tears by night.
To prison camps and barracks they all stream—
a trickle will come back.
Children look pale and sick,
like young banana leaves.
Of plowing women take full charge.
In hamlets not a glimpse of younger men.
Death notices drop thick and fast on thatch.
Here all is grief—
only loudspeakers will spout joy.

Translated from the Vietnamese by Huynh Sanh Thông

The Model Children of the Regime

The model children of the regime
seemed darlings when they came to jail,
toddling around without their pants:
the prison blouses covered them
down to their feet.
But as time flies, they've reached the age of ten.
With noses in the air,
they're regular terrors now.
When gape their mouths,
curses come gushing out and spare no one.
And they can kill
for a potato, a cassava root.

Translated from the Vietnamese by Huynh Sanh Thông

Travel with Grief—Goodbye to Joy

Travel with grief—goodbye to joy!
For baggage you have sweat and dust.
Some pocket money: poems and sweet dreams.
A dark, foul car—enjoy the smell.
Above the train a red flash glows:
somewhere, a storm is running wild?

Translated from the Vietnamese by Huynh Sanh Thông

from Sundry Notes

25

The Party holds you down and you lie still.
When all are equal—scholars, dunces, beasts—
the paramount, hair-graying question is:
two meals, oh for two meals!

26

But who are you? The minute I saw you
I felt a sorrow I could not escape.
Your eyes revived so many thirsts
I thought I'd smothered long ago.

48

The Party's wrapped all dreams inside a shirt
and packed men's purpose in a crock of rice.
Sound maintenance—still, the Party feels unsafe:
it stores away all dreams and men in jails.

68

Short measure get all sentiments in jail,
where friendship weighs less than a cigarette,
where loyalty, like a report card, spreads thin,
where self-respect a spoon of rice knocks down.

Translated from the Vietnamese by Huynh Sanh Thông

BEI DAO

China (b. 1949)

Bei Dao is the pen name of Zhao Zhenkai, the most prominent of the so-called Misty Poets, who turned away from Maoist social realism to explore the subjective world of private feelings. Bei was born in Beijing. The Cultural Revolution interrupted his education; he joined the Red Guard and was put to work on construction projects. In 1978, with his friend Mang Ke, he started the influential underground literary magazine *Jintian* (Today). All during China's Democracy Movement in the late 1970s, Bei Dao was a leading voice. If his early poems of love and political rebellion seem sentimental at times, his more mature work has kept its mysterious, even private aura while providing an acute analysis of the contradictory forces of historic change. By the mid-1980s he had become a member of the Chinese Writers' Association and gained a measure of official acceptance. But during the summer of 1989, while he was in Berlin for a writers' conference, the massacre in Tiananmen Square occurred and he decided to exile himself from China. Since then he has lived in Scandinavia and the United States, and opened his poems to a range of Western images.

Answer

The scoundrel carries his baseness around like an ID card.
The honest man bears his honor like an epitaph.
Look—the gilded sky is swimming
with undulant reflections of the dead.

They say the ice age ended years ago.
Why are there icicles everywhere?
The Cape of Good Hope has already been found.
Why should all those sails contend on the Dead Sea?

I came into this world with nothing
but paper, rope, and shadow.
Now I come to be judged,
and I've nothing to say but this:

Listen. *I don't believe!*
OK. You've trampled
a thousand enemies underfoot. Call me
a thousand and one.

I don't believe the sky is blue.
I don't believe what the thunder says.
I don't believe dreams aren't real,
that beyond death there is no reprisal.

If the sea should break through the sea-wall,
let its brackish water fill my heart.
If the land should rise from the sea again,
we'll choose again to live in the heights.

The earth revolves. A glittering constellation
pricks the vast defenseless sky.
Can you see it there? that ancient ideogram—
the eye of the future, gazing back.

Translated from the Chinese by Donald Finkel

The August Sleepwalker

On the sea-floor a stone bell, tolling,
tolling, roils the waves.

It's August tolling.
That isn't the noon-high August sun,

it's a sail billowing with milk
over floating corpses.

It's August billowing,
August apples tumbling from the heights.

Now the long-dead beacon's
agleam with sailors' eyes.

It's August gleaming,
a country fair, presaging the first frost.

On the sea-floor a stone bell, tolling,
tolling, roils the waves.

The August sleepwalker has seen
the midnight sun.

Translated from the Chinese by Donald Finkel

Accomplices

After all those years
mica glints in the mud,
evil as it is bright,
tiny suns in vipers' eyes.

Branch roads appear and disappear
in the hands of trees.
Where did that fawn go?
Only cemeteries could assuage
this desolation, like tiny cities.

Freedom is only the distance
between the hunter and his prey.
As we turn to look,
a bat describes a sweeping arc
across the vast canvas of our inheritance
and vanishes into the dusk.

Nor are we free of guilt.
Long since, in history's mirror,
we became accomplices,

awaiting the day we might
seep down through the layers of stone
into subterranean pools
to contemplate darkness again.

Translated from the Chinese by Donald Finkel

The Collection

The window makes a frame for the sky
the sky's in my collection

A black rubber mountain range
the century's evening
people who name stars can hear
the bugle sobbing
the metal's difficult breathing
a metal infant is born
inside earth's fence
on the open book of mankind
a peasant's hut curses loudly to the fields
the fan falls ill
the wind which interrogates the seasons drowns in the sea
shifting the thousands of lanterns which
light the way for the souls of the dead

The window makes a frame for me
I'm in the sky's collection

Translated from the Chinese by Bonnie S. McDougall and Chen Maiping

An Evening Scene

On the electrified ocean
the fleet laden with messengers holding lamps
presses on towards the details of the dark

the moment's knife-edge
pares away the flames on each cypress
the branches curve towards the darker side

after having changed the night's direction
the stone house on the cliff
opens its doors and windows on all sides

the souls who've come from afar
collect on the bright clean china plate
a long-legged mosquito stands in the middle

Translated from the Chinese by Bonnie S. McDougall and Chen Maiping

Discovery

City cactus
(these affectionate migrants)
scatter, but use thorns to form an alliance with flowers
taking ice from the mouth of the drowned
drawing heat from the gold's low flame
God is—smoke like a dragon
the woman leading a dog
is the last train, with no destination
what the drunks get on is a dream

I come back home from landscapes and atrocities
passing through the four seasons' revolving door
in the room where it is snowing
I find my childhood toys
and a secret mark on the clockwork springs

Translated from the Chinese by Bonnie S. McDougall and Chen Maiping

SHU TING

China (b. 1952)

Shu Ting is the pen name of Gong Peiyu, who was born in Fujian. During the Cultural Revolution, when she had not yet finished high school, she was sent to the countryside because her father was accused of political nonconformity. She was soon put to work in a cement factory and later in a textile mill. During these years—stimulated by reading foreign poetry— she began to write poems, and in 1979 she started publishing her work. She quickly established a reputation for lyrics at once powerful and delicate. By 1983 she was asked to join the official Chinese Writers' Association. In both 1981 and 1983, she won the National Poetry Award. Shu lives in Xiamen and has traveled extensively in Europe and the United States. Her poems search the emotional life for signs of what lies beneath and beyond the self.

Missing You

A multi-colored chart without a boundary;
An equation chalked on the board, with no solution;
A one-stringed lyre that tells the beads of rain;
A pair of useless oars that never cross the water.

Waiting buds in suspended animation;
The setting sun is watching from a distance.
Though in my mind there may be an enormous ocean,
What emerges is the sum: a pair of tears.

Yes, from these vistas, from these depths,
Only this.

Translated from the Chinese by Carolyn Kizer

Assembly Line

In time's assembly line
Night presses against night.
We come off the factory night-shift
In line as we march towards home.
Over our heads in a row
The assembly line of stars
Stretches across the sky.
Beside us, little trees
Stand numb in assembly lines.

The stars must be exhausted
After thousands of years
Of journeys which never change.
The little trees are all sick,
Choked on smog and monotony,
Stripped of their color and shape.
It's not hard to feel for them;
We share the same tempo and rhythm.

Yes, I'm numb to my own existence
As if, like the trees and stars
—perhaps just out of habit
—perhaps just out of sorrow,
I'm unable to show concern
For my own manufactured fate.

Translated from the Chinese by Carolyn Kizer

The Singing Flower

Thanks to your shining my agony has a faint halo.

I

I am already a singing flower
Upon your breast
Stirred by the breeze of your breath
As the moonlit fields are stirred.

Cover me, please
With your wide palm
For the time being.

II

Now permit me to dream:
Snow. Huge forest.
Ancient windbell. Slanting tower.
May I ask for a genuine Christmas tree?
Ice skates on its branches,
Fairy tales, magic flutes,
Fireworks vaunting their ardent fountains.
May I rush through the streets laughing loudly?

III

What has become of my little basket
Heaped with weeds from my Bumper Crop Allotment?
What has become of my old army canteen?
O those thirsty naps under the scaffolding!
The barrettes I never had a chance to wear.
My English exercises: I LOVE YOU LOVE YOU.
My shadow, stretched or shortened under the streetlamp
And my tears
        that flowed so many times, so many times choked back.

And more
And more

Don't ask me
Why I toss lightly in my dreams.
The past, like a cricket in the corner
Whines in its low, persistent voice.

IV

Permit me a calm dream.
Don't leave me alone.
That short street—so short!
We have been walking for years.

Permit me a quiet dream.
Don't disturb me.
Those wheeling crows that pester us—
Pay no attention if your eyes are clear.

Permit me a dream of absurdity.
Don't laugh at me.
Each day, newly green, I walk into your poem.
Each evening I return to you, bright rose.

Let me have an indecent dream.
Tolerate my tyranny
When I say, You're mine, you are mine!
Don't reproach me, beloved . . .
I even confess my eagerness to see
    A thousand waves of passion
    Drown you a thousand times.

V

When our heads touch
As if we were on a speeding train to the moon

The world falls back with a shriek.
The avalanche, Time, swirls madly
        then plunges to pieces.

When our eyes meet
Our souls are like a painting on a gallery wall:
Watery sunlight spreads in rings
        across our field,
Luring us deeper, deeper
        into harmony, silence and renewal.

VI

Just like this
We sit in the darkness, clasping hands
And let the voice of our love, ever old and new
Pierce our hearts.
No need to stir, even though
An emperor is knocking at the door,

Nevertheless . . .

VII

Wait! What is that? What sound
Rouses the scarlet pulsing in my veins?
        Now I am dizzy with love
        On the ever-sober ocean.
What is that? Whose will
Forces open the lids of my soul and body?
    "You must carry the cross on your back
    Every day, and follow me."

VIII

The dream, umbrella-shaped, takes off
And flies away, a dandelion gone to seed
In a cratered moonscape.

IX

Wild plum branch: my passionate love,
You choose the precarious life
On a storm-swept slope
Not the elegant pose in a vase.

Wild swan: my temperament,
You vow to confront winter, unprotected
Even with a bullet wound
Rather than linger in the cage of Spring.

At any rate, my name and my belief
Are entered for the race,
A single runner, to represent my nation.
I have no right to rest.
In the marathon of life
Speed itself is the goal.

X

Towards heaven
Which will judge me in the end
I lift my head.

Wind may sweep me away
But for my heart I reserve the right
To refuse to be counted among the lucky.

XI

Raise your lamp, my love,
    and show the way
So that I and my poems may travel far.
Somewhere, beyond this morass, an ideal bell
Rings in the soft night.
Villages, towns, swarm into my arms:
    lights flicker and burn.

Let my poems travel with me,
But the tentacles of highways signal: do not pass!
Still I may walk through the fields
Guided by flowers.

XII

I walk to the square through the zig-zag streets, back
To the pumpkin shack I guarded, the work in the barley fields,
        deep in the desert (of exile).
Life never stops testing me.
On one side, the laurel wreath, the heavy yoke on the other.
But no one knows I am still that stupid girl
        bad at mathematics.
No matter how the great chorus seems to drown me,
You will hear my singular voice.

XIII

Still I stand
Intrepid, proud, younger than ever!
The bitter storm deep in my heart
But sunshine on my forehead:
My bright, transparent yellow skin,
My clean, luxuriant black hair!

Mother China,
This daughter requires a new name,
She who comes at your call.

XIV

So call me your birch sapling,
Your little blue star, Mother.
If the bullet comes
Let it strike me first.
I shall slide to the ground from your shoulder
Smiling, with clear eyes.

No tears. Red flowers in the grass.
Blood flaming on its crest.

XV

My lover, when that time comes
Don't weep
Though there is no one
       who flings up her pastel skirts,
       who comes through the narrow alley
       where cicadas sing like the rain
       to knock at your stained-glass window.
Then there will be no wicked hand
       to make the alarm clock ring
       saying angrily, "On your mark!
       Time to get back to work!"
But don't make a statue of me
On a jade pedestal
And never, to the sound of a lone guitar,
Turn back the calendar, page by page.

XVI

Your post
Is beneath the banner.
The ideal makes pain bright.
This is the final word
I asked the olive tree
To pass to you.

To find me
Follow the pigeons.
Come in the morning.
I'll be in the hearts
Of women and men.
There you'll find
       your singing flower.

Translated from the Chinese by Carolyn Kizer

Bits of Reminiscence

A toppled wine-cup,
A stone path floating beneath the moon
Where the grass was trampled:
One azalea branch left lying there . . .

Eucalyptus trees begin to spin
In a collage of stars
As I sit on the rusted anchor,
The dizzy sky reflected in my eyes.

A book held up to shut out candlelight;
Fingers lightly at your mouth;
In the fragile cup of silence
A dream, half-illumined, half-obscure.

Translated from the Chinese by Carolyn Kizer

Maple Leaf

Here is a heart-shaped leaf
Picked up by a gentle hand
On a very special hillside
At the edge of a special wood.
It may not mean very much,
This leaf with its trace of frost

But still the leaf reminds me
Of a twilit avenue,
A mind crowded with thoughts
Released on a gentle breath
That scattered from my shoulders
The rays of the setting sun.

Again, on a special evening
That touch alights on me

Having grown heavy with meaning.
This time I can't deny it,
Deny that intimacy.

Now, when the wind rises
I am prompted to turn my head
And listen to you, leaf,
As you quiver on your twig.

Translated from the Chinese by Carolyn Kizer

Gifts

My dream is the dream of a pond
Not just to mirror the sky
But to let the willows and ferns
Suck me dry.
I'll climb from the roots to the veins,
And when leaves wither and fade
I will refuse to mourn
Because I was dying to live.

My joy is the joy of sunlight.
In a moment of creation
I will leave shining words
In the pupils of children's eyes
Igniting golden flames.
Whenever seedlings sprout
I shall sing a song of green.
I'm so simple I'm profound!

My grief is the grief of birds.
The Spring will understand:
Flying from hardship and failure
To a future of warmth and light.
There my blood-stained pinions
Will scratch hieroglyphics

On every human heart
For every year to come.

Because all that I am
Has been a gift from earth.

Translated from the Chinese by Carolyn Kizer

Fairy Tales

for Gu Cheng

You believed in your own story,
then climbed inside it—
a turquoise flower.
You gazed past ailing trees,
past crumbling walls and rusty railings.
Your least gesture beckoned a constellation
of wild vetch, grasshoppers, and stars
to sweep you into immaculate distances.

The heart may be tiny
but the world's enormous.

And the people in turn believe—
in pine trees after rain,
ten thousand tiny suns, a mulberry branch
bent over water like a fishing-rod,
a cloud tangled in the tail of a kite.
Shaking off dust, in silver voices
ten thousand memories sing from your dream.

The world may be tiny
but the heart's enormous.

Translated from the Chinese by Donald Finkel

GU CHENG

China (1956–1993)

Son of the poet Gu Gong, Gu Cheng was born in Beijing. In 1969 he and his family went to Shandong Province, where Gu Cheng worked as a swineherd and read poetry. Five years later he returned to Beijing and worked as a carpenter. He started writing at an early age, and his poems began to appear in 1977, at first anonymously. After the Tiananmen Square massacre in 1989, he emigrated to New Zealand, and his work began to appear abroad. Obsessed with his wife's attention, he insisted that their child be cared for by a Maori nurse and that his wife devote herself to him. In the grip of that obsession, he finally murdered her and then hanged himself.

A Generation

The pitch black night gave me two deep black eyes
with which to search for light.

Translated from the Chinese by Sam Hamill

Discovery

Of all the people who went into the snowy mountains,
Only Bulin discovered the path.
Though there's just a few meters of it,
Though Venus
Broke a tooth there,
None of this prevented
An Englishman from dying,
Lying in the middle of the road, smiling,
Orchids and tender leaves sprouting

From his ears,
And a rosy glow on his face.

What did that mean?
Bulin frowned
And at last he remembered:
When he was nine, he had come
To spend summer, and had planted a box of matches.
They sprouted, and bore
Berries the size of match heads.
The Englishman gobbled them up
Out of greed.

What a discovery!
Unprecedented, perhaps—
  the berry a match bears is poisonous!
Bulin started the trip downhill
And reached the Lama temple made of manure.
He stood stock still, ready to be robbed of his secret
At knifepoint.
But it didn't work out that way. He could only
Sob his heart out
And lash thin copper cables around his stockings
To escape into the deep marshes.

There
Slippers clamored in a frenzy
And turned into a cluster of frogs.

Translated from the Chinese by Eva Hung

Ark

The ship you've boarded
is doomed to go under—
vanish into the breathing sea.

But you still have time to stare at the flag,
or at the dark, unfolding plain,
or at the white birds twittering
over their watery grave.

You still have time to lean on the rail,
puzzled by a sound in the passageway—
though the whole ship is empty,
though every door is ajar—

till cool flames float up
from every cabin.

Translated from the Chinese by Donald Finkel

Forever Parted: Graveyard

In Chunqing, at Shapingba Park among weeds and scrub trees, a good way from the Cemetery of the Revolutionary Martyrs at Geyue Shan, there is a stretch of graves of Red Guards.

No sign that anyone has been here
but me, and my poems, and what can, what should
I say . . .

1. A Labyrinth of Byways Brought Me Here Among You

A labyrinth of byways
brought me here
among you
like a solitary shaft of sunlight
where the tall grass
and the short trees

rise up together.
I do not represent History
or the sounds
that issue from high places.
I came . . .
because it was time for me to come.

You fell in a heap here
on this ground, together,
tears of joy in your eyes,
grasping imaginary guns.
Your hands were
soft, your nails clean,
the hands of those who'd opened school books
and storybooks, books about heroes.
And maybe just out of habit, a habit
we share, on the last page you wrote
your name, your life, your own story.

Now, on my heart's page
there is no grid to guide my hand,
no character to trace,
only the moisture,
the ink blue dew
that has dripped from
the leaves.
To spread it I
can't use a pen,
I can't use a writing brush,
can only use my life's
gentlest breath
to make a single line of
marks worth puzzling over.

2. The Clouds at Geyue Shan Are Cold

The clouds at Geyue Shan
are cold

like a bloodless hand
pointing toward the graves.
In fire and in molten lead
sunken, silent, mother and father
so
caress the beloved child.
You didn't forget
the words they bequeathed you;
maybe it was just those voices
that called on you to die.
You breathed the same faith
with your very last breath.
You don't really lie so far apart
but on the one side there are still fresh flowers,
lively Sunday visitors
and the Young Pioneers,
and on the other, burrs and beggars' lice,
ants and lizards.

You're all so young,
heads of raven hair,
death's dark night
will keep you so, so pure
forever.

I can wish, I can hope
for the Young Pioneer
for the new fruit
or I can wish I were you,
a wedding picture,
fortunate instant,
that lingers forever,
but I go on living,
mind drawn on, drawn out
like a little boat
bearing slowly
through the dusk
toward the shore.

3. I Don't Have a Brother, but I Believe . . .

I don't have an older brother
but I believe you
are my older brother.
In the sandpile,
in the cicada's shrill,
you made a clay tank
and gave it to me.
You made me a paper plane, too.
You taught me to write
characters, to string them artfully
together.
You were a giant
already in sixth grade.

I have an older sister
but I believe you are also
my older sister,
in the dazzle of morning light
skipping rope,
jumping so high,
turning from side to side
as part of the game
as if the brightly colored strands
could catapult you straight up to the sky,
but they were stretched too tight
and I ended up tangled
from standing too close.

And *him*?
Who is *he*?
who pulled the golden feathers from
the reed finch's wing,
spattering the whole earth
with tiny drops of blood,
or teased the borer beetle
with bounds and flame
and forced him to totter
across a window sill stage

for the crime of eating wood chips?
Who was that?
I don't know him,
a man, only.

4. You Lived Among the Peaks

You lived among the peaks.
You lived behind walls.
Every day you went the way you *should* go,
away from the sea you'd never seen.
You never knew love,
never dreamed of another continent,
another world,
only saw *evils* afloat in a fog;
down the middle of every desk, in chalk
ran the "battle line" of the chess game.
You walked it;
you smiled,
and hid whatever you might be moved to think
if you thought it not right.
Moonlight hidden in the shade of branches:
your law
was unfeeling, pitiless,
and you took that cold sparkle for your festival, your fireworks,
and then, one fine morning
with a handful of dry leaves
you polished bright
the bronze buttons on your leather coat
and departed.

Everybody knew
it was the Sun who led you,
to the tune of a marching song,
off to Paradise.
Later, halfway there
you tired, tripped
over a bed whose frame was inlaid

with stars and bullet holes.
It had seemed to you
a game, a game to play,
a game where you could always start all over.

5. Do Not Interrogate the Sun

Don't question the sun.
Yesterday was not his fault;
yesterday there was another star,
a star that burned away
in the fearsome fire of hope.
Today's shrine holds
carefully selected potted plants
and perfect silence,
the silence of
an iceberg
afloat on a warm current.

When will the raucous bazaar,
when will the patched-up merry-go-round
come to life, start to move again
carrying the dancers or the silent
young, the toothless infants
and the toothless old.
Maybe there are always a few lives
destined to be shed
by the world,
the white crane's feathers
found every day at the camp site.

Tangerine, and pale green,
sweet and bitter
the lights come on.
In the fog-soaked dusk
time heals and we go on living.
Let's go home
and go back to living.

I haven't forgotten;
I'll walk carefully past the graves.
The empty eggshell of the moon
will wait there
for the birds that have left to return.

6. Yes, I Go Also

Yes, I am going as well,
to another world, another generation
stepping over your hands.
Though there are fallen leaves
and a scanty snow on the winter sky
I will go on as before.
Beside me—the stones, and the dark grove
and little town as pretty as a cupcake.
I am going to love
and to seek out my soul mates
because it is time for me to go, and to seek.

I believe
that you are the fortunate ones
because the wide earth
cannot flow off
with that arrogant, that innocent grin,
nor will it float up
from the red clay
and be gone.
November's misting rain
when it trickles down to you
will filter out life's doubts.
Eternal dreams
are purer, simpler than life.

I left the cemetery,
left behind the night
and the tangled vines of darkness
still groping

stroking the words engraved on your stones,
groping for you
groping for that life of yours.
Farther off, farther off, the burying ground.
I wish you peace.
I wish the labyrinth of byways
may one day be lost
beneath the new young green of Spring.

Translated from the Chinese by J. P. Seaton and Mu Yi

SO CHONG-JU

Korea (b. 1915)

Sŏ Chŏng-ju was born in the village of Sŏnun, in the southwestern part of Korea, and is now often considered Korea's most important living poet. For most of this century, Korea has been beset by war, occupation, and politics. Sŏ Chŏng-ju looked to Western poets, especially Baudelaire, for ways to write about the experience of an often brutal modernity while striving to keep in the balance a traditional Korean literary sensibility. His early work was noted for its sensuality and realism; his later work is more autobiographical, nostalgic and pastoral, indulging a folkish Buddhism. "The poet," he explains, "in return for having but little, discovers an expanding, deepening longing for things. The poet makes a lamp of that longing, of that singular love, and sets it alight in his heart. With that light, the poet explores numerous levels of inner feeling, gives them names, and in naming them, with the strength derived from that exercise, broadcasts his earnest longing for things to a world afflicted with disinterest."

Flower-Patterned Snake

A back path, steeped in musk and mint.
A beautiful snake.
Into what monstrous sorrow must you have been born
to bear a form so repulsive.

Like flower-patterned anklets.
Your grandfather's eloquent, Eve-beguiling tongue,
voiceless, flickers round your red mouth.
The blue skies—bite them,
in your resentment bite them

and flee, take your face away!

I follow,
hurling stone upon stone after you

down the scented, grass-choked path,
gasping as if I had swallowed oil,
but not because Eve was an ancestor's wife.

How I would like to wear your colors
more lovely than flower-patterned anklets.

The lovely mouth, gleaming red
as if wet with Cleopatra's blood.
Sink down, my snake!

Twenty-year-old Sunie's mouth, beautiful
as a cat's . . . Sink down, my snake!

Translated from the Korean by David R. McCann

Beside a Chrysanthemum

To bring one chrysanthemum
to flower, the cuckoo has cried
since spring.

To bring one chrysanthemum to bloom,
thunder has rolled
through the black clouds.

Flower, like my sister returning
from distant, youthful byways
of throat-tight longing
to stand by the mirror:

for your yellow petals to open
last night such a frost fell,
and I could not sleep.

Translated from the Korean by David R. McCann

Winter Sky

With a thousand nights' dream
I have rinsed clear the gentle brow
of my heart's love,
to transplant it
into the heavens.
A fierce bird
knows, and in mimicry
arcs through the midwinter sky.

Translated from the Korean by David R. McCann

Peony Afternoon

Where you are
a wind
stirs,
becomes a still lake . . .

mountain peak
between us rests its soothing,
today draws near, quietly
becoming a lake . . .

in that lake
the hill and the mountain's shade
cover us, two . . .

Hwem!
        Hwem!
                the peonies' deep
                        red
                                cough . . .

in stately tempo
the mountains hasten
toward you . . .

heaven and
earth
time
now becoming
the flicker of your lashes
as you wake . . .

Translated from the Korean by David R. McCann

A Sneeze

Somewhere
is someone
saying my words?

I stepped out
into the blue autumn day's
winds that touched the ricepaper door.
I sniffed at the weather,
and sneezed.

Somewhere
is someone
saying my words?

Somewhere
as someone says my words,
has a flower overheard and passed them along?

The clouds split as I look up—
a shining brassy spot of sun
on the mountain's back.

Traces that stir
the waves of an old love.

Is someone
somewhere
saying my words?

As someone says them
has an ox overheard?
Does he pass them along?

Translated from the Korean by David R. McCann

If I Became a Stone

If I became
a stone

stone would become
lotus

lotus,
lake

and if I became
a lake

lake would become
lotus

lotus,
stone.

Translated from the Korean by David R. McCann

Untitled

"Pine flower's blooming," says
a friend on the phone
a hundred miles away.
"Just think of the scent!"

"I am
        thinking of it," I say
to myself, facing
a thousand years away.
"Can you imagine
                    this scent?"

Translated from the Korean by David R. McCann

RYUICHI TAMURA

Japan (b. 1923)

Ryūichi Tamura was born in Otsuka, a suburb of Tokyo, and he grew up in the back room of a restaurant run by his mother. This was during an era of natural disasters, economic hardship, and militarism in Japan. In an effort, he said, to "break away from the conservatism and anachronism" of his culture, he began writing self-consciously modernist poems in school and fell in with a group of poets who looked to T. S. Eliot's work for inspiration. He studied at Meiji University but before graduation was drafted into the navy during the last two years of World War II. In postwar Tokyo writers questioned all the old values. "We were glad to be the living dead," he has said of that time, "with nothing to lose. We wanted to question the basic principles behind an industrial society based on war and imperialism. I tried to make my poems into holes or windows that would let me see through the indefinable spiritual waste as well as the obvious spiritual destruction." Since that time Tamura has continued to explore alternatives to the industrialized mechanisms of contemporary life.

Every Morning After Killing Thousands of Angels

I

I read a boy's poem called
"Every Morning After Killing Thousands of Angels"
I forget the poem, but the title won't leave me
I drink some coffee
read a paper read by millions
all the misery
all the destruction in the world
herded into headlines and catch phrases
the only part I trust
is the financial page

a completely blank space governed
by the mechanics of capital and pure speculation

2

That boy's mornings
and my mornings—
how are they different?

3

But the boy can see the angels' faces

4

What do you do
after you kill them?

I go out walking

Where?

To a river with a very big bridge over it

Every morning?

Every morning
while my hands are still bloody

5

I can't kill thousands of angels
but I walk a dry path to the beach
the hot sky's still filled
with sweating typhoon clouds
the sea's a later color

fall is not summer at the horizon
narrow streams run through
spaces silted with darkness
weak-looking capillaries float on my thin hands:
no place to anchor a big bridge

6

Noon at this end of the bridge
everything shines
shirt buttons
decayed tooth
an air rifle
broken sunglass lens
pink shells
smells of seaweed
river water mixing with the sea
sand
and
as far
as my footprints

7

It's my turn now
I'll tell you about the world
at the far end of the bridge
the shadow world
things and concepts totally shadow
shadows feeding on shadows
spreading, radiating like cancer cells
decomposing organs of drowned bodies
green thought swelling and distending
medieval markets surging with merchants and prostitutes and
        monks
cats, sheep, hogs, horses, cows
every kind of meat on the butcher shop hooks
but no blood anywhere

8

So I can't see the bridge
unless I kill thousands of angels?

9

What sight excites me most sexually?
the bridge has disappeared
a riderless black horse
crosses the world of light
slowly, toward the shadow world
but exhausted, it falls
crying animal tears but not rotting
gleaming directly to bone
pure white bone
and then to earth
and then
dawn comes
I've got to go out and live
after killing
killing thousands of angels

Translated from the Japanese by Christopher Drake

My Imperialism

I sink into bed
on the first Monday after Pentecost
and bless myself
since I'm not a Christian

Yet my ears still wander the sky
my eyes keep hunting for underground water
and my hands hold a small book
describing the grotesqueness of modern white society

when looked down at from the nonwhite world
in my fingers there's a thin cigarette—
I wish it were hallucinogenic
though I'm tired of indiscriminate ecstasy

Through a window in the northern hemisphere
the light moves slowly past morning to afternoon
before I can place the red flare, it's gone:
darkness

Was it this morning that my acupuncturist came?
a graduate student in Marxist economics, he says he changed
to medicine to help humanity, the animal of animals, drag itself
    peacefully to its deathbeds
forty years of Scotch whiskey's roasted my liver and put me
into the hands of a Marxist economist
I want to ask him about *Imperialism, A Study*—
what Hobson saw in South Africa at the end of the nineteenth
    century
may yet push me out of bed
even if you wanted to praise imperialism
there aren't enough kings and natives left
the overproduced slaves had to become white

Only the nails grow
the nails of the dead grow too
so, like cats, we must constantly
sharpen ours to stay alive
Only The Nails Grow—not a bad epitaph
when K died his wife buried him in Fuji Cemetery
and had To One Woman carved on his gravestone
true, it was the title of one of his books
but the way she tried to have him only
to herself almost made me cry
even N, who founded the modernist magazine *Luna*
while Japan prepared to invade China
got sentimental after he went on his pension;
F, depressed
S, manic, builds house after house
A has abdominal imperialism: his stomach's colonized his legs

M's deaf, he can endure the loudest sounds;
some people have only their shadows grow
others become smaller than they really are
our old manifesto had it wrong: we only looked upward
if we'd really wanted to write poems
we should have crawled on the ground on all fours—
when William Irish, who wrote *Phantom Lady,* died
the only mourners were stock brokers
Mozart's wife was not at his funeral

My feet grow warmer as I read
Kōtoku Shūsui's *Imperialism, Monster of the Twentieth
    Century,* written back in 1901
when he was young N wrote "I say strange things"
was it the monster that pumped tears from his older eyes?

Poems are commodities without exchange value
but we're forced to invade new territory
by crises of poetic overproduction

We must enslave the natives with our poems
all the ignorant savages under sixty
plagued by a surplus of clothes and food—
when you're past sixty
you're neither a commodity
nor human

Translated from the Japanese by Christopher Drake

Human House

I guess I'll be back late
I said and left the house
my house is made of words
an iceberg floats in my old wardrobe
unseen horizons wait in my bathroom
from my telephone: time, a whole desert

on the table: bread, salt, water
a woman lives in the water
hyacinths bloom from her eyeballs
of course she is metaphor herself
she changes the way words do
she's as free-form as a cat
I can't come near her name

I guess I'll be back late
no, no business meeting
not even a reunion
I ride ice trains
walk fluorescent underground arcades
cut across a shadowed square
ride in a mollusk elevator
violet tongues and gray lips in the trains
rainbow throats and green lungs underground
in the square, bubble language
foaming bubble information, informational information
adjectives, all the hollow adjectives
adverbs, paltry begging adverbs
and nouns, crushing, suffocating nouns
all I want is a verb
but I can't find one anywhere
I'm through with a society
built only of the past and future
I want the present tense

Because you open a door
doesn't mean there has to be a room
because there are windows
doesn't mean there's an interior
doesn't mean there's a space
where humans can live and die—
so far I've opened and shut
countless doors, going out each one
so I could come in through another
telling myself each time
what a wonderful new world lies just beyond
what do I hear?   from the paradise on the other side

dripping water
wingbeats
waves thudding on rocks
sounds of humans and beasts breathing
the smell of blood

Blood
it's been a while
I'd almost forgotten what it smells like
silence gathers around a scream
on the tip of a needle
as he walks slowly toward me
the surgeon puts on his rubber gloves
I close my eyes, open them again
things falling through my eyes
both arms spread like wings
hair streaming out full length
things descending momentary gaps of light
connecting darkness and darkness

I rise slowly from a table in a bar
not pulled by a political slogan or religious belief
it's hard enough trying to find my eyes
to see the demolition of the human house
the dismemberment of my language

My house, of course, isn't made of your words
my house is built of my words

Translated from the Japanese by Christopher Drake

CHIMAKO TADA

Japan (b. 1931)

The nuanced narrative or resonant image has always dominated the aesthetic of Japanese literature. "Intellectual" poetry has never been fashionable. But Chimako Tada—the skilled translator of works by Marguerite Yourcenar and Claude Lévi-Strauss—has sought in her poems to bring cultures and ideas to bear on experience. The results work a strange transformation: Tada can tell the story of Odysseus and make it sound like a No drama; or take the tradition of the flower poem, give it a hit of LSD, and reinvent things. "In poetry," she writes, "all the elements work functionally, each word having a numerical value that changes constantly along with the changes of syntax. When dealing with even a short poem the reader must engage his intellectual energy to follow an equation of almost infinite complexity. How does such difficult work come to be experienced as pleasure? Because the concrete images and situations and structures presented by the poem satisfy not only the senses and the emotions but also the brain's capacity for performing intellectually delicate work. And when to that satisfaction with decoding is added the poetic impact of glimpses of the utterly unexpected, of some other world, the resulting pleasure can approach that bliss which is among the most sublime experiences available to humans."

Wind Invites Wind

wind invites wind
to devour the wolf
blue flesh   quick blood
oh cedar of night   tower of the night

the pollen irresistibly swells and falls
and the moon rounds a white eye
let wind eat wind
let bone bite bone

the breathing gropes and the monkeys cower
piling one fossilized cry on another
oh cedar of night   tower of the night
a glass bird shatters into splinters

rails pierce the forest
red cracks the oven
again wind invites wind
to devour the wolf

Translated from the Japanese by Naoshi Koriyama and Edward Lueders

A Poetry Calendar

I who wait for myself
I who don't appear
again today I turn a page of the sea
throw away a tight-lipped dead clam

    the day   not quite dawn   the beach white
    a mother's barren womb   a broken oar

I who wait for myself
I who don't appear
again today I turn a page of the horizon
throw away a snake's too light slough

    the day   not quite dawn   a useless parasol
    a suspicious laugh   cold fried food

I who wait for myself
I who don't appear
again today I turn a page of the sky
sweep together and throw away all the sooty stardust

    the day   not quite dawn   the grass full of hanging tears
    I leaf and leaf through a calendar

yet I don't appear
I who wait for myself
world of imaginary numbers   love without arms

Translated from the Japanese by Naoshi Koriyama and Edward Lueders

The Odyssey or "On Absence"

1

You, Odysseus trainer of the wooden horse of pleasure
you made your wife swoon in ecstasy with the ardor of your breath
when the shadowy warriors jumped
every night from the broken sides of the wooden horse
Troy burned in the name of Penelope

You who started home a long time ago
wearing around your neck ornaments of the dead gods killed by
      fire
you were always on the waves
always in the shade of rocks
Did that seashell dissolve
in the clear acid sea
and the bittersweet pearl in the shell too
Is Ithaca still swaying on your brow
like a distant star
Is the small island still on your tongue
surrounded by bubbles
not dissolved in the sour saliva
on your broad warm tongue

2

The son grew up perched on the tallest treetop on the island
looking out over the open sea
Every ship could be the Royal one bearing his absent father
the god who did not even have to exist in order to rule

In an angelic moment
Telemachus flew through the sky
alighting on the mast of a ship on the sea
Oh how much like his thoughtful father
the rising grey head of the cresting wave
The mast abruptly tilts
like a scale that has lost its balance

When someday Odysseus returns
his son will for the first time doubt his father's presence
He will fall like a live bird with its wings torn off

But now
by the flowing current bringing along the seasons
by all the silver fish living in the sea
every ship could be that Royal one bearing his absent father

3

In the lonely womb—the warm water clock—
your wife crushes grapes one by one
trickling the juice into the empty space
thereby she is gradually relieved of weight
During the long years of absence
the clusters of grapes have all been crushed
and Penelope is no longer even a woman

In her hands worn out in the act of waiting
the thread will snap one day
the spindle that has been turning will stop
and you will appear out of the shade of the rocks
a man who is husband father and king
white hair streaming over your face like the crest of a breaking
      wave

The suitors will recede muttering like an ebb tide
With doubtful wondering eyes she will look at you

from silence as wide and white as her sandy beach
in sunlight as thick as swarming flies
at Odysseus no longer the hero of the tale

4

The slaughter is finished   Let us have music
The uninvited are all murdered in the course of the banquet
by another uninvited guest

Stepping over the slain bodies
you call the musicians   Let us have music
(All this while Penelope sleeps)

The feast must go on
Lukewarm blood is poured into the wine jar
Let the water and sponge cleanse the foul remembrance
while Penelope sleeps
And oh for some music
oh for a flute to comb her hair
oh for a harp to relax her cheeks
after the ceremony of murder
Closing her eyes to all this
Penelope sleeps on
reluctant to wake from a twenty year dream

Translated from the Japanese by Naoshi Koriyama and Edward Lueders

Universe of the Rose

lysergic acid diethylamide

Each of these microscopic points and lines is in itself a complete
    world;
so size and density exist there in precisely inverse proportion.

Prologue

one rose—
here is the whole range of crimson tones
this sweep of colored petals is a chain of being
joining sky to earth, future to past
I go down the scale, glissando
glimpse the compound eyed prime mover
concealed in folds of flower petals still unborn
immortal spider weaving its web toward infinity. . . .

Universe of the rose

one rose—universe rotating round the ever opening center of a
        flower
wriggling out of dense red darkness
sevenfold eightfold petals evolving toward gossamer rarity

then abruptly from the depths of the rose
a whirlwind rises
words that like a calyx had covered the flower
unable to endure any more   burst

bend backward and weep
(bloodshot compound eyes of the petals!)
the intestines of the rose are a coiled snake
glittering scales in bloom
odor of smoldering pollen
(sunspots multiply)

the countless dead buried in the flower core
in orderly piles spread like a fan
slowly regain their color and one by one stand

out of obscure folds in the undulating waves
simultaneously surges a multitude of coral insects
climbing the flesh-colored atoll

what kind of existence could be a balance
at the center of this ever-expanding rose universe

(place a polished bronze mirror
before the pollen-covered soul)

this flower born from me continually giving birth to me
when stepping on the color tones I follow the spiral staircase
innumerable butterflies rise from the dense grass of my hair
my eyes are dazzled by fragrance
then the spider
huge spider with radially extended legs hangs over me

oh whirlwind   overturning all the ships
funnel sucking them down the purple abyss
slowly rotating
aimed at a shoal of fish in the air
the cast net swiftly spreads

in consummate darkness
the rose had shaken off its withered words
on Libra the Balance
tilted strongly toward daybreak it stood
and roared   all its petals trembling

Epilogue

the universe is the work of an instant
as are all dreams
the divine dream also is short
infinity like rose nectar is hidden in this moment

even in the recreating of daily life
every fragment is given endless shades of color
the dream again and again survives the explosions
my bones will be adorned with the rose

Translated from the Japanese by Kirsten Vidaeus

SHUNTARO TANIKAWA

Japan (b. 1931)

Shuntaro Tanikawa was born in Tokyo, the son of a distinguished philosopher. He scorned the idea of attending college and pursued his writing. By age nineteen he was already a famous poet. When he began writing, poetry was dominated by the so-called Wasteland group, who brooded over Japan's wartime devastation. As a young member of the postwar generation, Tanikawa realized that "after the defeat, all the values that the Japanese believed in were totally destroyed," and he turned to Western culture, fascinated by both high and low. His poems abound with allusions to icons as different as Billy the Kid and Miles Davis, Rilke and Beethoven. He was searching for what he has called a "universal consciousness," a state of being beyond past and future, beyond cultural divisions, beyond poetic schools of thought. If that sounds ponderous, it should be remembered that Tanikawa insists: "In my own work I have had a dislike for the tragic, pathetic, and exaggerated that a lot of younger writers prefer. Even when I write exaggerated things I still hope to maintain feelings of objectivity in a sort of humorous way." He has written a great deal for children and worked in radio, film, and television. Today he is considered Japan's most popular poet.

Sadness

Sadness
A half-peeled apple
Not a metaphor
Not a poem
Merely there
A half-peeled apple
Sadness
Merely there
Yesterday's evening paper
Merely there
Merely there
A warm breast

Merely there
Nightfall
Sadness
Apart from words
Apart from the heart
Merely here
The things of today.

Translated from the Japanese by Harold Wright

Concerning a Girl

from a little basket on the kitchen shelf   I was about to
pick a star   the girl insisted she didn't care about a
harvest   I thought I had planted a seed but perhaps we too
had been planted seeds   without realizing it we were raised
and ripened and will probably wither away   later we're nothing
more than a tiny clod of earth in the middle of the world's
garden   yet this time we are the ones that will raise   someone
will stand on us and grope for a star with a huge hand   perhaps
even check for ripeness   however we are not fertilizer for
stars   even at that time a girl wise beyond doubt will be there
to plant her naked feet within us   then she herself will become
a flower   and when ripe   a star will naturally fall   the
flower knows all about this   and so will not be afraid of
dying   when standing on my tiptoes about to pick a star   I
was called by the girl

Translated from the Japanese by Harold Wright

Request

Turn inside out   turn me
Plow the fields inside me
Dry up the wells inside me

Turn inside out   turn me
Wash out my insides
And maybe you'll find a splendid pearl
Turn inside out   turn me
Is the inside of me the sea?
Is it the night
Is it a distant road
Is it a polyethylene bag
Turn inside out   turn me
What is growing inside of me
A field of overripe cactus plants?
A premature offspring of a unicorn?
A buckeye tree that failed to become a violin?
Turn inside out   turn me
Make the wind blow through me
Let my dreams catch cold
Turn inside out   turn me
Let my concepts weather away.

Turn inside out
Turn inside out please   turn me
Please shelter my skin
My forehead is frostbitten
My eyes are red with bashfulness
My lips are weary of kisses

Turn inside out
Turn inside out please turn me
Let my insides worship the sun
Spread my stomach and pancreas over the grass
Evaporate the reddened darkness!
Stuff the blue sky into my lungs!
With my spermaduct all entangled
Have me trampled by black stud horses
Please have my heart and brain,
                              using chopsticks of plain wood,
Be eaten by the one I love.

Turn inside out
Turn inside out please   turn me

Let all the words within me
Be chatted completely away   and quickly
Let the singing quartet of instruments
Be resounded completely away
Let the aged birds within me
Be flown completely away
Let the love within me
Be lost in an evil gambling den.

Turn inside out, please turn, inside out, turn me
I'll give away the fake pearl inside me
So turn inside out, please turn, inside out, turn me
Silence alone speaks softly within me
Let me depart
Outside of myself
To that shade of trees
Over that woman
Into that sand.

Translated from the Japanese by Harold Wright

Family Portrait

Filled with water
There's a jar
Eating of gruel begins
Wooden spoons
Berry wine
All is supported
By a heavy table.

There's a man
Wearing coarse cloth
Sitting
Strong arms
Fierce beard
Eyes fixed

In a gaze
At a field still dark.

There's a woman
Large breasts
Coiled-up hair
Hot hands
On the man's shoulders.

There's a child
His curved brow
Smeared with dirt
As if surprised
He turns around.

The old people
In a picture on the wall
Beside a calendar
Are gently waiting
A dog like a bear
Yawns by the door.

At a simple altar
A flame is glowing
The night is quietly
Beginning to dawn.

Translated from the Japanese by Harold Wright

River

Mother,
Why is the river laughing?

Why, because the sun is tickling the river.

Mother,
Why is the river singing?

Because the skylark praised the river's voice.

> Mother,
> Why is the river cold?

It remembers being once loved by the snow.

> Mother,
> How old is the river?

It's the same age as the forever young springtime.

> Mother,
> Why does the river never rest?

Well, you see it's because the mother sea
is waiting for the river to come home.

Translated from the Japanese by Harold Wright

Stone and Light

> The stone doesn't repel the light,
> The stone doesn't absorb the light.
> On the stone sits a deerfly,
> The light is radiant in its downy hair.
>
> The light just now arrived on earth.

Translated from the Japanese by Harold Wright

LATIN AMERICA

OCTAVIO PAZ

Mexico (b. 1914)

Born and educated in Mexico City, Octavio Paz lived for periods of time
in Spain, France, and the United States as a young man, absorbing their
literary traditions. After World War II, he entered the Mexican diplo-
matic service and was posted to Japan and India, cultures with decisive
influence on his subsequent work. In 1968 he resigned as ambassador to
India to protest his government's repressive brutality against student
demonstrations in Mexico City. He has since taught at Cambridge Uni-
versity and at Harvard. His voluminous output of poems and essays has
long since made him the leading man of letters in Latin America—a fact
recognized in 1990, when he was awarded the Nobel Prize for Literature.
Paz's career has been devoted to the idea that as "an operation capable of
changing the world, poetic activity is revolutionary by nature; a spiritual
exercise, it is a means of interior liberation." Although poetry reveals the
world and its *correspondences,* it denies history. It is simultaneously the
voice of the people, the language of the elect, and the word of the solitary.
Paz has preferred the fragmentary and ecstatic, the discoveries of chance
and dream, the infernal landscape of the city, nostalgic glimpses of par-
adisal literature from the past, the unredeemable self in extremis. His
technique, once surrealist, remains a rhetoric of images—in his phrase,
"the apple of fire on the tree of syntax." Poetry, he has maintained, "is
not truth, it is the resurrection of presences."

The Key of Water

> After Rishikesh
> the Ganges is still green.
> The glass horizon
> breaks among the peaks.
> We walk upon crystals.
> Above and below
> great gulfs of calm.
> In the blue spaces
> white rocks, black clouds.

You said:
> *Le pays est plein de sources.*
That night I dipped my hands in your breasts.

Translated from the Spanish by Elizabeth Bishop

Along Galeana Street

for Ramón Xirau

Hammers pound there above
    pulverized voices
From the top of the afternoon
    the builders come straight down

We're between blue and good evening
    here begin vacant lots
A pale puddle suddenly blazes
    the shade of the hummingbird ignites it

Reaching the first houses
    the summer oxidizes
Someone has closed the door   someone
    speaks with his shadow

It darkens   There's no one in the street now
    not even this dog
scared to walk through it alone
    One's afraid to close one's eyes

Translated from the Spanish by Elizabeth Bishop

Small Variation

Like music come back to life—
who brings it from over there, from the other side,

who conducts it through the spirals
of the mind's ear?—
like the vanished
moment that returns
and is again the same
presence erasing itself,
the syllables unearthed
make sound without sound:
and at the hour of our death, amen.

In the school chapel
I spoke them many times
without conviction. Now I hear them
spoken by a voice without lips,
a sound of sand sifting away,
while in my skull the hours toll
and time takes another turn around my night.
I am not the first man on earth—
I tell myself in the manner of Epictetus—
who is going to die.
And as I say this
the world breaks down in my blood.

                        The sorrow
of Gilgamesh when he returned
from the land without twilight
is my sorrow. On our shadowy earth
each man is Adam:
                    with him the world begins,
with him it ends.
                Between after and before—
brackets of stone—
for an instant that will never return I shall be
the first man and I shall be the last.
And as I say it, the instant—
bodiless, weightless—
opens under my feet
and closes over me and is pure time.

Translated from the Spanish by Mark Strand

I Speak of the City

for Eliot Weinberger

a novelty today, tomorrow a ruin from the past, buried and
    resurrected every day,
lived together in streets, plazas, buses, taxis, movie houses,
    theaters, bars, hotels, pigeon coops and catacombs,
the enormous city that fits in a room three yards square, and
    endless as a galaxy,
the city that dreams us all, that all of us build and unbuild and
    rebuild as we dream,
the city we all dream, that restlessly changes while we dream it,
the city that wakes every hundred years and looks at itself in the
    mirror of a word and doesn't recognize itself and goes back
    to sleep,
the city that sprouts from the eyelids of the woman who sleeps at
    my side, and is transformed,
with its monuments and statues, its histories and legends,
into a fountain made of countless eyes, and each eye reflects the
    same landscape, frozen in time,
before schools and prisons, alphabets and numbers, the altar and
    the law:
the river that is four rivers, the orchard, the tree, the Female and
    Male, dressed in wind—
to go back, go back, to be clay again, to bathe in that light, to
    sleep under those votive lights,
to float on the waters of time like the flaming maple leaf the
    current drags along,
to go back—are we asleep or awake?—we are, we are nothing
    more, day breaks, it's early,
we are in the city, we cannot leave except to fall into another city,
    different yet identical,
I speak of the immense city, that daily reality composed of two
    words: *the others,*
and in every one of them there is an I clipped from a we, an I adrift,
I speak of the city built by the dead, inhabited by their stern
    ghosts, ruled by their despotic memory,
the city I talk to when I talk to nobody, the city that dictates these
    insomniac words,

I speak of towers, bridges, tunnels, hangars, wonders and
  disasters,
the abstract State and its concrete police, the schoolteachers,
  jailers, preachers,
the shops that have everything, where we spend everything, and it
  all turns to smoke,
the markets with their pyramids of fruit, the turn of the seasons,
  the sides of beef hanging from the hooks, the hills of spices
  and the towers of bottles and preserves,
all of the flavors and colors, all the smells and all the stuff, the tide
  of voices—water, metal, wood, clay—the bustle, the haggling
  and conniving as old as time,
I speak of the buildings of stone and marble, of cement, glass and
  steel, of the people in the lobbies and doorways, of the eleva-
  tors that rise and fall like the mercury in thermometers,
of the banks and their boards of directors, of factories and their
  managers, of the workers and their incestuous machines,
I speak of the timeless parade of prostitution through streets long
  as desire and boredom,
of the coming and going of cars, mirrors of our anxieties, busi-
  ness, passions (why? toward what? for what?),
of the hospitals that are always full, and where we always die alone,
I speak of the half-light of certain churches and the flickering
  candles at the altars,
the timid voices with which the desolate talk to saints and virgins
  in a passionate, failing language,
I speak of dinner under a squinting light at a limping table with
  chipped plates,
of the innocent tribes that camp in the empty lots with their
  women and children, their animals and their ghosts,
of the rats in the sewers and the brave sparrows that nest in the
  wires, in the cornices and the martyred trees,
of the contemplative cats and their libertine novels in the light of
  the moon, cruel goddess of the rooftops,
of the stray dogs that are our Franciscans and *bhikkus,* the dogs
  that scratch up the bones of the sun,
I speak of the anchorite and the libertarian brotherhood, of the
  secret plots of law enforcers and of bands of thieves,
of the conspiracies of levelers and the Society of Friends of Crime,
  of the Suicide Club, and of Jack the Ripper,

of the Friend of the People, sharpener of the guillotine, of Caesar,
    Delight of Humankind,
I speak of the paralytic slum, the cracked wall, the dry fountain,
    the graffitied statue,
I speak of garbage heaps the size of mountains, and of melancholy
    sunlight filtered by the smog,
of broken glass and the desert of scrap iron, of last night's crime,
    and of the banquet of the immortal Trimalchio,
of the moon in the television antennas, and a butterfly on a filthy
    jar,
I speak of dawns like a flight of herons on the lake, and the sun of
    transparent wings that lands on the rock foliage of the
    churches, and the twittering of light on the glass stalks of the
    palaces,
I speak of certain afternoons in early fall, waterfalls of immaterial
    gold, the transformation of this world, when everything loses
    its body, everything is held in suspense,
and the light thinks, and each one of us feels himself thought by
    that reflective light, and for one long moment time dissolves,
    we are air once more,
I speak of the summer, of the slow night that grows on the hori-
    zon like a mountain of smoke, and bit by bit it crumbles,
    falling over us like a wave,
the elements are reconciled, night has stretched out, and its body
    is a powerful river of sudden sleep, we rock in the waves of
    its breathing, the hour is tangible, we can touch it like a fruit,
they have lit the lights, and the avenues burn with the brilliancy of
    desire, in the parks electric light breaks through the branches
    and falls over us like a green and phosphorescent mist that il-
    luminates but does not wet us, the trees murmur, they tell us
    something,
there are streets in the half-light that are a smiling insinuation, we
    don't know where they lead, perhaps to the ferry for the lost
    islands,
I speak of the stars over the high terraces and the indecipherable
    sentences they write on the stone of the sky,
I speak of the sudden downpour that lashes the windowpanes and
    bends the trees, that lasted twenty-five minutes and now, up
    above, there are blue slits and streams of light, steam rises

from the asphalt, the cars glisten, there are puddles where
ships of reflections sail,

I speak of nomadic clouds, and of a thin music that lights a room
on the fifth floor, and a murmur of laughter in the middle of
the night like water that flows far-off through roots and
grasses,

I speak of the longed-for encounter with that unexpected form
with which the unknown is made flesh, and revealed to each
of us:

eyes that are the night half-open and the day that wakes, the sea
stretching out and the flame that speaks, powerful breasts:
lunar tide,

lips that say *sesame,* and time opens, and the little room becomes
a garden of change, air and fire entwine, earth and water
mingle,

or the arrival of that moment there, on the other side that is really
here, where the key locks and time ceases to flow:

the moment of *until now,* the last of the gasps, the moaning, the
anguish, the soul loses its body and crashes through a hole in
the floor, falling in itself, and time has run aground, and we
walk through an endless corridor, panting in the sand,

is that music coming closer or receding, are those pale lights just
lit or going out? space is singing, time has vanished: it is the
gasp, it is the glance that slips through the blank wall, it is the
wall that stays silent, the wall,

I speak of our public history, and of our secret history, yours and
mine,

I speak of the forest of stone, the desert of the prophets, the ant-
heap of souls, the congregation of tribes, the house of mir-
rors, the labyrinth of echoes,

I speak of the great murmur that comes from the depths of time,
the incoherent whisper of nations uniting or splitting apart,
the wheeling of multitudes and their weapons like boulders
hurling down, the dull sound of bones falling into the pit of
history,

I speak of the city, shepherd of the centuries, mother that gives
birth to us and devours us, that creates us and forgets.

Translated from the Spanish by Eliot Weinberger

MANUEL ULACIA

Mexico (b. 1953)

Born in Mexico City, where he still lives and teaches, Manuel Ulacia first studied to become an architect and later pursued his graduate studies in literature at Yale, where his dissertation dealt in part with his grandfather, the distinguished poet Manuel Altolaguirre. Ulacia is the author of three collections of poems: *La Materia como ofrenda* (1980), *El Río y la piedra* (1989), and *Origami para un día de lluvia* (1991). In addition, he is an important critic, editor, and translator. His early work was guided by avant-garde models; more recent poems, with their transparent, often autobiographical textures, have more narrative heft and cadenced rhythms. Luis Cernuda and Octavio Paz have been abiding influences on Ulacia's work, as it seeks the shimmering boundary between desire and contemplation.

The Stone at the Bottom

As my father's breathing
fails little by little,
the probes and needles
and oxygen mask removed—
between systole and diastole,
on the stage of memory
one after another
the images like photos come to life.
The trip to school at eight A.M.
with its enigmas
of the Yellow River,
the gardens of Mesopotamia,
the Great Wall and Newton's apple,
and later, at recess,
while talking with other children
in the cool shade of tall trees,
the image of my father transformed
into the author of heroic feats,

and at home again,
the family reunited,
my father tells of the thousand and one discoveries
of his laboratory,
essence of rose, musk, lavender,
and the adventures of his mother as a child,
on the revolutionary trains
from Campeche to Mexico City,
the cockfights
that his father liked so much,
the excursions to mountains and rivers,
the forgotten image of his grandfather
who painted fans in Valencia,
his brief childhood in an immense garden,
stories of immigrants of almost a century ago
who left behind
the gothic tower, the olive grove and the cattle
and who never returned.

And at the end of the day
I watch how my parents get ready
to go to a party,
and after the goodnight kiss,
lost in the movie
on the black-and-white television
I imagine that life is like this,
and that my parents are dancing
on a moonlit terrace,
to a waltz by Augustín Lara,
and that my father is a movie star,
a pirate in a sea-battle,
Tarzan in the Amazon jungle,
and that someday I too will be big
and I will smell the scent of violets
on a girl's neck
and I will embody my fate
the way they explained to me.

As my father's breathing
fails little by little

and his pulse slows,
between systole and diastole
time extends outward
like the concentric circles that form
when a stone is thrown into the mirror that water makes.
Every instant is an hour,
every hour a lifetime.
The time that goes by, brief.
Those sunny days in the country,
the weathered walls of the house,
the stable, the corral,
the dam for the watering pond
with its reflections of moving clouds,
where one day my father showed me
how to measure the water's depth
by the time it takes
a tossed stone to reach bottom.
And the woman who shells the corn
as if she were shelling the seeds of time.
Into what waters do we fall
when we leave, if time does not exist?
What is the depth of heaven?
Where was the germination of the hours we live?
And then at dusk,
together in a dimly lit room,
in the loud steam of hot irons
over white sheets
my father told me
that in the next room
his father had just died:
first image of finite time,
a falling stone,
immense measuring that we disavow,
the sharp profile of my father's face,
the white sheet that shrouded his father,
the secret glance between the two ironing-women,
the hand and the clock that take the pulse.
My father sits up in bed
and asks, What time is it?,
and without listening he says, Tomorrow at the same time.

Shaking with cold his body begins
to give birth to another body,
an invisible butterfly with white wings
that awaits the precise hour
when out of him it will take flight
for its wedding with the void.

As my father's breathing fails,
an anguish revives—
a sharp-edged stone in the throat.
Those meals, in my youth,
when the only sound one heard
was the clink of porcelain serving dishes;
the sidelong glances
that hid the blushing
of fleshly passion
and my secret games in the bedroom;
while the wounding light coming in through the window
lit up the clouds on the pitcher,
the empty plates, the crumbs,
because, awakened in my lascivious dreams,
my singular desire had been revealed to me.

Now I would not be the image of the hero
dancing with a girl on the movie screen
nor the captain of industry
nor the man of discretion of whom society approves
nor the prey of virginities lying in wait for me
nor the father who perpetuates the species.
And later the quarrels—
freedom does not make men happy,
my mother says, *it only makes them men.*
My father is silent:
indifference is fragile armor.

My father lives inside the ideogram of his world,
he constructs other dreams
without thinking about the finitude of time,
about the stone, and its falling,
about the dark bedroom.

Tomorrow, tomorrow, always tomorrow
and the house grows larger,
while my mother's hair turns gray,
and in the mirror my sister discovers
her beginning breasts,
and my grandmother becomes a child again.
Tomorrow, tomorrow, always tomorrow.

As my father's breathing
fails little by little,
I want to tell him
that the only thing I wanted
was to live truly the truth of my loving,
but now he hears nothing,
he says nothing,
silence has taken over his body,
the body of my mother,
the circle that formed around their bed,
the dark room,
the clear mirror of water
where the stone keeps falling
in the fragile gravity of this instant.

As my father's breathing fails,
the transparency of the windowpane
reminds me that outside there is the world.
I contemplate the brightly lit city,
the cars going by,
the teenager who meets
his girlfriend on a corner,
the passing bicyclist,
the athlete running across the park meadow.
Pondering the fragility of time
I contemplate the world,
the window again,
the reunited family,
and I am thinking that my father no longer speaks
or sees or hears,
that his dead senses
are beginning to perceive the theater of the world

through us,
that the only memory of his life
is what lies in the fragments of our memory:
an immense puzzle with missing pieces.
What must he be thinking about as he leaves himself behind?
My mother's skin?
Newsreels from the Second World War?
First communion and the commandments?
The tumors spreading through his body?
My father, stammering,
says he has a stone in his throat,
it won't fall,
he's going to fall with it.
To where? In what place?

As my father's breathing fails him,
he seems to begin to forget everything:
the chemotherapy and the welts,
the waiting rooms and operating rooms,
the portrait of his grandmother and the young legs
of girls,
stone from Oaxaca and the song of the canary,
the red rattle and first cry.
Or, in his forgetting—
the last dream that time will devour—
perhaps he goes down a road
looking for his father.
But already that road is another road,
the house another house.
His life fits into one instant, now.
All the parts are reconciled.
A single sun shines in his consciousness,
a frozen fire that the world consumes.
In the mirror of water
the last wave is traced.
The stone, falling,
has hit bottom.

Translated from the Spanish by Reginald Gibbons

VERONICA VOLKOW

Mexico (b. 1955)

Verónica Volkow was born in Mexico City. She graduated from the National University of Mexico and studied further at Columbia University. Her first collection of poems, *La Sicilia de cumas*, appeared in 1974; *Litoral de tinta* appeared in 1979; a long sequence of poems, *El Inicio*, was published four years later; her most recent collection is entitled *El Principio*. Volkow has also written a travel book on South Africa, and among the works she has translated are the poems of Elizabeth Bishop and John Ashbery. The rhetorical precision of her images and rhythms—of her mind's eye and ear—is matched by an ambitious range of subject: her voice is magnanimous and compelling.

The Washerwoman

She feels her hands, scabrous as fish,
blind fish striking against the rock,
incessantly against the rock for years and years;
she watches the night pierced with eyes,
humid, slippery glances,
the mute faces shifting, disappearing,
brilliant glances of girls,
the dazed look of exhausted mothers.
The day ends and people return to their houses
and water runs from the faucet monotonously as a song,
the water has lost the shape of pipes,
lost the memory of its mountain source
and has pounded out its course,
besieged by obstacles
like the feet, like the eyes, like the hands.
She looks at shadows people drag along,
shadows on the walls, corners, the streets,
fugitive ink that marks the beaten roads,

desperate roads, laborious,
looking for only, perhaps, a fidelity.

Translated from the Spanish by Forrest Gander

from The Beginning

I

Hunger is the original eye of the body
primeval eye in the dark of the body
the eye with which flesh first beholds flesh

and a sanguinary darkness draws us inward

       the eye
with which my feet see you   my teeth
          my fingers

       the eye
with which I discover you   centuries long
in one night of touching
       that night
so like the night of the fish
       the tiger
       the snake
so like the first night of life

we close our eyes and are beast again
and our bodies are clamped like throats
       choking on the shapely flavors

VI

The lovers
have hands solely for loving
       they have only their hands

hands that are feet and wings over their bodies
hands that constantly seek
the breathing animal behind buried eyes
fingers that set their bodies on fire
that are branches on which caresses flower
flowers that are birds that are flames that are hands
hands that are lost in their lightning writing

hands that travel the flesh of bodies
like stars touching at daybreak
like suns rising   like shooting stars
like secret gods who draw the night

X

Between your body my body
is the print of your body
is the eye   the sound of your body
          I hear your forearms
             your teeth
             your tongue
             your thighs
I hear the shape of your body with all my skin

between my body your body
is another form of your body
like water turned to incandescent ice
or the open faucet of flames
             your body
cries out in my body
           and you, a loosed scream
             a shouted star
a mute cry   of flesh   in my body

tell me   isn't the flame
the seed of distant worlds
the peculiar and sudden nearness of the stars?

XI

You are nude
and your smoothness is infinite
you tremble to my fingers
your breath flies inside your body

      you are
like a bird in my hands
        vulnerable
as only desire could make you vulnerable
that exquisite pain with which we touch one another
that surrender in which we know
the abandon of victims

pleasure like a tongue
licks us   devours us
and our eyes burn out
      are lost

Translated from the Spanish by Martha Christina

ERNESTO CARDENAL

Nicaragua (b. 1925)

One of the most vital poets in Latin America, Ernesto Cardenal was born in Granada, Nicaragua. He studied at the University of Mexico and at Columbia University. There were three great North American influences in his life. One was the poetry of Ezra Pound. It was Pound's documentary collages that led Cardenal to adopt an aesthetic method he called *exteriorismo*. Although his earliest poems were epigrams that elegantly combine erotic and political barbs, he later broadened his range to write cantos filled with history and social criticism. The second major influence was the poet and Trappist monk Thomas Merton. Cardenal converted to Christianity in 1956 and went to Gethsemani, Kentucky, to study to become a priest. (He was ordained in 1965.) Merton's advocacy of nonviolence—and, later, the tenets of liberation theology—were crucial in shaping Cardenal's role as both activist priest and Marxist poet. The third influence was the pre-Columbian culture of the American Indians, those in North America as well as the more powerful civilizations of the south. Cardenal's poems evoking this culture embody the values he seeks to promote in the modern world. He has also used the Bible—its moral teachings as well as its rhetoric—to create rich, expressive poems that detail the life of the campesinos, analyze the social ills of political repression, and seek ways to transform the old order. During his country's struggles of the late 1970s, Cardenal became field chaplain for the Sandinista National Liberation Front, and when the Sandinistas took power, he served as minister of culture. Throughout his career he has passionately sought to balance the harsh realities of the world and the sense of the sacred that underpins them.

Mosquito Kingdom

The coronation ceremony was in Belize this time,
the king riding on a white horse in procession to the church
with the uniform of a British major, the others on foot
with red frock coats (castoff) of British officers
of all ranks and wearing sailor pants.

His Majesty was placed on a seat next to the altar
and the coronation rites were performed by the chaplain
acting on this occasion as the Archbishop of Canterbury.
When they reached the part that says: "And all the people said:
'May the King live forever, long live the King' "
the frigates shot off their cannon, and the Indian
and black vassals shouted: "Long live King Robert!
God save the King!" His Majesty meanwhile
seemed absorbed in looking at his lace. After the anointing
he kept touching with his finger the holy oil (which was
castor oil) and then putting his finger to his nose
but he did not flee in the midst of the ceremony to climb a
    coconut tree
as his illustrious ancestor had done in Jamaica.
After the ceremony the crowd
went to the schoolhouse for the gala banquet
in which no food other than rum was served
until King and court rolled dead drunk on the floor.

Vanderbilt never in his whole wretched life had had a vacation
and this time he determined to have one in Europe and therefore
a special ship was built. No one had ever seen anything
more fabulous on earth. The newspapers were stunned.
No private yacht could be compared with the *North Star*
in size or luxury: 2,500 tons; 300 feet long;
enormous paddle wheels moved by two motors. And the
walls of the vast saloons: of marble and granite.
The coffered ceilings of rosewood and sandalwood; in the ceiling
medallions of American heroes; the staterooms
like the apartments of Cosimo de'Medici
(even though his carpet in Washington Place was frayed)
and with a great cargo of ice, wines, rare foods, famous
chefs from New York, and a chaplain who blessed the food.
This time Vanderbilt "spent without his usual inhibitions."
In London the *Daily News* saluted the floating palace
with an editorial. He was given a reception in Mansion House
with many flunkies and with Carlyle. The Lord Mayor drank a
    toast to
"Mr. Vanderbilt the foe of monopolies" and Vanderbilt
made a speech—the only time in his life that he did so.

He saw Victoria and Prince Albert only at the Opera.
But in Russia Czar Alexander lent him his carriage
and Grand Duke Constantine, his son, inspected the ship
and asked permission to make a sketch of it. Emperor Napoleon
    (Louis)
paid him no attention because he was busy with the Crimean War.
They did not open the Tuileries for them and Mrs. Vanderbilt
did not see the wardrobes of the Empress Eugénie. Summer on the
Mediterranean . . . King Bomba of the Two Sicilies . . . then
Greece, etc., and the millionaire got bored and went back home.

But the British agents got screwed because the monarch
began to sell great portions of his kingdom
for barrels of rum.
In 1839 the sovereign "in the fourteenth year of his reign"
(having already sold a third of Nicaragua
half of Costa Rica
and a limitless stretch of Honduras)
was forced by McDonald to make his will
naming McDonald and others as "Regents"
in case His Majesty should die before the Heir Apparent
came of age
and shortly after this the King was kind enough to die
and his Eminence Colonel McDonald published a decree
in the name of the child king George William declaring
". . . the said surrender of territories null and void . . .
because the grantees obtained them at a time when the king
was bereft of reason [drunk]." But the decrees of one king
were worth as much as those of another, and one Shepperd, an
    old British
sailor, almost blind, in his Greytown house (San Juan del Norte)
years later still kept in a cupboard those old papers, with
    "X his mark"
        (because the sovereign couldn't sign)
of King Robert Charles Frederick,
that made him the owner of a third of the Mosquito Kingdom
("We, by our special grace, do give and grant . . .")
from Bluefields Bay to Colombia (Panama)
a total of twenty-two million acres
and a Texan named Kinney, who speculated in cattle and enormous

chunks of Texas, acquired the moth-eaten papers of the
sea-wolf through the promise of a half million dollars
(the biggest real-estate speculation in his whole life)
and he organized a so-called Central American Company
with authorized capital of $5,625,000 and 21 directors
and two hundred twenty-five thousand shares at $25.00 a share;
each share would bring 100 acres of land
on being presented at the company office in Greytown.
On Wall Street they believed he was a partner of Walker
but he was more a rival.
"I have land titles to begin legally," he said.
"I'm going to create a government and the rest is easy."
President Pierce, it was said, was on his side.
But the "Transit Company" was not . . .

In New York he recruited 500 men to capture Greytown
but before he could do it he was shipwrecked opposite Greytown
he reached Greytown shipwrecked and bankrupt to boot
with only 13 men and a printing press that he saved from the
    wreck.
But even so he had himself elected civil and military governor
by the handful of lazy inhabitants, in "a democratic election"
and he organized a provisional government while they were draw-
    ing up
the new constitution inspired by that of the United States.
Ten days later the press began to publish
the newspaper (bimonthly) *The Central American* with ads
for commercial firms in Greytown, import & export houses,
hotels, schools, bars, lawyers, banks,
clubs, doctors, bookstores, nightclubs, etc., etc.,
to attract immigrants. Alsop & Co., on California Street
(Buy and Sell Exchange) . . . Benicia-Boarding School
for young gentlemen—*The Atlantic Loan & Security Bank*
        The Ocean House (. . . on a romantic Lagoon . . .)
CAFE FRANÇAIS (every kind of refreshment)
to attract immigrants to that place which was nothing but
a swamp with 50 houses (thatched roofs) and 300 inhabitants
of all colors, nearly all blacks (ex-slaves from Jamaica,
fugitives from justice, and an occasional European) on the shore
    of a

noxious lagoon, full of alligators and surrounded by the forest,
a place that had been described as "one of the saddest
and most desolate on earth . . . so much so that, however varied
the experiences that the traveler had had with lugubrious places
the memory of Greytown would stay with him
as among the most melancholy and dismal . . ." The only banks
were sand banks covered with shark bones
that obstructed the sea view. The lively dance halls,
the lively dance halls of *Delmonico's* (open till dawn)
were probably the frog-filled swamps.
The monkeys: perhaps they were the music at *Mike's*
("Visit Mike's—The Best Restaurant"). Language Schools:
the cockatoos! *The Green Resort* perhaps wild boars
and tigers. Royal Caribbean with its enchanting singers
the Jamaica Grill, Jimmy's Café, so many more puddles
(or the luxurious St. John) with crocodiles, with mosquitoes
("Make your reservation . . .") but the immigrants did not arrive.

Vanderbilt had given up the presidency
of the Transit Company when he went to Europe
and he had made Morgan president and while he was traveling
Morgan and Garrison had made the shares fluctuate
earning enormous sums at Vanderbilt's expense
and he (who said "I don't give a shit for the law,
I've got the power") when he came back just sent them a note:
            "Gentlemen: I will ruin you. Sincerely Yours,
                Cornelius Van Derbilt"
The Transit Company had never paid Nicaragua
the 10% of the profits claiming that there weren't any profits
and Nicaragua couldn't claim that there *were* profits
because of the peculiar way the company kept its books,
which consisted of never recording either passengers or cargo.
Toward the end of December '56 the bar of the Hotel St. Charles
in New Orleans had more noise and more cocktails
than usual because the steamship *Texas* was leaving
with recruits for Walker toward the lands of the sunny South,
the hot, sensuous South, with the laudable intention
of robbing them (but those who went to Nicaragua almost never
        came back)
Italians who fought in Novara, Prussians

from the campaigns in Holstein, Englishmen from the Crimean
    War,
Yankees from the expedition to Cuba . . . (They carried the rifles
    in boxes
shaped like coffins.) And on the very same seas of Kidd
    and Morgan—
the other Morgan, the pirate—they would scan with their
    telescopes
the western, wood-covered coast of Cuba
saying that it would "sooner or later belong to Uncle Sam."
(And when they got to Nicaragua they would open the coffins.)
    Morgan
and Garrison who were losing control of the company
courted Walker so that he would confiscate it from Vanderbilt
who had never paid anything to Nicaragua, which now belonged
    to Walker,
and would deliver to the two partners the dead corporation with
a new contract that would set them up as a new company.
A plan of unscrupulous captains of industry against
a rival equally unscrupulous. A shark fight
like those of the reef of San Juan del Norte. There was stupor
on Wall Street when they learned of Walker's confiscation.
Panic among the investors. They all rushed
to sell their shares. On January 1st they had been at 18,
on February 14th at 23¼. On March 14th (when
the news arrived) they went down to 19, and on the 18th, to 13.
    In 4 days
15,000 shares changed hands. Vanderbilt, wounded,
attacked Walker. Oh, the bastard, said Vanderbilt
I'm going to screw Walker. No more boats to Nicaragua.
And as Morgan and Garrison weren't ready with theirs
the filibusterer with the gray, empty eyes ("that in daguerreotypes
seem to be without eyelashes") and a mouth that under no
    circumstances
did anyone ever see smile, was left trapped in Nicaragua.

The immigrants didn't arrive. And the British agents
didn't recognize the "provisional government," and besides
Walker was now in control of Nicaragua, and Kinney had no
    funds anymore

and besides he was ill, and many of his followers
went off with Walker. For some months he vegetated in
    Greytown.
Then he went away sick and without one cent.
          Sick and penniless.

Afterward Vanderbilt sold his ships and snapped up railroads,
       and forgot about Nicaragua.
His wife asked him: "Aren't you rich enough?"
      "Not yet."
Just about then a newsboy ran by under his window on
Washington Place shouting: CIVIL WAR!

The newspaper from San Juan del Norte with its fantastic ads
is disintegrating in the Library of Congress in Washington,
the librarians say, and it can't be Xeroxed; you touch it
       and it turns to ashes.

Translated from the Spanish by Donald D. Walsh

Vision from the Blue Window

From the round window, everything is blue,
the earth bluish, blue-green, blue
                (sky-blue)
       everything is blue
blue lakes and lagoons
         blue volcanoes
the further away the land, the bluer it is
     blue islands in a blue lake.
This is the face of the liberated land.
And where all the people fought, I think:
            for love!
To live without exploitation's
         hatred.
To love each other in a lovely land
very lovely, not only for the land
      but for its people

above all for its people.
That's why God rendered it so lovely
for its society.
And in all those blue places they fought, they suffered
                    for a society of love
                              here in this land.
A bit of blue has greater intensity . . .
And it seemed to me I was seeing the places of all the battles,
and all the deaths,
that, behind this glass, small, round,
                              blue
                    I was seeing all the shades of blue.

Translated from the Spanish by Marc Zimmerman

Tahirassawichi in Washington

In 1898 Tahirassawichi went to Washington
"only to speak about religion"
                    (as he told the American government)
          only to preserve the prayers.
And the Capitol did not impress him.
The Library of Congress was all right
but not fit to keep the sacred objects
which could only be kept in his mud hut
          (which was crumbling).
When by the Washington Monument they asked him
if he wanted to go up the elevator or the stairs
he answered: "I will not go up. White men heap
stones to climb on them. I shall not climb up.
     I have climbed the mountains that Tirawa made."
And Tahirassawichi told the State Department:
"Tirawa's Hut is the round blue sky
          (we do not like to have clouds between Tirawa and us)
The first thing to do
is to choose a sacred place to live in
a place devoted to Tirawa, where man

may be silent and meditate.
Our round hut represents the nest
       (a nest to be together in and keep little children)
In the center is the fire which makes us one family.
The door is for anyone to enter
and visions enter through it.
Blue is the color of Tirawa's Hut
and we mix blue dust with river water
for the river stands for life running
through the generations.
The bowl of blue paint is the curve of the sky
and we paint a corncob which is the strength of the earth.
Yet that strength comes from above, from Tirawa
that is why we paint the corncob with the color of Tirawa.
Afterwards we offer tobacco smoke to Tirawa.
       Earlier one did not smoke for pleasure but in prayer
        white men taught the profanation of tobacco to us.
On our way we greet all things with songs
for Tirawa is in all things. We greet the rivers:
from afar the rivers are a line of trees
       and we sing to those trees
closer we see the water line, and we hear it
and we sing to the rippling water.
And we sing to the buffalo, but not on the prairies
we sing the *Song of the Buffalo* in the hut
for there are no buffalo left.
And we sing of the mountains, made by Tirawa.
We climb the mountains alone, when we go to pray.
From there we can spot the enemy. Friends as well.
We sing of the mountains for they are good for men.
And we sing of the plateaus, but we sing of them in the hut
for we have not seen plateaus
       those mountains flat on their peaks
but we have been told our fathers saw many plateaus
and we remember what they saw far away, in their journeys.
And we sing of dawn when it breaks in the east
and renews all life
(this is very mysterious, I am telling you
       about something very sacred)
We sing to the morning star

the star is like a man and painted red
    the color of life.
We sing when animals awake
and come out of their lairs where they were asleep.
The doe comes out first, followed by the fawn.
We sing when the sun enters through the door of the hut
and when it reaches the skylight in the center of the hut
and in the evening when there is no more sun in the hut
and it is on the edge of the mountains which are like the wall
of a big round hut where people live.
We sing in the night when dreams come.
For visions visit us more easily at nighttime.
They travel better through the sleeping earth.
They approach the hut and stop at the door
and enter the hut, filling it.
If it were not true that dreams came
we would have long forsaken the songs.
And we sing in the night when the Pleiades come out.
The seven stars are always together
and guide the lost, far from their village
(and teach men to be as united as they are).
Tirawa is the father of all our dreams
and extends our tribe through our children.
With blue water we paint Tirawa's symbol
(an arch with the descending line in the center)
on the face of a child.
            The arch on the forehead and the cheeks
            and the straight line on the nose
(the arch is the blue dome where Tirawa lives
and the straight line his breath that descends and gives us life).
The child's face represents the new generation
and the river water is the passing of the generations
and the blue earth we mix is the sky of Tirawa
(and the blue sketch thus made is Tirawa's face).
Later we ask the child to look at river water
and in the water he sees his own image
as if seeing in his face his children and his children's children
but he is also seeing Tirawa's blue face
portrayed on his face and the future generations.
I told you our hut is like a nest

and if you climb the mountain and look around
you will see the sky surrounds all the earth
and that the earth is round and like a nest
so all tribes may live together and united.
The storm may cast the eagle's nest to the wind
but the oriole's nest only rocks in the wind
      and nothing happens to it."

Tahirassawichi's words, I suppose, did not mean anything
        to the State Department.

Translated from the Spanish by Carlos Altschul and Monique Altschul

CLARIBEL ALEGRIA

El Salvador (b. 1924)

Although she was born in Estelí, Nicaragua, Claribel Alegría's family was forced into political exile when she was less than a year old. They moved to Santa Ana, in El Salvador, a country she has since adopted as her own. She has also lived in Mexico, Chile, Uruguay, and Spain. She came to the United States in 1943 and studied at George Washington University. In 1978 she was awarded Cuba's Casa de las Américas Prize. She is a poet with a stark, urgent style who has written out of her obsessions—love, family, and, above all, a horror at the political violence that has beset Central America during her lifetime. "Central American reality is incandescent," she has written, "and if there be no place there for 'pure art' and 'pure literature' today, then I say so much the worse for pure art and pure literature. I do not know a single Central American writer who is so careful of his literary image that he sidesteps political commitment at this crucial moment in our history, and were I to meet one, I would refuse to shake his hand." The witness Alegría has borne to her region's history has been steadfast and compelling in its lyrical power. She has called herself a cemetery, in whose work the dead are embedded and reborn.

Savoir Faire

for Erik

My black cat doesn't know
he will die one day
he doesn't cling to life
as I do
he leaps from the rooftop
light as air
climbs the tamarind tree
barely scratching it
doesn't dread crossing bridges
or dark alleyways
nor the perfidious scorpion
my black cat falls in love

with every cat he meets
he refuses to be snared
by a single love
the way I did.

Translated from the Spanish by D. J. Flakoll

Nocturnal Visits

I think of our anonymous boys
of our burnt-out heroes
the amputated
the cripples
those who lost both legs
both eyes
the stammering teen-agers.
At night I listen to their phantoms
shouting in my ear
shaking me out of lethargy
issuing me commands
I think of their tattered lives
of their feverish hands
reaching out to seize ours.
It's not that they're begging
they're demanding
they've earned the right to order us
to break up our sleep
to come awake
to shake off once and for all
this lassitude.

Translated from the Spanish by D. J. Flakoll

From the Bridge

I have freed myself at last
it has been hard to break free:
near the end of the bridge
I pause
the water flows below
a turbulent water
sweeping fragments with it:
the voice of Carmen Lira
faces I loved
that disappeared.
From here
from the bridge
the perspective changes
I look backward
toward the beginning:
the hesitant silhouette
of a little girl
a doll
dangling from her hand
she lets it drop
and walks toward me
now she's an adolescent
gathers up her hair
and I recognize this gesture
stop girl
stop right there
if you come any closer
it will be difficult to talk
Don Chico died
after seven operations
they let him die
in a charity hospital
they closed Ricardo's school
and he died
during the earthquake
his heart failed.
Do you remember the massacre

that left Izalco without men?
You were seven.
How can I explain to you
nothing has changed
they keep on killing people daily?
It's better if you stop there
I remember you well at that age
you wrote honeyed poems
were horrified by violence
taught the neighborhood children
to read.
What would you say
if I told you that Pedro
your best student
rotted in jail
and that Sarita
the little blue-eyed girl
who made up stories
let herself be seduced
by the eldest son
of her employers
and afterwards sold herself
for twenty-five cents?
You've taken another step
you wear your hair short
have textbooks under your arm
poor deluded thing
you learned the consolations
of philosophy
before understanding
why you had to be consoled
your books spoke to you
of justice
and carefully omitted
the filth
that has always surrounded us
you went on with your verses
searched for order in chaos
and that was your goal

or perhaps your sentence.
You are coming closer now
your arms filled with children
it is easy to distract yourself
playing mother
and shrink the world
to a household.
Stop there
don't come any closer
you still won't recognize me
you still have to undergo
the deaths of Roque
of Rodolfo
all those innumerable deaths
that assail you
pursue you
define you
in order to dress in this plumage
(my plumage of mourning)
to peer out
through these pitiless
scrutinizing eyes
to have my claws
and this sharp beak.
I never found the order
I searched for
but always a sinister
and well-planned disorder
a prescribed disorder
that increases in the hands
of those who hold power
while the others
who clamor for
a more kindly world
a world with less hunger
and more hope
die tortured
in the prisons.
Don't come any closer

there's a stench of carrion
surrounding me.

Translated from the Spanish by D. J. Flakoll

Documentary

Come, be my camera.
Let's photograph the ant heap
the queen ant
extruding sacks of coffee,
my country.
It's the harvest.
Focus on the sleeping family
cluttering the ditch.
Now, among trees:
rapid,
dark-skinned fingers
stained with honey.
Shift to a long shot:
the file of ant men
trudging down the ravine
with sacks of coffee.
A contrast:
girls in colored skirts
laugh and chatter,
filling their baskets
with berries.
Focus down.
A close-up of the pregnant mother
dozing in the hammock.
Hard focus on the flies
spattering her face.
Cut.
The terrace of polished mosaics
protected from the sun.
Maids in white aprons

nourish the ladies
who play canasta,
celebrate invasions
and feel sorry for Cuba.
Izalco sleeps
beneath the volcano's eye.
A subterranean growl
makes the village tremble.
Trucks and ox-carts
laden with sacks
screech down the slopes.
Besides coffee
they plant angels
in my country.
A chorus of children
and women
with the small white coffin
move politely aside
as the harvest passes by.
The riverside women,
naked to the waist,
wash clothing.
The truck drivers
exchange jocular obscenities
for insults.
In Panchimalco,
waiting for the ox-cart to pass by,
a peasant
with hands bound behind him
by the thumbs
and his escort of soldiers
blinks at the airplane:
a huge bee
bulging with coffee growers
and tourists.
The truck stops in the market place.
A panorama of iguanas,
chickens,
strips of meat,
wicker baskets,

piles of *nances,*
nísperos,
oranges,
zunzas,
zapotes,
cheeses,
bananas,
dogs, *pupusas, jocotes,*
acrid odors,
taffy candies,
urine puddles, tamarinds.
The virginal coffee
dances in the millhouse.
They strip her,
rape her,
lay her out on the patio
to doze in the sun.
The dark storage sheds
glimmer.
The golden coffee
sparkles with malaria,
blood,
illiteracy,
tuberculosis,
misery.
A truck roars
out of the warehouse.
It bellows uphill
drowning out the lesson:
A for alcoholism,
B for battalions,
C for corruption,
D for dictatorship,
E for exploitation,
F for the feudal power
of fourteen families
and etcetera, etcetera, etcetera.
My etcetera country,
my wounded country,

my child,
my tears,
my obsession.

Translated from the Spanish by D. J. Flakoll

I Am Root

More than polished stone
more than morning dusk
more than the dream of the tree
and those of flower and fruit
I am root
a winding, crawling root
without luster, without a future
blind to any vision
hardening the ground
as I work through it
testing the fallen bread
of misfortune
the opacity of wingless birds
the overshadowed dawn
and its leaden clouds
hours that pass without dark messages
an undulating, twining root
perhaps bringing up from the ground
that lightning, that stone
once on the beach moving among
weeds, alone among rubbish, searching
cinereous root, mortal root
diver of my darkest regions
obscure calligraphy
inheritance of gallows, of cabala
poison root, imprisoned
by the time of a place
mirror of myself without water, thirsty

your blood tastes of the earth
your bark, summer
imprisoned, you don't look
for openings, you look for death
a quiet death, disguised
as days without omens
and as time without dates
and the gray willing faces of the hours
without birds where an instant
simply dissolves
the life I've yet to live
does not inspire me
in my lips there are crevices
and my face is stone
I do not allow a storm to enter
silently, I submerge myself
in a sea which no longer moves
the murmur ends
the appearances and disappearances
all dreams in which we can only
dream of ourselves
the remains of that daggered love
and the other, hidden love
the names of Eros and Thanatos
everything vanishes
your crystal song never reaches me
nor your wet touch, nor your lips
nor the teeth of your love
I gather my fragments and slip away,
I slither, I smell the sea
in which one day my memory will be
buried and I will not know pain
demands, or fear
and I will be then no more
than a calm spin in a tomb of water.

Translated from the Spanish by Carolyn Forché

ROBERTO JUARROZ

Argentina (b. 1925)

Roberto Juarroz was born in Coronel Dorrego, a small country town near Buenos Aires. His father was railroad stationmaster. "I had a relatively happy childhood," he recalls, "with waves or presentiments of solitude and mystery." At eighteen he took a job as a librarian at the Colegio Nacional, and he has been a librarian ever since. He now teaches library science at the University of Buenos Aires and has worked as a consultant in the field for UNESCO and the Organization of American States. He has spent time in New York and in Paris, where he studied at the Sorbonne. In his own country he has been praised but also punished by various regimes because he has "detested politics, and believe[s] it to be—whatever its color—the greatest adversary of poetry." Juarroz's first book of poems was published in 1958 and titled *Vertical Poetry;* his second book appeared in 1963 and was called *Second Vertical Poetry;* subsequent books—there are now eleven collections—have similar, cumulative titles. The poems are likewise all without titles, simply numbered as if part of a lifelong series. The abstract manner of their publication is matched by the austerity of the poems themselves: gnomic outtakes, elegantly ominous aphorisms, philosophical asides that do without description or narrative, experience distilled to a crystalline drop of paradox. Octavio Paz has called Juarroz "a great poet of absolute instants."

from Vertical Poetry

The bottom of things is neither life nor death.
My proof is
the air that goes barefoot in the birds,
a roof of absences that makes room for the silence,
and this look of mine that turns around at the bottom
as everything turns around at the end.

And my further proof is
my childhood that was bread before wheat,
my childhood that knew

that there were smokes that descend,
voices that nobody uses for talking,
roles in which a man does not move.

The bottom of things is neither life nor death.
The bottom is something else
that sometimes comes out on top.

Translated from the Spanish by W. S. Merwin

from Third Vertical Poetry

A lamp lit
in the middle of the day,
a light lost in the light.

And the theory of light is broken:
it's the greater light that recedes
as though a tree were to fall away from its fruit.

Translated from the Spanish by W. S. Merwin

from Fifth Vertical Poetry

The emptiness of the day
condenses into a point
that falls like a drop
into the river.

The fullness of the day
condenses into a minute orifice
that sucks that drop
out of the river.

From what fullness to what emptiness
or from what emptiness to what fullness
is the river flowing?

The eye draws on the white ceiling
a little line.
The ceiling takes up the eye's illusion
and turns black.
Then the line erases itself
and the eye closes.

Thus solitude is born.

Translated from the Spanish by W. S. Merwin

from Sixth Vertical Poetry

The bell is full of wind
though it does not ring.
The bird is full of flight
though it is still.
The sky is full of clouds
though it is alone.
The word is full of voice
though no one speaks it.
Everything is full of fleeing
though there are no roads.

Everything is fleeing
toward its presence.

Translated from the Spanish by W. S. Merwin

from Seventh Vertical Poetry

The prompting of my shadow
has taught me to be humble.
It doesn't care whether it draws me
on the bony seats of the trains
early in the morning,
on the seamless walls of the cemeteries
or on the penumbras of short cuts
that betray the city.

The frame doesn't matter to it,
nor the stilted epigraphs.
My shadow impersonates me step by step,
misleads me into the sockets of all the corners,
never answers my questions.

My shadow has taught me to adopt other shadows.

My shadow has put me in my place.

Translated from the Spanish by W. S. Merwin

from Ninth Vertical Poetry

To die, but far away.
Not here
where everything is a perverse
conspiracy of life,
even the other dead.

To die far away.
Not here
where death by now is a betrayal,
a greater betrayal than anywhere else.

To die far away.
Not here
where solitude rests now and then
like an animal stretched out
forgetting its spur of madness.

To die far away.
Not here
where everyone always
goes to sleep in the same place
yet always wakes up somewhere else.

To die far away.
Not here.
To die where nobody is waiting for us
and there may be a place to die.

Translated from the Spanish by W. S. Merwin

Snow has turned the world into a cemetery.
But the world already was a cemetery
and the snow has only come to announce it.

The snow has only come to point,
with its slender jointless finger,
at the truly outrageous protagonist.

The snow is a fallen angel,
an angel who has lost patience.

Translated from the Spanish by Mary Crow

from Tenth Vertical Poetry

Any movement kills something.

It kills the place that is abandoned,
the gesture, the unrepeatable position,

some anonymous organism,
a sign, a glance,
a love that returned,
a presence or its contrary,
the life always of someone else,
one's own life without others.

And being here is moving,
being here is killing something.
Even the dead move,
even the dead kill.
Here the air smells of crime.

But the odor comes from farther away.
And even the odor moves.

Translated from the Spanish by Mary Crow

from Eleventh Vertical Poetry

Every word is a doubt,
every silence another doubt.
However,
the intertwining of both
lets us breathe.

All sleeping is a sinking down,
all waking another sinking.
However,
the intertwining of both
lets us rise up again.

All life is a form of vanishing,
all death another form.
However,
the intertwining of both
lets us be a sign in the void.

Translated from the Spanish by Mary Crow

PABLO NERUDA

Chile (1904–1973)

The career of Pablo Neruda flourished earlier than that of most poets in this book, but his influence continues as a sort of international literary field of force. Not only was he the greatest Latin American poet of his century but from the 1930s until the present his work has shaped the imaginations and styles of poets around the world. He was born Neftalí Ricardo Eliecer Reyes Basoalto in Parral, in southern Chile, the son of a railway worker. He began writing at an early age and, to conceal his vocation, adopted the pen name Pablo Neruda; he said he just picked it out of a magazine. By the age of eighteen, he had moved to Santiago, and soon after his first collections appeared: simple and immediately celebrated poems about love. He joined the Chilean diplomatic corps and was posted to Asia; it was there he fell under the sway of European surrealist writers. During the 1930s he served as consul in Barcelona and Madrid, and his reputation grew. The Spanish Civil War drove him home and fired him to enlist his poetry in political causes. After serving as consul general to Mexico, Neruda was elected a senator in Chile, and in 1945 he joined the Chilean Communist party. Until his death his Marxism was fervent. The publication of *Canto general* in 1950 confirmed his position as the leading poet in the Spanish language. In the early 1970s he served as his country's ambassador to France, and in 1971 he was awarded the Nobel Prize for Literature. His poems have an unmatched sweep and intimacy, a sensualist's love of the physical world, a muralist's grasp of history, and a visionary's rhapsodic voice. He wanted, he said, a poetry "corroded as if by an acid, by the toil of the hand, impregnated with sweat and smoke, smelling of urine and lilies." With Walt Whitman, he is the quintessential American poet. He was an artist, he said, "of bread, truth, wine, dreams."

from Twenty Love Poems

I remember you as you were that final autumn.
You were a gray beret and the whole being at peace.
In your eyes the fires of the evening dusk were battling,
and the leaves were falling in the waters of your soul.

As attached to my arms as a morning glory,
your sad, slow voice was picked up by the leaves.
Bonfire of astonishment in which my thirst was burning.
Soft blue of hyacinth twisting above my soul.

I feel your eyes travel and the autumn is distant:
gray beret, voice of a bird, and heart like a house
toward which my profound desires were emigrating
and my thick kisses were falling like hot coals.

The sky from a ship. The plains from a hill:
your memory is of light, of smoke, of a still pool!
Beyond your eyes the evening dusks were battling.
Dry leaves of autumn were whirling in your soul.

Translated from the Spanish by Robert Bly

Walking Around

It happens that I am tired of being a man.
It happens that I go into the tailors' shops and the movies
all shriveled up, impenetrable, like a felt swan
navigating on a water of origin and ash.

The smell of barber shops makes me sob out loud.
I want nothing but the repose either of stones or of wool,
I want to see no more establishments, no more gardens,
nor merchandise, nor glasses, nor elevators.

It happens that I am tired of my feet and my nails
and my hair and my shadow.
It happens that I am tired of being a man.

Just the same it would be delicious
to scare a notary with a cut lily
or knock a nun stone dead with one blow of an ear.

It would be beautiful
to go through the streets with a green knife
shouting until I died of cold.

I do not want to go on being a root in the dark,
hesitating, stretched out, shivering with dreams,
downwards, in the wet tripe of the earth,
soaking it up and thinking, eating every day.

I do not want to be the inheritor of so many misfortunes.
I do not want to continue as a root and as a tomb,
as a solitary tunnel, as a cellar full of corpses,
stiff with cold, dying with pain.

For this reason Monday burns like oil
at the sight of me arriving with my jail-face,
and it howls in passing like a wounded wheel,
and its footsteps towards nightfall are filled with hot blood.

And it shoves me along to certain corners, to certain damp houses,
to hospitals where the bones come out of the windows,
to certain cobblers' shops smelling of vinegar,
to streets horrendous as crevices.

There are birds the color of sulphur, and horrible intestines
hanging from the doors of the houses which I hate,
there are forgotten sets of teeth in a coffee-pot,
there are mirrors
which should have wept with shame and horror,
there are umbrellas all over the place, and poisons, and navels.

I stride along with calm, with eyes, with shoes,
with fury, with forgetfulness,
I pass, I cross offices and stores full of orthopedic appliances,
and courtyards hung with clothes on wires,
underpants, towels and shirts which weep
slow dirty tears.

Translated from the Spanish by W. S. Merwin

We Are Many

Of the many men whom I am, whom we are,
I cannot settle on a single one.
They are lost to me under the cover of clothing,
They have departed for another city.

When everything seems to be set
to show me off as a man of intelligence,
the fool I keep concealed in my person
takes over my talk and occupies my mouth.

On other occasions, I am dozing in the midst
of people of some distinction,
and when I summon my courageous self,
a coward completely unknown to me
swaddles my poor skeleton
in a thousand tiny reservations.

When a stately home bursts into flames,
instead of the fireman I summon,
an arsonist bursts on the scene,
and he is I. There is nothing I can do.
What must I do to single out myself?
How can I put myself together?

All the books I read
lionize dazzling hero figures,
always brimming with self-assurance.
I die with envy of them;
and, in films where bullets fly on the wind,
I am left in envy of the cowboys,
left admiring even the horses.

But when I call upon my dashing being,
out comes the same old lazy self,
and so I never know just who I am,
nor how many I am, nor who we will be being.
I would like to be able to touch a bell

and call up my real self, the truly me,
because if I really need my proper self,
I must not allow myself to disappear.

While I am writing, I am far away;
and when I come back, I have already left.
I should like to see if the same thing happens
to other people as it does to me,
to see if as many people are as I am,
and if they seem the same way to themselves.
When this problem has been thoroughly explored,
I am going to school myself so well in things
that, when I try to explain my problems,
I shall speak, not of self, but of geography.

Translated from the Spanish by Alastair Reid

Too Many Names

Mondays are meshed with Tuesdays
and the week with the whole year.
Time cannot be cut
with your weary scissors,
and all the names of the day
are washed out by the waters of night.

No one can claim the name of Pedro,
nobody is Rosa or Maria,
all of us are dust or sand,
all of us are rain under rain.
They have spoken to me of Venezuelas,
of Chiles and of Paraguays;
I have no idea what they are saying.
I know only the skin of the earth
and I know it is without a name.

When I lived amongst the roots
they pleased me more than flowers did,

and when I spoke to a stone
it rang like a bell.

It is so long, the spring
which goes on all winter.
Time lost its shoes.
A year is four centuries.

When I sleep every night,
what am I called or not called?
And when I wake, who am I
if I was not I while I slept?

This means to say that scarcely
have we landed into life
than we come as if new-born;
let us not fill our mouths
with so many faltering names,
with so many sad formalities,
with so many pompous letters,
with so much of yours and mine,
with so much signing of papers.

I have a mind to confuse things,
unite them, bring them to birth,
mix them up, undress them,
until the light of the world
has the oneness of the ocean,
a generous, vast wholeness,
a crepitant fragrance.

Translated from the Spanish by Alastair Reid

from The Heights of Macchu Picchu

Stone within stone, and man, where was he?
Air within air, and man, where was he?

Time within time, and man, where was he?
Were you also the shattered fragment
of indecision, of hollow eagle
which, through the streets of today, in the old tracks,
through the leaves of accumulated autumns,
goes pounding at the soul into the tomb?
Poor hand, poor foot, and poor, dear life . . .
The days of unraveled light
in you, familiar rain
falling on feast-day banderillas,
did they grant, petal by petal, their dark nourishment
to such an empty mouth?
                              Famine, coral of mankind,
hunger, secret plant, root of the woodcutters,
famine, did your jagged reef dart up
to those high, side-slipping towers?

I question you, salt of the highways,
show me the trowel; allow me, architecture,
to fret stone stamens with a little stick,
climb all the steps of air into the emptiness,
scrape the intestine until I touch mankind.
Macchu Picchu, did you lift
stone above stone on a groundwork of rags?
coal upon coal and, at the bottom, tears?
fire-crested gold, and in that gold, the bloat
dispenser of this blood?

Let me have back the slave you buried here!
Wrench from these lands the stale bread
of the poor, prove me the tatters
on the serf, point out his window.
Tell me how he slept when alive,
whether he snored,
his mouth agape like a dark scar
worn by fatigue into the wall.
That wall, that wall! If each stone floor
weighed down his sleep, and if he fell
beneath them, as if beneath a moon, with all that sleep!

Ancient America, bride in her veil of sea,
your fingers also,
from the jungle's edges to the rare height of gods,
under the nuptial banners of light and reverence,
blending with thunder from the drums and lances,
your fingers, your fingers also—
that bore the rose in mind and hairline of the cold,
the blood-drenched breast of the new crops translated
into the radiant weave of matter and adamantine hollows—
with them, with them, buried America, were you in that
    great depth,
the bilious gut, hoarding the eagle hunger?

Translated from the Spanish by Nathaniel Tarn

Poet's Obligation

To whoever is not listening to the sea
this Friday morning, to whoever is cooped up
in house or office, factory or woman
or street or mine or harsh prison cell:
to him I come, and, without speaking or looking,
I arrive and open the door of his prison,
and a vibration starts up, vague and insistent,
a great fragment of thunder sets in motion
the rumble of the planet and the foam,
the raucous rivers of the ocean flood,
the star vibrates swiftly in its corona,
and the sea is beating, dying and continuing.

So, drawn on by my destiny,
I ceaselessly must listen to and keep
the sea's lamenting in my awareness,
I must feel the crash of the hard water
and gather it up in a perpetual cup
so that, wherever those in prison may be,
wherever they suffer the autumn's castigation,

I may be there with an errant wave,
I may move, passing through windows,
and hearing me, eyes will glance upward
saying "How can I reach the sea?"
And I shall broadcast, saying nothing,
the starry echoes of the wave,
a breaking up of foam and of quicksand,
a rustling of salt withdrawing,
the grey cry of sea-birds on the coast.

So, through me, freedom and the sea
will make their answer to the shuttered heart.

Translated from the Spanish by Alastair Reid

Poetry

And it was at that age . . . Poetry arrived
in search of me. I don't know, I don't know where
it came from, from winter or a river.
I don't know how or when,
no, they were not voices, they were not
words, nor silence,
but from a street I was summoned,
from the branches of night,
abruptly from the others,
among violent fires
or returning alone,
there I was without a face
and it touched me.

I did not know what to say, my mouth
had no way
with names,
my eyes were blind,
and something started in my soul,
fever or forgotten wings,
and I made my own way,

deciphering
that fire,
and I wrote the first faint line,
faint, without substance, pure
nonsense,
pure wisdom
of someone who knows nothing,
and suddenly I saw
the heavens
unfastened
and open,
planets,
palpitating plantations,
shadow perforated,
riddled
with arrows, fire and flowers,
the winding night, the universe.

And I, infinitesimal being,
drunk with the great starry
void,
likeness, image of
mystery,
felt myself a pure part
of the abyss,
I wheeled with the stars,
my heart broke loose on the wind.

Translated from the Spanish by Alastair Reid

Ode to the Cat

The animals were
imperfect,
long of tail, sorrowful
of head.
Little by little they got

adjusted,
made landscape,
acquired spots, graces, flight.
The cat only,
the cat
appeared complete
and proud:
born fully finished
he walked by himself and knew what he wanted.

Man wants to be fish and bird,
the serpent had wanted wings,
the dog is a displaced lion,
the engineer wants to be a poet,
the fly studies how to be a swallow,
the poet tries to imitate flies,
but the cat
wants only to be cat
and every cat is cat
from whiskers to tail,
from presentiment to living rat,
from the night right up to his golden eyes.

Nothing has his
unity,
nothing
lunar or floral
has such a texture:
he is one whole
like the sun or the topaz,
and the springing curve of his contour
firm and subtle as
the line of a ship's prow.
His yellow eyes
leave a single
slot
through which the coins of night drop.

Oh little
emperor without a realm,

conquistador without a country,
smallest tiger in the salon, and nuptial
sultan of the heaven
of erotic housetops.
Love's wind
you claim
in the wild weather
when you pass
and place
four feet, delicate,
on the ground,
sniffing,
distrusting
the whole universe
as if it all
were too dirty
for a cat's immaculate foot.

Oh proud Independent
of the house, haughty
remnant of night
lazy, athletic
and alien,
profoundest cat,
secret police
of the dwellings flag
of a
vanished velvet,
surely there is no
enigma
in your manner,
perhaps no mystery,
the whole world knows you and you belong
to the least mysterious of householders
perhaps all feel that,
all who feel themselves owners,
masters, uncles
of cats, companions,
colleagues,

students or friends
of the cat.

I don't—
I don't buy that,
I don't understand cats.
All these I know: life and its archipelago,
the sea and the unmeasurable city,
botany—
the pistil and its deviations,
the for and the minus of mathematics,
the world's volcanic funnels,
the crocodile's unreal rind,
the fireman's unknowable goodness,
yet I cannot decipher a cat.
My understanding slips on his indifference,
his eyes hold golden numbers.

Translated from the Spanish by John Hollander

Past

We have to discard the past
and, as one builds
floor by floor, window by window,
and the building rises,
so do we go on throwing down
first, broken tiles,
then pompous doors,
until out of the past
dust rises
as if to crash
against the floor,
smoke rises
as if to catch fire,
and each new day

it gleams
like an empty
plate.
There is nothing, there is always nothing.
It has to be filled
with a new, fruitful
space,
then downward
tumbles yesterday
as in a well
falls yesterday's water,
into the cistern
of all still without voice or fire.
It is difficult
to teach bones
to disappear,
to teach eyes
to close
but
we do it
unrealizing.
It was all alive,
alive, alive, alive
like a scarlet fish
but time
passed over its dark cloth
and the flash of the fish
drowned and disappeared.
Water water water
the past goes on falling
still a tangle
of bones
and of roots;
it has been, it has been, and now
memories mean nothing.
Now the heavy eyelid
covers the light of the eye
and what was once living
now no longer lives;
what we were, we are not.

And with words, although the letters
still have transparency and sound,
they change, and the mouth changes;
the same mouth is now another mouth;
they change, lips, skin, circulation;
another being has occupied our skeleton;
what once was in us now is not.
It has gone, but if they call, we reply:
"I am here," knowing we are not,
that what once was, was and is lost,
is lost in the past, and now will not return.

Translated from the Spanish by Alastair Reid

NICANOR PARRA

Chile (b. 1914)

The son of a teacher, Nicanor Parra was born in the small southern
Chilean town of Chillán. After graduating from the University of Chile
with a degree in mathematics and physics, he pursued advanced studies in
the United States and England. For many years he was professor of theo-
retical physics at the University of Chile, and he has taught as well at
New York University, Columbia, and Yale. All along he has pursued his
career as a poet and since 1937 has been singled out for his country's
most prestigious literary honors. But unlike his great countryman Pablo
Neruda, he has always considered himself what he calls an antipoet. "Let
the birds do the singing," he says. Like Catullus or Villon or Brecht, he
prefers to write about real problems in a flat, biting, wryly ironic style,
and he has crossed that with a peculiarly Latin American brand of fantasy
and dark humor. After the 1960s his poems took on a more political cast.
"I don't support the right or the left," he has written, "I just break the
molds." As a result he was unpopular with both the Allende and the
Pinochet regime, and his poems have adopted sly strategies to address a
range of issues in contemporary Chilean life. More recently he has been
concerned with ecology. His iconoclasm has remained hallucinatory and
feisty, his wit mordant and moving. After every poetry reading he says,
"Me retracto de todo lo dicho" (I take back everything I told you).

The Pilgrim

Your attention, ladies and gentlemen, your attention for one
     moment:
Turn your heads for a second to this part of the republic,
Forget for one night your personal affairs,
Pleasure and pain can wait at the door:
There's a voice from this part of the republic.
Your attention, ladies and gentlemen! Your attention for one
     moment!

A soul that has been bottled up for years
In a sort of sexual and intellectual abyss,
Nourishing itself most inadequately through the nose,
Desires to be heard.
I'd like to find out some things,
I need a little light, the garden's covered with flies,
My mental state's a disaster,
I work things out in my peculiar way,
As I say these things I see a bicycle leaning against a wall,
I see a bridge
And a car disappearing between the buildings.

You comb your hair, that's true, you walk in the gardens,
Under your skins you have other skins,
You have a seventh sense
Which lets you in and out automatically.
But I'm a child calling to its mother from behind rocks,
I'm a pilgrim who makes stones jump as high as his nose,
A tree crying out to be covered with leaves.

Translated from the Spanish by W. S. Merwin

The Tablets

I dreamed I was in a desert and because I was sick of myself
I started beating a woman.
It was devilish cold, I had to do something,
Make a fire, take some exercise,
But I had a headache, I was tired,
All I wanted to do was sleep, die.
My suit was soggy with blood
And a few hairs were stuck among my fingers
—They belonged to my poor mother—
"Why do you abuse your mother," a stone asked me,
A dusty stone, "Why do you abuse her?"
I couldn't tell where these voices came from, they gave me the
    shivers,

I looked at my nails, I bit them,
I tried to think of something but without success,
All I saw around me was a desert
And the image of that idol
My god who was watching me do these things.
Then a few birds appeared
And at the same moment, in the dark, I discovered some slabs of
    rock.
With a supreme effort I managed to make out the tablets of the
    law:
"We are the tablets of the law," they said,
"Why do you abuse your mother?
See these birds that have come to perch on us,
They are here to record your crimes."
But I yawned, I was bored with these warnings.
"Get rid of those birds," I said aloud.
"No," one of the stones said,
"They stand for your different sins,
They're here to watch you."
So I turned back to my lady again
And started to let her have it harder than before.
I had to do something to keep awake.
I had no choice but to act
Or I would have fallen asleep among those rocks
And those birds.
So I took a box of matches out of one of my pockets
And decided to set fire to the bust of the god.
I was dreadfully cold, I had to get warm,
But that blaze only lasted a few seconds.
Out of my mind, I looked for the tablets again
But they had disappeared.
The rocks weren't there either.
My mother had abandoned me.
I beat my brow. But
There was nothing more I could do.

Translated from the Spanish by W. S. Merwin

A Man

A man's mother is very sick
He goes out to find a doctor
He's crying
In the street he sees his wife in the company of another man
They're holding hands
He follows a few steps behind them
From tree to tree
He's crying
Now he meets a friend from his youth
It's years since we've seen each other!
They go on to a bar
They talk, laugh
The man goes out to the patio for a piss
He sees a young girl
It's night
She's washing dishes
The man goes over to her
He takes her by the waist
They waltz
They go out into the street together
They laugh
There's an accident
The girl's lost consciousness
The man goes to telephone
He's crying
He comes to a house with lights on
He asks for a telephone
Somebody knows him
Hey stay and have something to eat
No
Where's the telephone
Have something to eat, hey eat something
Then go
He sits down to eat
He drinks like a condemned man
He laughs
They get him to recite something

He recites it
He ends up sleeping under a desk

Translated from the Spanish by W. S. Merwin

The Poems of the Pope

I

They just elected me Pope:
I'm the most famous man in the world!

II

Now I'm at the top of the ecclesiastical profession
and I can die in peace

III

The Cardinals are angry
because I don't treat them like I used to
too solemn?
but I'm the Pope goddamn it . . .

IV

First thing tomorrow
I'll move into the Vatican

V

The title of my address:
How to Succeed in the Ecclesiastical Profession

VI

Congratulations are pouring in
every newspaper in the world
has my picture on the front page

and one thing's for sure:
I look much younger than I really am

VII

Ever since I was a boy
I wanted to be Pope
why's everybody so surprised
I worked like a dog
to get what I wanted

VIII

Holy Mother of God
I forgot to bless the multitude!

Translated from the Spanish by Edith Grossman

ENRIQUE LIHN

Chile (1929–1988)

Born in Santiago, Enrique Lihn started out to be a painter while at the
university but abandoned that career to write. In addition to being a pop-
ular poet, he was well known as a novelist and playwright, and taught lit-
erature at the University of Chile. In a country of strong poets, he
developed a personal voice—ample, nostalgic, eerie. As he once wrote in a
poem about Kafka, "I explore, coldly, the taste and feel of death." Both
the past and the future are forms of death, and Lihn kept both in his
sights. During the years when Chile was governed by a military junta, his
work increasingly dealt with the social and human cost of the dictator-
ship. His final book, *Diario de muerte (A Diary of Dying)*, was written in
the six weeks preceding his death from cancer. The evening before he
died, he corrected the proofs.

The Dark Room

The air's heaviness in the dark room, as if a vague bloodlike
drizzle threatened to come down from the ceiling.
We inhaled some of that brew, our noses dirty, a symbol of
    children acting like grownups
to go on secretly with our struggle, for some cause we did and
    didn't know;
a game of hands and feet, twice as rough, but just as sweet
as paying back tooth and nail for the first blood drawn or for a
    young girl
sweet as the first trickle of her blood.

And that's how the old wheel—symbol of life—began to turn,
    getting stuck between one generation and the next
as if it couldn't fly off, caught in the wink of bright and dim eyes
with an imperceptible, mossy sound.
Pulling into its center, imitating us, kids spinning around two at a

time, our ears red—symbols of a modesty that delights in its
crime—furiously tender,
the wheel gave a few false turns as in the age before the invention
of the wheel
clockwise, and then counter clockwise.
For a second confusion ruled over time. I slowly bit into the neck
of my cousin Isabel,
in the wink of the eye of he who sees everything, as in the age
before sin
because we pretended to struggle in the belief that this is what we
were doing; a belief bordering on faith as the game on truth
and the facts could hardly dare to prove us wrong
with our ears red.

We stopped rolling around on the floor, my cousin Angel winner
over my sister Pauline; and I over Isabel, two nymphs
wrapped up in a cocoon of blankets that made them sneeze—the
mothball smell on a fruit's downy skin—.
Those were our victorious and their defeated weapons each taken
for the other, like nests for cells, cells for hugs, hugs for
chains tying down hands and feet.
We stopped rolling around, overcome by a strange feeling of
shame, without managing to come up with another reproach
than the one for finding such an easy victory.
The wheel was already turning perfectly, as in the age it appeared
in the myth, as in the day it was first carved in wood
with a sound of medieval sparrows' song;
time was flying in the right direction. You could hear it moving
toward us
quicker than the dining room clock whose ticking grew louder to
break so much silence.
Time flew as if to roll us up with a sound of foaming water that
rushed faster near the mill's wheel, with sparrows' wings—
symbols of savage free order—with itself as the only
overflowing thing
and life—symbol of the wheel—moved ahead to storm by making
the wheel turn faster and faster, as in a mill furiously grinding
time.
I let my captive go and fell on my knees, as if I had suddenly
grown old, seized by a sweet, cloying panic

as if I had known, beyond love in its prime the heart's cruelty in
the fruit of love, the fruit rotting and then . . . the bloody pit,
feverish and dried out.

What has become of the children we were? Someone hurried to
turn on the light, faster than the thoughts of grownups.
They were already looking for us inside the house, around the
mill: the room dark as a clearing in a forest.
But there was always time to win before the never quitting child
hunters got there. When they came into the dining room there
we were, angels sitting around the table,
looking at the pictures in our magazines—men at one end, women
at the other—
in perfect order, before the bloodshed.

Going counter clockwise, the wheel broke loose before it began
turning and we couldn't even find each other on the other
side of dizziness, when we entered time
as in calm waters, serenely quick;
we scattered ourselves forever in the waters, just like pieces of the
same shipwreck.
But part of me hasn't turned in time with the wheel, gone along
with the current.
Nothing is real enough for a ghost. Part of me is that boy who
falls down on his knees
softly crushed by unbearable omens
and I haven't come of age yet
nor will I reach it like him
once and for all.

Translated from the Spanish by David Unger

Cemetery in Punta Arenas

Not even death could make these men alike
who give their names to different gravestones
or shout them into the sun's wind that rubs them out:

some more dust for a fresh gust of wind.
Here, by the sea that is just like marble,
between this double row of bowing cypresses,
peace rules, a peace struggling to shatter itself,
ripping the burial parchments in a thousand pieces
to reveal the face of an ancient arrogance
and to laugh at the dust.

This city had yet to be built when its first
settlers raised still another empty city
and, one by one, they settled deep into their places
as if anyone would even try taking it away from them.
Each one forever in his own place, waiting,
the tablecloths laid out, for his sons and grandsons.

Translated from the Spanish by David Unger

Six Poems of Loneliness

I

The unending loneliness from which others drink
during the cocktail hour
is my grave, not my glass, I bring it up to my lips
and thrash about in it till I disappear
into its morbid waves.
Loneliness is my monster, not my canary
as if I were living with an insane asylum.

II

Pure one, I would be lying if I didn't tell you:
you either eat a heart or throw it away
it's neither a vase with flowers nor a poem.
You were very near, you almost caught me
your body lagged behind.

I can't leave my heart in your little box
with your earrings and your photographs.
Soon enough someone will give you a better one.

III

Everything's ready for war except me.
The housewife ready for war
against the invading rat,
boys ready for the future, for a war ahead,
men standing ready for war with their banners and slogans.
Except me standing for what,
standing for poetry, standing for nothing.

IV

Living on the other side of a woman
I'm talking about this kind of suicide
on the edge of madness,
and, for one reason or another, time goes by
as the poet would say, without her.
Here in this town, in a glass honeycomb,
in my sealed cell
I steal hours of sanity from anguish, dying
in the poet's fruitless work,
in his plodding impotence.
Without a woman, with fright,
plodding on.

V

Next to a virgin who feeds me
her sweetness until exhausted,
tropical, wax fruits:
love almost made in the image
of what it should be,
but really just a talking doll,

and a dangerous game
of not turning into real fruits.
Punishment: impotence, sexual blunders,
sadness, wanting to die.

VI

Women
steeped in everything there is,
good or bad, it makes no difference.
Huge, obliging sponges.
They are my great resentment,
what my spiteful glands secrete,
my loneliness, my daily bread.

Translated from the Spanish by David Unger

Torture Chamber

Your alms are my salary
Your salary is the squaring of my circle, that I draw out
with my fingers to maintain their agility
Your calculator is my hand missing a finger with which
I keep myself from making calculation errors
Your alms are the capital I contribute when I go begging
Your appearance in Ahumada Mall is my debut
Your society is secret insofar as my tribe is concerned
Your personal security is my indecision
Your pocket handkerchief is my white flag
Your necktie is my gordian knot
Your brand name suit is my backdrop
Your right shoe is my left shoe a dozen years later
The crease of your pants is the edge I couldn't cross
even though I disguised myself as you
after tearing your clothes off
Your ascension up the staircase at the Bank of Chile
is my dream of Jacob's ladder on which a blond angel

with painted wings descends
to pay, in hand to hand combat, all my debts
Your checkbook is my sack of papers when I get stoned
Your signature is my illiterate's game
Your 2 + 2 = four is my 2 − 2
Your coming and going are my labyrinth in which
meditating I get lost pursued by a fly
Your office is the backstage where my name can be
condemned to death and transferred to another corpse
that will bear it in some friendly country
Your doctor's office is my torture chamber
Your torture chamber is the only hotel where I can be
received at any hour
without advance notice
Your order is my song
Your electric pen is what makes me a prolific author,
a goddam visionary, or the guy who remains silent—
depending on who I am at the moment
Your bad will is my blood
Your foot on my butt is my ascension to the heavens
that are what they are and not what God wants
Your tranquility is my being stabbed in the back
Your liberty is my everlasting flower
Your peace is mine forever and whenever I enjoy it eternally
and you for life
Your real life is the end of my imagination when I get stoned
Your house is my lost paradise which I'm going to feel I own
the next time I get stoned
Your wife is in that case my squashed kitten
Your toothpick is now my fork
Your fork is my spoon
Your knife is my temptation to slit your throat
when I suck on a joint
Your police dog is the guardian of my impropriety
Your German shepherd is my beheader at the door of your house
as if I weren't a cursed lost sheep
Your machinegun is the lover I fuck in my dreams
Your helmet is the mold in which they emptied
the head of my son when he was born
Your military march is my wedding processional

Your garbage dump is my pantheon
as long as the corpses aren't carried off.

Translated from the Spanish by Mary Crow

Of All Despondencies

Of all despondencies, death-despair must be the worst
it, and fear of death, no more of that
when now they can foretell the day and hour
There's an ugly probability that fear of death and death-despair
    may be
as a rule inseparable as flesh and nail
I remember a friend from other years he fled by night from his
    home and from hospital
with no more safe conduct than you would give a condemned man

he unloaded himself on the house of women friends who did not
    share his love for them, damnably beautiful
he insisted with arguments straight from the science of madness
that they receive him in their house as a normal guest
I seem to see the end of these impossible conversations
how he is led back to his lair by the women and their husbands
in a deep silence, he, the gnome in the black jungle of dawn
returned to his antihouse
or to the hospital airport so as not to miss his flight.

Translated from the Spanish by Alastair Reid

A Favorite Little Shrine

I have turned into a little shrine, a favorite
among truck drivers and their families
A little death house lit by candles, devoutly; with fresh flowers
    every day

I have turned into an actor who is going to die, really die, in the
    last act
a famous tightrope walker with no net who dances night after
    night on the loose wire
The telephone in my dressing room rings all the time.
They cannot call me to cancel my appearance in the show
they only call to ask me to keep them tickets if only for the third
    act
They call up, people close to my heart, now empty but not
    indifferent, and people thousands of miles from it
these last ones to make their peace with Jesus, their paralytic, by
    way of me
to obtain a last-minute absolution
Par délicatesse I am going to lose, in what is left of my life,
the joy of dying, receiving those big-mouths

Death is a hit with the public
Twelve people are enough for me
I don't want anyone else in the auditorium

Translated from the Spanish by Alastair Reid

Goodnight, Achilles

So, we got you in the heel.
Death, the one you keep fleeing from,
    will be running at your side, matching your every step

Goodnight, Achilles

Translated from the Spanish by Alastair Reid

CARLOS DRUMMOND DE ANDRADE

Brazil (1902–1987)

The son of a rancher, Carlos Drummond de Andrade was born in the small mining town of Itabira, in the province of Minas Gerais. He was expelled from a Jesuit school in Rio de Janeiro for "mental insubordination," a trait that came to shape his imagination. He eventually graduated with a degree in pharmacology and until his retirement in 1966 worked as a civil servant in the Ministry of Education. All along he was a translator, essayist, short-story writer, and poet. His first collection of poems appeared in 1934, but even during the 1920s he was a member of the Semana de Arte Moderna, a group of avant-garde poets determined to upend the heavy burdens of traditional verse and promote a poetry that was on the one hand popular, catching the flux of modern life ("prayers, / victrolas, / saints crossing themselves, / ads for a better soap, / a racket of which nobody / knows the why or wherefore"), and on the other hand charged with the exotic forces of surrealism and primitivism. Drummond's mature work, however, has its own stamp: inward, ironic, realistic, humorous, nostalgic. "Everything is possible, only I am impossible," he wrote, a motto for the sense of personal isolation and loneliness that pervades his work. Out of that loneliness was born his wry and gentle compassion.

Seven-Sided Poem

When I was born, one of the crooked
angels who live in shadow, said:
Carlos, go on! Be *gauche* in life.

The houses watch the men,
men who run after women.
If the afternoon had been blue,
there might have been less desire.

The trolley goes by full of legs:
white legs, black legs, yellow legs.

My God, why all the legs?
my heart asks. But my eyes
ask nothing at all.

The man behind the mustache
is serious, simple, and strong.
He hardly ever speaks.
He has a few, choice friends,
the man behind the spectacles and the mustache.

My God, why hast Thou forsaken me
if Thou knew'st I was not God,
if Thou knew'st that I was weak?

Universe, vast universe,
if I had been named Eugene
that would not be what I mean
but it would go into verse
faster.

Universe, vast universe,
my heart is vaster.

I oughtn't to tell you,
but this moon
and this brandy
play the devil with one's emotions.

Translated from the Portuguese by Elizabeth Bishop

Souvenir of the Ancient World

Clara strolled in the garden with the children.
The sky was green over the grass,
the water was golden under the bridges,
other elements were blue and rose and orange,
a policeman smiled, bicycles passed,

a girl stepped onto the lawn to catch a bird,
the whole world—Germany, China—
    all was quiet around Clara.

The children looked at the sky: it was not forbidden.
Mouth, nose, eyes were open. There was no danger.
What Clara feared were the flu, the heat, the insects.
Clara feared missing the eleven o'clock trolley:
She waited for letters slow to arrive,
She couldn't always wear a new dress. But she strolled in the
    garden, in the morning!
They had gardens, they had mornings in those days!

Translated from the Portuguese by Mark Strand

Motionless Faces

Father dead, loved one dead.
Aunt dead, brother born dead.
Cousins dead, friend dead.
Grandfather dead, mother dead
(hands white, portrait on the wall always crooked, speck of dust
    in the eyes).
Acquaintances dead, teacher dead.

Enemy dead.

Fiancée dead, girl friends dead.
Engineer dead, passenger dead.
Unrecognizable body dead: a man's? an animal's?
Dog dead, bird dead.
Rosebush dead, orange trees dead.
Air dead, bay dead.
Hope, patience, eyes, sleep, movement of hands: dead.

Man dead. Lights go on.
He works at night as if he were living.

Good morning! He is stronger (as if he were living).

Dead without an obituary, secretly dead.
He knows how to imitate hunger, and how to pretend to love.

And how to insist on walking, and how well he walks.
He could walk through walls, but he uses doors.

His pale hand says good-bye to Russia.
Time enters and leaves him endlessly.

The dead pass quickly; they cannot be held on to.
As soon as one leaves, another one is tapping your shoulder.
I woke up and saw the city:
the dead were like machines,
the houses belonged to the dead,
drowsy waves,
an exhausted chest smelling of lilies,
feet bound up.
I slept and went to the city:
everything was burning,
crackling of bamboo,
mouth dry, suddenly puckering.
I dreamt and returned to the city.
But it wasn't the city anymore.
They were all dead, the medical examiner was checking the tags
    on the corpses.
The medical examiner himself had died years ago but his hand
    continued implacably.
The awful stench was everywhere.

From this veranda without a railing I watch both twilights.
I watch my life running away with a wolf's speed, I want to stop
    it, but would I be bitten?
I look at my feet, how they have grown, flies circulate among
    them.
I look at everything and add it up, nothing is left, I am poor, poor,
    poor,
but I cannot enter the circle,

I cannot remain alone,
I shall kiss everyone on the forehead,
I shall distribute moist flowers,
after . . . There is no after or before.
There is cold on all sides,
and a central cold, whiter still.
Colder still . . .
A whiteness that pays well our old anger and bitterness . . .
Feeling myself so clear among you, kissing you and getting no dust
    in my mouth or face.
Peace of wispy trees,
of fragile mountains down below, of timid riverbanks, of gestures
    that can no longer annoy,
sweet peace without eyes, in the dark, in the air.
Sweet peace within me,
within my family that came from a fog unbroken by the sun
and returns to their islands by underground roads,
in my street, in my time—finally—reconciled,
in the city of my birth, in my rented rooms,
in my life, in everyone's life, in the mild and deep death of myself
    and everyone.

Translated from the Portuguese by Mark Strand

Residue

From everything a little remained.
From my fear. From your disgust.
From stifled cries. From the rose
a little remained.

A little remained of light
caught inside the hat.
In the eyes of the pimp
a little remained of tenderness,
very little.

A little remained of the dust
that covered your white shoes.
Of your clothes a little remained,
a few velvet rags, very
very few.

From everything a little remained.
From the bombed-out bridge,
from the two blades of grass,
from the empty pack
of cigarettes a little remained.

So from everything a little remains.
A little remains of your chin
in the chin of your daughter.

A little remained of your
blunt silence, a little
in the angry wall,
in the mute rising leaves.

A little remained from everything
in porcelain saucers,
in the broken dragon, in the white flowers,
in the creases of your brow,
in the portrait.

Since from everything a little remains,
why won't a little
of me remain? In the train
traveling north, in the ship,
in newspaper ads,
why not a little of me in London,
a little of me somewhere?
In a consonant?
In a well?

A little remains dangling
in the mouths of rivers,

just a little, and the fish
don't avoid it, which is very unusual.

From everything a little remains.
Not much: this absurd drop
dripping from the faucet,
half salt and half alcohol,
this frog leg jumping,
this watch crystal
broken into a thousand wishes,
this swan's neck,
this childhood secret . . .
From everything a little remained:
from me; from you; from Abelard.
Hair on my sleeve,
from everything a little remained;
wind in my ears,
burbling, rumbling
from an upset stomach,
and small artifacts:
bell jar, honeycomb, revolver
cartridge, aspirin tablet.
From everything a little remained.

And from everything a little remains.
Oh, open the bottles of lotion
and smother
the cruel, unbearable odor of memory.

Still, horribly, from everything a little remains,
under the rhythmic waves
under the clouds and the wind
under the bridges and under the tunnels
under the flames and under the sarcasm
under the phlegm and under the vomit
under the cry from the dungeon, the guy they forgot
under the spectacles and under the scarlet death
under the libraries, asylums, victorious churches
under yourself and under your feet already hard

under the ties of family, the ties of class,
from everything a little always remains.
Sometimes a button. Sometimes a rat.

Translated from the Portuguese by Mark Strand

Family Portrait

Yes, this family portrait
is a little dusty.
The father's face doesn't show
how much money he earned.

The uncles' hands don't reveal
the voyages both of them made.
The grandmother's smoothed and yellowed;
she's forgotten the monarchy.

The children, how they've changed.
Peter's face is tranquil,
that wore the best dreams.
And John's no longer a liar.

The garden's become fantastic.
The flowers are gray badges.
And the sand, beneath dead feet,
is an ocean of fog.

In the semicircle of armchairs
a certain movement is noticed.
The children are changing places,
but noiselessly! it's a picture.

Twenty years is a long time.
It can form any image.
If one face starts to wither,
another presents itself, smiling.

All these seated strangers,
my relations? I don't believe it.
They're guests amusing themselves
in a rarely-opened parlor.

Family features remain
lost in the play of bodies.
But there's enough to suggest
that a body is full of surprises.

The frame of this family portrait
holds its personages in vain.
They're there voluntarily,
they'd know how—if need be—to fly.

They could refine themselves
in the room's chiaroscuro,
live inside the furniture
or the pockets of old waistcoats.

The house has many drawers,
papers, long staircases.
When matter becomes annoyed,
who knows the malice of things?

The portrait does not reply,
it stares; in my dusty eyes
it contemplates itself.
The living and dead relations

multiply in the glass.
I don't distinguish those
that went away from those
that stay. I only perceive
the strange idea of family

traveling through the flesh.

Translated from the Portuguese by Elizabeth Bishop

JOAO CABRAL DE MELO NETO

Brazil (b. 1920)

Born in Pernambuco in northeastern Brazil, João Cabral de Melo Neto grew up on a sugar plantation and moved to Rio de Janeiro in 1942. Three years later he entered the diplomatic service. Over four decades, until his retirement in 1987, he was posted to Spain, England, France, and Switzerland; he has been his country's ambassador to both Senegal and Honduras. His books of poems began appearing when he was in his twenties, and he has since published more than two dozen collections. In 1992 he was awarded both the São Paulo Literary Prize and the Neustadt Prize for Literature. Incantatory syntax and echoing images give his poetry the power of song, but an abstract song. Contemporary Brazilian poetry has been resolutely experimental, but Cabral's innovative work has never abandoned traditional verse forms, however austerely conceptual it has been. And the landscape around Recife and the Capibaribe River continues to draw from him evocative memories. But poetry, he has written in a defense of what he calls the *antilyric,* "is the exploration of the materiality of words and of the possibilities of organization of verbal structures, things that have nothing to do with what is romantically called inspiration, or even intuition. In this respect, I believe that lyricism, upon finding in popular music the element that fulfills it and gives it its prestige, has liberated written poetry and has allowed it to return to operate in a territory that once belonged to it. It has made possible too the exercise of poetry as emotive exploration of the world of things and as rigorous construction of lucid formal structures, lucid objects of language."

Daily Space

In the daily space
the shadow eats the orange
the orange throws itself into the river,
it's not a river, it's the sea
overflowing from my eye.

In the daily space
born out of the clock

I see hands not words,
late at night I dream up the woman,
I have the woman and the fish.

In the daily space
I forget the home the sea
I lose hunger memory
I kill myself uselessly
in the daily space.

Translated from the Portuguese by W. S. Merwin

The End of the World

At the end of a melancholy world
men read the newspapers.
Indifferent men eating oranges
that flame like the sun.

They gave me an apple to remind me
of death. I know that cities telegraph
asking for kerosene. The veil I saw flying
fell in the desert.

No one will write the final poem
about this private twelve o'clock world.
Instead of the last judgment, what worries me
is the final dream.

Translated from the Portuguese by James Wright

Landscape of the Capibaribe River

The city is crossed by the river
as a street

is crossed by a dog,
a piece of fruit
by a sword.

The river called to mind
a dog's docile tongue,
or a dog's sad belly,
or that other river
which is the dirty wet cloth
of a dog's two eyes.

The river was
like a dog without feathers.
It knew nothing of the blue rain,
of the rose-colored fountain,
of the water in a water glass,
of the water in pitchers,
of the fish in the water,
of the breeze on the water.

It knew the crabs
of mud and rust.
It knew silt
like a mucous membrane.
It must have known the octopus,
and surely knew
the feverish woman living in oysters.

The river
never opens up to fish,
to the shimmer,
to the knifely unrest
existing in fish.
It never opens up in fish.

It opens up in flowers,
poor and black
like black men and women.
It opens up into a flora
as squalid and beggarly

as the blacks who must beg.
It opens up in hard-leafed
mangroves, kinky
as a black man's hair.

Smooth like the belly
of a pregnant dog,
the river swells
without ever bursting.
The river's childbirth
is like a dog's,
fluid and invertebrate.

And I never saw it seethe
(as bread when rising
seethes).
In silence
the river bears its bloating poverty,
pregnant with black earth.

It yields in silence:
in black earthen capes,
in black earthen boots or gloves
for the foot or hand
that plunges in.

As sometimes happens
with dogs, the river
seemed to stagnate.
Its waters would turn
thicker and warmer,
flowing with the thick
warm waves
of a snake.

It had something
of a crazy man's stagnation.
Something of the stagnation
of hospitals, prisons, asylums,
of the dirty and smothered life

(dirty, smothering laundry)
it trudged through.

Something of the stagnation
of decayed palaces,
eaten
by mold and mistletoe.
Something of the stagnation
of obese trees
dripping a thousand sugars
from the Pernambuco dining rooms
it trudged through.

(It is there,
with their backs to the river,
that the city's "cultured families"
brood over the fat eggs
of their prose.
In the complete peace of their kitchens
they viciously stir
their pots
of sticky indolence.)

Could the river's water
be the fruit of some tree?
Why did it seem
like ripened water?
Why the flies always
above it, as if about to land?

Did any part of the river
ever cascade in joy?
Was it ever, anywhere,
a song or fountain?
Why then
were its eyes painted blue
on maps?

Translated from the Portuguese by Richard Zenith

A Knife All Blade

for Vinícius de Moraes

Like a bullet
buried in flesh
weighting down one side
of the dead man,

like a bullet
made of the heaviest lead
lodged in some muscle
making the man tip to one side,

like a bullet fired
from a living machine
a bullet that had
its own heartbeat,

like a clock's
beating deep down in the body
of a clock who once lived
and rebelled,

clock whose hands
had knife-edges
and all the pitilessness
of blued steel.

Yes, like a knife
without pocket or sheath
transformed into part
of your anatomy,

a most intimate knife
a knife for internal use
inhabiting the body
like the skeleton itself

of a man who would own it,
in pain, always in pain,
of a man who would wound himself
against his own bones.

Translated from the Portuguese by Galway Kinnell

Education by Stone

An education by stone: through lessons,
to learn from the stone: to go to it often,
to catch its level, impersonal voice
(by its choice of words it begins its classes).
The lesson in morals, the stone's cold resistance
to flow, to flowing, to being hammered:
the lesson in poetics, its concrete flesh:
in economics, how to grow dense compactly:
lessons from the stone (from without to within,
dumb primer), for the routine speller of spells.

Another education by stone: in the backlands
(from within to without and pre-didactic place).
In the backlands stone does not know how to lecture,
and, even if it did would teach nothing:
you don't learn the stone, there: there, the stone,
born stone, penetrates the soul.

Translated from the Portuguese by James Wright

The Emptiness of Man

I

The emptiness of man is not like
any other: not like an empty coat

or empty sack (things which do not stand up
when empty, such as an empty man),
the emptiness of man is more like fullness
in swollen things which keep on swelling,
the way a sack must feel
that is being filled, or any sack at all.
The emptiness of man, this full emptiness,
is not like a sack of bricks' emptiness
or a sack of rivets', it does not have the pulse
that beats in a seed bag or bag of eggs.

2

The emptiness of man, though it resembles
fullness, and seems all of a piece, actually
is made of nothings, bits of emptiness,
like the sponge, empty when filled,
swollen like the sponge, with air, with empty air;
it has copied its very structure from the sponge,
it is made up in clusters, of bubbles, of non-grapes.
Man's empty fullness is like a sack
filled with sponges, is filled with emptiness:
man's emptiness, or swollen emptiness,
or the emptiness that swells by being empty.

Translated from the Portuguese by Galway Kinnell

THE CARIBBEAN

HEBERTO PADILLA

Cuba (b. 1932)

Heberto Padilla was born in Pinar del Rio and had published his first volume of poetry by the age of seventeen. He studied journalism at the University of Havana and wrote movie scripts. In 1957 he came to the United States to work, first as a radio commentator in Miami and later as a language teacher in New York. But in 1959, with the revolution in Cuba a success, he returned eagerly and worked for Prensa Latina, the Cuban press agency. For several years he was the agency's correspondent in Moscow and London. In the late 1960s, however, his differences with the Castro regime led to his dismissal as a foreign correspondent. He was called home but also given his country's highest literary prize for a new volume of poems. By 1971 he had been arrested and beaten, and he was released only after "confessing" his errors. This sort of intellectual barbarism prompted sixty of the world's most famous writers to protest on Padilla's behalf. During the 1970s he was unable to publish in Cuba and worked as a ghostwriter and translator. Finally, in 1980 he was expelled from Cuba and joined his family in the United States. His sensibility was formed by refined models—Rainer Maria Rilke, Wallace Stevens, Luis Cernuda, and Cuba's greatest modern poet, José Lezama Lima. Padilla has tempered the natural exuberance of Latin American poetry in favor of direct emotion. He has continually drawn his lyricism into history's arena and used his own experience to represent the plight of the troubled conscience and the moral exile.

A Prayer for the End of the Century

We who have always looked with tolerant irony
    on the mottled objects of the end of the century:
                                the vast structures
    and men stiff in dark clothes
We for whom the end of the century was at most
    an engraving and a prayer in French
We who thought that after a hundred years there would be only
    a black bird lifting a grandmother's bonnet

We who have seen the collapse of
                                parliaments
        and the patched backside of liberalism
We who learned to distrust illustrious myths
        and who see as totally impossible
        (uninhabitable)
        halls with candelabra
        tapestries
        and Louis XV chairs
We children and grandchildren of melancholy terrorists
        and superstitious scientists
We who know that the error exists today
        that someone will have to condemn tomorrow
We who are living the last years of this century
        wander about unable to improvise
                                movements
        not already planned in advance
        we gesture in a space more straitening
        than the lines of an etching;
        we put on formal clothes again,
        as though we were attending another parliament,
        while the candelabra sputter at the cornice
        and the black birds
        tear at the bonnet of that hoarse-voiced girl.

Translated from the Spanish by Alastair Reid and Andrew Hurley

Landscapes

    You can see them everywhere in Cuba.
    Green or red or yellow, flaking off from the water
    and the sun, true landscapes of these times
    of war.
    The wind tugs at the Coca-Cola signs.
    The clocks courtesy of Canada Dry are stopped
    at the old time.
    The neon signs, broken, crackle and splutter in the rain.

Esso's is something like this
       S   O   S
and above there are some crude letters
reading   PATRIA   O   MUERTE.

Translated from the Spanish by Alastair Reid and Andrew Hurley

Self-Portrait of the Other

Is it anxiety, nausea,
raptures?
Or is it just wanting
sometimes to shout out?
I don't know. I come back onstage.
I walk toward the footlights
as if toward yesterday,
        swifter than a squirrel,
with my child's drool
and a tricolor flag on my breast,
        agitator, irascible,
                among the students.

The truth is that they finally
        managed to lock me up
in that baroque garden I hated so much
and this opal gleam
        in my eyes
makes me unrecognizable.
The little gladiator (bronze)
which I have put on the table
—a scowling hero, master
of his short white blade—
and his snarling bitch
        are now my only buddies.
But when my troupe of jugglers
        appears
we will file through the bars

and I will break out.
Doors are things there are too many of!

Under the plastic moon
have I become a parrot
or a nylon clown
that bumbles and loses the password?
Or is it not true?
Is it a nightmare
that I myself could destroy,
opening my eyes
suddenly
and rolling through the dream in a barrel,
and the world mixed now with these seethings?
Or is it just wanting
sometimes to shout out?

The Right praises me
     (in no time they will defame me)
The Left has given me a name
     (have they not begun to have doubts?)
But at any rate
I warn you I'm alive in the streets.
I don't wear dark glasses.
And I don't carry time bombs in my pockets
or a hairy ear—a bear's.
Give me room, now.
Don't greet me, I beg you.
Don't even speak to me.
If you see me, keep to one side.

Translated from the Spanish by Alastair Reid and Andrew Hurley

Man on the Edge

He is not the man who goes over the wall,
feeling himself enclosed by his times,
nor is he the fugitive breathing hard
hidden in the back of a truck
fleeing from the terrorists,
nor is he the poor guy with the canceled passport
who is always trying to cross a new border.
He lives on this side of heroics
—in that dark part—
but never gets rattled or surprised.
He does not want to be a hero,
not even a romantic
around whom we might
weave a legend.
He is sentenced to this life, and, what terrifies him more,
condemned irretrievably to his own time.
He is headless at two in the morning,
going from one room to another
like an enormous wind
which barely survives in the wind outside.
Every morning he begins again
as if he were an Italian actor.
He stops dead
as if someone had just stolen his being.
No looking glass would dare reflect
this fallen mouth, this wisdom gone bankrupt.

Translated from the Spanish by Alastair Reid and Alexander Coleman

The Discourse on Method

If, after the bombardment is over,
walking on the grass that can grow just as well
among ruins

as in your bishop's hat,
you are able to imagine that you are not seeing
what is going to take root
inevitably before your eyes,
or that you are not hearing
what you will have to hear for a long time still,
or, worse,
you think that cunning and good judgment
will be enough to get by,
avoiding the one day when, entering your house,
you find only a broken chair,
a pile of torn books,
I recommend that you run out immediately
and get hold of a passport, a baggage check,
a sickly child,
anything that might justify you
as you face the policeman off his guard for the moment
(the police these days are all peasants and laborers)
and you get out once and for all.

Scramble down the garden stairs,
make sure nobody sees you.
Don't bring anything.
      They won't help, in any case—
an overcoat, a glove, a last name,
a gold bar, or a musty diploma.
Don't waste time hiding jewels in the walls,
because they'll find them sooner or later.
Don't bury your manuscripts in the cellar;
the militia will dig them out afterwards.
Don't trust your most faithful maid.
Don't hand over the keys to a chauffeur
or leave the dog with the gardener.
Don't get worked up at the news on the short wave.

Stand in front of the tallest mirror in the living room
and contemplate your life,
and contemplate yourself as you are now,
because this will be the last time.

They are taking down the barricades in the parks.
Those who have seized power are now appearing on the balcony.
The dog, the gardener, the chauffeur, and the maid
    are all there, applauding.

Translated from the Spanish by Alastair Reid and Alexander Coleman

Daily Habits

Every morning
I get up and go to the basin,
run the water,
    and, always, a single word
pops out at once,
    vengeful,
and drowns out the faucet where my eye has wandered.

Translated from the Spanish by Alastair Reid and Alexander Coleman

A Fountain, a House of Stone

(Zurbarán)

A fountain, a house of stone,
a bridge, a chapel with a weather vane
and a squeaking hinge in the door,
a road bordered by flowers
and, farther on, a river.

Can we describe the world this way,
eyes wide open, shoes up on the table
with a dusky halo like a lantern,
and the still face, distant and ever-demanding,
nailing us down with its eyes,
hunting down in our innards

the cowardly swagger of allegory?
It is possible. The world can be described
        in any way you like. You might
come out with one last twist of the facts, as they say,
our last coin
to take us back again to that river
        that attends our childhood as it does old age.
One might cross the bridge
among the bamboo which creaks once again
like a bridge across a river,
in such a way that the hinge we have hung on to
        since we were children
        becomes stronger as time passes.
The house, the road bordered by flowers, and the chapel
        thereby belong to us,
or we belong to them. It's all the same.

Translated from the Spanish by Alastair Reid and Alexander Coleman

MARIA ELENA CRUZ VARELA

Cuba (b. 1953)

The child of campesinos, María Elena Cruz Varela was born on a farm in Colón, in the province of Matanzas. Her education was patchy, but by the age of forty she had written four books of poems and had been awarded, in 1989, her country's National Award for Poetry, given by the Union of Cuban Writers and Artists. But two years later that organization expelled her. In 1991, as a member of an intellectual opposition group called Criterio Alternativo, Cruz Varela published a manifesto attacking the Castro regime and what she called the "closed system of impossibilities" that Cuban society had become. For this act soldiers broke into her house, dragged her into the streets, beat her, and tried to make her swallow a copy of her manifesto; she was then arrested and imprisoned for two years. "I am a *balsera* [raft person] who drowned her life on land," she wrote in 1994. "Here I am: forty-one years old, my spinal column damaged as a result of the events of November 19, 1991; an irreversible vitamin deficiency, acquired in prison; and an anxiety for my compatriots that does not leave me night or day. And over there is my country, an improbable raft in the middle of the ocean, waiting for a sign of hope before the inevitable shipwreck, trying to hear a coherent voice beyond the stale ideologies." Her voice is less a direct, simplistic attack on ideology than an ecstatic, keening witness and defense of the private soul. Her poems are series of small, lyric explosions, unpredictable and powerful. Since 1994 she has lived in Puerto Rico.

Love Song for Difficult Times

Antonio
cuánto me dueles siendo hombre.
        Albis Torrez

So hard to say I love you madly.
Until I reach my marrow. What would happen to my body
if I lose your hands? What would happen to my hands
if your hair is lost? So hard. Very hard

a love poem on these days.
It happens that you exist. Ferocious in your evidence.
It happens that I exist. Counterfeited. Insisting.
And it happens that we exist. The law of gravity doesn't forgive us.
So hard to say I love you these days.
I love you with urgency. I want to make a side.
Without doubts. And without traps.
To say I love you. Like that. Plainly.
And that our love shall save me from the nocturnal howl
when, like a maddened she-wolf, the fever will grab me.
I don't want to be hurt by the absence of tenderness.
But love. So hard to write that I love you.
Like this. "Between so much gray, so many hunches together."
How can I aspire to transparency.
To retake this worn-out voice.
This ancient custom of saying I love you.
Like this. Plainly. Anciently. I say.
If everything is so hard. If everything hurts so much.
If one man. And another man. And again another. And another.
Destroy the spaces where love is kept.
If it weren't hard. Hard and tremendous.
If it weren't impossible to forget this rage.
My clock. Its tick-tock. The route to the scaffold.
My ridiculous sentence with this false cord.
If it weren't hard. Hard and tremendous.
I would cast this verse with its cheap cadence.
If it were this simple to write that I love you.

Translated from the Spanish by Mairym Cruz-Bernal and Deborah Digges

Kaleidoscope

All of us were there:
the one who fell marked by the water spurt
the one who ruined his countenance through ineptitude
the one who did not strike a flame
and violated the city in martial law.

The one who suffered the sin of clairvoyance
the one who fertilized with bizarre feces
the one who could not give more nails to the torture
the one who was not on time for the demolitions
the one who came early
the one who didn't come
and resolved by saying he wasn't informed.

All of us were there:
the innocent ones because they didn't know
and the guilty ones for legal ignorance
the more cultivated accomplices
the ones who fed themselves with prejudices
the more elaborated ones
the more cyclic ones
the singers with the lagger tone
the blind blind from not wanting to see
the ones subject to criticism
the critics subject to their dogmas
the denominators with their tabula rasa
the unbeaten facade
the marked backs

All of us were there
waiting for medals, and judgments.

Translated from the Spanish by Mairym Cruz-Bernal and Deborah Digges

Invocation

*Estoy como la casa del guardabosque
donde el hacha es la culpa y los árboles caen.*
                    Lina de Feria

Nobody knocks at my door. Nobody comes to hit me.
To curse me. To want me. To cry in my hands.
Nobody blanches if I blaspheme.

If I deny God. Already without a name
I return to the door boarded up, mute.
Nobody shares my platform destiny. Of railway guard.
Of a forgotten pebble. Of a confused string.
Nobody's obliged to my house arrest.
Outside, a light. An open window.
My door. Its muteness. Its iron fierceness.
This is my destiny.
This silence from which no one saves me frightens me.
The next station was also a lie.

Translated from the Spanish by Mairym Cruz-Bernal and Deborah Digges

AIME CESAIRE

Martinique (b. 1913)

Born and raised in Martinique, Aimé Césaire went to Paris as a scholarship student in 1930. It was there he became friends with the young African poets Léopold Senghor and Léon Gontian Damas, and with them he formulated the concept of *négritude,* both an idea and a movement aimed at transcending colonialist fragmentation and urging blacks around the world to cherish the social and cultural traditions of their common African heritage. It was in Paris too that he fell under the sway of the surrealists and wrote his long poem *Return to My Native Land,* which first announced his themes of exile and defiance. Césaire returned to Martinique in 1939 and plunged into politics, first as a Communist and later as leader of his own political party. During his long and distinguished political career, he has served as both mayor of Fort-de-France and a deputy in the French National Assembly, posts he has held simultaneously for decades. His vision of both the African and the Antillean past remains richly extravagant, and his style ranges over the extremes of the French language to create poems at once turbulent and luxuriant.

Different Horizon

Night forked stigmata
night telegraphic bush planted in the ocean
for the scrupulous love-making of cetaceans
night locked
splendid muck heap
where with all its strengths with all its wild beasts
the purple muscle of the monkshood of our sun prepares to spring

Translated from the French by Clayton Eshleman and Annette Smith

Bucolic

Then very gently the earth grows a mane, swivels maneuvering its well-oiled octopus head, turns over in its brain an idea clearly visible in the area of circumvolutions, then rushes on at full speed, carrying away in a sinister flight of rocks and meteors, the river, the horses, the horsemen and the houses.

And as the silver of chests blackens, as the water of piscinas swells, as the tombstones are unsealed, as the bucolic installs in the hollow a sea of mud which nonchalantly smokes the best maccaboy of the century, gigantic lights flash off in the distance and, under their black mushroom helmets, observe a hill, good russet shepherd, who with a phosphorescent bamboo pushes a tall herd of shivering temples and cities into the sea.

Translated from the French by Clayton Eshleman and Annette Smith

On the Islands of All Winds

lands which leap very high
not high enough however to keep their feet from remaining caught
    by the peculium of the sea
    booming its assault of irremediable faces

hunger of man heard by the mosquitoes and his thirst
for they are loaves laid out for a bird feast
sand saved against all hope or arms bent
to gather to one's breast all that lingers of
the out of season heat

O justice noon of reason too slow it does not matter
that nameless to the resinous torch of tongues
they do not know that their dirt offering
is in this too distant song recklessly achieved

the morning in the unbeknown of my voice will unveil
the bird which it nevertheless carries and Noon

why my voice remained encrusted with the blood of my panting
    throat

                              from the islands from all of them you will say
that according to the heart a supernumerary of vertiginous birds

for a long long time seeking between sheets of sand
the wound at the coveted crossroad of the undermining sea
you found through the hiccup
the pit of the insult included in the bitter blood
that finally exulting in the wounded kine of the stars
overheated in our feverish breath and a challenge
to a sobbing richer than the bars, we knew
crying land clinging to the most slippery of the wall of being
always speaking beautifully as we die
the carnal and kinky black head of the sun

Translated from the French by Clayton Eshleman and Annette Smith

In Memory of a Black Union Leader

Let no tempest subside no rock stagger
for this chest which was firm
whose bugle of fire neither in the dark
nor in coarse fate faded

O people observed from the highest mirador
who were defying with the canes of blindmen
        the native noun of enormous injustice

I once placed you
in the center of a landscape against a background of cane fields
standing in the middle of the sod of our enlarged
eyes and somehow resembling
the black gold Haitian face
of a god

Look, in the sleepless forest
friends have sprung up, patient,
you used to squint you're still squinting
you hardly ever spoke you hardly speak any less now

you were content to smile you're still smiling the same way very
    tenderly
a smile born strong from the intermingled sheaves of the kindred
    earth and sea

what wages have you just again discussed
on your black and serene breast
have you again just revived supreme
as a sacred knot of benumbed grass snakes
the angers of the rainy season and the cutlass of strikes

and into what coolness did you again dare to dip
your dew-like smile
how in the midst of the great debacle did you shrewdly shelter
your great secret strength
your hard peasant face
the calm waters imprisoned by the half-laughter of your eyes
    in me a doubt trembles
    from hearing a dream find its way
    in the jungle of flowers

Mastermind of runaway clarities
will we have the strength this spring to hoist
our pure limbs up to the womb
where dormant the fecund climates are waiting

our impatient skies
    tradewinds or southwinds
    are you awakening our dead races

briefly a seducer of stars
a foul wind blows from the rotten bagasse
your people are hungry are thirsty stumble your people
are a hand truck which constantly tears itself from the mud

covered with curses and lashed along the mute edge of the black
    night of sugar cane
by a saber sensation

       you the rejection of somber defeat
       tough leader protector of huts
       god of the dubbins breadfruit tree of the errand-girls
in unrotable fern I have carved you
to be worshiped sylvan
when May gilds chabin-like the large kinky heads
of its rarest mango trees

the dream arose you are walking you the fervor of a name
under the tenacious science of a land of silence
every dog sniffs at you not one dares stand in your way
your walls have collapsed the paths are muddy
in the balisiers great red hearts are committing suicide
you are walking pilgrim you walk and you smile
at the blackbirds of the last ray which peck at the ticks on the
    zebus' backs

Ringmaster
the whole sky has long been extinguished
the sea down there in the cove slopes the swaying of a roof
restoring it to lost birds and the light
the light you redistribute all of it
to the orphan reefs to the leaves filtering it for them
to the barely cooled volcano stones reborn as gems
to the eyes of comrades, varnished light vaguely tinged with blood

Translated from the French by Clayton Eshleman and Annette Smith

In Order to Speak

  In order to revitalize the roaring of phosphenes
  the hollow heart of comets

in order to revive the solar verso of dreams
their roe
in order to activate the cool flux of saps the memory of silicates

Anger of the people outlet of the Gods their recoil
be patient the word his or his orle
—until vomiting fire—
his mouth.

Translated from the French by Clayton Eshleman and Annette Smith

Lagoonal Calendar

I inhabit a sacred wound
I inhabit imaginary ancestors
I inhabit an obscure will
I inhabit a long silence
I inhabit an irremediable thirst
I inhabit a one-thousand-year journey
I inhabit a three-hundred-year war
I inhabit an abandoned cult
between bulb and bulbil I inhabit the unexploited space
I inhabit not a vein of the basalt
but the rising tide of lava
which runs back up the gulch at full speed
to burn all the mosques
I accommodate myself as best I can to this avatar
to an absurdly botched version of paradise
        —it is much worse than a hell—
I inhabit from time to time one of my wounds
Each minute I change apartments
and any peace frightens me

        whirling fire
        ascidium like none other for the dust of strayed worlds

having spat out my fresh-water entrails
a volcano I remain with my loaves of words and my
secret minerals

I inhabit thus a vast thought
but in most cases I prefer to confine myself
to the smallest of my ideas
or else I inhabit a magical formula
only its opening words
the rest being forgotten
I inhabit the ice jam
I inhabit the ice melting
I inhabit the face of a great disaster
I inhabit in most cases the driest udder
of the skinniest peak—the she-wolf of these clouds—
I inhabit the halo of the Cactaceae
I inhabit a herd of goats pulling
on the tit of the most desolate argan tree
To tell you the truth I no longer know my correct address
Bathyale or abyssal
I inhabit the octopuses' hole
I fight with the octopus over an octopus hole

Brother lay off
a kelpy mess
twining dodder-like
or unfurling porana-like
it's all the same thing
which the wave tosses
to which the sun leeches
which the wind whips
sculpture in the round of my nothingness

The atmospheric or rather historic pressure
even if it makes certain of my words sumptuous
immeasurably increases my plight.

Translated from the French by Clayton Eshleman and Annette Smith

KAMAU BRATHWAITE

Barbados (b. 1930)

Edward Kamau Brathwaite was born in Bridgetown, Barbados, and was
educated there at Harrison College and later as a scholarship student at
Pembroke College, Cambridge. In addition to his work as poet and play-
wright, he has been an important historian of the development of Creole
society in the West Indies. His passion for history gleams throughout his
densely allusive poems. From 1955 until 1962, he worked with the Min-
istry of Education in Ghana, and during this time he studied how African
traditions were passed on to Caribbean life and culture. He has made his
journeys and displacements the subject of his poems. Often those poems
are coruscating collages of description, protest, celebration, and analysis.
Their insistent, incantatory lyricism is allied to jazz and folk rhythms, and
their vivid wordplay gives voice to both the variety of political and emo-
tional experience and the single meditative mind brooding on it. Brath-
waite was awarded the 1993 Neustadt Prize for Literature.

Citadel

I

So
we are learning
we are learning

surrounded by thickets
clustered against my brothers
muskets growing our own thorns

and from each spike and sparkle
each drip of star and lighted water candle
the petals of dead planets broken

cusps from which i have now stumbled
links fragments obscure breastplates
still hearting us together

o sisyphus o herculean labourer

unto the humble herb and straggeling idiot of the tribe
the vultures flying over christophe's citadel
itself still sailing where the islands float

unmoored and moisture lidded laden with dream and dew
and find no anchor of love here no hope in our back
yard we find no safe no hollow

but here in the cup of my word
on the lip of my eyelid of light
like a star in its syllable socket

there is a cripple crack and hobble
whorl
of colour   eye
at last   cool harbour

death of the trapped fish is not its meaning
dearth of the quetzalcoatl wing is not within its memory
safe for ships the fishermers windjammer

soft cloud   high shadow

ulysses cuts his white teeth towards it
as does my father and the caribs and yemajaa

there is the smell of tar of mango tang
locked sun of oranges and leaking muscovado casks

graph stains of charcoal from the castries mountain
the stretched skin of the brown decks creaking with wave heave

the seas drummers

softly softly on sound fire of spar in the star
light blazed by white bellows the black bulk heaving starboard

it is a beginning

forests canefields move over the waters towards it
seeds of our salt fruit cashew seagrape fatpork macca quickstick

palm

with its blind tendril freedom
a long way the one eyed stare of the coconut will travel

steered by its roots what its milk teaches

till its stalk with its flag and its cross
sword its mailed head and chained feet

walks over the arawaks beaches

2

so write this poem wood
that inches out towards its edges rule the rule
that will need blood the blood

that will devour iron the iron
metal speaking freely of the fire the fire
harp blaze howling hot and long and lambent in the grip of god

so we make pots
potients against the sound of lamentations
against the maljo blowing from the devil's ridge

against thij history that will not write us up unless we lying
down
beneath your raj and spur and raleigh beneath your hiss of drake

across the land
and from this tennament this sipple spider space we hold
we make this narrow thread of silver spin the long time of sand

Colombe

C
olumbus from his after-
deck watched stars, absorbed in water,
melt in liquid amber drifting

through my summer air
Now with morning shadows lifting
beaches stretched before him cold & clear

Birds circled flapping flag & mizzen
mast. birds harshly hawking. without fear
Discovery he sailed for. was so near

C
olumbus from his after-
deck watched heights he hoped for
rocks he dreamed. rise solid from my simple water

Parrots screamed. Soon he would touch
our land. his charted mind's desire
The blue sky blessed the morning with its fire

But did his vision
fashion as he watched the shore
the slaughter that his soldiers

furthered here? Pike
point & musket butt
hot splintered courage. bones

cracked with bullet shot
tipped black boot in my belly. the
whips uncurled desire?

C

olumbus from his after-
deck saw bearded fig trees. yellow pouis
blazed like pollen & thin

waterfalls suspended in the green
as his eyes climbed towards the highest ridges
where our farms were hidden

Now he was sure
he heard soft voices mocking in the leaves
What did this journey mean. this

new world mean. dis
covery? or a return to terrors
he had sailed from. known before?

I watched him pause

Then he was splashing silence
Crabs snapped their claws
and scattered as he walked towards our shore

LORNA GOODISON

Jamaica (b. 1947)

Lorna Goodison was born in Kingston. She has worked as a painter,
prose writer, and screenwriter, a teacher and government official. In 1986
she was awarded the Commonwealth Poetry Prize. Her work has always
been rooted in Jamaica, the inflections of its language and the colors of its
landscape. Of particular interest is that fact that, as she says, she has
borne witness "to the experience of women in Jamaica, and indeed
throughout the West Indies, and to the heritage of struggle and resistance,
of patience and fortitude and independence, which has been an important
part of the history of my people since the dislocations and dispossessions
of slavery."

The Road of the Dread

That dey road no pave
like any other black-face road
it no have no definite color
and it fence two side
with live barbwire.

And no look fi no milepost
fi measure you walking
and no tek no stone as
dead or familiar

for sometime you pass a ting
you know as . . . call it stone again
and is a snake ready fi squeeze yu
kill yu
or is a dead man tek him
possessions tease yu.
Then the place dem yu feel
is resting place because time

before that yu welcome like rain,
go dey again?
bad dawg, bad face tun fi drive yu underground
wey yu no have no light fi walk
and yu find sey that many yu meet who sey
them understand
is only from dem mout dem talk.
One good ting though, that same treatment
mek yu walk untold distance
for to continue yu have fe walk far
away from the wicked.

Pan dis same road ya sista
sometime yu drink yu salt sweat fi water
for yu sure sey at least dat no pisen,
and bread? yu picture it and chew it accordingly
and some time yu surprise fi know how dat full
man belly.

Some day no have no definite color
no beginning and no ending, it just name day
or night as how you feel fi call it.

Den why I tread it brother?
well mek I tell yu bout the day dem
when the father send some little bird
that swallow flute fi trill me
and when him instruct the sun fi smile pan me first.

And the sky calm like sea when it sleep
and a breeze like a laugh follow mi.
Or the man find a stream that pure like baby mind
and the water ease down yu throat
and quiet yu inside.

And better still when yu meet another traveler
who have flour and yu have water and man and man
make bread together.
And dem time dey the road run straight and sure
like a young horse that cant tire

and yu catch a glimpse of the end
through the water in yu eye
I wont tell yu what I spy
but is fi dat alone I tread this road.

Always Homing Now Soul Toward Light

Always homing now soul toward light,
want like wings beating
against the hold-back of dark.

Above the face of yet another city
bright with bright points of seduction
I hover, and know from having been there
that the lights of cities go under,
their brilliance is not what
this soul is after.
Night swallows the sunset now
the lips of the horizon come together
and there is in all this dark sky
only one thin line of glow.
When the lips close finally
it will seem (be warned)
it will seem like the dark has won.
But is only the interim
before the true shining comes.
Light is close sometimes,
it seems to burnish my limbs
some nights.
And for wanting it so
I'm a child then
who must sleep with some
small part of light
from a connection above
my head.
Surround us while we sleep, light
encircling

602 • CONTEMPORARY WORLD POETRY

light in rings marrying me to
source.
To me, I say, fold the dark dresses
of your youth
let the silver run like comets'
tails through your hair.
For me, I know, the light in me
does not want to be hidden anymore,
anywhere.

Birth Stone

The older women wise and tell Anna
first time baby mother,
"hold a stone upon your head and follow
a straight line go home."

For like how Anna was working in the
field, grassweeder
right up till the appointed hour
that the baby was to come.

Right up till the appointed hour
when her clear heraldic water
broke free and washed her down.

Dry birth for you young mother;
the distance between the field and home
come in like the Gobi desert now.
But your first baby must born abed.

Put the woman stone on your head
and walk through no man's land
go home. When you walk, the stone
and not you yet, will bear down.

Songs of the Fruits and Sweets
of Childhood

O small and squat
with thin tough skin
containing the slick flesh
of mackafat
which makes fillings
like putty between
the teeth.

Cream pink pomander
like a lady's sachet
is the genteel roseapple
scenting the breath.

Jade green lantern
light astringent
is the tart taste
of the jimbelin.

Tough skinned
brown pods
of stinking toe
you broke open hard
upon stone
to free the pungent
dry powdery musk
called by some,
locust.

A brittle sweet cup
brims
with a sweetish slime
in which
tiny grey-eyed seeds
seem to wink.

And coolie plums
and red/yellow
coat plums
and plums called
for June time
and apples
O taheti.

But of all fruit
the most perfect is
the dark ocher
taste like rosewater
color like logwood honey
that is a naseberry.

The starapple
wears a thick coat
of royal purple
and at its center
sports a star
of many points.

This is a lover's fruit
because it runs
with a sweet
staining milk
and the flesh
if bitten too deep,
has been known to bind you.

Of the sweets
the sweets
now sing,
beginning with the sour
fleshed tamarind.

Which if rolled
into sugar
becomes balanced

into being
the yin and yang
of sweets.

A soft brown square
of rare delight
is a wedge
of guava cheese.
O guava cheese
make you sneeze.
Penny a cut
full yu gut?

And in singing
the lungs will fill
with the sweet dust
of corn,
pounded, parched
blended with
cane sugar
to tickle the
channels of breathing.
Inhale, sneeze
sing so
"Asham O."

The rise
of the palette's roof
is a nice height
under which
to tuck the pink backed
paradise plum.
Its smooth
white underbelly
melting level
with the tongue.

A mint ball
is divided by thin

varicolored stripes
like the porcelain
marble of a prince.

A shaggy
grater cake
can be rich brown
if it takes
its color
from burnt sugar.

But if it holds
its coconut milk
to itself
and mixes only
with white sugar,
it becomes
what some consider
a greater cake.
It is then topped
with a show off hat
of cochineal or magenta.

A Bustamante backbone
is a stubborn mixture
of coconut
and caramelized sugar.
One side wears
a thin skin
of grease proof paper
which you peel off
before chewing.

Hard on the jawbone
it is,
tying up the teeth.

But the tie-teeth
is another kind
of sweet.

Tangled and sweet
like some things
tempting
but so tangled.

Hot pink
stretcher
like a fuchsia lipstick.

Whole peanuts
suspended
in crystalized sugar
is a wangla.

And the ring game
or join up
of pink top
candy bump
going round and round
in a ring
of the fruits and sweets
of childhood
sing.

From the Garden of the Women
Once Fallen

Thyme

Woman alone, living
in a tenement of enmity.
One room of back-biting
standpipe flowing strife.

Recall one dry Sunday
of no rice and peas no meat

how you boiled a handful
of fresh green thyme

to carry the smell of Sunday
as usual.
Thyme, herb of contraction
rising as steaming incense
of save-face.

When you dwell among enemies
you never make them salt your pot.
You never make them know
your want.

Of Bitterness Herbs

You knotted the spite blooms into a bouquet-garni
to flavor stock for sour soups and confusion stews.
Now no one will dine with you.

A diet of bitterness is self consuming. Such herbs
are best destroyed, rooted out from the garden
of the necessary even preordained past.

Bitter herbs grow luxuriant where the grudgeful crow
dropped its shadow, starting a compost heap of need in you
to spray malicious toxins over all flowers in our rose gardens.

Bitterness herbs bake bad-minded bread, are good for little
except pickling green-eyed gall stones, then eaten alone
from wooden spoons of must-suck-salt.

In the Time of Late-Blooming Pumpkins

In this garden, water walks
and water walking enters
belly of pumpkin.

This means you are growing
big from within, all ripeness,
though somebody (Jeremiah?)

shouts from outside the garden wall
"You are all conceived in sin"
but that is just some false prophet

negative and bad mouthing.
For in this new garden
of fresh start over

with its mysteries of walking water,
give thanks for late summer's
rose afternoons shading
into amethyst, then deepening
into red water grass evenings,
time of late-blooming pumpkins.

DEREK WALCOTT

St. Lucia (b. 1930)

Derek Walcott was born in Castries, the capital of St. Lucia, in the West Indies. It was an island with no ruins, no museum, no dates. "It was," he has said, "a country without a history." The task he set himself as a young poet, then, was not to discover his history but to create one, and to make it out of himself, out of his circumstances and his birthright. He has called himself a "divided child"—a black with a white grandfather, raised as a Methodist in a Catholic country, part of the educated middle class in a backwater of poverty. There were other divisions as well that he sought to reconcile. He grew up with three languages—English, French Creole, and English Creole—and he has worked the patois of the islands into his poems. His style could be called English speech with a West Indian inflection, a style, rooted in the traditions of classic English verse, that reaches out to the life of the islands, to its sensuous beauty and native theatricalism. Two long poems punctuate his career: the autobiographical *Another Life* (1973) and *Omeros* (1990), a Caribbean reworking of the Homeric epic. The grandiloquence of Walcott's early work has yielded to a more clipped and severe tone; it has lost none of its allure but gained in authority. His style now has a range and a grave radiance that transfigure the smallest detail. And although his poems are built up from details, they have challenged their own fluency by addressing the large, intractable problems of modern history—exile, injustice, the lurid terrorism of the mind, the ordinary treason of the heart. In 1992 Walcott was awarded the Nobel Prize for Literature. In his acceptance speech he said, "For every poet it is always morning in the world, and History a forgotten insomniac night; History and elemental awe are always our early beginning, because the fate of poetry is to fall in love with the world, in spite of History."

Crusoe's Island

I

The chapel's cowbell
Like God's anvil

Hammers ocean to a blinding shield;
Fired, the sea grapes slowly yield
Bronze plates to the metallic heat.

Red, corrugated-iron
Roofs roar in the sun.
The wiry, ribbed air
Above earth's open kiln
Writhes like a child's vision
Of hell, but nearer, nearer.

Below, the picnic plaid
Of Scarborough is spread
To a blue, perfect sky,
Dome of our hedonist philosophy.
Bethel and Canaan's heart
Lies open like a psalm.
I labour at my art.
My father, God, is dead.

Past thirty now I know
To love the self is dread
Of being swallowed by the blue
Of heaven overhead
Or rougher blue below.
Some lesion of the brain
From art or alcohol
Flashes this fear by day:
As startling as his shadow
Grows to the castaway.

Upon this rock the bearded hermit built
His Eden:
Goats, corn crop, fort, parasol, garden,
Bible for Sabbath, all the joys
But one
Which sent him howling for a human voice.
Exiled by a flaming sun
The rotting nut, bowled in the surf,
Became his own brain rotting from the guilt

Of heaven without his kind,
Crazed by such paradisal calm
The spinal shadow of a palm
Built keel and gunwale in his mind.

The second Adam since the fall,
His germinal
Corruption held the seed
Of that congenital heresy that men fail
According to their creed.
Craftsman and castaway,
All heaven in his head,
He watched his shadow pray
Not for God's love but human love instead.

II

We came here for the cure
Of quiet in the whelk's centre,
From the fierce, sudden quarrel,
From kitchens where the mind,
Like bread, disintegrates in water,
To let a salt sun scour
The brain as harsh as coral,
To bathe like stones in wind,
To be, like beast or natural object, pure.

That fabled, occupational
Compassion, supposedly inherited with the gift
Of poetry, had fed
With a rat's thrift on faith, shifted
Its trust to corners, hoarded
Its mania like bread,
Its brain a white, nocturnal bloom
That in a drunken, moonlit room
Saw my son's head
Swaddled in sheets
Like a lopped nut, lolling in foam.

O love, we die alone!
I am borne by the bell
Backward to boyhood
To the grey wood
Spire, harvest and marigold,
To those whom a cruel
Just God could gather
To His blue breast, His beard
A folding cloud,
As He gathered my father.
Irresolute and proud,
I can never go back.

I have lost sight of hell,
Of heaven, of human will,
My skill
Is not enough,
I am struck by this bell
To the root.
Crazed by a racking sun,
I stand at my life's noon,
On parched, delirious sand
My shadow lengthens.

III

Art is profane and pagan,
The most it has revealed
Is what a crippled Vulcan
Beat on Achilles' shield.
By these blue, changing graves
Fanned by the furnace blast
Of heaven, may the mind
Catch fire till it cleaves
Its mould of clay at last.

Now Friday's progeny,
The brood of Crusoe's slave,
Black little girls in pink

Organdy, crinolines,
Walk in their air of glory
Beside a breaking wave;
Below their feet the surf
Hisses like tambourines.

At dusk, when they return
For vespers, every dress
Touched by the sun will burn
A seraph's, an angel's,
And nothing I can learn
From art or loneliness
Can bless them as the bell's
Transfiguring tongue can bless.

Midsummer, Tobago

Broad sun-stoned beaches.

White heat.
A green river.

A bridge,
scorched yellow palms

from the summer-sleeping house
drowsing through August.

Days I have held,
days I have lost,

days that outgrow, like daughters,
my harbouring arms.

The Hotel Normandie Pool

I

Around the cold pool in the metal light
of New Year's morning, I choose one of nine
cast-iron umbrellas set in iron tables
for work and coffee. The first cigarette
triggers the usual fusillade of coughs.
After a breeze the pool settles the weight
of its reflections on one line. Sunshine
lattices a blank wall with the shade of gables,
stirs the splayed shadows of the hills like moths.

Last night, framed in the binding of that window,
like the great chapter in some Russian novel
in which, during the war, the prince comes home
to watch the soundless waltzers dart and swivel,
like fishes in their lamplit aquarium,
I stood in my own gauze of swirling snow
and, through the parted hair of ribboned drapes,
felt, between gusts of music, the pool widen
between myself and those light-scissored shapes.

The dancers stiffened and, like fish, were frozen
in panes of ice blocked by the window frames;
one woman fanned, still fluttering on a pin,
as a dark fusillade of kettledrums
and a piercing cornet played "Auld Lang Syne"
while a battalion of drunk married men
reswore their vows. For this my fiftieth year,
I muttered to the ribbon-medalled water,
"Change me, my sign, to someone I can bear."

Now my pen's shadow, angled at the wrist
with the chrome stanchions at the pool's edge,
dims on its lines like birches in a mist
as a cloud fills my hand. A drop punctuates
the startled paper. The pool's iron umbrellas

ring with the drizzle. Sun hits the water.
The pool is blinding zinc. I shut my eyes,
and as I raise their lids I see each daughter
ride on the rayed shells of both irises.

The prayer is brief: That the transparent wrist
would not cloud surfaces with my own shadow,
and that this page's surface would unmist
after my breath as pools and mirrors do.
But all reflection gets no easier,
although the brown, dry needles of that palm
quiver to stasis and things resume their rhyme
in water, like the rubber ring that is a
red rubber ring inverted at the line's center.

Into that ring my younger daughter dived
yesterday, slithering like a young dolphin,
her rippling shadow hungering under her,
with nothing there to show how well she moved
but in my mind the veer of limb and fin.
Transparent absences! Love makes me look
through a clear ceiling into rooms of sand;
I ask the element that is my sign,
"Oh, let her lithe head through that surface break!"

Aquarian, I was married to water;
under that certain roof, I would lie still
next to my sister spirit, horizontal
below what stars derailed our parallel
from our far vow's undeviating course;
the next line rises as they enter it,
Peter, Anna, Elizabeth—Margaret
still sleeping with one arm around each daughter,
in the true shape of love, beyond divorce.

Time cuts down on the length man can endure
his own reflection. Entering a glass
I surface quickly now, prefer to breathe
the fetid and familiar atmosphere

of work and cigarettes. Only tyrants believe
their mirrors, or Narcissi, brooding on boards,
before they plunge into their images;
at fifty I have learnt that beyond words
is the disfiguring exile of divorce.

II

Across blue seamless silk, iron umbrellas
and a brown palm burn. A sandalled man comes out
and, in a robe of foam-frayed terry cloth,
with Roman graveness buries his room key,
then, mummy-oiling both forearms and face
with sunglasses still on, stands, fixing me,
and nods. Some petty businessman who tans
his pallor a negotiable bronze,
and the bright nod would have been commonplace

as he uncurled his shades above the pool's
reflecting rim—white towel, toga-slung,
foam hair repeated by the robe's frayed hem—
but, in the lines of his sun-dazzled squint,
a phrase was forming in that distant tongue
of which the mind keeps just a mineral glint,
the lovely Latin lost to all our schools:
"*Quis te misit, Magister?*" And its whisper went
through my cold body, veining it in stone.

On marble, concrete, or obsidian,
your visit, Master, magnifies the lines
of our small pool to that Ovidian
thunder of surf between the Baltic pines.
The light that swept Rome's squares and palaces,
washing her tangled fountains of green bronze
when you were one drop in a surf of faces—
a fleck of spittle from the she-wolf's tooth—
now splashes a palm's shadow at your foot.

Turn to us, Ovid. Our emerald sands
are stained with sewage from each tin-shacked Rome;
corruption, censorship, and arrogance
make exile seem a happier thought than home.
"Ah, for the calm proconsul with a voice
as just and level as this Roman pool,"
our house slaves sigh; the field slaves scream revenge;
one moves between the flatterer and the fool
yearning for the old bondage from both ends.

And I, whose ancestors were slave and Roman,
have seen both sides of the imperial foam,
heard palm and pine tree alternate applause
as the white breakers rose in galleries
to settle, whispering at the tilted palm
of the boy-god, Augustus. My own face
held negro Neros, chalk Caligulas;
my own reflection slid along the glass
of faces foaming past triumphal cars.

Master, each idea has become suspicious
of its shadow. A lifelong friend whispers
in his own house as if it might arrest him;
markets no more applaud, as was their custom,
our camouflaged, booted militias
roaring past on camions, the sugar-apples
of grenades growing on their belts; ideas
with guns divide the islands; in dark squares
the poems gather like conspirators.

Then Ovid said, "When I was first exiled,
I missed my language as your tongue needs salt,
in every watery shape I saw my child,
no bench would tell my shadow 'Here's your place';
bridges, canals, willow-fanned waterways
turned from my parting gaze like an insult,
till, on a tablet smooth as the pool's skin,
I made reflections that, in many ways,
were even stronger than their origin.

"Tiled villas anchored in their foaming orchards,
parched terraces in a dust cloud of words,
among clod-fires, wolfskins, starving herds,
Tibullus' flute faded, sweetest of shepherds.
Through shaggy pines the beaks of needling birds
pricked me at Tomis to learn their tribal tongue,
so, since desire is stronger than its disease,
my pen's beak parted till we chirped one song
in the unequal shade of equal trees.

"Campaigns enlarged our frontiers like clouds,
but my own government was the bare boards
of a plank table swept by resinous pines
whose boughs kept skittering from Caesar's eye
with every yaw. There, hammering out lines
in that green forge to fit me for the horse,
I bent on a solitude so tyrannous
against the once seductive surf of crowds
that no wife softens it, or Caesar's envy.

"And where are those detractors now who said
that in and out of the imperial shade
I scuttled, showing to a frowning sun
the fickle dyes of the chameleon?
Romans"—he smiled—"will mock your slavish rhyme,
the slaves your love of Roman structures, when,
from Metamorphoses to Tristia,
art obeys its own order. Now it's time."
Tying his toga gently, he went in.

There, at the year's horizon, he had stood,
as if the pool's meridian were the line
that doubled the burden of his solitude
in either world; and, as one leaf fell,
his echo rippled: "Why here, of all places,
a small, suburban tropical hotel,
its pool pitched to a Mediterranean blue,
its palms rusting in their concrete oasis?
Because to make my image flatters you."

III

At dusk, the sky is loaded like watercolor paper
with an orange wash in which every edge frays—
a painting with no memory of the painter—
and what this pool recites is not a phrase
from an invisible, exiled laureate,
where there's no laurel, but the scant applause
of one dry, scraping palm tree as blue eve-
ning ignites its blossoms from one mango flower,
and something, not a leaf, falls like a leaf,

as swifts with needle-beaks dart, panicking over
the pool's cloud-closing light. For an envoi,
write what the wrinkled god repeats to the boy-
god: "May the last light of heaven pity us
for the hardening lie in the face that we did not tell."
Dusk. The trees blacken like the pool's umbrellas.
Dusk. Suspension of every image and its voice.
The mangoes pitch from their green dark like meteors.
The fruit bat swings on its branch, a tongueless bell.

The Season of Phantasmal Peace

Then all the nations of birds lifted together
the huge net of the shadows of this earth
in multitudinous dialects, twittering tongues,
stitching and crossing it. They lifted up
the shadows of long pines down trackless slopes,
the shadows of glass-faced towers down evening streets,
the shadow of a frail plant on a city sill—
the net rising soundless as night, the birds' cries soundless, until
there was no longer dusk, or season, decline, or weather,
only this passage of phantasmal light
that not the narrowest shadow dared to sever.

And men could not see, looking up, what the wild geese drew,
what the ospreys trailed behind them in silvery ropes
that flashed in the icy sunlight; they could not hear
battalions of starlings waging peaceful cries,
bearing the net higher, covering this world
like the vines of an orchard, or a mother drawing
the trembling gauze over the trembling eyes
of a child fluttering to sleep;
                                 it was the light
that you will see at evening on the side of a hill
in yellow October, and no one hearing knew
what change had brought into the raven's cawing,
the killdeer's screech, the ember-circling chough
such an immense, soundless, and high concern
for the fields and cities where the birds belong,
except it was their seasonal passing, Love,
made seasonless, or, from the high privilege of their birth,
something brighter than pity for the wingless ones
below them who shared dark holes in windows and in houses,
and higher they lifted the net with soundless voices
above all change, betrayals of falling suns,
and this season lasted one moment, like the pause
between dusk and darkness, between fury and peace,
but, for such as our earth is now, it lasted long.

SELECTED BIBLIOGRAPHY

Adonis

Transformations of the Lover, trans. Samuel Hazo. International Poetry
    Forum, Byblos Editions, rev. ed., 1982.
Victims of a Map: Mahmud Darwish, Samih al-Qasim, Adonis, trans. Ab-
    dullah al-Udhari. Al Saqi Books, 1984.
An Introduction to Arab Poetics (criticism). Al Saqi Books, 1990.
The Pages of Day and Night, trans. Samuel Hazo. Marlboro Press, 1994.

Claribel Alegría

Flowers from the Volcano, trans. Carolyn Forché. University of Pittsburgh
    Press, 1982.
Woman of the River, trans. D. J. Flakoll. University of Pittsburgh Press, 1989.
Fugues, trans. D. J. Flakoll. Curbstone Press, 1993.
Thresholds, trans. D. J. Flakoll. Curbstone Press, 1996.

Yehuda Amichai

Selected Poetry of Yehuda Amichai, trans. Chana Bloch and Stephen
    Mitchell. Harper & Row, 1986.
Amen, trans. Ted Hughes and the author. Milkweed Editions, 1987.
Poems of Jerusalem and *Love Poems,* trans. Assia Guttmann et al. Sheep
    Meadow Press, 1988.
Even a Fist Was Once an Open Palm with Fingers, trans. Benjamin Har-
    shav and Barbara Harshav. HarperCollins, 1991.
Yehuda Amichai: A Life of Poetry, 1948–1994, trans. Benjamin Harshav
    and Barbara Harshev. HarperCollins, 1994.

Eugénio de Andrade

Inhabited Heart: The Selected Poems of Eugénio de Andrade, trans. Alexis
    Levitin. Perivale Press, 1985.
White on White, trans. Alexis Levitin. Quarterly Review of Literature, Po-
    etry Series VIII, 1987.
Memory of Another River, trans. Alexis Levitin. New Rivers Press, 1988.
The Slopes of a Gaze, trans. Alexis Levitin. Apalachee Press, 1992.

Solar Matter, trans. Alexis Levitin. QED Press, 1995.
The Other Name for Earth, trans. Alexis Levitin. QED Press, 1995.
The Shadow's Weight, trans. Alexis Levitin. Gavea-Brown, 1995.

Kofi Awoonor

Until the Morning After: Collected Poems, 1963–1985. Greenfield Review
    Press, 1987.

Ingeborg Bachmann

In the Storm of Roses: Selected Poems by Ingeborg Bachmann, trans. Mark
    Anderson. Princeton University Press, 1986.

Bei Dao

The August Sleepwalker, trans. Bonnie S. McDougall. New Directions, 1990.
Waves (stories), trans. Bonnie S. McDougall and Susette Ternent Cooke.
    New Directions, 1990.
Old Snow, trans. Bonnie S. McDougall and Chen Maiping. New Directions,
    1991.
A Splintered Mirror: Chinese Poetry from the Democracy Movement, trans.
    Donald Finkel. North Point Press, 1991.
Forms of Distance, trans. David Hinton. New Directions, 1994.
Landscape Over Zero, trans. David Hinton and Yanbing Chen. New Di-
    rections, 1996.

Yves Bonnefoy

Poems, 1959–1975, trans. Richard Pevear. Vintage Books, 1985.
The Act and the Place of Poetry (essays), ed. John Naughton. University of
    Chicago Press, 1989.
Early Poems, 1947–1959, trans. Galway Kinnell and Richard Pevear. Ohio
    University Press, 1991.
In the Shadow's Light, trans. John Naughton. University of Chicago Press,
    1991.
Beginning and End of Snow, trans. Lisa Sapinkopf. Quarterly Review of Lit-
    erature, Poetry Series XI, 1992.
The Lure and Truth of Painting: Selected Essays on Art, ed. Richard Stamel-
    man. University of Chicago Press, 1995.
New and Selected Poems, ed. John Naughton and Anthony Rudolf. Uni-
    versity of Chicago Press, 1995.

Kamau Brathwaite

The Arrivants: A New World Trilogy. Oxford University Press, 1973.
Other Exiles. Oxford University Press, 1975.
Mother Poem. Oxford University Press, 1977.
Sun Poem. Oxford University Press, 1982.
Third World Poems. Longman, 1983.
X/Self. Oxford University Press, 1987.
MiddlePassages. New Directions, 1993.
Dream Stories. Longman, 1994.
Black & Blues, New Directions, 1995.

Breyten Breytenbach

In Africa Even the Flies Are Happy: Selected Poems, 1964–1977, trans. Denis Hirson. John Calder, 1977.
And Death White as Words, ed. A. J. Coetzee. Rex Collings, 1978.
A Season in Paradise (memoir), trans. Rike Vaughan. Persea Books, 1980.
Mouroir: Mirrornotes of a Novel (novel). Farrar, Straus and Giroux, 1984.
The True Confessions of an Albino Terrorist (memoir). Farrar, Straus and Giroux, 1985.
End Papers: Essays, Letters, Articles of Faith, Workbook Notes. Farrar, Straus and Giroux, 1986.
Judas Eye and *Self-Portrait/Deathwatch.* Farrar, Straus and Giroux, 1988.
Return to Paradise (memoir). Harcourt Brace, 1993.
The Memory of Birds in Time of Revolution (essays), Harcourt Brace, 1995.

Joseph Brodsky

Selected Poems, trans. George L. Kline. Penguin, 1973.
A Part of Speech, trans. George L. Kline et al. Farrar, Straus and Giroux, 1980.
Less Than One (essays). Farrar, Straus and Giroux, 1986.
To Urania, trans. George L. Kline et al. Farrar, Straus and Giroux, 1988.
Watermark (prose). Farrar, Straus and Giroux, 1992.
On Grief and Reason (essays). Farrar, Straus and Giroux, 1995.
So Forth. Farrar, Straus and Giroux, 1996.

Dennis Brutus

Letters to Martha. Heinemann, 1968.
A Simple Lust. Heinemann, 1973.
Stubborn Hope. Three Continents Press, 1978.
Still the Sirens. Pennywhistle Press, 1993.

João Cabral de Melo Neto

Selected Poetry, 1937–1990, ed. Djelal Kadir. Wesleyan University Press, 1994.

Ernesto Cardenal

Apocalypse and Other Poems, ed. Robert Pring-Mills and Donald D. Walsh. New Directions, 1977.
Zero Hour and Other Documentary Poems, ed. Donald D. Walsh. New Directions, 1980.
Flights of Victory, ed. Marc Zimmerman. Orbis Books, 1985.
Golden UFOs: The Indian Poems, trans. Carlos Altschul and Monique Altschul. Indiana University Press, 1992.
Cosmic Canticle, trans. John Lyons. Curbstone Press, 1993.
The Doubtful Strait, trans. John Lyons. Indiana University Press, 1995.

Paul Celan

Last Poems, trans. Katherine Washburn and Margret Guillemin. North Point Press, 1986.
Poems, trans. Michael Hamburger. Persea Books, 1989.
Collected Prose, trans. Rosmarie Waldrop. Sheep Meadow Press, 1990.

Aimé Césaire

Aimé Césaire: The Collected Poetry, trans. Clayton Eshleman and Annette Smith. University of California Press, 1983.

María Elena Cruz Varela

Ballad of the Blood: The Collected Poems of María Elena Cruz Varela, trans. Mairym Cruz-Bernal and Deborah Digges. Ecco Press, 1996.

Sándor Csoóri

Memory of Snow, trans. Nicholas Kolumban. Penmaen Press, 1983.
Selected Poems, trans. Len Roberts. Copper Canyon Press, 1992.

Mahmoud Darwish

Selected Poems, trans. Ian Wedde and Fawwaz Tuqan. Carcanet, 1973.

The Music of Human Flesh, trans. Denys Johnson-Davies. Heinemann, 1980.

Victims of a Map, trans. Abdullah al-Udhari. Al Saqi Books, 1984.

Sand and Other Poems, trans. Rana Kabbani. KPI, 1986.

Memory of Forgetfulness, trans. Ibrahim Muhawi. University of California Press, 1995.

Carlos Drummond de Andrade

Travelling in the Family: Selected Poems, ed. Thomas Colchie and Mark Strand. Random House, 1986.

Jacques Dupin

Selected Poems, ed. Paul Auster. Wake Forest University Press, 1992.

Odysseus Elytis

The Axion Esti of Odysseus Elytis, trans. Edmund Keeley and George Savidis. University of Pittsburgh Press, 1974.

The Sovereign Sun: Selected Poems, trans. Kimon Friar. Temple University Press, 1974.

Selected Poems, ed. Edmund Keeley and Philip Sherrard. Viking Press, 1981.

Open Papers (essays), trans. Olga Broumas and T. Begley. Copper Canyon Press, 1995.

Hans Magnus Enzensberger

Poems for People Who Don't Read Poems, trans. Michael Hamburger, Jerome Rothenberg, and the author. Atheneum, 1968.

The Sinking of the Titanic, trans. the author. Houghton Mifflin, 1980.

Critical Essays, ed. Reinhold Grimm and Bruce Armstrong. Continuum, 1982.

Mediocrity and Delusion: Collected Delusions, trans. Martin Chalmers. Verso, 1992.

Selected Poems, trans. Michael Hamburger and the author. Bloodaxe Books, 1994.

Faiz Ahmed Faiz

Poems by Faiz, trans. V. G. Kiernan. George Allen & Unwin, 1971.

The Rebel's Silhouette, trans. Agha Shahid Ali. Peregrine Smith, 1991.

Ángel González

"Harsh World" and Other Poems, trans. Donald D. Walsh. Princeton University Press, 1977.
Astonishing World: The Selected Poems of Ángel González, 1956–1986, ed. Steven Ford Brown. Milkweed Editions, 1993.

Lorna Goodison

Selected Poems. University of Michigan Press, 1992.
To Us, All Flowers Are Roses. University of Illinois Press, 1995.

Gu Cheng

Selected Poems of Gu Cheng. Renditions Press, 1990.
The Red Azalea: Chinese Poetry Since the Cultural Revolution, ed. Edward Morin. University of Hawaii Press, 1990.
A Splintered Mirror: Chinese Poetry from the Democracy Movement, trans. Donald Finkel. North Point Press, 1991.
Out of the Howling Storm: The New Chinese Poetry, ed. Tony Barnstone. University Press of New England, 1993.

Paavo Haavikko

Selected Poems, ed. Anselm Hollo. Carcanet, 1991.
Contemporary Finnish Poetry, ed. Herbert Lomas. Bloodaxe Books, 1991.

Zbigniew Herbert

Report from the Besieged City and Other Poems, trans. John Carpenter and Bogdana Carpenter. Ecco Press, 1985.
The Barbarian in the Garden (essays), trans. Michael March and Jaroslav Anders. Carcanet, 1985.
Selected Poems, trans. Czesław Miłosz and Peter Dale Scott. Ecco Press, 1986.
Still Life with a Bridle (essays and apocrypha), trans. John Carpenter and Bogdana Carpenter. Ecco Press, 1991.
Mr. Cogito, trans. John Carpenter and Bogdana Carpenter. Ecco Press, 1993.

Nâzim Hikmet

The Epic of Sheik Bedreddin, trans. Randy Blasing and Mutlu Konuk. Persea Books, 1977.

Human Landscapes, trans. Randy Blasing and Mutlu Konuk. Persea Books, 1982.
Rubaiyat, trans. Randy Blasing and Mutlu Konuk. Copper Beech Press, 1985.
Selected Poetry, trans. Randy Blasing and Mutlu Konuk. Persea Books, 1986.
Poems of Nâzim Hikmet, trans. Randy Blasing and Mutlu Konuk. Persea Books, 1994.

Miroslav Holub

Selected Poems, trans. Ian Milner and George Theiner. Penguin, 1967.
Although, trans. Ian Milner and Jarmila Milner. Jonathan Cape, 1971.
Sagittal Section, trans. Stuart Friebert and Dana Habova. FIELD Translation Series, 1980.
Interferon, or On Theater, trans. Dana Hábová and David Young. FIELD Translation Series, 1982.
On the Contrary, trans. Ewald Osers. Bloodaxe Books, 1984.
Vanishing Lung Syndrome, trans. David Young and Dana Hábová. Faber and Faber, 1990.
The Dimension of the Present Moment (essays), ed. David Young. Faber and Faber, 1990.
Poems Before & After: Collected English Translations, trans. Ian Milner, Jarmila Milner, Ewald Osers, and George Theiner. Bloodaxe Books, 1990.

Philippe Jaccottet

Breathings: The Poems of Philippe Jaccottet, trans. Cid Corman. Grossman, 1974.
Seedtime, trans. André Lefevere and Michael Hamburger. New Directions, 1977.
Selected Poems, trans. Derek Mahon. Wake Forest University Press, 1988.

Roberto Juarroz

Vertical Poetry, trans. W. S. Merwin. North Point Press, 1988.
Vertical Poetry: Recent Poems, trans. Mary Crow. White Pine Press, 1992.

Rutger Kopland

A World Beyond Myself, trans. James Brockway. Enitharmon Press, 1991.

Enrique Lihn

The Dark Room and Other Poems, ed. Patricio Lerzundi. New Directions, 1978.

Jayanta Mahapatra

A Rain of Rites. University of Georgia Press, 1976.
Life Signs. Oxford University Press (New Delhi), 1983.
Selected Poems. Oxford University Press (New Delhi), 1987.

Claire Malroux

First and Last Things, trans. Marilyn Hacker. Wake Forest University Press, 1996.

Sophia de Mello Breyner

Marine Rose: Selected Poems, trans. Ruth Fainlight. Black Swan Books, 1988.

Nijolė Miliauskaitė

Four Poets of Lithuania, trans. Jonas Zdanys. White Birch Press, 1995.

Czesław Miłosz

The Captive Mind (prose), trans. Jane Zielonko. Alfred A. Knopf, 1953.
Native Realm (autobiography), trans. Catherine Leach. Doubleday, 1968.
Bells in Winter, trans. Lillian Vallee and the author. Ecco Press, 1978.
The Issa Valley (novel), trans. Louis Iribarne. Farrar, Straus and Giroux, 1981.
Nobel Lecture. Farrar, Straus and Giroux, 1981.
The Witness of Poetry (essays), Harvard University Press, 1983.
The Separate Notebooks, trans. Robert Hass, Robert Pinsky, Renata Gorczynski, and the author. Ecco Press, 1984.
The Land of Ulro (essays), trans. Louis Iribarne. Farrar, Straus and Giroux, 1984.
Unattainable Earth, trans. Robert Hass and the author. Ecco Press, 1986.
The Collected Poems, 1931–1987, trans. Robert Hass and the author. Ecco Press, 1988.
Provinces: Poems 1987–1991. Ecco Press, 1991.
The Year of the Hunter (diaries), trans. Madeline G. Levine. Farrar, Straus and Giroux, 1994.
Facing the River, trans. Robert Hass and the author. Ecco Press, 1995.

Taslima Nasrin

The Game in Reverse, trans. Carolyne Wright. George Braziller, 1995.

Ágnes Nemes Nagy

Selected Poems, trans. Bruce Berlind. University of Iowa Press, 1980.
Between: Selected Poems, trans. Hugh Maxton. Dedalus Press, 1988.

Pablo Neruda

The Heights of Macchu Picchu, trans. Nathaniel Tarn. Farrar, Straus and Giroux, 1967.
Selected Poems, ed. Nathaniel Tarn. Delacorte Press, 1972.
Residence on Earth, trans. Donald D. Walsh. New Directions, 1973.
Memoirs (prose), trans. Hardie St. Martin. Farrar, Straus and Giroux, 1977.
Canto general, trans. Jack Schmidt. University of California Press, 1991.
Odes to Common Things, trans. Ken Krabbenhoft. Little, Brown, 1994.
Fully Empowered, trans. Alastair Reid. New Directions, 1995.

Henrik Nordbrandt

Selected Poems, trans. the author and Alexander Taylor. Curbstone Press, 1978.
God's House, trans. the author and Alexander Taylor. Curbstone Press, 1979.
Armenia, trans. the author and Alexander Taylor. Curbstone Press, 1984.

Christopher Okigbo

Collected Poems. Heinemann, 1986.

Heberto Padilla

Legacies: Selected Poems, trans. Alastair Reid and Andrew Hurley. Farrar, Straus and Giroux, 1982.
Heroes Are Grazing in My Garden (novel), trans. Andrew Hurley. Farrar, Straus and Giroux, 1983.
Self-Portrait with the Other (memoir), trans. Alexander Coleman. Farrar, Straus and Giroux, 1990.
A Fountain, a House of Stone, trans. Alastair Reid and Alexander Coleman. Farrar, Straus and Giroux, 1991.

Dan Pagis

Variable Directions: The Selected Poetry of Dan Pagis, trans. Stephen Mitchell. North Point Press, 1989.
Last Poems, trans. Tsipi Keller. Quarterly Review of Literature, Poetry Series XI, 1992.

Nicanor Parra

Emergency Poems, trans. Miller Williams. New Directions, 1972.
Sermons and Homilies of the Christ of Elqui, trans. Sandra Reyes. University of Missouri Press, 1984.
Antipoems: New and Selected, ed. David Unger. New Directions, 1985.

Pier Paolo Pasolini

Poems, trans. Norman MacAfee and Luciano Martinengo. Random House, 1982. Farrar, Straus and Giroux, 1996.
Roman Poems, trans. Lawrence Ferlinghetti and Francesca Valente. City Lights Books, 1986.

Octavio Paz

The Labyrinth of Solitude (prose), trans. Lysander Kemp. Grove Press, 1961.
Early Poems, 1935–1955, trans. Muriel Rukeyser et al. New Directions, 1973.
Alternating Current (essays), trans. Helen R. Lane. Viking Press, 1973.
The Bow and the Lyre (essays), trans. Ruth L. C. Simms. University of Texas Press, 1973.
Conjunctions and Disjunctions (essays), trans. Helen R. Lane. Viking Press, 1974.
Children of the Mire (prose), trans. Rachel Phillips. Harvard University Press, 1974.
The Collected Poems of Octavio Paz, 1957–1987, ed. Eliot Weinberger. New Directions, 1987.
Sor Juana (critical study), trans. Margaret Sayers Peden. Harvard University Press, 1988.
The Other Voice (essays), trans. Helen R. Lane. Harcourt Brace Jovanovich, 1990.

György Petri

Night Song of the Personal Shadow: Selected Poems, trans. Clive Wilmer and George Gömöri. Bloodaxe Books, 1991.

Vasko Popa

Collected Poems, 1943–1976, trans. Anne Pennington. Carcanet, 1977.
Homage to the Lame Wolf: Selected Poems, trans. Charles Simic. Oberlin College Press, 1987.

A. K. Ramanujan

Selected Poems. Oxford University Press (New Delhi), 1976.
Second Sight. Oxford University Press (New Delhi), 1986.
Collected Poems. Oxford University Press (New Delhi), 1995.

Dahlia Ravikovitch

A Dress of Fire, trans. Chana Bloch and Ariel Bloch. Sheep Meadow Press, 1978.
The Window: New and Selected Poems, trans. Chana Bloch and Ariel Bloch. Sheep Meadow Press, 1989.

Yannis Ritsos

Gestures and Other Poems, 1968–1970, trans. Nikos Stangos. Cape Goliard Press, 1971.
Chronicle of Exile, trans. Minas Savvas. Wire Press, 1977.
Ritsos in Parentheses, trans. Edmund Keeley. Princeton University Press, 1979.
Subterranean Horses, trans. Minas Savvas. International Poetry Forum, 1980.
Exile and Return: Selected Poems, 1967–1974, trans. Edmund Keeley. Ecco Press, 1985.
Selected Poems, 1938–1988, trans. Kimon Friar and Kostas Myrsiades. BOA Editions, 1989.
Repetitions, Testimonies, Parentheses, trans. Edmund Keeley. Princeton University Press, 1991.
The Fourth Dimension, trans. Peter Green and Beverly Bardsley. Princeton University Press, 1993.

Tadeusz Różewicz

Faces of Anxiety, trans. Adam Czerniawski. Swallow Press, 1969.
"The Survivor" and Other Poems, trans. Magnus J. Krynski and Robert A. Maguire. Princeton University Press, 1976.
Unease, trans. Victor Schanilec. New Rivers Press, 1980.

Conversation with the Prince, trans. Adam Czerniawski. Anvil Press Poetry, 1982.

Pentti Saarikoski

Poems, 1958–1980, trans. Anselm Hollo. Toothpaste Press, 1983.
Contemporary Finnish Poetry, trans. Herbert Lomas. Bloodaxe Books, 1991.

Léopold Sédar Senghor

The Collected Poetry, trans. Melvin Dixon. University Press of Virginia, 1991.

Shu Ting

The Red Azalea: Chinese Poetry Since the Revolution, ed. Edward Morin. University of Hawaii Press, 1990.
A Splintered Mirror: Chinese Poetry from the Democracy Movement, trans. Donald Finkel. North Point Press, 1991.
Out of the Howling Storm: The New Chinese Poetry, ed. Tony Barnstone. University Press of New England, 1993.

Elena Shvarts

"Paradise": Selected Poems, trans. Michael Molnar. Bloodaxe Books, 1993.

Sŏ Chŏng-ju

Winter Sky, trans. David R. McCann. Quarterly Review of Literature, Poetry Series III, 1981.

Marin Sorescu

Selected Poems, trans. Michael Hamburger. Bloodaxe Books, 1983.
The Biggest Egg in the World, trans. Seamus Heaney, Ted Hughes et al. Bloodaxe Books, 1987.

Wole Soyinka

Idanre and Other Poems. Hill and Wang, 1968.
The Shuttle in the Crypt. Hill and Wang, 1972.
Mandela's Earth and Other Poems. Random House, 1988.
Art, Dialogue and Outrage: Essays on Literature and Culture. Pantheon, 1994.

Wisława Szymborska

Sounds, Feelings, Thoughts: Seventy Poems by Wisława Szymborska, trans. Magnus J. Krynski and Robert A. Maguire. Princeton University Press, 1981.
Selected Poems, trans. Grazyna Drabik, Austin Flint, and Sharon Olds. Quarterly Review of Literature, Poetry Series IV, 1982.
People on a Bridge, trans. Adam Czerniawski. Forest Books, 1990.
View with a Grain of Sand, trans. Stanislaw Baranczak and Clare Cavanagh. Harvest Books, 1995.

Novica Tadić

Night Mail: Selected Poems, trans. Charles Simic. FIELD Translation Series, 1992.

Ryūichi Tamura

Dead Languages: Selected Poems, 1946–1984, trans. Christopher Drake. Katydid Books, 1984.

Shuntaro Tanikawa

The Selected Poems of Shuntaro Tanikawa, trans. Harold Wright. North Point Press, 1983.

Nguyen Chi Thiên

Flowers from Hell, trans. Huynh Sanh Thông. Yale Southeast Asia Studies, 1984.

Tomas Tranströmer

Selected Poems, 1954–1986, ed. Robert Hass. Ecco Press, 1987.
Collected Poems, trans. Robin Fulton. Dufour Editions, 1988.

Eddy van Vliet

Farewell and Fall, trans. John van Tiel et al. Dedalus Press (Dublin), 1994.

Andrei Voznesensky

Antiworlds, ed. Patricia Blake and May Hayward. Basic Books, 1966.
Nostalgia for the Present, ed. Vera Dunham and Max Hayward. Doubleday, 1978.

An Arrow in the Wall: Selected Poetry and Prose, ed. William Jay Smith and
    F. D. Reeve. Henry Holt, 1987.

Derek Walcott

The Gulf. Farrar, Straus and Giroux, 1970.
Dream on Monkey Mountain and Other Plays (drama). Farrar, Straus and
    Giroux, 1970.
Another Life. Farrar, Straus and Giroux, 1973.
Sea Grapes. Farrar, Straus and Giroux, 1976.
The Joker of Seville and *O Babylon!* (drama). Farrar, Straus and Giroux, 1979.
The Star-Apple Kingdom. Farrar, Straus and Giroux, 1979.
Remembrance and *Pantomime* (drama). Farrar, Straus and Giroux, 1980.
The Fortunate Traveller. Farrar, Straus and Giroux, 1981.
Midsummer. Farrar, Straus and Giroux, 1984.
Collected Poems, 1948–1984. Farrar, Straus and Giroux, 1986.
*Three Plays: The Last Carnival; Beef, No Chicken; A Branch of the Blue
    Nile* (drama). Farrar, Straus and Giroux, 1986.
The Arkansas Testament. Farrar, Straus and Giroux, 1987.
Omeros. Farrar, Straus and Giroux, 1990.
The Antilles: Fragments of Epic Memory (prose). Farrar, Straus and Giroux,
    1993.
The Odyssey (drama). Farrar, Straus and Giroux, 1993.

Yevgeny Yevtushenko

The Collected Poems, 1952–1990, ed. Albert C. Todd with the author and
    James Ragan. Henry Holt, 1991.

Adam Zagajewski

Tremor: Selected Poems, trans. Renata Gorczynski. Farrar, Straus and
    Giroux, 1985.
Solidarity, Solitude (essays), trans. Lillian Vallee. Ecco Press, 1990.
Canvas, trans. Renata Gorczynski, Benjamin Ivry, and C. K. Williams. Far-
    rar, Straus and Giroux, 1991.
Two Cities: On Exile, History, and the Imagination (essays), trans. Lillian
    Vallee. Farrar, Straus and Giroux, 1995.

Andrea Zanzotto

Selected Poetry of Andrea Zanzotto, trans. Ruth Feldman and Brian Swann.
    Princeton University Press, 1975.

ACKNOWLEDGMENTS

No book is an island. Causeways of advice and practical help linked this project to the expertise of many people. Particular thanks are due to Yehuda Amichai, John Balaban, Bruce Berlind, Susan Bianconi, Kenneth Bleeth, Mario Corradi, Marilyn Hacker, John Hollander, Edmund Keeley, Chip Kidd, Alexis Levitin, Tom Mellers, Patrick Merla, So Young Park, Robert Pinsky, Alastair Reid, Jonathan Spence, Lorin Stein, and Huỳnh Sanh Thông. Seth Lobis's energy and imagination brought the project to completion. Maxine Groffsky was its constant friend. LuAnn Walther's patience was its muse, and her intelligence its model.

Permissions Acknowledgments

"Fable" from *The Slopes of a Gaze,* trans. Alexis Levitin. Copyright 1992 Eugénio de Andrade and Alexis Levitin. Used by permission of Apalachee Press.

Sections V, XII, XIII, XXX, and XXXV from *White on White,* from *Quarterly Review of Literature,* vol. XXVII, Poetry Book Series, 1987. © Eugénio de Andrade. Used by permission of Quarterly Review of Literature, Poetry Book Series.

Awoonor, Kofi: "At the Gates," "This Earth, My Brother," "The First Circle," "They Shall Know," and "So the World Changes" from *Until the Morning After: Collected Poems 1963–1985:* © 1987 Kofi Awoonor. Used by permision of Kofi Awoonor.

Bachmann, Ingeborg: "Paris," "Psalm," "Invocation of the Great Bear," "Songs from an Island," "Aria I," and "A Kind of Loss" from *In the Storm of Roses: Selected Poems of Ingeborg Bachmann,* translated, edited, and introduced by Mark Anderson. Copyright © 1986 by Princeton University Press. All rights reserved. Reprinted by arrangement with Mark Anderson, c/o Joan Daves Agency as agent for the proprietor.

Bei Dao: "Answer," "The August Sleepwalker," and "Accomplices" from *A Splintered Mirror,* translated by Donald Finkel. Translation copyright © 1991 by Donald Finkel. Reprinted by permission of North Point Press, a division of Farrar, Straus & Giroux, Inc. "The Collection," "An Evening Scene," and "Discovery" from *Old Snow,* trans. Bonnie S. McDougall and Chen Maiping. Copyright © 1991 by Bei Dao. Reprinted by permission of New Directions Publishing Corp.

Bonnefoy, Yves: "The Tree, the Lamp" and "The Words of Evening" from *Poems, 1959–1975,* trans. Richard Pevear. Copyright © 1985 by Random House, Inc. Reprinted by permission of the publisher. "Summer Again," "De Natura Rerum," and "The All, the Nothing" from *Quarterly Review of Literature,* Poetry Series XI (1992). Trans. Lisa Sapinkopf. Copyright ©. Used by permission of Quarterly Review of Literature, Poetry Book Series.

"A Stone," "The Well," and "The Top of the World" from *In the Shadow's Light,* trans. John Naughton. © 1991 by The University of Chicago. All rights reserved. Used by permission of The University of Chicago Press.

Braithwaite, Kamau: "Citadel" from *X/Self* by Kamau Braithwaite. © 1987. Reprinted by permission of Oxford University Press (England).

"Tahirassawichi in Washington" from *Golden UFOs: The Indian Poems*.
Poem © by Ernesto Cardenal. English translation copyright © 1973 by The
Johns Hopkins University Press. Used by permission of the publisher, Indiana University Press.

Cavalli, Patrizia: "But first one must free oneself," "The Moroccans with
the carpets," "Now that time seems all mine," "To simulate the burning of
the heart," "This time I won't permit the blue," "Far from kingdoms," and
"Ah, yes, to your misfortune" from *New Italian Poets*, ed. Dana Gioia and
Michael Palma. © 1991. Used by permission of Story Line Press.

Celan, Paul: "Death Fugue," "I am the first," "Tenebrae," "Language
Mesh," "Matière de Bretagne," "Alchemical," "Thread suns," "In Prague,"
"When you lie," "Little night," and "All those sleep shapes" from *Poems
of Paul Celan*, translated by Michael Hamburger, copyright © 1972, 1980,
1988. Reprinted by permission of Persea Books and Suhrkamp Verlag.

Césaire, Aimé: "Different Horizon," "Bucolic," "On the Islands of All
Winds," "In Memory of a Black Union Leader," "In Order to Speak," and
"Lagoonal Calendar" from *Aimé Césaire: Collected Poetry*,
translated/edited by Clayton Eshleman and Annette Smith. Copyright ©
1983 The Regents of the University of California. Reprinted by permission
of the University of California Press.

Cruz Varela, María Elena: "Love Song for Difficult Times," "Kaleidoscope," and "Invocation" from *Ballad of the Blood* by María Elena Cruz
Varela. Copyright © 1996 by María Elena Cruz Varela. First published in
1996 by The Ecco Press. Reprinted by permission.

Csoóri, Sándor: "My Masters," "A Thin, Black Band," "Postponed Nightmare," "We Were Good, Good and Obedient," and "Everyday History"
from *Selected Poems*, trans. Len Roberts. © 1992 by Sándor Csoóri.
Reprinted by permission of Copper Canyon Press, P.O. Box 271, Port
Townsend, WA 98368.

Darwish, Mahmoud: "Identity Card," "On Wishes," "Victim Number 48,"
and "Steps in the Night" from *The Music of Human Flesh* (Three Continents
Press). © in selection and translation Denys Johnson-Davies 1980. Used by
permission of Denys Johnson-Davies. "We Walk Towards a Land," "Sirhan
Drinks his Coffee in the Cafeteria," and "Words" from *Sand and Other*

Poems. Translation © Rana Kabani 1986. Used by permission of Kegan Paul International, London and New York.

"Guests on the Sea" from *Anthology of Modern Palestinian Literature* edited by Khadra Jayyusi. Copyright © 1992 by Columbia University Press. Reprinted with permission of the publisher.

Drummond de Andrade, Carlos: "Seven-Sided Poem" and "Family Portrait" from *The Complete Poems 1927–1979* by Carlos Drummond de Andrade, translated by Elizabeth Bishop. Copyright © 1979, 1983 by Alice Helen Methfessel. Reprinted by permission of Farrar, Straus & Giroux, Inc.

"Souvenir of the Ancient World" from *Travelling in the Family: Selected Poems* by Carlos Drummond de Andrade. Copyright © 1986 by Carlos Drummond de Andrade and Thomas Colchie. Reprinted by permission of Random House, Inc.

"Motionless Faces" and "Residue" from *Travelling in the Family: Selected Poems* by Carlos Drummond de Andrade, translated by Mark Strand. Copyright © 1976 by The New Yorker Magazine, Inc. Originally published in *The New Yorker.* Reprinted by permission of Random House, Inc.

Dupin, Jacques: "Mineral Kingdom," "My Body," "Waiting with lowered voice" from *The Random House Book of Twentieth-Century French Poetry,* edited by Paul Auster: Copyright © 1982 by Paul Auster. Used by permission of Paul Auster.

Twelve prose sections (1, 2, 3, 17, 19, 20, 43, 44, 45, 51, 54, 56) from "Songs of Rescue" from *Selected Poems,* edited by Paul Auster. Translations copyright Paul Auster and Wake Forest University Press, 1992. Used by permission of Wake Forest University Press.

Elytis, Odysseus: "Aegean Melancholy," excerpt from "The Axion Esti," and "The Origin of Landscape or the End of Mercy" from *Odysseus Elytis: Selected Poems* by Odysseus Elytis, translated by Edmund Keeley and Philip Sherrard, *et al.* Translation copyright © 1981 by Edmund Keeley and Philip Sherrard. Used by permission of Viking Penguin, a division of Penguin Books USA Inc.

Enzensberger, Hans Magnus: "For the Grave of a Peace-Loving Man," "Middle-Class Blues," "Song for Those Who Know," "At Thirty-three," "The Holiday," "Short History of the Bourgeoisie," "Vanished Work," and "The Poison" from *Selected Poems.* English translation © Hans Magnus Enzensberger 1980, 1981, 1994 & Michael Hamburger, 1966, 1968, and

1994. German text copyright © Suhrkamp Verlag, Frankfurt am Main 1960, 1964, 1971, 1978, 1980, 1983, 1991, 1994. Used by permission of Bloodaxe Books, Ltd.

Faiz, Faiz Ahmed: "Don't Ask Me for That Love Again," "A Prison Evening," "Fragrant Hands," "Vista," "So Bring the Order for My Execution," and "*You* Tell Us What to Do" from *The Rebel's Silhouette,* trans. Agha Shahid Ali. © 1991.

González, Ángel: "Before I Could Call Myself Ángel González," "City," "Yesterday," "The Future," "Inventory of Places Propitious for Love," "Whatever You Want," and "Diatribe Against the Dead" from *Astonishing World: The Selected Poems of Ángel González,* translated from the Spanish and edited by Steven Ford Brown (Milkweed Editions, 1993). Copyright © 1993 English language translation by Steven Ford Brown and Gutierrez Revuelta. Reprinted with permission from Milkweed Editions.

Goodison, Lorna: "Always Homing Now Soul Toward Light" from *Heartease* by Lorna Goodison. Copyright ©. Published by New Beacon Books Ltd. in 1988. Used by permission of New Beacon Books Ltd.
   "The Road of the Dread" from *Selected Poems* by Lorna Goodison (New Beacon, 1992). Copyright © by Lorna Goodison 1992. Used by permission of Lorna Goodison.
   "Birth Stone," "Songs of the Fruits and Sweets of Childhood," and "From the Garden of the Woman Once Fallen" from *To Us, All Flowers Are Roses.* © 1995 by Lorna Goodison. Reprinted by permission of the author and the University of Illinois Press.

Gu Cheng: "Ark" from *A Splintered Mirror,* translated by Donald Finkel. Translation copyright © 1991 by Donald Finkel. Reprinted by permission of North Point Press, a division of Farrar, Straus & Giroux, Inc.
   "A Generation," "Discovery," and "Forever Parted: Graveyard" from *Out of the Howling Storm: The New Chinese Poetry,* ed. Tony Barnstone. © 1993 by Wesleyan University Press by permission of University Press of New England.

Haavikko, Paavo: Excerpts from "The Short Year" and from *Darkness* from *Contemporary Finnish Poetry* (Bloodaxe), ed. Herbert Lomas. © 1991. Used by permission of Herbert Lomas.

Section X from *The Heights of Macchu Picchu* by Pablo Neruda. Translation © 1966 and renewed © 1994 by Nathaniel Tarn. Reprinted by permission of Farrar, Straus & Giroux, Inc., and Jonathan Cape Limited.

"Ode to the Cat," translated by John Hollander. Translation © 1996 by John Hollander. Used by permission of John Hollander and Carmen Balcells Agencia Literaria S.A.

Nordbrandt, Henrik: "China Observed Through Greek Rain in Turkish Coffee," "No Matter Where We Go," "Our Love Is Like Byzantium," "Streets," and "Sailing," from *Selected Poems,* translated by Alexander Taylor and the author (Curbstone Press, 1978). Translation © 1978 by Alexander Taylor and Henrik Nordbrandt. Reprinted with permission of Curbstone Press. Distributed by Consortium.

Okigbo, Christopher: "Elegy of the Wind," "Come Thunder," and "Elegy for Alto" from *Collected Poems* (Heinemann): Copyright © Estate of Christopher Okigbo 1986.

Padilla, Heberto: "A Prayer for the End of the Century," "Landscapes," "Self-Portrait of the Other," from *Legacies* by Heberto Padilla. English translation copyright © 1991 by Alastair Reid and Andrew Hurley. Reprinted by permission of Farrar, Straus & Giroux, Inc.

"Man on the Edge," "The Discourse on Method," "Daily Habits," and "A Fountain, a House of Stone" from *A Fountain, a House of Stone.* English translation copyright © 1991 by Alastair Reid and Alexander Coleman. Reprinted by permission of Farrar, Straus & Giroux, Inc.

Pagis, Dan: "Autobiography," "Footprints," "Conversation," and "Picture Postcard from Our Youth" from *Selected Poetry,* trans./ed. by Stephen Mitchell. Copyright © 1996 The Regents of the University of California, © 1989 by Stephen Mitchell. Used by permission of the University of California Press.

"Wall Calendar," trans. Tsipi Keller from *Quarterly Review of Literature,* Poetry Series XI, vol. XXXI. Used by permission of the Quarterly Review of Literature, Poetry Book Series.

Parra, Nicanor: "The Pilgrim," "The Tablets, "A Man," and "The Poems of the Pope" from *Antipoems: New and Selected.* Copyright © 1985 by Nicanor Parra. Reprinted by permission of New Directions Publishing Corp.

Pasolini, Pier Paolo: "Prayer to My Mother," "Southern Dawn," "Civil Song," and "Lines from the Testament" from *Poems* by Pier Paolo Pasolini, translated by Norman MacAfee. Translation copyright © 1982 by Norman MacAfee. Reprinted by permission of Farrar, Straus & Giroux, Inc.

"Part of a Letter to the Codignola Boy" from *Poetry*, CVL, 1-2 (Oct./Nov. 1989). Translated by David Stivender and J. D. McClatchy. © 1989. Used by permission of J. D. McClatchy.

"The Day of My Death" from *Roman Poems*, trans. Lawrence Ferlinghetti and Francesca Valente. Copyright © 1986 by City Lights Books. Reprinted by permission of City Lights Books.

Paz, Octavio: "The Key of Water," "Along Galeana Street," "Small Variation," and "I Speak of the City" from *The Collected Poems of Octavio Paz: 1957–1987*, ed. Eliot Weinberger. Copyright © 1986 by Octavio Paz and Eliot Weinberger. Reprinted by permission of New Directions Publishing Corp.

Petri, György: "To an Unknown Poet from Eastern Europe, 1955," "To S. V.," "Gratitude," "To Be Said Over and Over Again," "Night Song of the Personal Shadow," "Christmas 1956," "Electra," and "Morning Coffee" from *Night Song of the Personal Shadow*: Translation copyright © Clive Wilner & George Gömöri. Copyright © György Petri 1971, 1974, 1982, 1985, 1991. Used by permission of Bloodaxe Books, Ltd.

Popa, Vasko: "In the Ashtray" and "Pig" from *Collected Poems*. Translation copyright © Anne Pennington. Published by Anvil Press Poetry in 1995. Used by permission of Anvil Press Poetry.

"Heaven's Ring" from *Homage to the Lame Wolf*, trans. Charles Simic. Copyright © 1987 by Oberlin College. Used by permission of Oberlin College Press.

"Burning Shewolf" from *The Horse Has Six Legs: An Anthology of Serbian Poetry*. Translation copyright © 1992 by Charles Simic. Reprinted with the permission of Graywolf Press, St. Paul, Minnesota.

Ramanujan, A. K.: "Elements of Composition," "In the Zoo," "Pleasure," "At Forty," and "Some People" from *Second Sight*. © Oxford University Press 1986. Used by permission of Oxford University Press (India).

Ravikovitch, Dahlia: "Trying Again," "Surely You Remember," "A Dress of Fire," "The Sound of Birds at Noon," "You Can't Kill a Baby Twice," and "Hovering at Low Altitude" from *The Window: New and Selected Poems* by Dahlia Ravikovitch, trans. Chana Bloch and Ariel Bloch. Copyright © 1989 by Chana Bloch and Ariel Bloch. Used by permission of Chana Bloch.

Ritsos, Yannis: "Miniature," "Penelope's Despair," "The End of Dodona II," "Marpessa's Choice," "Requiem on Poros," and "The Distant" from *Repetitions, Testimonies, Parentheses,* trans. Edmund Keeley. Copyright © 1991 by Princeton University Press. Reprinted by permission of Princeton University Press.

Różewicz, Tadeusz: "Who Is a Poet," "Draft of a Modern Love Poem," "Among Many Tasks," and "Homework Assignment on the Subject of Angels" from *"The Survivor" and Other Poems,* trans. Magnus J. Krynski & Robert A. Maguire. Copyright © 1976 by Princeton University Press. Reprinted by permission of Princeton University Press.

Saarikoski, Pentti: "Potato Thief" and excerpts from *The Dance Floor on the Mountain* and from *Invitation to the Dance* from *Contemporary Finnish Poetry* (Bloodaxe Books), ed. Herbert Lomas. © 1991. Used by permission of Herbert Lomas.

Senghor, Léopold Sédar: "Pearls," "I Am Alone," "Before Night Comes," and "Song of the Initiate" from *The Collected Poetry,* trans. Melvin Dixon. © 1991. Used by permission of the University Press of Virginia.

Shu Ting: "Missing You," "Assembly Line," "The Singing Flower," "Bits of Reminiscence," "Maple Leaf," "Gifts," and "Fairy Tales" from *A Splintered Mirror* translated by Donald Finkel. Translation copyright © 1991 by Donald Finkel. Reprinted by permission of North Point Press, a division of Farrar, Straus & Giroux, Inc.

Shvarts, Elena: "What That Street Is Called," "Remembrance of Strange Hospitality," "Elegy on an X-ray Photo of My Skull," and "Elegies on the Cardinal Points" from *Paradise* by Elena Shvarts. English translations © Michael Molnar. Russian poems copyright © Elena Shvarts 1989, 1990, 1993. Reprinted by permission of Bloodaxe Books Ltd.

Sŏ Chŏng-ju: "Flower-Patterned Snake," "Beside a Chrysanthemum," "Winter Sky," "Peony Afternoon," "A Sneeze," "If I Became a Stone," and

"Untitled" from *Winter Sky,* trans. David R. McCann, in *Quarterly Review of Literature,* Poetry Series III, vol. XXII. © 1981 Quarterly Review of Literature. Used by permission of the Quarterly Review of Literature, Poetry Book Series.

Sorescu, Marin: "With a Green Scarf" and "Start" from *Selected Poems.* Translations © Michael Hamburger 1983. Copyright © Marin Sorescu 1965, 1966, 1968, 1970, 1972, 1973. All rights reserved. "Precautions," "Fresco," "Perseverance," "Map," "Fountains in the Sea," and "The Tear," from *The Biggest Egg in the World.* Translations copyright © 1987. Copyright © Marin Sorescu 1968, 1975, 1979, 1982, 1987. Selection copyright © Bloodaxe Books Ltd. 1987. All poems reprinted by permission of Bloodaxe Books Ltd.

Soyinka, Wole: "The Hunchback of Dugbe" from *Idanre & Other Poems* by Wole Soyinka. Copyright © 1967 by Wole Soyinka. Reprinted by permission of Hill and Wang, a division of Farrar, Straus & Giroux, Inc.

"Funeral Sermon, Soweto" from *Mandela's Earth and Other Poems* by Wole Soyinka. Copyright © 1988 by Wole Soyinka. Reprinted by permission of Random House, Inc.

Szymborska, Wisława: "Unexpected Meeting," "The Women of Rubens" "Pietà," "Theater Impressions," and "Under a Certain Little Star" from *Sounds, Feelings, Thoughts: Seventy Poems,* trans. Magnus J. Krynski & Robert A. Maguire. Copyright © 1981 by Princeton University Press. Reprinted by permission of Princeton University Press.

"Reality Demands" from *The New Yorker,* March 1, 1993. Trans. Stanislaw Baranczak and Clare Cavanagh. Reprinted by permission. © 1993 Stanislaw Baranczak and Clare Cavanagh.

"The End and the Beginning" from *The New Republic,* January 18, 1993. ©. Used by permission of Stanislaw Baranczak.

Tada, Chimako: "Wind Invites Wind," "A Poetry Calendar," "The Odyssey or 'On Absence,' " and "Universe of the Rose" from *A Play of Mirrors: Eight Major Poets of Modern Japan,* edited by Ooka Makoto and Thomas Fitzsimmons. Copyright © 1987. All rights reserved. Used by permission of Katydid Books.

Tadić, Novica: "Dogs Gambol," "Nobody," "Man from the Death Institute," "Jesus," "Antipsalm," "Little Picture Catalogue," and "Laocoon/Ser-

Women, edited by Forrest Gander (Milkweed Editions). © 1993. Reprinted by permission of Forrest Gander.

Voznesensky, Andrei: "I Am Goya" and "Someone Is Beating a Woman" from *Antiworlds and the Fifth Ace: Poetry* by Andrei Voznesensky and edited by Patricia Blake and Max Hayward. © 1966, 1967 by Basic Books, Inc. © 1963 by Encounter Ltd. Copyright renewed. Reprinted by permission of BasicBooks, a division of HarperCollins Publishers, Inc.

"The Call of the Lake," "A Chorus of Nymphs," and "Two Poems" from *An Arrow in the Wall, Selected Poetry and Prose* by Andrei Voznesensky. Edited by William J. Smith and F. D. Reeve. "Two Poems" copyright © 1987 by Henry Holt and Co., Inc. Poetry translation copyright © 1987 by William J. Smith, F. D. Reeve, and Patricia Blake. Reprinted by permission of Henry Holt and Co., Inc.

"Old Song" from *Nostalgia for the Present,* ed. V. Dunham and Max Hayward (HarperCollins, 1987).

Walcott, Derek: "Crusoe's Island," "Midsummer, Tobago," "The Hotel Normandie Pool," and "The Season of Phantasmal Peace" from *Collected Poems: 1948–1984* by Derek Walcott. Copyright © 1986 by Derek Walcott. Reprinted by permission of Farrar, Straus & Giroux, Inc.

Yevtushenko, Yevgeny: "Babii Yar," "The Heirs of Stalin," "Hand-Rolled Cigarettes," and "Siberian Wooing" from *The Collected Poems 1952–1990,* edited by Albert C. Todd with Yevgeny Yevtushenko and James Regan. Copyright © 1991 by Henry Holt and Co., Inc.

Zagajewski, Adam: "Betrayal" from *Tremor: Selected Poems* by Adam Zagajewski, translated by Renata Gorczynski. Translation copyright © 1985 by Farrar, Straus & Giroux, Inc. Reprinted by permission of Farrar, Straus & Giroux, Inc.

"At Daybreak," "Electric Elegy," "Watching *Shoah* in a Hotel Room in America," and "When Death Came," from *Canvas* by Adam Zagajewski, translated by Renata Gorczynski. Translation copyright © 1985 by Farrar, Straus & Giroux, Inc. Reprinted by permission of Farrar, Straus & Giroux, Inc.

Zanzotto, Andrea: "How Long," "Distance," and "Campèa" from *Selected Poetry of Andrea Zanzotto.* Copyright © 1975 by Princeton University

Press. Used by permission of Andrea Zanzotto and the translators, Ruth Feldman and Brian Swann.

"Epiphany" from *Selected Poetry of Andrea Zanzotto*. Copyright © 1975 by Princeton University Press. Reprinted by permission of Princeton University Press.

"If It Were Not" from *Selected Poetry of Andrea Zanzotto*. Copyright © 1975 Princeton University Press. The poem was originally published in *Mundus Artium: A Journal of International Literature and the Arts,* Volume VII, #1, 1974. Used by permission of Mundus Artium, The University of Texas at Dallas.

"Behold the Thin Green" from *Selected Poetry of Andrea Zanzotto*. Reprinted with permission from *The Nation* magazine. © The Nation Company L.P.

About the Editor

J. D. McClatchy is the author of three collections of poems, *Scenes From Another Life* (1981), *Stars Principal* (1986), and *The Rest of the Way* (1990), and a book of criticism, *White Paper* (1989). He has edited several other books as well, including *The Vintage Book of Contemporary American Poetry*. A recipient of awards and fellowships from the American Academy and Institute of Arts and Letters, the National Endowment for the Arts, and the Guggenheim Foundation, he has taught at Princeton, Yale, UCLA, and other universities. He is a Chancellor of the Academy of American Poets, and is editor of *The Yale Review*.